E. Anderson.

THE PRIMORDIAL OCEAN

THE
PRIMORDIAL OCEAN

An Introductory Contribution
to Social Psychology

by

W. J. PERRY, M.A., D.Sc.

READER IN CULTURAL ANTHROPOLOGY
IN THE UNIVERSITY OF LONDON

METHUEN & CO. LTD. LONDON
36 Essex Street W.C.

First published in 1935

PRINTED IN GREAT BRITAIN

PREFACE

THE aim of this book is to study some of the general principles underlying the development of human society in its various phases.

I hope to have succeeded in making it easier for the student to find his way through the jungle of facts with which he is confronted; and that he will thereby gain a clearer understanding of the nature and meaning of human culture. The most pressing need of the moment is not the accumulation of facts but the gaining of insight into their meaning and relationships.

Synthetic work such as is carried out in this investigation obviously derives its inspiration from various sources. In this case the initial impulse came from Rivers and Elliot Smith. During the past ten years the deepening of our knowledge of social processes has been made possible by the work of Hocart, as set out in his *Kingship*, and other works.

Hocart has greatly advanced the study of social structure, and the effects of this new development are apparent in several recent studies, for instance, in the series of lectures by various authorities, edited by Professor S. H. Hooke, and published in the volume entitled ' Myth and Ritual.'

Although I gratefully acknowledge my indebtedness to various sources, I have tried in this book to sum up my own attitude towards the vast problems of the interactions between men and society.

I have not attempted to criticize other schools of thought. In particular, I have not tried to bridge the gap between the Functionalist School, led by Malinowski and Radcliffe-Brown, on the one hand, and the Historical, or Diffusionist, or Comparative School on the other. I feel certain, however, that those who seek to found general principles on a limited basis of fact will be forced, sooner or later, to broaden their outlook. I feel confident, moreover, that the candid reader will agree with me that the gap between the two Schools is not nearly as wide as might appear.

I owe much to my helpers, prominent among them the late Miss Mary Levin. Dr. M. Gompertz stepped into the breach caused by her untimely death, and has helped much in the preparation of the book, as well as in the proof-correcting and indexing. Mr. G. A. Cheshire has kindly revised the chapter on 'Acquisition.' Professor A. M. Blackman and Miss Winifred Blackman have generously helped me in some Egyptological matters.

W. J. PERRY

UNIVERSITY COLLEGE
LONDON, W.C.1
March, 1935

CONTENTS

vii

INTRODUCTION

WE are apt to take ourselves for granted. Brought up in certain social surroundings, we tend to adopt customs and beliefs without question. We regard our actions as ' natural ' to normal human beings. We read books ; we enjoy the theatre ; we play games and derive satisfaction from exercising our skill, as well as from the company of our opponents and of our partners. There grow up from these activities certain mental connexions which seem to us inevitable. These associations between the drama, games, literature and certain human feelings are obvious, but we must be very careful how we interpret any particular association.

For example, children spend much time in play ; so we easily assume that the tendency to play games is innate. It must be realized, however, that children rarely invent games, but merely imitate the actions of grown-ups ; and even adult games are not spontaneous, and have to be learned. Football, to take a well-known case, has been spread abroad from England throughout the world : and its presence, say, in Spain, is due to the fact that it has been adopted because it is a form of sport agreeable to the youth of Spain.

A similar conclusion is suggested by the study of the novel, the theatre, and so forth. These activities give pleasure, and persist for that reason ; but we cannot say that they originated solely because of the pleasures experienced.

We are thus led to ask what social activities are common to the whole of mankind, and what are due to special circumstances ? The answer to this question may be found by comparing the behaviour of the two great groups of people into which mankind may be divided, viz. Food-Gatherers and Food-Producers ; that is, peoples without cultivated plants or domesticated animals, and those with them.

The food-gatherers are ' natural ' men. They usually have no chiefs ; no organized social groupings ; no pottery-making ; no metal-working. In short they spend their lives in getting food, and living in groups of relatives.

The food-producers, on the other hand, have cultures of differing complexities. They possess what may be termed Social Institutions, such as religion, kingship, clans, magic, arts and crafts —that is to say, forms of organized behaviour; but these social institutions have mostly arisen in the first instance in connexion with the production of food and the family grouping. We thus see that human nature is fundamentally simple, whatever complexities it may present among more civilized peoples.

Certain alterations in human behaviour have been produced by social institutions. Various causes have made food-producing men more acquisitive and more violent than their food-gathering fellows. They have been guilty of deliberate cruelties that are practically unknown among food-gatherers : witch-burning in Western Europe and the cannibalism of the Aztecs of Mexico are cases in point.

It is found that, as a general rule, those social activities which are not characteristic of food-gatherers, but belong to food-producers, are ultimately based upon some theory, religious or otherwise. The witch-burners and the cannibals were satisfied that their actions were entirely logical according to their established beliefs.

The playing of games such as football would seem, at first sight, to be the direct outcome of the resulting pleasure, and would thus appear to contradict the generalization just laid down. But football has a history ; it is derived from ceremonial games formerly played in Christian Churches at certain times of the year. Savages in some parts of the world still play ball games on ceremonial occasions, and although pleasure is derived from them, they are rarely, if ever, played merely as games.

We thus see that certain social activities that might seem to have arisen spontaneously owing to their immediate emotional appeal were formerly part of organized institutions from which they have become detached. Indeed it is becoming increasingly clear to students that the social institutions of most peoples, savage and civilized, are the products of a vast organized system of thought. All manner of activities come within its scope. Political groupings, religion, arts and crafts, and other forms of social organization, form part of this great growth.

The chief factor in the construction and acceptance of this system of thought was the conviction that it was possible, by various procedures, to procure more ' life '—more health, longer life, good crops, healthy flocks and herds, and all manner of advantages. The founders of civilization were led, in the course of this process, to formulate ideas concerning gods, the sky-world, immortality, creation, and to achieve such triumphs as the alphabet and the solar calendar. The core of this many-sided growth was the kingship. The earliest known kings were sources of ' life ' to their peoples, and also were the first scientists, lawgivers, and administrators.

The majority of social institutions of modern savages and semi-civilized peoples centre round their rulers, and are also ' life-giving ' ; and so these institutions are retained intact as far as possible, because they are the only known ways of procuring ' life ' in its various aspects.

Such communities ascribe their social institutions to the past ; and those societies which have kings or chiefs attribute their beginnings to the divine ancestors of their rulers. They look back, in short, to an Age of the Gods. This transmission of culture from the past to the present, from gods to men, may be studied over a period of five thousand years, that is, from the earliest historical times.

Many peoples, separated by vast distances, and long periods of time, agree, in the main, concerning the mode of origin of their culture. Their creation stories state that a community of beings in a sky-world drew up the first land from the depths of a Primordial Ocean which lay beneath them, in much the same way as the First Chapter of Genesis recounts the separation of land from the water. This incident is widespread in the creation stories of America, Northern Asia, Oceania, as well as of Japan, Ancient India, Babylonia, and Egypt. This unanimity, occurring, as it does, in a long chain of communities which, for the greater part, owe their culture to the past, is striking. It suggests that, in spite of many differences, such peoples look back to a common source of inspiration. As the argument proceeds it will be seen that the incident of bringing up land out of the Primordial Ocean must have had a definite historical basis. It will be seen, more-over, that this original Ocean played a fundamental part in the organization of the early thought of food-producing men. Since the idea of unity of culture emerges from the discussions, it seems but fitting to express it in the title of this book. I have accordingly chosen The Primordial Ocean as the most striking symbol of that unity.

CHAPTER I

MAN IN SOCIETY

MAN is born into this world, not as an isolated individual, but as a member of a community. He lives his life in social surroundings, and therefore cannot be considered apart from them. From the day of his birth a child is surrounded by parents, brothers and sisters, maiden aunts, nurses, or whoever minister to his wants. He derives much information from them, directly or indirectly ; he imitates them incessantly ; and his relationships with them are productive of attitudes towards other people which will duly influence his social behaviour in the future. If, therefore, we wish to understand the reasons for his actions, both as an individual and as a member of a group, we cannot for a moment leave out of mind the action on him of some social group or other from the day of his birth to the time of his death.

The first group with which he usually comes into contact is the family of which he is a member. As time goes on he enlarges his social horizon, and comes under the influence of other groups —playfellows, the school, which play their part in producing in him certain ideas and certain forms of behaviour. As he develops and grows up to manhood, he comes into contact with still wider groups ; he becomes a member perhaps of a church, or of a political organization, and is duly influenced by them.

Although it is evident that every member of society belongs to some social group or other from the day of his birth, yet the meaning of the relationship between him and any one of these groups is not so easy to appreciate as it would at first appear to be.

In the first place, it is evident that a member of society is not merely plastic material in the hands of objective forces. He is born with an equipment, the result of the experience of the human race in its evolution from less advanced forms. This innate equipment is concerned with certain tendencies to action, which will manifest themselves at the right times. Man possesses certain nervous mechanisms, the aim of which is to further his own ends, either as an individual or as a member of a group.

1

Some of these mechanisms enable him to provide himself with food and protect himself from danger, while others serve for the perpetuation of the species. Generally speaking, he possesses these innate tendencies, instincts they are called, in common with other members of the mammalian group ; and they represent the result of the evolutionary process. But while resembling the apes and other mammals in some ways, he also differs from them. His intellectual equipment is far superior, and it is to this fact that he owes his advancement : for example, the acquisition of stereoscopic vision, of articulate speech, and other faculties have made him what he is, a creature related to, yet different from, the rest of the animal world.

By virtue of his innate equipment man reacts in certain ways to the world, social and physical, into which he is born. Although he finds social groups already there, yet he does not come entirely under their sway. His ancestors, beings similar to himself, were responsible for the inauguration of these groups, as well as their perpetuation. Somehow or other man has built up the complex of knowledge and social relationships which we call society. He is of it, and therefore must react to it in his own peculiar way, the manner of the reaction being dependent on several factors. This innate equipment is common to the human species, and is only absent in very rare instances where there has been a breakdown in growth, especially in the pre-natal stages.

It must not be forgotten that as man developed his intellectual powers, he developed also certain physical characteristics which serve to distinguish the native inhabitants of different parts of the earth. There are definite differences between a Mongol and a Negro, between a man of Mediterranean race and a Nordic. The shape of the skull, the pigmentation of the skin, and the height are different. It is therefore possible that, in addition to the innate capacities and tendencies which have resulted from the biological history of mankind, each section of the human family may have some peculiar characteristics or innate tendencies to action that have resulted from this racial experience. But it is patent that these innate tendencies cannot be so pronounced as those which men possess in common.

In addition to the innate equipment that man has received from his ancestors, as the result of the experience of the human race in its onward march, each of us receives from his parents, and through them from a long line of ancestors, certain combinations of qualities that mark him off from the rest of man, and make of him an individual. This is the case both physically and mentally. Innate capacity for learning, inborn mental tendencies can be detected in all of us, and in a certain measure these are the peculiar property of the individual, and not the result of education in any sense of the term. Originality of any sort is inborn in individuals, and no one can predict where it will appear.

Every one of us, therefore, comes into the world with an inborn equipment, a biological inheritance, it may be called. Certain tendencies we possess in common with the rest of normal human beings; we may possess perhaps certain characteristics because of our racial ancestry in the narrower sense of the term; we may also possess personal idiosyncrasies; and the combination makes up a personality who has to face the world of society.

Apart from the Racial Inheritance of man, there is what is called the Social Inheritance. Human society is vastly different from that of the nearest relatives of the human race, the anthropoid apes. It is infinitely more complicated, both as regards the possession of knowledge and as regards relationships between various members of a society. Apes have knowledge; they know the habits of their neighbours; they recognize each other; they know how to get food; but they do not think constructively. Their social relationships are simple, being mostly confined to the family, in the narrow sense of the term.[1] Man, on the other hand, possesses vast stores of knowledge; and he has elaborated vast complexes of human relationships, some of which influence each of us.

When we begin to study the relationship between the social heritage, on the one hand, and man himself on the other, we are met by a problem of fundamental importance, namely, the determination of the relation of cause and effect in the social behaviour of mankind.

In some instances it is possible to determine fairly easily which is cause and which is effect. But, in many instances, it is very difficult to solve the problem. When a man displays a particular type of behaviour, are we to say that it is part of his innate mental equipment, or is it a mode of behaviour induced in him by the action of some social institution or other? We know that the way of a man with a maid is innate, generally speaking; we take an interest in the opposite sex because we possess an innate equipment so to do. But we cannot say the same where man joins a political party, or wears certain types of dress, or affects certain manners of speech. Either the Conservative party is composed

[1] Zuckerman 315–16.

of men drawn together on account of their similar mental make-up ; [1] or else the party produces the type ; or the result may be due to a combination of the two factors. When a man beats his child because it is naughty, it may be because he has an innate tendency so to do on such occasions, or it may be a mode of behaviour that he has acquired from the society in which he lives. It may be that industry can only proceed on the basis of greed and need, that man only works because he has to ; so that, if production for profit were to be abolished, the vast majority of mankind would do as little work as possible. Or it may be that the present industrial system has induced in men such a mode of behaviour that the hope of gain is the main stimulus that causes the industrial machine to work.

One problem that we have to face therefore is that of cause and effect in human society. We find certain social institutions in existence, and in conjunction with them certain types of behaviour. Are we to say, in any given case, that the group has arisen in the midst of people with similar modes of behaviour, or are we to say that the group has produced the behaviour ? In some cases the one, in other cases the other answer would seem to be indicated.

This problem will have to be solved if ever we are to possess a true science of society that will enable us to formulate the conditions under which human beings can live the best possible lives, in which they can maintain harmony with their fellows, and develop their capacities to the fullest possible extent. Until that happens social psychology will be mostly guess-work, and politics will never advance beyond the empirical stage.

It is also necessary for us to determine the relationship between the two main divisions of the social heritage, knowledge and institution. Certain social groupings, for instance the family, can immediately be put on one side as being the direct products of our innate instinctive equipment. But institutions are the result of the development of society. Man has, for some reason, developed the class-system, religion and so forth. He has also acquired stores of knowledge. We have to inquire if there is any relationship between the two processes of development, the social and the intellectual, and if so, what is the nature of that relationship. We must determine, on the one hand, what effect the advance of knowledge has had upon social relationships ; on the other hand, we must determine how social groupings have affected the acquisition of knowledge. Here again we are faced

[1] As seems to be suggested by Mr. W. Trotter in his work, ' Instincts of the Herd in Peace and War '.

with the problem of cause and effect, and till that is solved the relationship will necessarily be obscure in many cases. Indeed we shall find that many explanations of the nature of social institutions are false because of the neglect on the part of their propounders to ask themselves whether they are dealing with cause or effect.

Only when we have attained to fair certainty on these two main points will it be possible to approach the problem of the relationship between the individual and society. This problem is peculiarly difficult, for the individual is confronted with the product of the activities of his forbears, near and remote. He does not reconstruct society anew for himself; he is partly a passive agent in the matter. At the same time he transmits the society that he finds around him more or less intact to his descendants. He is, as it were, the nexus between the past and the future.

What general principle are we to adopt in order to solve the riddles with which we are confronted ? If we are to found a science, it is imperative that an experimental method be adopted. We obviously cannot take human society and examine it in a laboratory. That path is closed to us. But we are fortunately able to apply a method which should in time provide stable results. For many centuries mankind in various parts of the earth has been living in societies of different kinds. Some of these societies are highly complicated, while others are simple. Many societies have become extinct, and therefore cannot be examined by us as minutely as those which still exist. But we know enough of past and present communities to enable us to institute a comparative method of study of the behaviour of men in society, using the term ' behaviour ' in the widest possible sense. This method enables us to compare communities of the most varied sorts, and thus to detect causal relationships. Moreover, it is possible, in many instances, to range societies in a historical sequence, and in that way to understand the interplay between men and society, to watch the changes in behaviour that accompany changes in institutions, and thereby to detect the causal relationship between them. We can inquire why some societies have no class-system, while others have it ; why some peoples have rudimentary ideas of property, while others make that institution the core of their culture ; we may inquire why some peoples treat their children with all kindness, while others are brutal towards them ; we may ask why the penal codes of peoples differ so, and why they differ at various times in the history of the same people. We can inquire on these and a thousand other

2

topics with the hope of gaining definite answers in the course of time, and thus we shall learn something of the working of the human mind in society.

It is evident, at the outset of our inquiry, that some method of dealing with this vast group of problems must be formulated. The first classification of human behaviour is fairly obvious. A cursory survey of human society shows that the behaviour of men may be divided into three main divisions. First there is that derived from his ancestry, a type that is usually called *Instinctive* or *Innate*. This is possessed in common by the whole human race. Then there is that type of behaviour which differs from one social group to another, which I propose to term *Institutional*. Man's brain, with its highly developed cerebral cortex, makes possible a vast range of behaviour, in the general sense of the term, that is unknown in the rest of the animal kingdom. Much of his behaviour is obviously the product of society, and is associated with certain social institutions. The third type of behaviour is what may be termed *Individual*. This is the combination of the two preceding with the personal qualities of the individual.

The Individual type of behaviour will largely be left on one side ; for it is the concern of the psychologist, who has to take account of factors not directly accessible to those who deal mainly with the comparison between societies and with the development of culture as a whole. At the same time, it is interesting to note that the order of introduction of the forms of behaviour, innate, institutional and individual, corresponds well with the logical development of the subject. For it is evident that human culture owes much to the innate tendencies. They form the substructure on which the rest depends for support. Out of them have come the social institutions on which depend the institutional types of behaviour. I do not mean to say that the development of human society has been entirely instinctive. That is obviously false. This process is to be explained as the result of intelligence. All I mean is that the initial functioning of intelligence in the formation of society must have been closely bound up with the innate side of behaviour.

Given an adequate account of the innate behaviour of man, it is possible to proceed then to study the relationships between the products of his intelligence and of his innate tendencies. This task is of peculiar complexity. For while we are studying the behaviour of man, as a member of society, while we are trying to account for this behaviour, we must not forget that man has produced the institutions whose effect we are studying. This duality in human society constitutes its peculiarity and its interest. The study of this relationship can therefore be undertaken only after the mode of innate behaviour has been determined, and not till then.

The behaviour of the individual obviously comes last. For how can the psychologist, faced with the complicated interaction of innate and institutional factors, together with that individual contribution that some of us make, hope to guide his steps through the maze of cause and effect, without some preliminary analysis of the racial and social heritage into which each of us enters.

The first problem, then, is that of inquiring into the innate type of human behaviour. When that has been determined, it will be possible to go further, and to inquire into the second type of behaviour, the institutional. We must try to formulate the standard type of human behaviour. We must try to catch men so primitive that they have hardly made any steps toward the foundation of civilization.[1] It is certain that human beings once lived in a ' state of nature ', as it is called, and were devoid of any of the fundamental social institutions. Their behaviour was as nearly instinctive as we can hope to encounter. If we can formulate that original type of behaviour, then we shall have gone far on our way. We shall have established a standard to which other forms of behaviour can be referred.

[1] I mean by ' civilization ' a form of society based upon food-production.

CHAPTER II

THE STANDARD OF BEHAVIOUR

THE search for the type of behaviour that rests directly upon the innate equipment of men, and is not the outcome of the action of social institutions on the individual, must now be undertaken. For, it seems to me, only in that direction can we hope to unravel the tangle of cause and effect that confronts the student of human society in its many aspects. If it is possible to formulate that standard type of behaviour, even approximately, then a step forward can be taken, and divergencies from it may be explained by the influence of some social institution or other. This Standard of Behaviour constitutes the base to which all other types may be referred. It will act as the ' control ' which every student of biology must utilize ; and is not the student of human behaviour a biologist ?

The determination of a Standard of Behaviour will settle, once and for all, the debate concerning ' human nature '. It is said that ' human nature is unchangeable ', and also that it is ' the most changeable thing on the face of the earth '. Both state-ments are probably true. The one assumes that there is a funda-mental uniform mode of behaviour common to all men, that cannot be altered except to a very slight degree ; while the other asserts that men can vary enormously in their behaviour.

Where are we to seek for this standard type of behaviour ? It sounds hopeless, at this time, to inquire into matters that concern human beings in a condition so primitive that they represent something very near the beginning of culture. Yet we have to seek for our evidence from existing peoples, for the remains left behind by those who have gone before do not help us very much. It is not long before we find, however, that, in spite of the fact that civilization, rooted in agriculture, has existed for about six thousand years,[1] there are still peoples low enough in culture to provide ample material upon which to base a generalization.

[1] It is only in the Ancient East that so remote a date can be assigned to the foundation of food-production. The dates of beginnings elsewhere vary enormously.

The accompanying Sketch Map (p. 10) serves as a rough guide to illustrate the general nature of the distribution of culture throughout the world in the days before the expansion of the modern peoples of Western Europe. This geographical distribution of culture is important. There are three zones. The central area, the Ancient East, was the scene of the earliest known civilizations. Then come the peoples of the lower culture, who depend upon agriculture and stock-rearing, or on the latter only, for their sustenance. On the outskirts are peoples ignorant of agriculture or stock-rearing, who gain their living by hunting or by gathering the fruits of the earth. I have proposed the term Food-Gatherers for the last group, and Food-Producers for the first two.[1]

It is generally admitted that agriculture began about six thousand years ago,[2] so that, before that time, the earth was tenanted by peoples who were simply food-gatherers. For untold thousands of years men had wandered about, and had never thought how much easier it would be to cultivate or breed food than to depend upon natural supplies. We shall see soon that early man had tackled the problem of his food supply, but on wrong lines. It was only with agriculture that any real advance was made.

The manner of inception of agriculture and stock-rearing in the outlying parts of the world is an occasion of dispute. But this dispute is confined within very narrow limits. Some think that agriculture began, or might have begun, in more than one spot. But certain areas are definitely excluded as possible homes of cultivation. Europe is one. It is known that agriculture was introduced there by people who brought with them the cultivation of wheat and barley, both of which plants had been grown previously, in Egypt and Babylonia at least, for hundreds of years.[3] In like manner the southern part of Africa is excluded, for the reason that agricultural peoples arrived there only a few centuries ago.[4] China in all probability received agriculture from the west, and diffused it throughout the larger part of eastern Asia. The eastern Pacific was colonized from the west by peoples who brought with them their own food-plants, including bread-fruit, taro, banana, coco-nut and yam.[5] Agriculture spread from the Maya of Central America throughout Mexico and up into the United States. It probably diffused from some centre throughout South America. In short, there is no area of the whole world,

[1] See Perry vi., 2nd ed., 5.   [2] Gompertz, 6–23.
[3] Breasted iv. 27, 46, 47 ; ii. 28, 32 ; Gordon Childe, 48 e.s.
[4] Haddon ii. 62 e.s.
[5] See Perry vi. cap. iv. for list of authorities.

outside the central ring, which can lay valid claim to have been the scene of the beginning of agriculture.

Agriculture was flourishing before 3000 B.C. in Egypt, Mesopotamia, Elam, and probably elsewhere in Western Asia. The rest of the world was, we may conclude, still in the food-gathering stage of culture. It is asserted by some that agriculture was begun independently by the Maya of America.[1] But if they accomplished that feat, it could not have been much before the beginning of our era, and possibly later. It still leaves us face to face with the fact that the out-lying parts of the world were tenanted by food-gatherers only, while agriculture and stock-rearing were flourishing in the central area.

The fact that agriculture has demonstrably been introduced into Europe, eastern Asia, the Pacific, South Africa, and into many other parts of the world, leaves but little likelihood of the independent origin of food-production in places lying outside the area of the earliest known civilizations. This has an important bearing upon the general theory of the development of civilization, but it need not be discussed at this point.[2] What we have to pay attention to is the relationship between the food-producers as a whole and the food-gatherers. This is necessary in order to make it possible to decide what value is to be given to the food-gatherers as evidence of the early condition of mankind.

The map suggests that the presence of food-gatherers on the outskirts of the world is to be explained by the fact that the knowledge of agriculture and of stock-rearing had not yet penetrated so far, when Europeans stepped in and altered the original balance, and prevented the agricultural and stock-rearing natives from advancing any further. The inference is that the food-gatherers on the periphery would ultimately have been absorbed into the mass of food-producers. They represent, it might be said, the last relics of the original state of affairs, in the days before agriculture began to spread throughout the world.

This view is supported by the work of Professor Sollas who, in his work on 'Ancient Hunters and their Modern Representatives', has urged that two groups at least of modern hunters, the Bushmen of South Africa, and the Eskimo of Greenland, Canada and Alaska, are related to the men of the Old Stone Age of Europe and North Africa.[3]

---

[1] S. G. Morley 28.

[2] A discussion of this point will be found in my 'Growth of Civilization', Chaps. III, V.

[3] Sollas, *op. cit.* (1924), Ch. VIII (Bushmen), 438–39, 443 ff. ; Ch. IX, 490 ff., 599 ; Ch. XII (Eskimo), 581 n., 583–5.

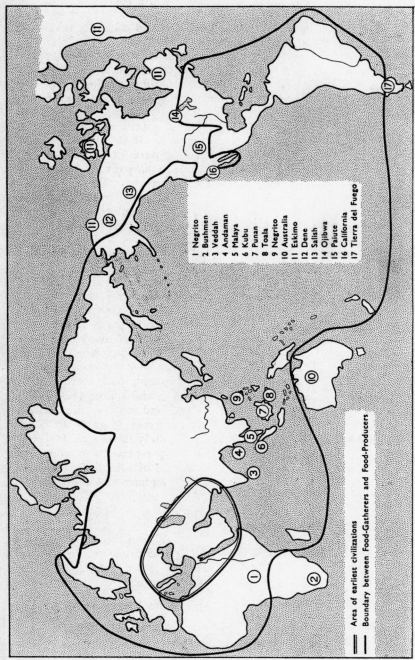

1	Negrito
2	Bushmen
3	Veddah
4	Andaman
5	Malaya
6	Kubu
7	Punan
8	Toala
9	Negrito
10	Australia
11	Eskimo
12	Dene
13	Salish
14	Ojibwa
15	Paiute
16	California
17	Tierra del Fuego

═══ Area of earliest civilizations

─── Boundary between Food-Gatherers and Food-Producers

SKETCH MAP.   RELATIVE DISTRIBUTION OF FOOD-GATHERERS AND FOOD-PRODUCERS

The Old Stone Age is divided into two main divisions, according to whether the population belonged to the species Homo Sapiens, that of man proper, or not.[1] These two stages have been termed Palaeoanthropic and Neoanthropic, or Lower and Upper Palaeolithic respectively. The first members of Homo Sapiens in Europe possessed what is termed the Aurignacian stage of culture. This stage has parallels in North Africa. It would seem that the Bushmen of South Africa have some affinities with this stage of culture.[2] It may even be possible, as has been said, that the ancestors of the Bushmen were formerly themselves in Europe.[3]

The closing stage of the Old Stone Age in Europe was what is termed the Magdalenian stage of culture. This is equated by Sollas to the culture of the Eskimo. If the conclusions of Sollas be correct, then the Bushmen and the Eskimo have in their culture something that connects them with the peoples of the Old Stone Age in Europe.

They have, like their fellows, lingered behind while the rest of mankind moved forward towards the foundation of civilization.

I do not propose, however, to lay any stress upon this supposed connexion between certain peoples of low culture of to-day and the vanished peoples of the Old Stone Age of Europe. I shall give another direction to the argument, and shall urge that all we need to do is to discover mankind in as simple a stage of culture as possible, and then to see what form of behaviour is exhibited by the societies that are in that low state of culture. That is to say, any people examined may be really primitive, or may have lost their former culture. The essential characteristic that will be considered will be, primarily, the absence of agriculture and stock-rearing.

An objection may be raised against this mode of procedure. Surely, it might be urged, there is a profound difference between a people that has always been primitive and one that has once been more highly civilized and has, for some reason or other, lost its knowledge. It would seem that in so deciding upon the criterion to be adopted, we shall be comparing entirely different things. In answer, it may be urged that the sole preoccupation at this point is to see what sort of behaviour is manifested by peoples in this low stage of culture, and to decide when that

[1] Elliot Smith iv. Ch. III. 92 seq. [2] Childe 35.
[3] It must not be forgotten that the Bushmen made pottery resembling that of the pre-dynastic Egyptians (Peringuey, Pl. 24). The hunting scenes shown in their cave paintings are remarkably like those carved on a slate palette, of protodynastic date, now in the British Museum. Cf. Tongue. Also E. S. Thomas for parallels between pre-dynastic Egypt, north-west Africa and Spain, 385.

evidence has been examined whether it is necessary to make a further analysis.

Another difficulty must be faced at this point. The existing food-gatherers belong to certain racial types, but not to all racial types. This suggests that certain races have advanced far towards civilization because of some inherent superiority, as yet undefined, while those who have remained behind have done so because of their inherent incapacity for advance.

Man may be divided into six groups, based upon a general description of the types. These are :

(1) Australoid.
(2) Negroid.
(3) Mongoloid.
(4) Alpine.
(5) Mediterranean.
(6) Nordic.[1]

The Australoid race includes the natives of Australia and of Tasmania, the Toala of Celebes, the Sakai and Senoi of Malaya, the Veddas of Ceylon and certain of the jungle tribes of southern India. It therefore occupies a continuous area, but has, in India and Indonesia, been largely displaced by peoples of other racial divisions, such as the Mediterranean in India, and Mongoloid and Mediterranean in Indonesia.

The Negroid race is divided into two physical divisions :

(1) Negrito.
(2) Normal Negro.

The Negritos are found in the basin of the Congo, and, as the Bushmen, in South Africa. They also live in the Andaman Islands ; in Malaya ; in the Philippines ; in certain islands between Timor and New Guinea ; and in New Guinea itself. The Negrito is practically always a food-gatherer.

The Negro proper lives in Africa, in the Sudan and the country to the south ; also in Melanesia. The Negro is practically always a food-producer.

The third racial type to be considered is the Mongoloid. This race has an enormous range. It is usually divided into two broad geographical divisions in Asia, the Northern and the Southern.

The Northern Mongols extend from Japan to Lapland, and from the Arctic Ocean to the Great Wall of China ; they occupy also the Aralo-Caspian basin ; parts of Irania ; Asia Minor ; East Russia and the Balkans.

---

[1] The classification is that made by Elliot Smith. See his ' Human History.' New York, 1929. London, 1930. Ch. IV, 120 sqq.

THE STANDARD OF BEHAVIOUR 13

The Southern Mongols inhabit Tibet; the southern slopes of the Himalayas; Assam; Upper Burma; Indo-China, to the Isthmus of Kra; Formosa; the Philippines; and Indonesia.

The Mongoloid race includes both food-gatherers and food-producers. In Asia itself the Punan and allied tribes of Central Borneo, and the Kubu of Sumatra, are food-gatherers. Several groups of tribes in America are still ignorant of agriculture and stock-rearing. Indeed, none of the peoples of the northern half of the continent ever domesticated any animals, except the dog, prior to the coming of Columbus. The tribes of California and of some of the western states of the United States are still food-gatherers. This is also the case with many of the peoples of eastern Canada.

The next racial group to be considered, that called Alpine in Europe, and Armenoid in western Asia, has had a chequered career. Its home was probably in central Siberia, with the Mongols to the East, and the Nordics to the West. This racial type has been dispersed far and wide in historical times. It forms part, for example, of the Russians, Turks, Armenians, Serbs, Bavarians, Savoyards, Egyptian aristocrats of the Pyramid Age, Assyrians, Ainu of Japan, Todas of India, and Polynesians.

This race and the two to be described, the Mediterranean and the Nordic, do not possess any food-gathering members. In this they present a definite contrast to the dark and yellow-skinned members of the human family.

The Mediterranean race extends from Ireland, through Spain and Portugal, southern France and the Mediterranean generally, North Africa, Arabia, Baluchistan, to India and thence into Indonesia.

The Nordic race is spread over Scandinavia, north-west Germany, Holland, Belgium, and Britain, together with the colonies of these countries.

Those are the principal racial divisions of mankind. When their distributions are compared with those of the different stages of culture, it is evident that the light-skinned races, the Alpine, Mediterranean and Nordic, lie within the area of high culture as a general rule, while the three darker-skinned races, the Mongoloid, Negroid and Australoid, lie on the periphery. The food-gatherers are confined to the darker-skinned races.

It would be extremely dangerous at the present stage of our knowledge, to try to draw any conclusions from the last fact as to the relative intellectual characters of these two main divisions of the human species. For, while the food-gatherers are certainly confined to the three darker-skinned types, these types are not exclusively food-gathering. On the contrary, the greater mass of the Mongoloid race practises agriculture or stock-rearing. Those Mongoloid peoples who even now do not practise agriculture or rear stock, owe their condition to the fact that they have not been taught these crafts. They do not lack the mental capacity. The same may be said with regard to the Negro proper. Even the Negrito sometimes takes up agriculture, and therefore has sufficient intelligence for that purpose. The only people who seemingly are strongly resistant to the sedentary or pastoral life, are the Bushmen and Australian blacks. It does not seem possible to teach them agriculture or stock-rearing.

Two out of three of the darker-skinned races therefore are quite capable of practising agriculture and stock-keeping, and when they fail to possess these crafts it is usually because they have not happened to learn them from their neighbours. From these considerations, therefore, it would seem that the food-gathering peoples can be taken as a fair sample of the human species as a whole. Any conclusions that can be derived from a study of them can be applied to the three other types.

The factor of intelligence, or rather, ability, or originality, is apt to be used in a lighthearted manner by those who deal with the problems of civilization. It is safe to say that we know little about the subject, and that we have to rid our minds of many prepossessions concerning it. It must be remembered that the capacity for originality may be there, and yet lie dormant, while inferior capacity may exhibit originality. For instance, it is reasonably certain that the Punan, a Mongoloid food-gathering people of Central Borneo, never invented any art or craft, nor ever contributed to the development of such.

On the other hand, the Neanderthal race, a sub-human type, that is associated in Europe with the Mousterian type of implement, was associated with the remarkable technique of the manufacture of implements from a core.[1] This technique enabled users of flint implements henceforth to improve their industry and to gain an enormously enhanced control over their material. The reason for this display of originality need not occupy us at this stage. It can serve simply as a warning against any argument which states that because certain people have not displayed any originality, therefore they are incapable of it. The problem of originality and its occurrence must be reserved for separate treatment, until other matters have been discussed.

---

[1] I formerly assumed that the invention of the ' core ' was the work of Neanderthal man. A paper recently published by Mr. Goodwin contains some interesting views on this subject. See Goodwin ii.

For the reasons already stated, it will be best, from the point of view of method, to make no preliminary assumptions concerning the value of the evidence to be gained from the food-gatherers, but simply to set it down and then study it. After this examination it will be possible to discuss its bearing upon the problem of the determination of a Standard of Behaviour. We can simply take them as people at the bottom of the cultural scale, living in a state as near to the primordial as we can get. We need not worry overmuch whether or not they are really primitive. All we seek is to understand how men behave in the simplest forms of society which can now be found on the earth. At the same time it must be understood that, since these people are, in a sense, modern, their culture may have been permeated with the influence of more advanced peoples. This certainly is the case in some instances, as for example, in Australia and among the Bushmen of South Africa. But such perturbations tend to cancel out one another in the general mass of evidence.

CHAPTER III

FOOD-GATHERERS : AFRICA, INDIA AND INDONESIA

THE food-gatherers live mainly on the outskirts of the world, far from the great centres of civilization.   In some cases they occupy countries, such as Australia, that show little or no traces of a higher civilization ; in others they dwell in territories that formerly were visited or occupied, or are now occupied, by peoples with an advanced civilization.   Their distribution is world-wide ; for they are found in Africa, India, Malaya, Indonesia, Australia, and America.

These primitive populations include the Negritos of the Congo Basin and adjoining regions ; Bushmen of South Africa ; Veddahs of Ceylon ; pre-Dravidian jungle tribes of southern India ; Semang of Malaya (Negrito) ; Sakai, Senoi, Jakun of Malaya (Australoid) ; Andaman Islanders ; Kubu of Sumatra ; Punan and cognate tribes of Borneo ; Negritos of the Philippines and New Guinea ; Australians ; Tasmanians (now extinct) ; Eskimo ; Déné of the Mackenzie Basin ; the interior Salish of British Columbia ; the northern Ojibway ; the Paiute of Nevada, Utah and Arizona ; the Paviotso of Nevada ; the indigenous peoples of California ; and the inhabitants of Tierra del Fuego.[1]

I do not propose to give an exhaustive account of these peoples, for that would extend to a whole book.   To avoid exposing myself to the charge of selecting my facts, or colouring my descriptions, I shall use the actual words of those who describe them, concentrating attention upon the essential features of their social grouping and their general behaviour.

Certain food-gathering peoples have adopted beliefs and practices from their more highly civilized neighbours.   The Bushmen of South Africa, for example, formerly made pottery with tubular handles.   Pottery-making is not found as a rule among peoples of this stage of culture, and there is little doubt that, in this case, there has been borrowing from other peoples.[2]   Some of these

---

[1] References to the literature concerning these tribes will be given in this and the following chapters.

[2] See p. 11n.

16

exceptions to the general type of culture characteristic of food-gatherers as a whole will be dealt with at length, for they are of theoretical importance.

The food-gatherers as a whole conform, on the material side, to a general cultural scheme. They have, of course, no agriculture and no domesticated animals except the dog. They do not build permanent houses, and at the most make rough shelters. They would seem formerly to have gone about naked. They are ignorant of pottery-making and of metal-working. They have no social classes, and usually no organization into clans or other social groupings. In fact, their stage of culture can legitimately be said to be one in which there are practically no social institutions.

Certain African pygmies of the east Congo Basin, known as the Mambuti, or Bambuti, are typical food-gatherers. They are forest dwellers, and, for the most part, find all the shelter they need under trees and boughs. In some instances they make primitive huts, by twisting twigs and leaves together ; but, as a rule, they appear to be equally contented without shelter.[1]

Little has been noted about the social organization of these people, but family life plays an important part. ' The strangest thing about them is that they are monogamous.'[2] It has also been observed that pygmies of the Ituri forest are without chiefs, and that the family, in its widest sense, forms the basis of their society.[3] ' They have large families. I saw one family of four children and spoke to a mother who had raised nine. They have great respect for their elders, and in this connexion I noted that a girl whom I pushed ahead to lead a dance withdrew, made a place for the oldest woman in the party, and took her own place near the rear of the line. The same rank was in order with the men, the oldest always in the lead, and when he fell out another grey-haired elder took his place. When we went to their forest home a young woodman led the way, but he withdrew in favour of the oldest in the village, who led us on and found the intricate path which wound its way to their abode.'[4]

A similar description of the Negrito is given by Schebesta :
' Here I was, living with a group of people who were absolutely primitive, relics, almost, of a prehistoric age, but who were, in fact, " savages " in name only ; men, who would never dream of snatching food from one another, but who would stand by one another ; men, whose hearts glowed with kindly feelings towards one another. I could see that among these people there were strong family ties. The affection for father and mother, brother and sister, meant to them exactly what it means to us, differing

[1] Bergh 238.   [2] *Ibid.*, 244.   [3] Christy 47.   [4] Bergh 263–4.

only in that their demonstrations of love and affection were more naïve, more undemonstrative, and, possibly, therefore, more real than ours.   This poor little camp had an air of contentment and peace about it, only because it was the sanctuary of men, not one of whom possessed more than his brother ; little men, linked together by their harsh elemental environment in a communal existence, where there was scant scope for envy or greed.' [1]

The fundamental social unit is the small group of relatives. The oldest man acts as a kind of leader.   Each family has its own hunting-grounds, including an anthill.   There is no chiefly class, and no tribal unity.[2]

Fighting sometimes takes place between family groups—' it sometimes happens that whole groups wipe each other out in such disputes. . . .   Once they are thoroughly aroused, the passions of these primitive men are often uncontrollable.' [3]

Regarding the behaviour of the Mambuti, Van den Bergh continues : ' What struck me most forcibly was that they are not devoid of an ethical code.   Indeed, the contrast of their ideas of morality with those of other African tribes is so great as to be astounding.   It has for some time been a conviction with me that among most of the African tribes, especially those with which I have come into contact, there is almost a complete absence of morality.' . . . ' For this reason I was, to say the least, surprised to find the Mambuti imbued with such high moral instincts. Stealing is so far foreign to their habits that the Wanyari chiefs give them their goats and sheep to mind whenever a tribe lingers for any length of time in the same locality.   This they do because they can rest more easily having their flocks in the hands of the Mambuti than in the hands of men of their own villages.   Adultery seems to be almost unheard of among them.   That they do not indulge in excesses we found out when they received tobacco and native banana beer from the chief.   They drank the beer in moderate quantities and they smoked of the tobacco very frugally.' [4]

' Their manners are very gentle and they have a sense of delicacy.   I am told also that they do not kill among themselves, and my information went so far as to state that the oldest Mambuti of the two villages with which I came into contact had never known of such an act being committed among themselves.   It is true that a couple of Wanyari had become the victims of their poisoned arrows, but they were explained as cases of warfare rather than homicides, because they had intruded into the forest

---

[1] Schebesta ii. 53.   [2] *Ibid.*, 119–24.   [3] *Ibid.*, 96.
[4] Bergh 252–3.

which the dwarfs consider their inviolable domain. In cases where one Mambuti has wounded another with a poisoned arrow they had always applied an antidote in the making of which they are experts.'[1]

The relations of these people to the Wanyari tribes are of interest. ' Originally they (the Mambuti) had a free hand in this country and roamed about as they pleased, occupying a stretch of open land now and then, or retiring to the forest, as the spirit moved them. They resented the settlement of the Wanyari (a group of negroes) in their territory to such an extent that even now they kill the Wanyari whenever they feel so inclined, if intruders dare to enter the domains of the Pygmy forest. This they do only by sniping, because they dare not fight their foe in the open, where they know that they would not be the equal to the Wanyari. They lie in wait for them in the forest, and from ambush it is an easy matter, comparatively, to land one of their poisoned arrows in the anatomy of their hated enemies. At present, however, the Pygmies are not, as a race, quite so hostile to the Wanyari. They have taken their ejection philosophically for the past half-century, and now look not only on the Wanyari as a race of conquerors, but almost as friends in general. But they do not soon forget a personal slight or injustice ; hence occasional vendettas.'[2]

P. H. G. Powell-Cotton gives a few more details concerning the way of life of these Negritos, and their strict code against trespass. He says : ' The Pygmies live in groups, numbering from 6 to 18 men, with their families. Each of these groups occupies a recognized part of the forest, which is their particular hunting-ground and into which any strange native trespasses at his peril. Each little community enters into a sort of compact with the headman of some other forest tribe, whom they supply with fresh meat and honey, leaves to thatch his houses, pliant creepers for use as ropes, and other forest produce in exchange for bananas, sweet potatoes, and maize.' . . .

' Their villages are of the most simple construction. Situated in some little clearing in the forest, they consist of a few primitive huts, each formed by thrusting pliant saplings into the ground, tying the ends together and thatching them with the broad, plantain-like leaf to be found everywhere in the forest.

' In one of these villages our attention was attracted by a hut, lower and smaller than the rest, which, it was explained, had been built for the children, who always sleep together.'[3]

[1] Bergh 254. This account of behaviour conflicts with the statements of Schebesta concerning internecine fights between groups.

[2] *Ibid.*, 237.   [3] Powell-Cotton 4.

The Bushmen of South Africa, now almost confined to the Kalahari desert, are a branch of the Negrito race. Formerly they occupied land much further north than their present range, but have gradually been driven southwards by advancing Bantu-speaking negroes, who have spread from the north. Their old area of occupation is shown by rock and cave paintings, in which they depicted some of the animals they were in the habit of hunting.

When the Dutch arrived at the Cape they found the Bushmen in possession ; but a war of extermination soon began. The first fight was in 1688. ' Regular commandoes were formed to hunt them down. The men were shot as wild beasts, and the women and children carried off as slaves. The reasons for this war to the knife was the cattle-stealing propensities of the Bush-men. As the Dutch occupied the land they drove away or slaughtered the game on which the Bushmen lived, and the latter took to looting the herds and flocks of the Colonists.' [1] . . . ' There is good reason to believe that the Bushmen were not originally thieves, that where they had plenty of other food they usually left the stock of both Bantu and European alone, and it was only when they saw their means of existence destroyed that they took to looting and murder.' [2]

The Bushmen formerly wore little clothing, sometimes even going naked ; in fact young boys did so up to puberty.[3] ' What little clothing they did wear was a skin thrown over the shoulders in cold weather, a fillet of skin round the head in the case of the men, in which they were accustomed to stick their arrow points, or a band of discs cut from ostrich shells in the case of the women, who also wore a girdle of the same round the loins, or a small piece of skin with fringes in front, usually made from the hide of a springbok or the skin of a jackal. Sometimes the men had a narrow piece of skin threaded on a sinew that went round the loins, the skin being passed between the legs and tied in front.' [4]

The Bushmen lived in small groups of relatives, rarely number-ing more than twenty.[5] They had no permanent dwellings, but used windscreens, rock-shelters, caves, or even holes in the ground for protection.[6]

Each group had its own hunting grounds, and bitterly resented any intrusion on them, either by other natives, or by Europeans. ' Each little family goes its own way, and the father is a despot as long as he can maintain his own authority, that is as long as he is in full possession of his physical powers, but once these show signs of decline he is soon displaced. Occasionally a man who

[1] Dornan 43.   [2] Ibid., 45.   [3] Ibid., 49, 87.
[4] Ibid., 48–9.   [5] Ibid., 90.   [6] Ibid., 90.

has shown great prowess in hunting or war may remain at the head of the family for some time after he has retired from active participation in the chase, but sometimes even this does not last long.' 'The Masatwas have such a struggle to maintain their existence, and to-day it is greater than ever, that they have no desire to be burdened with despots who cannot feed themselves. Fights between rivals for the possession of power in the family or clan were not infrequent in the old days and may occur even yet. Such ended in the victor either killing, or maiming, and driving out his opponent, who henceforth went off on his own, and nourished feelings of revenge, which he ever sought occasion to gratify. Sometimes he was able to carry out his desire, but his rival was usually too much on his guard, and too wary to be caught napping, realizing only too well what his own fate would be if he were, and that his tenure of power depended upon his ability to maintain it. Yet in spite of the impatience of the Bushmen to all forms of authority they were not naturally cruel or vindictive to each other, and in times of stress a leader once chosen was implicitly obeyed, and in his turn expected such obedience.' [1]

The Bushmen were, as a rule, monogamous ; but cases of polygamy occurred, especially among the peoples living near the Shashi and Motloutsi rivers.[2] 'Feats of hunting are regarded as of great importance in procuring a wife.' [3] 'The young man is most favoured who is the bravest or most successful hunter, but in any case ability to provide for the wife is an absolute necessity before marriage. In the old days marriage was often by capture. The strongest and bravest man in a clan could and did take as many of the women and girls as his power enabled him to do. . . .' [4]

The children as a rule are well treated. 'It has been stated that the Bushmen are wanting in feelings of affection towards one another. I have often heard the statement made that mothers are cruel to their children, sometimes destroying them if they prove too great a burden. This is not borne out by what I have seen. Often one sees Bushmen mothers kissing their babies just as European mothers do, and when they are sick they are tenderly cared for. The fathers are stern and rough often, but they are never brutal to their children.' [5]

The Bushmen were accused of cruelty to their neighbours, and conflicts occurred between them and the Bantu peoples and Europeans who surrounded them. These conflicts were due to the

---

[1] Dornan 85–6, 132.   [2] *Ibid.*, 124.   [3] *Ibid.*, 124.
[4] *Ibid.*, 127.   [5] *Ibid.*, 133–4.

3

pressure of a higher civilization upon a lower culture : deprived of their land hunting grounds, the Bushmen were forced to steal in order to live. ' The Bushmen of the Kalahari are not cruel, certainly far less cruel than the Cape Bushmen, according to what we read and hear, and I have never come across any well-authenticated statements of their atrocities upon the Bechuanas or Matabele. With the Makaranga they get on very well, and these people do not speak of them with the contempt that the Bechuanas do.' [1]

The Bushmen were, on the whole, a happy, lively people, capable of great bravery in hunting. ' They are light-spirited, full of merriment, especially the women, irresponsible, improvident and careless. They have much pleasure in their lives. On the other hand, they have equally great faults. They are wayward, obstinate, impatient of control, and when opposed or thwarted, savage, vindictive and cruel to a degree. Of their bravery there is no need to speak at length. They will do anything for a person who has earned their respect and confidence. If one is face to face with an angry lion, the Bushman tracker will stand by one's side and never quail. If the hunter goes down in the fight, so will the Bushman, and cases are on record where a Bushman has killed a lion on the body of his master.' [2]

The Bushmen rarely have serious quarrels among themselves, although easily roused to anger. ' They appear never to have had great wars against each other ; sudden quarrels among rival huntsmen, ending in lively skirmishes, which, owing to their nimbleness and presence of mind, caused little damage to life or limb, appear to have been the extent of their individual or tribal differences.' [3]

Turning from these now almost extinct peoples of South Africa to the jungle tribes of the Indian peninsula, we find the Veddahs of Ceylon leading the same kind of life. The Veddahs form a remnant of the earliest inhabitants of the country, called the pre-Dravidians, who as a whole belong to the Australoid race (see page 12). They live for the most part in rock shelters, in small groups of relatives. Each of these communities has its own hunting grounds, and trespass on to neighbouring grounds is rare.

Mr. J. Bailey, who describes these people from personal experience of them, says that ' they are as peaceful as it is possible to be. They are proverbially truthful and honest. They are fond of their children, who early become useful to them. . . . Their constancy to their wives is a very remarkable trait in a country where conjugal virtue is not classed as the highest of domestic

[1] Dornan 204.   [2] *Ibid.*, 205–6.   [3] Stow 38.

virtues. Infidelity, whether in the husband or the wife, appears to be unknown, and I was very careful in my inquiries on the subject. Had it existed the neighbouring Singhalese would have had no hesitation in accusing them of it, but I could not find a trace of it.' He goes on to say that the Kandyans divorce freely, that husbands and wives desert one another on account of sickness. ' But the Veddahs have not yet arrived at such a pitch of civilization. Divorce is unknown among them. They are kind and constant to their wives, and few of their Kandyan neighbours could say as I have heard a Veddah say, " Death alone separates husband and wife." The idea of such constancy was quite too much for one of the bystanders, an intelligent Kandyan chief, on one occasion when I was talking on these subjects to some Veddahs. " Oh, Sir," he exclaimed apologetically, " they are just like Wanderoos " (monkeys). He was perfectly scandalized at the utter barbarism of living with only one wife, and never parting till separated by death.' [1] Professor Seligman corroborates this point. ' It may be noted,' he writes, ' that even at the present day the sexual morality of the Veddahs is extremely high ; they are strictly monogamous, and both married and unmarried are habitually chaste.' [2]

The views of Mr. Atherton, a former Assistant Agent of the Government, are quoted by another authority. He ' spoke in favourable terms of their disposition. Notwithstanding an apparently almost complete indifference to morals, grave crimes, he said, were rarely committed. In case of theft the delinquent, if detected, must make restitution. Thus, if a girl be carried off from her parents, she is claimed and brought home. The husband of a faithless wife is content to receive her back, while his family punish the seducer by flogging him. Murder is almost unknown. In a general way these people may be described as gentle and affectionate one to another. They are strongly attached to both their children and their relatives. Widows are invariably supported by the local community, receiving their share of fruits or grain and the products of the chase. Altogether they appear to be a quiet and submissive race, obeying the slightest expression of a wish, and being very grateful for any assistance or attention. They consider themselves superior to their neighbours, and are unwilling to change their wild forest life for any other.' [3]

Professor and Mrs. Seligman describe them as ' Extremely courteous and merry . . . and in the main have retained their old virtues of truthfulness, chastity and courtesy.' Each Veddah ' readily helps all other members of his own community, and

[1] Bailey 291–3. [2] Seligman iii. 413. [3] L.R.M. 174.

shares any game he may kill or honey he may take ' with the rest.
' In every respect the women appear to be treated as equals of
the men ; they eat the same food ; indeed, when we gave presents
of food the men seemed usually to give the women and children
their share first.' . . . ' Veddahs are affectionate and indulgent
parents.' [1]

The pre-Dravidian tribes of India itself formerly lived under
similar conditions ; but in nearly all cases they have been subjected to slavery at the hands of their neighbours, and in their
service have learned the rudiments of agriculture and other arts.
The Malasirs of the Coimbatore district are typical of this condition. Buchanan sent for some of this tribe and they informed
him ' that they live in small villages of five or six huts. . . .
They collect drugs for the trader, to whom they are let ; and
receive from him a subsistence, when they can procure for him
any thing of value. . . . A great part of their food consists of
wild yams (Dioscoreas), which they dig when they have nothing
to give to the trader for rice. They cultivate some small spots
in the woods, after the *Cotu-cadu* fashion, both on their own
account and on that of the neighbouring farmers, who receive
the produce, and give the Malasirs hire. The articles cultivated
in this manner are Rali, Avaray, and Tonda. They are also hired
to cut timber and firewood. . . . They always marry girls of
their own village, and never take a second wife unless the first dies.
Marriage is indissoluble, except in the case of infidelity on the part
of the woman.' [2]

The Malay Peninsula, now called Malaya, is the home of several
food-gathering tribes, among whom are the Semang. These
peoples are of negrito stock. They live in the forest, making windscreens of branches to protect themselves, but having no permanent
dwelling places. They live chiefly on what vegetable products
they can collect in the forest, but occasionally do a little hunting.
To a very limited extent they practise agriculture.[3]

The Semang have no tribal organization. They simply live
together in small groups. There is no form of government, but
the father of the family is everywhere respected. ' Freedom, but
not licence, is the principle of the Semang group and the characteristic of each individual.' [4] All members of the group eat
in common, and share their food. If there is plenty it is said
that some is given to other families of the same ' clan ' (Sippe),
but not to members of other ' clans ' that happen to be with
them.[5]

[1] Seligman ii. 37, 44, 66, 88.   [2] F. H. Buchanan II. 384.
[3] Schebesta i. 158, 159, 278–9.   [4] *Ibid.*, 279.   [5] *Ibid.*, 84.

These people are monogamous.[1] Polygamy, however, is allowed but is rarely practised. Marriage is a condition of absolute equality between husband and wife, and adultery is regarded as a great crime, punishable by death. Children are highly prized, and are the link that holds the parents together. Newly married couples do, upon occasion, separate ; but after children have been born, the union is scarcely ever dissolved.

Murder, theft and drunkenness are unknown among the Semang. ' The better I knew the dusky dwarf, the less reason I had for thinking evil of him. He certainly is not evil, but is vain, disputatious and proud.' [2]

Major Enriquez gives a brief account of these people. ' But for a bark loin-cloth, they are naked.' [3] . . . ' Truly, in their miserable lean-to shelters in the forest they seem hardly human. They are nomadic, rarely stopping more than two or three days in one place, but it should be understood that the migrations of all these races are limited within fixed boundaries.' [4]

' They have, however, no form of agriculture whatever, and live upon jungle produce, and by hunting, fishing and trapping. Their distinctive weapon is the bow and poisoned arrow. They live under overhanging rocks or leaf-shelters, and build no houses.' [5]

In a few cases the food-gatherers learn the elements of agriculture through being employed by their neighbours to assist in cultivating their fields. ' It should be added, however, that in recent years civilization has begun to influence many of the Wild Tribes. . . . Some have begun to sow crops, which restricts their tendency to wander ; and that in turn leads to the construction of huts and houses. But the Semang have experienced these influences only to a very limited degree.' [6]

The Sakai, the Australoid neighbours of the Semang, lead a similar kind of life, but have been rather more influenced by the civilization of the Malays. They occupy the mountainous area of south-east Perak and north-west Pahang.

' Rock shelters and weather screens are used ; but, as a rule, the Sakai prefer huts, sometimes placing them up trees at a height of 30 feet from the ground. Their dress is a strip of Ipoh bark.' . . . ' They have the attractive simplicity and good-heartedness of many primitive folk, and are certainly far more intelligent than the Semang of Lengong. In Ulu Kinta the Sakai are quite civilized, and dress almost like the Malays.' . . . ' But even in this advanced state they still sometimes build their huts up trees.' [7]

[1] Skeat and Blagden I. 54, 66 ; II. 55 e.s.
[2] Schebesta i. 97, 190.   [3] Enriquez 75.   [4] Ibid., 76.
[5] Ibid., 76.   [6] Ibid., 76.   [7] Ibid., 81.

Another writer, Abraham Hale, says of these people . . .
' where not demoralized by Malay intercourse, [the Sakai are]
most kind and simple-hearted, always anxious to do their best to
assist any white man that happens to be in want of assistance,
and I find that the opinion of other people out here who have had
dealings with them coincides with mine in this respect.' [1]

These people are said to be very affectionate towards their
women and children. [2]

The Jakun, a proto-Malay tribe of the same district, though
more influenced by civilization, still show many of the characteristics of the food-gatherers. They are mild, and peaceful.
They are fairly strict monogamists, and very faithful. [3]

The next peoples to be considered are those living in the Andaman Islands, in the Bay of Bengal, on the track between southern
India and the Straits of Malacca. They will play a part in the
discussion concerning early warfare, so it will be necessary to
note their social and political organization. Although food-
gatherers, their social organization is more complicated than that,
say, of the Semang or Sakai, who have just been considered.

Professor Radcliffe-Brown has given a detailed account of the
social organization of the Andamanese. They live in villages
built on a definite plan, with separate bachelors' quarters. In
this they resemble the neighbouring food-producing tribes. Each
family occupies a hut in the village. [4]

These villages form the headquarters of a local group, [5] which
owns its hunting grounds in common, every member of the group
having equal rights over the whole of it. Other property, however, is privately owned. Thus a man's weapons are his own
personal property. He may reserve a tree for his own special
use ; or a pig is considered to belong to the man whose arrow
first hit it. In the same way anything a woman makes is her
property, and her husband cannot dispose of it without her permission. [6] Certain things, such as communal huts and canoes,
are held in common with special reservations.

Andaman communities have no organized government ; but
there is a great respect for seniority. ' Beside the respect for
seniority there is another important factor in the regulation of the
social life, namely the respect for certain personal qualities. These
qualities are skill in hunting and in warfare, generosity and
kindness, and freedom from bad temper.' There is, in each
community, no real authority ; influence is the force at work. [7]

---

[1] Hale 286.   [2] L.R.M. 96.
[3] Skeat and Blagden, *passim*, 79, 118, 342, 523, 528, 534, 559, 560.
[4] Radcliffe-Brown ii. 34.   [5] *Ibid.*, 31.   [6] *Ibid.*, 41.   [7] *Ibid.*, 47.

'Women may occupy a position of influence similar to that of the men.' [1]

The Andamanese are said not to practise marriage between relatives. They have premarital intercourse between the sexes, but 'the girls are always modest and childlike in their behaviour, and when married they make good wives and become models of constancy.' Sir Richard Temple states that they are monogamous, and that 'divorce is rare and unknown after the birth of a child, and there is no polygamy or incest.' [2]

The treatment of children is noteworthy. 'Andamanese children are reproved for being impudent and forward, but discipline is not enforced by corporal punishment ; they are early taught to be generous and self-denying, and the special object of the fasting period . . . seems to be to test the fortitude and powers of the lads and lasses before entering upon the cares and responsibilities of married life. The duties of showing respect and hospitality to friends and visitors being impressed upon them from their early years, all guests are well treated ; every attention is paid to their wants, the best food at their host's disposal is set before them, and, ere they take their leave, some tokens of regard or good will are bestowed, or, to speak more correctly, interchanged.' [3]

With regard to crime and punishment Radcliffe-Brown remarks, 'There does not seem to have been any such thing as punishment of crime. We may distinguish the two kinds of anti-social action which are regarded by the natives as being wrong. The first kind are those actions which injure in some way a private individual. The second are those which, while they do not injure any particular person, are yet regarded with disapproval by the society in general.'

Amongst the anti-social actions of the first kind are murder, or wounding, theft and adultery, and wilful damage of the property of another.

'No case of one Andamanese killing another has occurred in recent years. Quarrels sometimes occur between two men of the same camp. A good deal of hard swearing goes on, and sometimes one of the men will work himself up into a high pitch of anger, in which he may seize his bow and discharge an arrow near to the one who has offended him, or may vent his ill-temper by destroying any property he can lay his hands on, including not only that of his enemy, but also that of other persons and even his own. At such a display of anger the women and children flee into the jungle in terror, and if the angry man be at all a formidable person

[1] Radcliffe-Brown ii. 47.   [2] Temple 305.   [3] Man iii. 93–4.

the men occasionally do the same. It apparently requires more courage than the native usually possesses to endeavour to allay such a storm of anger. Yet I found that the slightest show of authority would immediately bring such a scene to an end. A man of influence in his village was probably generally equal to the task of keeping order and preventing any serious damage from taking place. It was probably rare for a man so far to give way to his anger as to kill his opponent.

'Such murders did, however, occasionally take place. The murderer would, as a rule, leave the camp and hide himself in the jungle, where he might be joined by such of his friends as were ready to take his part. It was left to the relatives and friends of the dead man to exact vengeance if they wished and if they could. If the murderer was a man who was much feared it is probable that he would escape. In any case the anger of the Andamanese is short-lived, and if for a few months he could keep out of the way of those who might seek revenge, it is probable that at the end of that time he would find their anger cooled.' [1]

E. H. Man describes these manifestations of anger on the part of the Andamanese as follows : ' When out of temper they do not defame relatives or use improper expressions, but merely indulge in mild terms of abuse such as the following, you liar, you log-head . . . you long-nose . . . you skin and bone.' [2] In cases of wrong-doing the aggrieved one sometimes flings a blazing faggot at the offender, or discharges an arrow at, or more frequently near him. All present flee and remain concealed until the quarrel is over. Sometimes friends interpose, and unarm the quarrellers, and do not return their weapons so long as there appears any risk of their misusing them. [3] In spite of the fact that the anger of the Andamanese usually blazes away as rapidly as it rises, there are exceptions in certain feuds of long standing. These feuds arise at tribal meetings, and are frequently centuries old.

Foreign influence has affected the Andamanese adversely. In their natural state ' they are gentle and pleasant to each other, but having no legal or other restraint on their passions are easily roused to anger and shoot and kill.' [4] But under Malay influence many of their natural virtues have been lost. Man writes, ' So widespread is the evil influence that has been exercised, that on no point probably will future writers differ so strongly as on the social and moral virtues of the Andamanese. I wish, therefore, to make it clear to my readers that my remarks and observations . . . are restricted to those living in their primitive state, and

---

[1] Radcliffe-Brown, *op. cit.*, 49.   [2] Man 27.
[3] *Ibid.*, 42.   [4] Portman i. 368.

who may therefore be fairly considered as representatives of the race, being unaffected by the virtues or vices of so-called civilization.' [1] The Malays taught the Andamanese to be pirates, and to raid the Nicobar Islands for plunder. [2]

The Kubu of Sumatra, a people still in the food-gathering stage of culture, with no social classes, who wander about in bands of relatives, are quite peaceful by nature, being shy and timid. They are monogamous. The elders settle disputes and impose punishments for offences. Until a few years ago they wore no clothes. [3] The same author states of them in another place, ' What struck me most in them was their extreme submissiveness, their want of independence and will ; they seemed too meek ever to act on the offensive. One cannot help feeling that they are harmless overgrown children of the woods. Within the memory of the chief of the village in which I first met these Kubus, have they only come to possess a sense of shame ; formerly they knew none, and were the derision of the villagers into whose neighbourhood they might come.' [4]

The Punan of Borneo are, culturally speaking, among the most primitive people in the world. For untold ages they have lived in the fastnesses of the forests of Borneo, well out of the way of the great movements that have swept through the Archipelago, carrying culture from India to the East. There is no reason to believe that they had been influenced strongly by any food-producing people until the Kayan and kindred tribes came up into the central watershed on their way down into Sarawak. The central part of Borneo is practically devoid of any archaeological remains, so far as is known, for the only objects that have been discovered are some carved stones of unknown origin on the banks of the Mahakam River. [5] It is probable that in the Punan we have a food-gathering people who have remained comparatively undisturbed, and present to us typical conditions obtaining among early food-gatherers generally.

We owe to Dr. Hose, and his collaborator, Professor McDougall, an account of these people.

The Punan have no social classes, no agriculture, no pottery making, no houses ; their property is communal. In regard to behaviour, ' The Punan is a likeable person, rich in good qualities and innocent of vices. He never slays or attacks men of other tribes wantonly ; he never seeks or takes a head, for his customs do not demand it ; and he never goes upon the warpath, except

[1] Man 264.   [2] Ibid., 266.
[3] Forbes ii. 232 e.s.   [4] Idem., i. 123.   [5] Perry v. 61.

when occasionally he joins a war-party of some other tribe in order to facilitate the avenging of blood. But he will defend himself and his family pluckily, if he is attacked and has no choice of flight.' [1] . . . 'Fighting between Punans, whether of the same or different communities, is very rare ; the only instances known to us are a few in which Punans have been incited by men of other tribes to join in an attack upon their fellows.' [2]

The Punan wander about in bands of relatives, numbering from forty to sixty. One of the elder men is the leader, but ' his sway is a very mild one ; he dispenses no substantial punishment ; public opinion and tradition seem to be the sole and sufficient sanctions of conduct among these Arcadian bands of gentle wary wanderers.' [3] . . . ' Harmony and mutual help are the rule within the family circle, as well as throughout the larger community ; the men generally treat their wives and children with all kindness, and the women perform their duties cheerfully and faithfully.' [4] . . . 'each shares with all members of the group whatever food, whether vegetable or animal, he may procure by skill or good fortune.' [5] Marriage is monogamous and for life. The authors remark, ' Those who are accustomed to all the complex comforts and resources of civilization, and to whom all these resources hardly suffice to make tolerable the responsibility and labour of the rearing of a family, can hardly fail to be filled with wonder at the thought of these gentle savages bearing and rearing large families of healthy well-mannered children in the damp jungle, without so much as a permanent shelter above their heads.' [6]

I have taken these extracts from what is certainly one of the most charming chapters ever written about the less civilized races of mankind. This information is especially valuable in that, as already mentioned, it concerns peoples who have been but little influenced by those of a more advanced stage of culture, and therefore represent what probably was the primitive condition of mankind.

Negrito tribes still linger in the Philippines. Schadenberg says of them, that they are monogamous and keep strictly to the union. The old are respected, and when they get beyond looking after themselves they are fed by their children.[7] Women are not so important as the men.[8]

Heer Morice Vanoverbergh, a missionary in the Philippines, has given a detailed account of the Negritos of northern Luzon.

[1] Hose and McDougall, II. 180.   [2] *Ibid.*, 183.
[3] *Ibid.*, 182.   [4] *Ibid.*, 185.   [5] *Ibid.*, 187.
[6] *Ibid.*, 184.   [7] Schadenberg 135.   [8] *Ibid.*, 137.

They have been considerably influenced by the neighbouring peoples, but retain enough of their original nature to show their cultural similarity to the other food-gatherers. Usually they live in houses, not commonly a trait of food-gathering culture, and one family to the house is the rule. One case is mentioned of a house occupied by four families, but these were related. The houses are scattered over a wide area, and never more than four of them together.

'. . . they never keep two wives at a time, although this practice is indulged in very often by Isneg and Kalinga alike ; married people very rarely separate, although this is a very general custom among the other pagan tribes.' [1]

As for their other morals. ' Two vices, generally recognized as being common to many uncivilized people, are lying and stealing. It would seem almost against the nature of the Negrito to tell a lie, and one reason for this is perhaps his apparent inability to conceal his own thoughts. Whatever he knows he, like the " enfant terrible," makes public.' . . . ' Stealing, if it occurs at all, is certainly very rare. The fact that we left our belongings for several days where every passing Negrito could have taken from them whatever he liked, is a sufficient proof of his honesty. Only once . . . have I heard the imputation of a Negrito having stolen something, and this was in the way of eatables, which might readily excuse hungry men, as everybody has a right to live ; but . . . this was told me by a Kagayan, a member of a race that is far from respecting the Negritos. Anyway, stealing is certainly abhorred by them. . . .' [2]

They are very peaceful. ' Whatever may be the case with other Negritos, and whatever writers may have said about them, the Negritos I saw are of a very peaceful character. Only on one occasion did I hear of a Negrito having wounded one of his fellow Negritos : it was Allapa, who had to arrest the other fellow ; as the latter was not willing to follow, Allapa became angry and wounded him ; he then gave himself up to the authorities and was sentenced to prison for one year.

' There is no question of warfare between the different Negrito groups ; they usually know one another ; and, even when unknown, they are always very friendly ; they seem to consider the whole Negrito race as a big family, any representatives of it being welcome to their homes at all times. . . . When I asked Masigun if they would allow even Negritos from Alkalá—and farther away to hunt in their forests, he candidly answered me in the affirmative and added : " We cannot forbid them ; if

[1] Vanoverbergh 199.   [2] *Ibid.*, 195.

they like to come here and hunt in our forests, they are allowed to do so ; why not ? "   When I asked him if his people would not object or shoot arrows at them, he simply laughed, seeming to find the idea a very funny one, and said, " No, never." [1]   ' To conclude, we find the Negritos living in happy intercourse with everybody else, but entirely isolated and kept away, from Isneg and Christians alike, by a deep social gulf.' [2]

His opinion of the Negrito may be summed up in his words. ' A Negrito is always happy, he laughs more than he weeps ; he is devoted to his friends (and he has no enemies), and is always ready to succour them ; he is very polite, and he is hospitable to a remarkable degree. . . .   To the Negrito life seems to be a very joyous affair, and he does not seem to have any preoccupations at all.   To him each day has its own cares, and, if he cannot find to-day what he is in need of, he expects to find it at some other time, not seeming to care a fig for disappointments of any kind.' [3]

[1] Vanoverbergh 187.   [2] *Ibid.*, 189.   [3] *Ibid.*, 191.

CHAPTER IV

FOOD-GATHERERS : AUSTRALIA

THE Australians are typical food-gatherers in all the details of everyday life. They are ignorant of pottery-making. They have no agriculture, nor do they depend on domesticated animals for food. Sir Baldwin Spencer, in his book on the Arunta, describes them in the following words : ' In their ordinary condition the natives are almost completely naked, which is all the more strange, as kangaroo and wallaby are by no means scarce, and one would think that their fur would be of no little use and comfort in the winter-time, when, under the perfectly clear sky, which often remains cloudless for weeks together, the radiation is so great that at night-time the temperature falls several degrees below freezing point. The idea of making any kind of clothing as a protection against cold does not appear to have entered the native mind.' [1]

The social organization of the Australian tribes forms one of the many interesting problems of social anthropology. The subject is complex and difficult, but recent work by Professor Radcliffe-Brown and his colleagues has thrown a flood of light on the obscurity. [2] Professor Malinowski has also made a signal contribution in his work on ' The Family among the Australian Aborigines.' [3]

It is not necessary here to enter into details, for there seems to be a general agreement that the social structure of these tribes is based on the family.

The family is the fundamental economic unit, as among food-gatherers in general. But the situation is somewhat complicated by the fact that Australian natives spend their lives in the company of the rest of the ' horde ' to which they belong.

The ' horde,' as defined by Radcliffe-Brown, is a local grouping possessing a common territory, and consisting normally of a single line of descent through the male line. ' The horde, . . . as an existing group at any moment consists of male members of all ages whose fathers and fathers' father belonged to the horde,

---

[1] Spencer ii. 14.   [2] Radcliffe-Brown iii.
[3] Malinowski i.

unmarried girls who are the sisters or daughters or son's daughters of the male members, married women, all of whom, in some regions, and most of whom, in others, belonged originally to other hordes, and have become attached to the horde by marriage.'[1]

The statements of Professor Radcliffe-Brown show that the Australian horde usually consists of a band of relatives; that is to say, the family group, in either the limited or extended sense of the term, is the basic unit of Australian tribal life.

The Australian natives usually had no ruling classes, although hereditary chiefs are mentioned in certain cases. Authority in the group was usually vested in the initiated men.[2]

Most Australian tribes possess two intermarrying divisions, termed moieties. This form of social institution is called The Dual Organization.[3]

The Australians have complicated marriage rules, based usually upon their division into two intermarrying groups. Monogamy is not quite so universal as among other food-gatherers. Some of the older men, becoming very powerful, claim several of the women for themselves, thus depriving the younger men of their chances of marriage for a long time. Nevertheless the family unit is preserved intact.

The children are well cared for. ' Both men and women are very fond of children, and the kindest attention is shown them by young and old alike. They are not spoilt by this kind treatment all round ; one word from the parent generally is sufficient to check a child when doing wrong, and the greatest respect is shown to parents by their children. Altogether, the treatment of children by these people, after they are once taken up and nursed, is judicious and very creditable.'[4] On the other hand, little affection is shown for the babies in the first months of their lives, and only when they grow older do the mothers take much notice of them.[5]

The Australian makes no provision for the future. ' He stores nothing, except for a few days, in preparation for a ceremony, and has no idea of agriculture or domestication, partly perhaps because the animals around him, such as kangaroos, are not adapted to act as beasts of burden or givers of milk, but still more because he believes that, by means of magic, which plays a large part in his life, he can increase their numbers when he wishes to do so. When food is abundant he eats to repletion; when it is scarce he tightens his waist-band and starves philosophically.'[6]

[1] Radcliffe-Brown, *op. cit.*, 3, 4, 5, 28, 105.   [2] Howitt Ch. VI.
[3] Radcliffe-Brown iii. 87.   [4] Bonney, F., 125, 6.
[5] Bischofs 35.   [6] Spencer ii. 14.

The food supply is divided out according to rule. Discussing this practice Howitt remarked : ' The instances given
in this chapter of the division of food among the kindred and
relations, and the special provision for the old people, give an
entirely different idea of the aboriginal character to that which
had been usually held. This latter is derived from what is seen
of the blacks under our civilization. The oft-repeated description
of the black fellow eating the white man's beef or mutton and
throwing a bone to his wife who sits behind him, in fear of a blow
from his club, is partly the new order of things resulting from
our civilization breaking down the old rules. But it is also, in
part, the old rule itself. I have shown that in some cases the
wife is fed by her own people, and the throwing of food to another
person is not an act of discourtesy. Its reason is that there is
a deep-seated objection to receive anything which can convey
evil magic from the hand of another person, and in many instances
that applies to the two sexes.

' Such contrasts between the old and the new conditions of
things struck me very forcibly at the Kurnai *Jeraeil*; there the
people lived in the manner of their old lives, certainly with the
addition of the white man's beef and flour, but without his
intoxicating drinks, which have been a fatal curse to the
black race. That week was passed without a single quarrel or
dispute.' [1]

According to the evidence of Dawson the women are not well
treated. ' These poor creatures,' he says, ' are made to do all
the drudgery. . . . They carry the wood for fires, make the
nets for fishing, and carry everything else that they move about
with, except their instruments of war.' [2]

According to one authority, ' The natives are a mild and harmless race of savages ; and where any mischief has been done by
them, the cause has generally arisen, I believe, in bad treatment
by their white neighbours. Short as my residence has been here,
I have, perhaps, had more intercourse with these people, and more
favourable opportunities of seeing what they really are, than any
other person in the colony. . . . They have usually been treated,
in distant parts of the colony, as if they had been dogs, and shot
by convict-servants . . . for the most trifling causes.' [3]

This treatment of the natives by the whites caused retaliation
on the part of the former, and led to the belief in the cruelty of the
natives. The natives are not very stable in character, and in
consequence are easily influenced, sometimes for the worse, by the
habits and customs of the whites. The Rev. John Mathew says

[1] Howitt 777.   [2] Dawson 67.   [3] *Ibid.*, 57–8.

about them that ' in the aboriginal character there are many admirable, meritorious elements, but there is a lack of strong, inherited, combining, marshalling will or self-determination, and, as a natural consequence, the moral qualities are prone to operate capriciously.   The natives are not insensible to promptings of honourable feeling, but generally, unless when repressed or constrained by fear, they act from impulse rather than from principle, and their best inclinations are easily overpowered by pressure from within or from without.   You could rely upon a black fellow being faithful to a trust only on condition that he were exempt from temptation.' [1]

Mr. Mathew further considers the testimony of James Davies. Mr. Davies knew them well, and he said of them, ' Hundreds of them would take your life for a blanket or a hundredweight of flour.   I wouldn't trust them as far as I could throw a bullock by the tail. . . .   They are so greedy that nothing can come up to them. . . .   They are the most deceitful people I ever came across. . . .   The father will beat his son and the son the father. The brother will lie in ambush to be avenged on the brother ; if he cannot manage him in fight he will lie in ambush with a spear or a club.'   Mr. Mathew dissents from this harsh judgment. ' This, I am sure, was stating the case against the poor creatures too strongly.   They are not wantonly untruthful ; they are not deficient in courage ; they are not excessively selfish ; and they are by no means lacking in natural affection.   But Mr. Davies corroborates what I have said of the presence of that defect of character which may be termed instability.   It may be said that the whole fabric of their moral character is in a position of unstable equilibrium.   The slightest strain will destroy the poise.' [2]   He goes on to say that they have courage which enables them to perform marvellous feats.   They may be covetous, but they are very generous. [3]   ' As a rule the blacks are sympathetic and affectionate, especially the women.   Sufficient evidence of this is the way in which white men have been treated who have been unfortunate enough to be cast upon their mercy.   Relatives are usually fondly attached to each other.   The attachment between parents and their offspring is very strong, and exhibits itself in kindness to the aged, who are tenderly cared for, and indulgence to little children.'   They are light-hearted people, very fond of a joke.   Their laughter is unrestrained, but easily turns to anger. [4]

' Settlement by the British has usually proceeded without much resistance.   The blacks have kindly assisted in their own dis-

[1] Mathew 79.   [2] *Ibid.*, 79.   [3] *Ibid.*, 79.   [4] *Ibid.*, 80.

possession and extermination, guiding the aliens through their forests, giving them much of their own strength at a beggarly rate of recompense, submitting contentedly to indignity and oppression, and rewarding injuries and insults with gentleness and service. They have committed robbery, rape, murder, and perpetrated several massacres. True, but they have often been trained to such offences by the lawless, brutal, indecent, tyrannical behaviour of the white men with whom they have come into contact, for as a matter of fact the outskirts of civilization have a strong admixture of barbarism.' [1]

Among themselves the Australian natives are extremely peaceful. Speaking of the natives of Victoria, about the year 1847, William Thomas wrote to the Governor of that province that the blacks were much in the habit of wandering through the land, settling down for the night in temporary encampments. At such times they behave in the most peaceful manner possible. ' The harmony that exists among them when none of another tribe is in the party is surprising. I have been out with them for months without a single altercation.' [2]

Sir Baldwin Spencer endorses this view of the natives. ' As a general rule,' he writes, ' the natives are kindly disposed to one another—that is, of course, within the limits of their own tribe ; and, where two tribes come into contact with one another on the borderland of their respective territories, there the same amicable feelings are maintained between the members of the two. There is no such thing as one tribe being in a constant state of enmity with another so far as the Central tribes are concerned. Now and again, of course, fights do occur between the members of different local groups who may belong to the same or to different tribes.' [3]

William Thomas points out that ' there is one particularly amiable trait in the aboriginal character, which is, that no animosity remains in their breasts nor does any shrink from punishment. At the close of a fight or punishment, those who have inflicted the wounds may be seen sucking them and doing any other kind office required.' [4]

The marriage rules of the Australians are carefully enforced, and are the chief cause of dispute between the two intermarrying groups that usually make up the tribe.[5] This fighting, however, is not very serious. ' Fighting being a pastime with them, a few blows or a deep cut or two are considered as nothing, and the men being in first-rate condition, the wounds soon heal.' Howitt

[1] Mathew 81.　　　　[2] Bride 66.　　　　[3] Spencer ii. 15, 28, 38.
　　　　[4] Bride 68.　　　　　　[5] Howitt 234.

4

concludes : ' Nearly all their fights were the result of the capture of women, either after the ceremonial combats, or in raids for that special object.' [1]

Trespass is very severely punished. Lesser crimes are also punished, usually by the offended person. Thomas writes : ' Theft is of rare occurrence, and is punished by blows on the head of the thief by the party wronged. I never knew but one case of this kind.' [2]

The death of a man is punished in the following manner. A meeting was arranged for the purpose, the guilty man was then placed before the members of his group, while members of the murdered man's group ranged themselves opposite, armed with spears. The spears were then thrown at the murderer, who had to protect himself as well as he could with his shield. Dawson describes one of these meetings, in which the name of the criminal was Corbon Wickie. After the spear-throwing a man named Wallis advanced on Wickie and challenged him to combat with his waddy (club). ' After some abuse and flourishing with their waddies, Wickie struck Wallis a tremendous blow on the crown of his head, which he purposely held forward without any defence. In an instant he was seen dancing in the face of his opponent like a harlequin, brandishing his waddy, while the blood streamed down his cheeks and chest. Wickie now held forward his head to Wallis, who struck him a similar blow, when Wickie was seen dancing and bleeding in like manner. At this moment I dashed in between them, and insisted upon their desisting. They were all instantly silent, and not the slightest opposition was made ; but Wallis, who had always shown great attachment towards me, entreated that I would allow him to give Corbon Wickie one blow more, which should not hurt him, and then Wickie would give him another also. " Only a little bit, massa," he said. " Bael hurt it, den no more coulor (anger) ; black pellow always do so."

' The sight was most sickening to me, and I would allow no more of it. I reasoned and argued with both of them, and told them to shake hands. They seemed to be quite astonished that I should suppose they were enemies. Wallis said, " I like Corbon Wickie always, dat good pellow." ' Why, then,' I said, " do you wish to hurt each other ? " They both laughed outright at this question, which, as well as my reasoning, appeared quite incomprehensible to them.' [3]

The spear-throwing on these occasions was always conducted very fairly. None was thrown without warning, and deaths were

[1] Howitt 236.   [2] Bride 67.   [3] Dawson 288.

very rare, so skilled were the natives at defending themselves. It was, in fact, more of the nature of an ordeal.[1]

The Australians believe that death is due to magic, and if anyone dies someone must be responsible. This theory leads to much needless killing, for it is thought that only the kidney fat of the wrong-doer will appease the dead man, and in order to obtain this another death has to occur. [2]

[1] Dawson 289, 64.
[2] Bride 68 ; Howitt 326 ; Spencer and Gillen 556.

CHAPTER V

FOOD-GATHERERS : AMERICA

AMERICA contains food-gathering peoples, both in the north and in the south. Those of the north include the Eskimo, whose territory stretches from Alaska in the west to Greenland in the east ; and some of the Indian tribes, such as the Déné, Salish, Ojibwa, Paiute, and the tribes of California.

The Eskimo have long been in contact with peoples of different cultures, and, like the Andamanese and the Australians, have been influenced by them. Unlike most food-gatherers, they wear very complete clothing.[1] They depend, however, for this, and for their food, entirely on their prowess as hunters. Their dwelling-places, also, are much more better built than those of the majority of the food-gatherers. In winter they live in snow houses, or iglu. In summer they use tents, generally made of skin.[2]

' The (Labrador) Eskimo never had any " chiefs " in the Indian sense of the word. They have had leaders, great hunters or enterprising shamans, who have been accorded their position by general appreciation of their worth. But the office has never carried any particular authority with it.

' In nearly every Eskimo village there is a head-man, who entertains strangers and transacts the village business with them, but he has no authority outside his own family. . . . When a shaman is also head of a village, he is quite a powerful personage, but may be deposed or killed if he plays the tyrant. The office is not hereditary, unless the son of the head-man shows equal merit. The office often passes from one family to another and entails the rather burdensome duty of feasting the villagers occasionally to keep them in a good humour.' [3]

According to Boas, ' The social order of the Eskimo is entirely founded on the family and on the ties of consanguinity and affinity between the individual families.' He adds that ' monogamy is everywhere more frequent than polygamy, only a very few men having two or more wives. According to Ross, polygamy occurs with the Netchillirmiut.' [4]

The children are well cared for. Boas writes, ' Children are

[1] Hawkes 38 e.s.   [2] Ibid., 58 e.s.   [3] Ibid., 110.   [4] Boas 578, 579.

40

treated very kindly and are not scolded, whipped, or subjected to any corporal punishment.' 'Besides the children properly belonging to the family, adopted children, widows, and old people are considered part of it. Adoption is carried on among this people to a great extent.' [1]

' In summer most families have each their own tent, but in the fall from two to four join in building a house. Frequently the parents live on one side, the family of the son-in-law on the other, and a friend or relative in a small recess.' [2]

Food is shared out equally among the whole village. 'When a seal is brought to the huts everybody is entitled to a share of the meat and blubber, which is distributed by the hunter himself, or carried to the individual huts by his wife. This custom is only practised when food is scarce. In time of plenty only the housemates receive a share of the animal.' [3]

There is no punishment for crime except blood vengeance. A man who is offended by another man may take revenge by killing the offender. It is then the right and the duty of the nearest relatives of the victim to kill the murderer. In certain quarrels between the Netchillirmiut and the Aivillirmuit, in which the murderer himself could not be apprehended, the family of the murdered man has killed one of his, the murderer's relations, in his stead. Such a feud sometimes lasts for a long time and is even handed down to a succeeding generation. It is sometimes settled by mutual agreement. As a sign of reconciliation both parties touch each other's breasts, saying Ilaga (my friend).

' If a man has committed a murder or made himself odious by other outrages he may be killed by anyone simply as a matter of justice. The man who intends to take revenge on him must ask his country-men singly if each agrees in the opinion that the offender is a bad man deserving death. If all answer in the affirmative he may kill the man thus condemned and no one is allowed to revenge the murder.

' Their method of carrying on such a feud is quite foreign to our feelings. Strange as it may seem, a murderer will come to visit the relatives of his victim (though he knows that they are allowed to kill him in revenge) and will settle with them. He is kindly welcomed and sometimes lives quietly for weeks and months. Then he is suddenly challenged to a wrestling match, and if defeated is killed, or if victorious he may kill one of the opposite party, or when hunting he is suddenly attacked by his companions and slain.' [4]

There is no law of trespass among the Eskimo. ' The Eskimo

[1] Boas 580.   [2] Ibid., 581.   [3] Ibid., 582.   [4] Ibid., 582.

do not have any strict divisions of hunting territory, such as characterize their near Indian neighbours, the Micmacs and Montagnais. Most of the hunting is done on the sea, which is free to everyone. The same condition applies to the vast interior where the Eskimo hunt for deer in the autumn and spring. The idea of restricting the pursuit of game is repugnant to the Eskimo, who hold that food belongs to everyone. This does not preclude them from having intricate laws for the division of game, when hunting in parties.

'Under ordinary conditions, a family may occupy a fishing station in summer year after year undisputed, but it does not give them any special right to it. Anyone else is free to come and enjoy its benefits, and, according to Eskimo ethics, they would move away before they would start a dispute about it. Quite often a poor young hunter is invited by a more fortunate family to share their camping ground, and is thus enabled to get a start in life.' [1]

There is a contrast between the Eskimo living in the east and their western kinsfolk. Among the Greenland and east Canadian Eskimo warfare is unknown, but with the Alaskan and Bering Straits tribes inter-tribal feuds are widespread. Speaking of the Greenland Eskimo, Nansen wrote : ' Fighting and brutalities are unknown among them, and murder is very rare. They hold it atrocious to kill a fellow-creature ; therefore war is in their eyes incomprehensible and repulsive, a thing for which their language has no word ; and soldiers and officers, brought up to the trade of killing, they regard as mere butchers.

' It has, indeed, as Egede says, " occurred now and then that an extremely malicious person, out of rankling hatred, has killed another." But when he adds that " this they regard with the greatest coolness, neither punishing the murderer nor taking the thing to heart in any way," I believe that he is not quite just to them. They certainly abhor the crime, and if they do not actively mix themselves up in the matter, it is because they regard it as a private affair between the murderer and his victim. It is not the business of the community, but simply of the murdered man's nearest relatives to take revenge for his death, if they are in a position to do so ; and thus we find, even among this peaceful folk, traces of a sort of blood-feud, though the practice is but slightly developed, and the duty does not, as a rule, seem to weigh heavily upon the survivors. In cases of extreme atrocity, however, the men of a village have been known to make common cause against a murderer, and kill him.

[1] Hawkes 25.

' Here, as elsewhere, women and love are among the most frequent causes of bloodshed. The attack often takes place at sea, the murderer transfixing his victim from behind with his harpoon, or capsizing his kaiak and cutting a hole in it. It does not accord with the Eskimo's character to attack another face to face, not so much because he is afraid as because he is bashful, and would feel it embarrassing to go to work under the other's eye.

' They do not regard it as criminal to kill old witches and wizards, who, they think, can injure and even kill others by their arts. Nor is it inconsistent with their moral code to hasten the death of those who are sick and in great suffering, or of those in delirium, of which they have a great horror.' [1]

The Bering Strait and Alaskan Eskimo present a great contrast in behaviour to their more easterly kinsfolk. When the Russians first appeared upon the north Pacific coast of America they found the Eskimo engaged in deadly blood-feuds. The causes of these feuds were similar to those which caused occasional strife among the Greenland and Labrador Eskimo ; but they were carried on in a very different manner. In the east once a murder had been revenged, all angry feelings were appeased. In the west one murder only led to another, forming a chain of reprisals that might be carried on for several generations. ' Blood revenge is considered a sacred duty among all the Eskimo, and it is a common thing to find men who dare not visit certain villages because of a blood-feud existing, owing to their having killed some one whose near relatives live in the place. . . . Owing to this custom, a man who has killed another watches incessantly, and in the end acquires a peculiar restless expression which the Eskimo have learnt to recognize at once. Several of them told me that they could always recognize a man who had killed another by the expression of his eyes, and from cases observed by myself I think this is undoubtedly true. The desultory feud existing between the Kotzebue sound Malemut and the Tinné of the interior partakes of the character of blood revenge, except that each side seeks to avenge the death of relatives or fellow tribesmen upon any of the opposing tribe.' [2] The constant feuds between these two tribes led to considerable damage being done to property. ' The people of the coast from the Yukon mouth to the Kotzebue sound have many tales of villages destroyed by war parties of Tinné. Back from the head of Norton bay and Kotzebue sound, during the time of my residence in that region, several Tinné were killed by Malemut while hunting reindeer on the strip of uninhabited tundra lying between the districts occupied by the

[1] Nansen 162-3.   [2] Nelson 293,

two peoples. During the summer of 1879 a party of three Malemut from the head of Kotzebue sound ambushed and killed seven Tinné who were found hunting reindeer in the interior.' [1]

Sometimes marauding parties would inflict considerable damage on the enemy, killing the males, and even the children lest they should grow up to be enemies, and taking the women into captivity. Young men, fighting in their first skirmish, were given drinks of enemies' blood, and made to eat small parts of enemies' hearts, in order to give them bravery.[2]

The Malemut are quarrelsome and have frequent bloody affrays among themselves. The Unalit and Yukon people regard them with the greatest fear and hatred and say that they are like dogs —always showing their teeth and ready to fight.[3]

Strangers were usually regarded with more or less suspicion, and in ancient times were commonly put to death. But among friends and relatives they are very hospitable. 'Hospitality is regarded as a duty among the Eskimo, as far as concerns their own friends in the surrounding villages, and to strangers in certain cases as well as to all guests visiting the village during festivals. By the exercise of hospitality to their friends and the people of neighbouring villages their goodwill is retained and they are saved from any evil influence to which they might otherwise be subjected.' [3] Nelson found them sometimes to be inhospitable to himself; but at Askinuk and Kaialigamut (in the same district) 'the people ran out at our approach, unharnessed our dogs, put our sledges on the framework, and carried our bedding into the Kashim with the greatest goodwill.' [4]

With regard to the general behaviour of these peoples Nelson says, 'The only feeling of conscience or moral duty that I noted among the Eskimo seemed to be an instinctive desire to do that which was most conducive to the general good of the community, as looked at from their point of view. Whatever experience has taught them to be best is done, guided by superstitious usages and customs.' [5] They are very honest, paying all debts contracted with traders. 'A curious part of this custom was that very often the same Eskimo who would be perfectly honest and go to great trouble and exertion to settle a debt would not hesitate to steal from the same trader. Among themselves this feeling is not generally so strong, and if a man borrows from another and fails to return the article he is not held to account for it. This is done under the general feeling that if a person had enough property to enable him to lend some of it, he has more than he needs.

The one who makes the loan under these circumstances does not even feel justified in asking for the return of the article, and waits for it to be given back voluntarily.' [1]

Moore sums them up by saying that on the whole they have many likeable qualities, and during his stay with them he became very much attached to them. 'They have many virtues, and their faults might better be called weaknesses which harm no one so much as themselves, while those factors which have made most for their moral and their physical degeneration have been introduced from without.' [2]

The contrast, therefore, between the eastern and the western groups of Eskimos lies in the fact that the peoples living near the Bering Straits and in Alaska have had superimposed upon their naturally harmonious temperaments a type of intermittent warfare due to blood-feuds. The reason for this change in character seems to be due to the contact with Indian tribes, who have introduced a different type of civilization. This is clear from the contrast between the Coppermine River and Mackenzie River tribes. The first of these groups are ' gentle and courteous ', but the others are ' as turbulent and fierce as the latter are peaceful and well-disposed '. This contrast is due to the fact that Indian influence has been at work in the west. ' The only reason I can assign for these Esquimaux (the Mackenzie River) being so different in temper and disposition from their countrymen to the east is, that they have always been at war with the Souchoux Indians, who hunt on the lands in proximity to the sea coast.' [3]

South of the Eskimo live the Athapascan Déné. With the exception of a few groups who have come into contact with alien cultures on the coast, these people are food-gatherers. They wander about in small groups, having no chiefs. They rank high in all moral qualities, with the exception of courage. They never resort to arms, but, in cases of conflict, opponents lay aside their knives and wrestle with each other. [4]

The Salish tribes are the south-western neighbours of the Déné. Some of them, living near the coast, have social classes, and are warlike, to a certain extent. The inland members of the tribe, however, are hunters, living in small groups. They were formerly described as ' well-regulated, peace-loving, and virtuous people, whose existence was far from being squalid or miserable '. [5] According to Father de Smet ' the beau-ideal of the Indian character, uncontaminated by contact with the whites, is found among them. What is most pleasing to the stranger is to see

[1] Nelson 294.   [2] Moore 375.   [3] Rae i, 150
      [4] Hill-Tout 43 e.s.   [5] Ibid., 43, 47.

their simplicity, united with sweetness and innocence, keep step with the most perfect dignity and modesty of deportment. The gross vices which dishonour the red men on the frontiers are utterly unknown among them. They are honest to scrupulosity. The Hudson's Bay Company during forty years that it has been trading in furs with them has never been able to perceive that the smallest object has been stolen from them. The agent takes his furs down to Colville every spring and does not return before autumn. During his absence the store is confided to the care of an Indian, who trades in the name of the company, and on the return of the agent renders him a most exact account of his trust. The store often remains without anyone to watch it, the door unlocked and unbolted and the goods are never stolen. The Indians go in and out, help themselves to what they want, and always scrupulously leave in place of whatever article they take, its exact value.' [1]

Some of the peoples of eastern Canada, such as the Ojibwa, are still food-gatherers. This, however, only applies to one section of the tribe, the Chippewas. This group was mild and harmless, little disposed to make war on the neighbouring tribes, and formed a great contrast to the remaining Ojibwa, who were an agricultural people, and who were, at the same time, extremely warlike. [2]

The Paiute of Nevada, Utah, and Arizona make no pottery and do not practise agriculture. 'As a people they are moral, industrious and peaceable, and are highly commended for their good qualities by those who have had the best opportunities for judging. While apparently not as bright in intellect as the prairie tribes, they appear to possess more solidity of character, . . . they have steadily resisted the vices of civilization. . . .' [3]

Professor Kroeber of California University says that ' from the time of the first settlement of California, its Indians have been described as both more primitive and more peaceful than the majority of the natives of North America.' [4]

Miss Hooper, speaking of the Cahuilla Indians, says ' unselfishness and respect for old people is their ideal of right living. Children are taught from infancy to be generous and kind to the old. . . . Liberality and generosity were considered the most important virtues. The man who was the best hunter was held in very high esteem. The woman who could do most work in the shortest time was the ideal woman. Nowadays these things do not seem to matter so much. There was always real affection

[1] Hill-Tout, C., 46.   [2] ' Arch. Rep. 1905,' 79.
[3] ' Handbook of American Indians,' II. 187.
[4] Kroeber, A. L., i. 81.

between the members of an Indian family but very little outward demonstration of it.'[1] Miss Hooper further adds that 'the Cahuilla, like most of the Californian Indians, have been a very peaceful people. Their main troubles were between villages, and were caused by boundary disputes '.[2]

Children on the whole are well treated among the Californians, especially while young.[3]

One characteristic of the Californians is reminiscent of the Australians. 'Warfare throughout California was carried on only for revenge, never for plunder or from a desire of distinction. The Mohave and Yuma must indeed be excepted from this statement, but their attitude is entirely unique. Probably the cause that most commonly originated feuds was the belief that a death had been caused by witchcraft. No doubt theft and disputes of various sorts also contributed. Once ill-feeling was established, it was likely to continue for long periods.'[4]

The Fuegians and their close neighbours, the Chonoans, are the chief food-gathering group of South America. In spite of the low latitudes at which these people live they have very little clothing. Their chief covering consists of a mantle made of skins. Among the Ona tribe this mantle reaches to the knees or feet ; but as in other tribes it only covers the shoulders or sometimes the breast. Among the Ona this mantle is discarded during hunting or wrestling. Other tribes frequently discard it altogether.[5]

These peoples sometimes build themselves beehive-shaped huts by covering a framework of branches with skins, grass or any other available material ; but among many tribes, especially the Ona, a skin windshield is more common. In this case there is no roof, but in bad weather extra skins are laid over the shields to give greater protection. In some cases the skins are merely tied to trees, and a rude shelter is thus formed.[6]

The Fuegians have no government, but sometimes ' the older men and the wizards wield a certain undefined influence or authority over the people. The only fixed authority is that of the man over his family ; this authority is in theory at least, if not always in practice, an absolute one.

' No distinct clan organization within the tribe exists, although certain groups of natives related apparently by blood and marriage occupy more or less fixed localities.'[7]

The marriage customs vary slightly from tribe to tribe, but

[1] Hooper 352–3.   [2] *Ibid.*, 355.
[3] Goddard 52.   [4] Kroeber ii. 296.
[5] Cooper 193–4.   [6] *Ibid.*, 192.   [7] *Ibid.*, 178.

' as to polygamy, there is no tribal sentiment apparently, at least among the Yahgans and Onas, against a man having two or even more wives, yet, *de facto*, monogamy is the more common rule '.[1] ' It is a common practice among both the Onas and the Yahgans for a man to marry two sisters,' or sometimes he ' marries a woman and her daughter by a former husband '.[2]

' Love for and good treatment of children are amply attested for all three Fuegian tribes. . . . Capt. Bove states that the Yahgan mother's love wanes as the child is weaned and ceases entirely at the child's seventh or eighth year.' [3]

' Among the three Fuegian tribes the aged are respected and well treated.' [4]   The women are said to be subject to the men, but this holds in theory only.   In practice they are allowed considerable power.   ' Brutality, where indulged in by the man, may be occasioned by jealousy ; but, on the other hand, the wife herself is not so tender at times with her sinning spouse.   A cruel husband gets into trouble with his wife's relatives.   Husbands have real affection for their wives but are chary of showing it, especially in the presence of strangers.' [5]

The Fuegians are not entirely peaceful in their behaviour. ' The custom of blood-revenge is emphatically prevalent.   In their daily relations the Fuegians are peaceful enough, yet quarrels are not infrequent—quarrels which often, especially among the Onas, pass from words to blows, and may end in homicide.

' Among the Yahgans murder is comparatively infrequent. Between 1871 and 1884 the Rev. Mr. Bridges found only 22 cases of homicide—this among a people who must of necessity take the law into their own hands.   The friends of the fighting parties intervene, both by persuasion and by force, to restore peace, but often the fight develops into a general mêlée.   A murderer becomes an outcast, abandoned by all, and will sooner or later be killed.

' Among the Onas homicide is much more common, Mr. Lucas Bridges stating that " there are few Onas over 30 years of age who have not killed one of their own people in revenge ".   The intrusion of white settlers into native hunting grounds has probably had something to do with this.' [6]

Inter-tribal feuds also exist among these people.   ' There is, or was, a good deal of bad feeling for one another between the members of the three Fuegian tribes, but as a rule on border territories the relations have been fairly peaceful.   In their relations with the whites both the Chonos and Fuegians have normally shown themselves peaceful, friendly and tractable, but

[1] Cooper 165.   [2] *Ibid.*, 165.   [3] *Ibid.*, 170.
[4] *Ibid.*, 170.   [5] *Ibid.*, 168.   [6] *Ibid.*, 174.

the Fuegians have often shown themselves hostile, aggressive, and treacherous, when they have felt they were numerically superior. More commonly, however, the white man has, deliberately or unwittingly, been the first to give offence.

' Deadly and long-standing intertribal feuds are common, particularly so among the Onas, but warfare, properly so called, cannot be said to exist. The vanquished men are usually killed outright and the women and children taken captive.' [1]

[1] Cooper 174.

CHAPTER VI

BEHAVIOUR IN FAMILY GROUPS [1]

IT is time now to examine the evidence put forward in this survey of the food-gatherers.

These people are, as we have seen, the most primitive known to us. They thus afford us the best chance of estimating the nature of the behaviour of primitive men.

I feel it necessary, however, in order to anticipate a criticism that is certain to be made, to mention once again, a matter of method. I have already pointed out that the simplicity of the culture of the food-gathering peoples may be due to two distinct causes. The food-gatherers who have come under review are modern people, living at the present time. They may have derived their cultural simplicity from the fact that they are the survivors of primitive groups that have remained at a low stage of culture, or they may be peoples who once had a more advanced culture, but have lost it in the course of time. Whichever is the true explanation the value of the evidence remains unaltered, for the aim is to study human beings under conditions of the simplest type that can be discovered. It does not matter whether these lowly peoples once had chiefs, or some other more compli-

---

[1] Some students will notice that my description of the food-gatherers as a whole agrees closely with the conclusions of Father W. Schmidt, the renowned Professor and Editor of ' Anthropos ', contained in his monograph on ' The Pygmies '.*

Father Schmidt's work appeared in 1910. My first contribution to the same subject was made in 1917.† Father Schmidt therefore has the prior claim to part of my thesis. I am not consciously aware that I knew of his views in detail till about the year 1924. I had studied his monograph on Indonesian religions in 1913, and therefore was well acquainted with his views on early religion, particularly as regards his ideas of monotheism.

I find myself unable to agree with Father Schmidt's views on this latter topic. At the same time, however, I fully agree with what he says concerning pygmies in general.

My conclusions, it will have been seen, are derived directly from the descriptions of those who have lived among food-gatherers ; they are not based on any *a priori* hypothesis.

---

* ' Die Stellung der Pygmaënvölker in der Entwickelungsgeschichte des Menschen ', 1910.   † Perry iv.

cated form of society; the point is that they lack them now. Their behaviour is that of people living without these more advanced social institutions. The obvious fact that certain of these food-gathering peoples have often learned something from their more advanced neighbours is of great importance, and reference will be made to it on more than one occasion. But for the present the aim is to discover, if possible, what appears to be the general type of food-gathering society.

From time to time during the survey it has been obvious that, in certain respects, it is not possible to lay down hard and fast generalizations concerning the culture of food-gatherers. The social organization of Australia, Bushman pottery, and the bachelors' houses of the Andamanese, are cases in point. But on the whole the evidence presents a well-defined picture.[1]

First, as to the arts and crafts. The food-gatherers are singularly lacking in material possessions. The Negritos in Africa and south-eastern Asia use bows and arrows. There does not seem to be as yet any evidence as to how they came by these weapons. As a whole they do not make pottery; they do not work metals; they do not weave; or even spin. It would appear that they formerly wore no clothes and made no proper houses, but at the most constructed shelters of branches. They usually practise no agriculture, and keep no domesticated animals for use as food.

To turn now to the social life. The predominant grouping is that of small bands of relatives. This may consist of a single family, parents and children. It may also be slightly more complicated, and consist of, say, grandparents, children and grandchildren, or of married brothers, or some such grouping: but in all cases the members of these groups are in the closest possible relationship to one another.

Each group has its own hunting ground, about which it moves, making temporary settlements here and there.

Food-gathering societies have no tribal organization. They do not possess chiefs or chiefly classes. It would appear that each group is equal to every other group. The senior members of the group exercise any necessary authority and guidance.

These groupings of food-gathering people therefore present us with a picture as simple as could well be imagined.

The general lack of material culture is a striking trait. I do not know of any one artefact that can be ascribed to food-gatherers as a whole. The only possible exception might be traps, or snares,

[1] Professor C. Daryll Forde's work on ' Habitat, Economy and Society ', may be read with profit in connexion with this and the following chapters.

but I know of no evidence on this point that would warrant any generalization. The bow and arrow of the Negrito certainly presents an interesting problem, but the other food-gatherers do not appear to have possessed this weapon.

To turn now to the family group. We are repeatedly informed that food-gatherers are monogamous, and that the union is for life. It would appear, however, that this stability is not due so much to an abiding affection between the parties as to the presence of children. We are told that newly united couples who have as yet had no children, may separate ; but once children are born separation is rare.

The family group is united by ties of affection. Usually the utmost harmony prevails within it. Witness, for example, the case of the large Eskimo families, shut up together in small huts throughout the long Arctic winter, with nothing to relieve the monotony of the dark months. They avoid family quarrels. The greatest friendliness is the rule, and all share alike in the resources of the group.

In the family groups there is considerable respect for the acquired wisdom of the elders. They are the natural leaders, and even when too old to lead in the hunting field are generally treated with courtesy and consideration, and their material needs are well provided for. The women are on an equality with the men. Children are kindly treated and are well behaved. They are taught to be kind and considerate, hospitable, to share with others.

Food-gatherers practise a kind of communism in certain of their belongings.[1] This never applies to personal possessions. A man's weapons are his own, and a woman's cooking utensils are her own. The communism applies chiefly to the food supply. The right of every one to his or her fair share is widely recognized, and generally acted upon. With certain other things, such as some of the large Eskimo canoes, too, there is a certain amount of general ownership, but such possessions are rare among food-gatherers, and therefore the question hardly ever arises. Food-gatherers do not display any marked tendency to accumulate property beyond immediate needs. They do not store up food to provide for the future. When there is food it is eaten ; when there is none they starve.

Since there are no chiefs or chiefly classes, there is nothing that can strictly be called government.

Food-gatherers are noted for their hospitality. Strangers are

[1] It should be noted that the word ' communism ' is used in a special sense. It applies here to groups of relatives, not to unrelated people.

welcomed, and are given due share of the food and shelter that their hosts possess. The children are early taught to observe this rule, which is one of great importance.

An apparent exception to the above rule is to be found in the strict laws of trespass that many of these people observe. Nearly all the groups have fairly clearly determined areas over which they alone have the right to hunt. Should their area be infringed by neighbouring groups, or by strangers, they are quick to retaliate, often even taking the life of the offender. A guest, so long as he does not attempt to infringe this rigid rule, is welcome.

Another amiable character of primitive peoples is their transparent honesty. In a natural state, with few needs, and few possessions, men show little tendency to covet what does not belong to them, and, with strongly developed views concerning the right of others to their share in the goods of the community, rarely attempt to take for themselves what really belongs to others. This obviates the need of subterfuge, and gives them a greater degree of integrity than is found among those who have been touched by civilization.

The last and most striking character of the food-gatherer is that, so long as he is left undisturbed by outside influences, he rarely indulges in violent behaviour. Within the family group all is peaceful. His emotions are apt to be somewhat uncontrolled, but violence usually only appears as a reaction to violence.

Warfare is not a characteristic of food-gathering society. Trespass may be resisted and murders avenged, but we do not find young men trained as warriors. I do not mean by this that food-gatherers are incapable of warlike behaviour. The history of the Bushmen of South Africa, the natives of Tasmania and others, shows that food-gatherers can display great ferocity when sufficiently aroused.

I have already pointed out that certain criticisms will be directed against the generalizations I am formulating. They crop up in conversation with unfailing regularity. One of these criticisms concerns violent behaviour. In spite of the fact that I have already pointed out that the evidence concerning food-gathering peoples is not unanimous, that there are apparent exceptions to all the rules, my critics will certainly point out these exceptions, as if I had ignored them. Those who do not believe that food-gathering man was peaceful will insist on the warlike behaviour of certain of the Eskimo tribes, of the Andamanese, and of the Australian natives. I shall therefore deal with these exceptions in the chapter on Violence, and shall show that these

5

exceptions, when studied, support the generalization based on the behaviour of food-gathering men as a whole.

This survey of food-gathering peoples, who still inhabit the more outlying regions of the earth, provides a fairly uniform type of behaviour. As has already been pointed out, the peoples that have been considered include Negritos in Africa, the Andaman Islands, Malaya, and the Philippines; Australoids in Ceylon, Malaya, and Australia; Mongoloids in Borneo and America. They are therefore found among three of the great racial divisions of mankind, the Alpine, Mediterranean, and Nordic being excluded.

The food-gatherers live under every possible variety of climatic condition. The Negritos usually inhabit tropical forest regions, either in Africa or Asia. The Eskimo and Fuegians live at the other extreme, and inhabit Polar or semi-Polar areas. Between these two every type of environment is experienced, from the woodlands of Canada, and the North American Plains to the arid districts of Central Australia.

Many characteristics that the food-gatherers may possess in common can therefore hardly be argued to depend upon race, or environment. They would appear, on the contrary, to be common to mankind. But it must not be forgotten that we have not been able to study the Mediterranean, Alpine and Nordic races in their food-gathering stages. It might be argued that existing food-gatherers belonging, as they do, to the dark-skinned races, represent a lower type of humanity. The same argument could not, however, be applied to the Mongoloid race, who are admittedly not below the light-skinned races in intelligence. I shall therefore assume, as a working hypothesis, that the standard of behaviour based on the study of existing food-gatherers, applies to the whole of mankind.

The Standard of Behaviour.

We may, I think, fairly deduce from the evidence the following types of behaviour as characteristic of mankind.

(1) *The Getting of Food.*—I have not dealt with this activity, for it merely needs to be mentioned once and for all. We depend for our daily existence upon our food. This law holds with every living organism. Hunger forces every living creature to take measures to supply itself with food at definite intervals, under pain of extinction. In the course of evolution various types of organisms have elaborated complicated mechanisms for the acquisition of food. Man is no exception to the rule. The food-gatherers display a high degree of intelligence in the acquisition of food. It is well known that the Bushmen, the Negritos, the

Australian blacks, possess a vast and intimate knowledge concerning their food supply. They are able to track their quarry with amazing skill. They have learned what is good to eat and what is poisonous. Radcliffe-Brown is of the opinion that the ' food-getting ' aspect of marriage is more important in the minds of Australian natives than the sexual aspect.[1]

The getting of food is based on an innate tendency. Every normal human being feels hunger, and will be forced into activity to satisfy it. It is the great fundamental urge to activity. It is remarkable, in view of these facts, that groups of normal intelligent human beings can persist for untold thousands of years, using their intelligence daily in the acquisition of food, and yet not realize how much easier it would be to domesticate animals and plants.[2]

(2) *The Family.*—One of the most striking results of the survey of human behaviour is to establish the family, or rather the grouping of relatives, as the fundamental group of mankind. It is deeply rooted, and is based, for the greater part, on innate tendencies. It is certain, of course, that the human family is partly the product of intelligence, but its broadest base is that of the innate tendency. I shall make no attempt to analyse this group.

I shall regard it as a biological grouping, and shall not include it among the social institutions. For instance, it may be true that man, as opposed to woman, is polygamous, and that woman is monogamous. I shall make no attempt to discuss this problem, but shall simply stress the fact that the normal human society as exhibited by the food-gatherers is based on monogamy, and that the children form the cement of society, that once children come on to the scene the union between the parents becomes stable. I shall assume that the normal, stable family grouping consists of parents and children. The reasons for the affection displayed between the parents themselves, and between the parents and children, will not be discussed. They will simply be accepted as characteristic of the simplest social grouping of which we have knowledge.

Other types of innate behaviour are certainly displayed by food-gatherers. Men take measures to protect themselves from danger. They exhibit what might be termed ' self-esteem '. A Bushman prides himself on being a good hunter. But these

---

[1] Radcliffe-Brown iii. 103.

[2] ' It seems exceedingly strange that the pygmies who have lived so long with the more civilized negro peasants have not imitated them, and improved their standard of living.'—Schebesta ii. 139.

traits are more particularly individualistic, and, therefore, do not need stressing in this analysis.

The Standard of Behaviour therefore is a very simple one. All that can be postulated of mankind is an active interest in food, and a social life spent among his relatives. It does not seem to me to be possible to go beyond that. He will tend to protect himself from danger, and will display marked signs of self-esteem in his desire to outstrip his fellows in various forms of social activity.

This mode of life is remarkably stable ; for it is obvious that food-gathering peoples have persisted for thousands of years on a cultural basis that is as near fundamental as we may conceive. It does not seem possible to detect in their culture any tendency to advance. We have found them markedly harmonious in their behaviour, happy in their family life, sharing food with their relatives, not desirous of acquiring property, men and women on terms of equality, none of which characteristics suggest a tendency to change.

It is interesting to examine this Standard of Behaviour in its negative aspects.

(1) *Herd Instinct.*—It is sometimes asserted that the social life of mankind is based, partly at least, on an innate tendency of human beings to congregate together. A well-known example of this type of theorization is found in Mr. W. Trotter's ' Instincts of the Herd in Peace and War '.[1] It is true, of course, that man is a social animal, and is not meant for solitude. He lives his life among his fellows. It is true, moreover, that an argument for the existence of the herd instinct may be based on the attraction of large towns for country people. Whatever may be the nature of this attraction, it certainly is not fundamental in human nature. For we have failed to detect any sign of it among the food-gatherers, whose daily life is lived among relatives. There is, therefore, no basis for such an instinct, if it is intended to apply to people not related to one another. If the term ' herd instinct ' is applied to the family groups of the food-gatherers it becomes meaningless, for this kind of behaviour obviously has its own basis.

(2) *Pugnacity.*—The harmonious behaviour of food-gathering groups has as its corollary a marked absence of violence. This does not mean to say that they are incapable of violent behaviour, for they have on occasion exhibited great ferocity towards their enemies. A widespread tendency to resist trespass suggests a possible direction in which warlike behaviour might develop, but

[1] Trotter 18–23.

in the absence of any aggressive action on the part of their neighbours the food-gatherers remain peaceful. They do not raid their neighbours for women or property. There is no evidence of fights for food. Slavery is unknown, and so are cannibalism and human sacrifice. The absence of chieftainship, based on birth or personal qualities, also harmonizes well with the peaceful habits of the food-gatherers ; for throughout the ages chieftainship and warfare have been closely linked. In short, it does not seem possible to detect in the food-gathering culture any tendency to violent behaviour, except as a sporadic occurrence within the group, or as a reaction to aggression from without.

(3) *Acquisition.*—Food-gatherers do not betray any tendency to acquire property beyond their immediate needs. They do not fight neighbouring groups for hunting grounds. Their possessions are mainly concerned with their mode of livelihood. A man does not store up bows and arrows beyond his personal needs. He does not acquire many wives to work for him. He does not think of the future. It is therefore not possible to speak of an instinct of acquisition among mankind.

(4) *Social Groupings.*—Every student of social institutions is aware of the existence among many peoples of ruling groups, of clans, moieties, and so forth. Food-gathering society consists of family groups in juxtaposition. We do not seem to find any tendency for one group to superimpose itself on another. Among the food-gatherers family groups give rise to family groups, all of them independent and on a basis of equality. This budding-off process goes on indefinitely. It is therefore hard to see in what direction chieftainship could arise spontaneously among, say, the Negritos of Central Africa. The groups do not fight one another, and so there could be no question of conquest. The acquisition of property, women, or slaves does not interest them. Yet somewhere or other, somehow or other, this superimposition must have taken place ; but, like the grouping of men into large cities, it cannot be a direct manifestation of the innate behaviour of mankind.

It does not need much knowledge to realize that innate tendencies centering round food, family, and self-preservation are not in themselves peculiar to mankind. They are possessed in common by the more highly organized groups of animals. Therefore it cannot be said, without qualification, that they alone account for the building-up of civilization. The element of intelligence must also be taken into account. While it is futile to deny intelligence and even constructive intelligence to, say, the higher mammals, yet we possess that quality in so markedly a superior degree as to distinguish us definitely from the rest of the animal kingdom. The explanation of civilization as such, must therefore take account of intellectual processes.

It is possible to observe the workings of intelligence among food-gatherers in more than one direction. It is well known that they always possess an accurate and detailed knowledge of the habits and properties of the plants and animals constituting their food supply. Indeed food must have been a constant topic of conversation among them, since they sought to feed at least once every day. It is remarkable, nevertheless, to think that people such as the Bushmen, who display such profound knowledge of their food supply, had never thought of providing for the future either by storing up food or by domestication. Their forefathers for thousands of years had hunted game, and yet had never succeeded in domesticating any species in order to supply a store of food. We know that the Aurignacian and Solutrean peoples of France killed and ate horses, and yet the domestication of the horse can hardly be traced back five thousand years. This lack of originality is indeed surprising. Primitive men seem to have been satisfied by appeasing their hunger in the most direct possible manner. This constant urge may have caused them to construct traps and snares. This certainly seems to have happened in the Aurignacian period of the Old Stone Age ; for the so-called tectiforms depicted on the walls of caverns in France and Spain have every appearance of being traps. Moreover, it is hard to conceive how these early men could have captured bears, tigers, rhinoceros, and mammoths without the use of traps and pit-falls. This suggests that these early men were actively thinking of how to capture their daily food supply.

We know, however, with much greater certainty, that this intelligent attitude had led these early men several steps forward on the path to civilization. The industry of the Old Stone Age reveals a long-continued process of invention of implements, all apparently connected with the food supply. Most of these artefacts are intended for the preparation of food. In the Aurignacian period the stone implement industry became further enriched by the invention of graving and modelling tools. These people engraved, painted, and modelled representations of the animals that they hunted and ate, on the walls, ceilings and floors of certain limestone caverns, particularly in western Europe. There is little doubt that the ideas at the back of the minds of these artists were what we should term magical. These representations may have been intended to increase the food supply ; they may have been intended to cause the animals to be captured with greater ease. There may have been some other aim, but beyond doubt the satisfaction of hunger was the main urge.

The working of self-esteem is apparent in this art. The artist evidently took a great delight in the skilful depicting of life as he saw it.

The burials of the people of the Aurignacian stage of culture reveal further suggestions of the working of intelligence. The dead were buried in shallow graves, usually under a rock shelter. The bodies had been packed round with red ochre (hæmatite); they had been adorned with necklaces of the canine teeth of deer and other animals, bits of bone, shells, and other objects; sometimes cowrie shells were arranged round the body near to the joints. All this suggests that these people possessed a certain attitude towards the dead person, and that they believed they could, by these means, influence the dead in some way or other.

There does not seem to be any direct evidence concerning the attitude of these early people towards illness; but the use of amulets is strongly suggested by the objects comprising the necklaces worn by the dead. Similar objects are in use to-day in London, as is shown by the collection of amulets and charms that is housed in the Wellcome Museum.

The traces of the emergence of religious ideas seem to be confined, in this period, to the small feminine figurines found in the graves of the people of the Upper Palaeolithic age. These appear to have developed into the great group of mother goddesses of historical times in the Ancient East.

It is evident that food-gathering men have, in one part of the world at least, accumulated knowledge and formulated theories in connexion with food-getting and self-preservation. It does not follow, however, that existing food-gatherers have achieved a like advance in culture. It is a truism that they know much about their food supply. They may have also acquired knowledge of the medicinal properties of certain plants, but it is not easy to say whether they have independently, in many places, begun to formulate theories of a magical or religious nature. One great difficulty in estimating their contributions lies in the fact that they are modern people. Magical and religious institutions have existed in various parts of the world for thousands of years. Most of these lowly peoples live in close proximity to food-producing peoples who have such institutions to a greater or less degree of complexity, and their culture reveals evidence of the influence of such peoples. The Punan of Borneo, for instance, resemble in their magic and religion the particular tribes in whose proximity they happen to live, and it is almost certain that they have derived their beliefs and practices entirely from such sources.[1] This is certainly borne out by their magical equipment. Similar considerations lead to the conclusion that the magic of Australian blacks has not been developed by them in isolation, but has been acquired from people of a higher culture. The evidence collected by Schebesta concerning the pygmies of the Congo Basin goes to show that their clan organization, tattooing, cannibalism, circumcision, lip-piercing, houses, as well as their magic, religion and burial practices, are wholly borrowed from neighbouring food-producers.[2] In fact, there is hardly any food-gathering tribe that can be assumed to have been untouched by influences from more advanced peoples.

It is evident that the problem of accounting for the magical and religious beliefs and practices of food-gatherers is difficult. We have seen that the men of the Old Stone Age, particularly in Europe, had made certain progress in these directions, and that modern food-gatherers also possess magical and religious ideas and practices. It is difficult, however, to come to conclusions concerning the food-gatherers of to-day. For that reason I shall leave it open. But it must be remembered that I am concerned in this book more particularly with method. I make no attempt to be exhaustive, but am simply concerned with the building up of provisional working hypotheses.

The discussion up to the present has suggested that food-gatherers possess a culture as simple as may be imagined. Their lives are spent in the midst of relatives, and are occupied with the getting of food. The arts and crafts, with certain exceptions, are mostly unknown to them. Whether they invariably bury their dead, practise magic, or possess religious beliefs and practices, I do not pretend to say.

The next task is to carry the inquiry over the border line into those societies which practise food-production. These societies, we shall find, are usually much more complicated than those of the food-gatherers. Nevertheless, we shall find them based ultimately on the same fundamental innate tendencies.

[1] Hose and McDougall II. 185–6.
[2] Schebesta ii. 101–3, 120, 123, 162, 236–7, Chaps. 7, 11.

CHAPTER VII

THE GETTING OF FOOD

The argument now takes another turn. The study of the food-gatherers has revealed that we can predict but little of mankind when dissociated from civilization. We can only postulate a lively interest in food and a closely knit family life. We cannot assume that man would necessarily wear clothes, build houses, work metals and so forth. Yet men have somehow or other come to display these activities. The next task is to understand how and why human behaviour has altered so profoundly since the change from food-gathering to food-production.

Civilization consists of social institutions of many kinds. It will be necessary before long to inquire into the meaning of these institutions; but before commencing that task it will be well to inquire what happens to the Standard of Behaviour once men have come to acquire these manifold new activities. To what extent, we may ask, has the need for food continued to influence men? What has happened to the family as civilization has developed? These problems must be faced first of all.

It is not necessary to delve deeply into the history of human culture to realize to what an extent the getting of food has entered into Man's activities. It is only natural that it should be so. Man has to live, and the insistent urge of hunger tends to direct his attention constantly towards his food supply.

The exact means by which the step was taken from food-gathering to food-production are not yet a matter of common agreement. We do not yet know how barley and wheat were first domesticated. The connecting links with their ancestors have yet to be discovered. There is no conclusive evidence as yet to show where the domestication of animals, including the dog, took place. The earliest agricultural societies had domesticated animals. Indeed it is interesting to note that the early food-producers, when emerging into history, not only already possessed an empirical knowledge of agriculture and the domestication of animals, but had woven them around with a tangle of magical and religious theories that is not yet entirely unravelled. But there is a general agreement that this momentous step took

61

place in the Ancient East, the region of the most ancient civilizations known to us.[1]

It does not take long to discover that early food-producing society was largely organized round agriculture and the domestication of animals. As Havelock Ellis says : ' For a primitive people the art of life is necessarily in large part concerned with eating.' [2] The kingship and the State, from the earliest known times down to the present day in some parts of the world, reveal clear traces of this preoccupation. Vast collections of examples are included in ' The Golden Bough ' of Sir James Frazer. Mr. A. M. Hocart in his work on ' Kingship ' has carried the examination of the connexion between state organization and food-production still further.

Examples are easy to find, and there is no need to multiply them.

In the first place the annual cycle of ceremonials is usually based on agriculture. We read of Peru under the Incas. ' Religion, in its ritual and ceremonial observances, was dependent on the annual recurrence of agricultural events such as the preparation of the land, sowing, and harvest, and both were dependent on the calendar. . . . The solstices and equinoxes were carefully observed.' [3]

The Incas, like other kings of early civilization, were the High Priests of the State cults. They inaugurated the various activities of the agricultural year, particularly those of seed-time and harvest. The Inca himself inaugurated the ploughing season by turning up a furrow with a golden plough.[4]

It will be interesting to quote another example from the other side of the world. A ploughing festival is recorded in the Buddhist Chronicles of Ancient India. The text runs as follows : ' The King was richly attired and attended by a thousand nobles. At this festival all the people were accustomed to attend, in the gayest dresses, and with every token of pleasure. About a thousand ploughs start at once ; of these, 108 are made of silver, and the horns of the bullocks that draw them are tipped with silver, and adorned with white flowers ; but the plough held by the king is of gold, and the horns of the bullocks attached are also tipped with gold. The king takes the handle of the plough in his left hand, and a golden goad in his right ; and the nobles do the same with their ploughs and goads of silver. The king

[1] Professor Gordon Childe's two works have some interesting discussions on this question.
[2] Ellis 14.   [3] Markham, C. R., iii. 115.
[4] Markham, C. R., ii. 25.

makes one furrow, passing from east to west ; the nobles make
three ; and the rest of the ploughmen then contend with each
other who shall perform their work in the best manner.' [1]

The Mikado of Japan is High Priest of the national cult of
Shinto. He is a descendant of the sun goddess Amaterasu, who
gave many of the food plants that the Japanese use. The ceremonies performed by the Mikado are mostly agricultural in nature.
For instance, the most important festival was called Ohonihe or
Daijowe, which means ' great food offering '. It was a ceremony
of first fruits, ' performed soon after the accession of a Mikado to
the throne, and, like our coronation ceremony, constituting the
formal religious sanction of his sovereignty.' [2]

These kings fulfilled functions both secular and religious. They,
or their high priests, decided the time for ploughing, for they
alone possessed the knowledge of the calendar. This calendar
was built up on an agricultural basis. The ruler decided not
merely the time of ploughing, but also the time of harvesting.
The king not merely took part in ceremonials of ploughing and
first fruits, but, in his very person, and particularly after his
marriage to the queen, was supposed to control the well-being
of the State. In his consecration ceremony he was supposed to
create supplies of food for his subjects, and to endow them all
with health, strength and prosperity. He was provided at his
consecration with the necessary vital energy.[3]

Man's early thought regarding gods and kings was largely bound
up with his agricultural and pastoral experiences. From the very
earliest times one of the sceptres of the Egyptian king was a
shepherd's crook. The king of Egypt was constantly referred
to as a bull. He was often said to have been suckled by the
goddess Hathor, the Divine Cow. The notion of the king being
suckled by Hathor finds a notable expression in the temple erected
by Queen Hatshepsut, of the Eighteenth Dynasty, at Deir-el-
Bahri. This temple contains representations of a cow-headed
Hathor engaged in suckling the young queen, who is always
represented as masculine.[4]

There is little doubt that this feature of the Egyptian kingship
was the source of the classical instances of twin heroes being
suckled by animals.[5] The crudity of the later beliefs is not a
sign of their more primitive nature, but of their derivation at

[1] R. Spence Hardy 150. Buddha was a royal prince of the Sakhya branch
of the solar line of India.
[2] Aston 268.   [3] See p. 232.
[4] Naville i. II. 17, Plate LIII.
[5] For example, Romulus and Remus.

second or third hand, from Egypt, by people who did not understand the original situation.

Elliot Smith has pointed out, that the early rulers and gods of the Ancient East were closely associated with a personage whom he termed the Great Mother.[1] This concept appears to have been based on the maternal characteristics of women. These great mothers have various names and qualities, often derived from domesticated plants and animals. For example, in addition to Hathor in Egypt, Aditi, the mother of the great gods of the Vedic period in India, who included Indra, Varuna, Vishnu, and Mitra, was looked upon as a cow in one of her manifestations.

It is well known that the mother goddesses in the various countries of the Ancient East were usually linked together. For instance, a Sumerian goddess, named Gestin-Anna, ' Heavenly Mother goddess of the Vine ', was also known as ' Nina Queen of Waters '. The two of them were connected with canals, irrigation, sheep, cattle, sacred song, incantation, and they were also identified with the Scorpion Goddess. The Vine Goddess was also the Grain Goddess. Many of these goddesses were simply the personifications of various attributes of an original goddess. For instance, Professor Langdon mentions of Innini, ' Having cast off many concrete qualities which were personified into female consorts of local gods, she retains for herself the commanding position of a detached deity mother of humanity, defender of her people.' [2]

An interesting example of this process is found in the Corn Mother of the western world, the Rice Mother of India and Indonesia, the Maize Mother of America. This being was represented by a few ears of the cereal bound together, and used for ceremonial purposes. The Rice Mother, for instance, was supposed to contain the ' life ' of the rice, and her function was that of maintaining the health of the crop.[3] The Maize Mother, represented by heads of maize, played an important part in the ritual of North America (see p. 184).

The oldest known Sanskrit writings of India include the Vedas, particularly the Rig-Veda, which consists of a series of hymns, composed as accompaniments to ceremonials. It is merely necessary to open a volume of these hymns to realize the intense preoccupation of these early people with food. The following texts bear this out.

[1] See Perry vii. 16 sqq. for a discussion of this concept, including reference to the writings of Elliot Smith dealing with this important topic, in particular, ' The Evolution of the Dragon '.

[2] Perry vi. 218.   [3] *Ibid.*, 228.

'Opulent Indra, encourage us in this rite for the acquirement of wealth, for we are diligent and renowned. Grant us, Indra, wealth beyond measure or calculation, inexhaustible, the source of cattle, of food, of all life. Indra, grant us great renown and wealth acquired in a thousand ways, and those (articles) of food (which are brought from the field) in carts.' Each deity in turn is importuned. 'Agni, granter of abundant sustenance . . .' 'Through Agni the worshipper obtains that affluence which increases day by day, which is the source of fame and the multiplier of mankind.' . . . Procure for us the food that is in heaven and mid-air, and grant us the wealth that is on the earth. Rudra is asked for food. 'When may we repeat a most grateful hymn to the wise, the most bountiful and mighty Rudra, who is (cherished) in our hearts ? By which earth may (be induced to) grant the gifts of Rudra to our cattle, our people, our cows, and our progeny.' Again Savitri is called on. 'We invoke Savitri, the enlightener of men, the dispenser of various home-insuring wealth. Sit down, friends ; Savitri verily is to be praised by us, for he is the giver of riches.' The Aswins, the heavenly twins are called on in their turn. 'Desiring food, I invoke (Aswins) to support my life. Your wonderful car, swift as thought, drawn by fleet horses, worthy of veneration, many-bannered, bringing rain, containing wealth, abundantly yielding delights, and conferring riches.' [1] Hundreds of such quotations could be given, showing that each and every deity in the Vedas was importuned for food. Moreover, the demands for food and wealth—usually in cattle—far exceed any others, which is a good sign of the real interests of these people.

The religious systems of modern peoples of the lower culture likewise reveal an intense preoccupation with food. A few examples will serve.

The Todas are a people living in the Nilgiri Hills of southern India who keep buffaloes, and live on the milk and butter produced from them. Rivers has shown how the ritual centres round the cattle on which the people depend for their daily food. One of the prayers will serve as an example. 'May it be well with the buffaloes, may they not suffer from disease or die, may they be kept from poisonous animals and from wild beasts and from injury by flood or fire, may there be water and grass in plenty.' [2]

The annual ceremonial cycle of the Pawnee tribe of the United States is described as follows. 'The routine of their daily life did not differ materially from year to year. Their year may be

[1] Wilson ii. 23, 122, 3, 69, 117, 51, 321.
[2] Rivers i. 216, 229.

said to have begun in the early spring, when Tirawa, their Creator, first spoke to them from the thunders. Then, in rapid succession, followed a number of ceremonies which had to do largely with the ceremonial preparation of the seed-corn and with the fields, after which ensued the planting. Next came the great summer buffalo hunt, with the return to the village for the gathering of the crops in the fall, after which the tribe again went upon the hunt in order to lay in their supply of winter meat and robes. This hunt was often prolonged until late in the winter, or, if successful at the outset, the hunters returned to the permanent village, where they remained throughout the winter.' [1]

The Zuñi Indians of New Mexico are expert agriculturists, practising irrigation, and exhibiting much skill in their craft. They have a very extensive ritual, which is centred round their food supply. They have a Sun priesthood, the High Priest of which is responsible for the calendar. The Zuñi pray chiefly for rain, which is of prime importance to them. Their chief priesthood is the Rain priesthood.[2]

The Tontemboan people of Minahassa, in north-eastern Celebes, may be taken as another example. Schwarz tells us that ' the old Minahassa religion had its centre in the various ceremonies which were concerned with the getting of crops. The " garden priest " and " garden priestess " were foremost of all those who were leaders and counsellors in religious matters.' [3]

These examples, selected more or less at random, serve to show the important part played by food in the ceremonials of savage peoples. It is interesting to note that the people just mentioned, the Tontemboan of Minahassa, say that formerly they grew no rice because they did not know the necessary ceremonies. The knowledge of growing rice is said to have come from the sky-world. Other peoples of Indonesia make a similar claim. Certain Toradja people of Central Celebes say that the knowledge of rice-growing was brought them by a culture hero. They also say that a man formerly found his way to the sky-world and was taught rice-growing.[4]

The eternal quest for food naturally determines the direction of human interests. Professor Hocart tells me that if a Fijian be asked about any particular animal or plant, he will reply ' it is good to eat ', or ' it is bad to eat '. Fijian society is characterized by a complicated clan organization. Each clan provides its quota for feasts. Fijian chiefs are closely connected with feasts.

[1] Dorsey i. xvii. [2] Stevenson 108 e.s.
[3] Schwarz 159. [4] Perry v. 139–40.

Dr. Audrey Richards has recently published a work dealing with the part played by food in the daily life of South African tribes, as well as in ceremonial. Each native settlement, those of chiefs excluded, houses a group of relatives. The daily meals are eaten more or less in common by each family of the group. Age and sex determine, in the family circle, the access to food, but there appears to be little formalism in this respect.[1]

These meals usually are vegetarian—maize and pumpkins being the staple diet. Meat is rarely eaten. Indeed, it is possible to say that, with the exception of stray birds and so forth, it is actually only eaten on ceremonial occasions such as initiations, beer-drinks and weddings. These ceremonials concern wider groups than the kraal itself, and the meat is shared out according to rule.

Dr. Richards' evidence agrees with the observations made by Mr. J. E. S. Griffiths and myself among the Bakwena Basuto of East Griqualand and the Pondo respectively. These peoples present, in their attitude towards food, an interesting contrast. They live principally on vegetables ; yet they have very little associated ceremonial. On the other hand, their cattle are important ceremonially, and are not eaten freely. Even the drinking of milk is subject to restrictions.

Throughout the whole range of the native reservations in the eastern part of Cape Colony, the cattle kraal is an integral part of the settlement. It is only a few yards away from the dwellings. The cultivated land, on the other hand, may be some miles away. On important ceremonial occasions, such as marriage, or initiation of boys or girls, cattle are killed and eaten, but, as a rule, no vegetable food is offered. Strict regulations exist as to the drinking of milk. Often we find that the bride may not drink the milk from the cattle of her husband's kraal for the first year of her married life. Sometimes she brings a cow with her from her father's kraal. The women are not allowed to have anything to do with the cattle. The boys act as herdsmen, and they or the men milk the cows.

The head of the kraal is usually buried close to the cattle kraal. Often when illness occurs, and a doctor is sent for, he says that the ghosts of the dead have caused the illness because they want meat. They do not appear to bother much about vegetable food.

The evidence from the Pondo and other peoples shows that men have built up a complex system of thought and behaviour around their food supply. This applies particularly to food-producers.

[1] Richards, A., 76 e.s.

This process of reasoning has so entangled men that they have, as in Mexico, offered their fellow-beings for the good of their crops ; or, as in India, have been driven again by their false reasoning, to refuse to kill cattle, thus depriving themselves of an important source of food.

It is obvious that the discovery of agriculture was the act of man's intelligence ; yet, from the very earliest times of which we have record, agriculture has been mixed up with a farrago of distorted logic. It would be a task of the greatest interest to unravel the threads of reasoning that has led the cow, a simple domesticated animal, to be an object of veneration, even of worship.

Realizing the powerful influence of ideas on behaviour, it is interesting to note the complacency with which the Pondo cultivates his crops, in spite of the disappearance of his agricultural ritual, while he accepts without question the restrictions on his flesh diet.

Tribal hunts are practically universal in negro Africa. There is, for instance, a close association, throughout that continent, between chiefs and leopards. Chiefs usually have the sole right to wear leopard skins.

There is every reason to believe that the interest that man took in the getting of food led him first of all to paint, draw and carve pictures of the animals that he wished to kill. He did not trouble to depict other animals that did not arouse his interest. Nor did he take much trouble over depicting human beings or plants. The dawn of art certainly began as one effect of the impulse to get food, not to satisfy an ' artistic impulse '. Many peoples have very little art. There is, for instance, no sign of any art before that of the Aurignacian cave-dwellers. What is more, after the period of the cave-dwellers, art sank to a very low ebb. It is not something that constantly arises in human society ; there is no reason to believe that men are impelled to express themselves by it. On the contrary, as we see, the earliest art was definitely utilitarian. It was splendid, but it was simply an imagined means of getting food.

It is evident, therefore, that hunting has exercised the mind of man from the earliest food-gathering days, down to our own times.

Some of the evidence on this point is interesting. Our knowledge of early art reaches back, as is well known, to the Aurignacian phase of the Old Stone Age. Somewhat later, a cave art, rather more sophisticated, appeared in Eastern Spain. This art was mainly concerned with hunting scenes. A similar form of art

has been shown by Mr. E. S. Thomas to have been present in
north-west Africa, as well as in pre-dynastic Egypt.[1] This art was
very similar to that of the Bushmen of South Africa.[2]

Some of the most striking evidence for ceremonial hunting
comes from Egypt. Certain flint knives from the pre-dynastic
period have gold or ivory handles on which scenes are depicted
that suggest organized hunts. In addition hunting scenes are
portrayed on the walls of a tomb excavated by Mr. J. E. Quibell
at Hieraconpolis in Upper Egypt. This tomb dated from just
before the beginning of the dynastic period. Its walls were
ornamented with hunting scenes that recall those of the Bushmen.
But still more striking were the carvings on a ceremonial slate
palette from this same time. These carvings were in low relief,
and depicted hunting scenes of a similar character to those already
mentioned.

The importance of these last-mentioned sets of carvings lies
in their association with kings. For other palettes and mace
heads have been found at Hieraconpolis, that are obviously intended for ceremonial purposes. These objects are derived from
the slate palettes and mace heads of earlier pre-dynastic times,
but they are much larger and are profusely ornamented with
low relief carvings depicting various kinds of royal ceremonial.
It is obvious therefore that the scene in question was that of a
royal hunt.

Throughout the ages State hunts have been a constant feature
of the kingship. They were practised in Egypt from the very
earliest known times. They were well known in ancient China,
throughout Africa, India, in fact throughout the world in all ages.

It would be interesting to know the relationship between these
historical hunting scenes and the art of the prehistoric period in
Europe. I do not propose to examine the question at this point,
but should like to mention an interesting example of continuity.
Herodotus mentions a people named the Scythians living in what
is now south-western Russia. These Scythians possessed a remarkable form of art. The chief *motif* of this art was the representation of wild animals, usually depicted in a more or less
conventional manner. This art ranges from Europe right across
to China. It was acquired by the ancient barbaric peoples.
Some years ago M. Salomon Reinach showed clearly that this
Scythian art was intimately connected with that of the Mycenaean
civilization of the eastern Mediterranean. One remarkable

[1] Thomas, E. S., 385 e.s.
[2] See, for example, the collection of Bushman paintings made by Miss
Helen Tongue.

6

feature of his demonstration was to show that throughout Mycenaean and Scythian art, horses were represented as galloping in an entirely unnatural manner. These animals galloped with their two hind legs and their two front legs together, like rocking-horses !

It is reasonable to suppose that the Scythian art was derived from the Mycenaean.[1]

The culture of the Mycenaean period in Crete, Greece and Asia Minor is permeated through and through with Egyptian influence; [2] so it is possible that the Mycenaeans derived their peculiar representation of galloping horses from that source; for Egyptian art of the Eighteenth Dynasty includes representations of kings riding in chariots drawn by horses in this fantastic attitude.[3] The Egyptian kings of that period also used hunting daggers, the sheaths of which were inlaid with pictures of wild animals and other forms of ornamentation.[4]

The study of this long series of hunting scenes opens up fascinating problems concerning the nature of early kingships. It would seem that not only are state hunts a constant feature of the kingship in all ages, but this association would appear to have existed in pre-dynastic Egypt before the beginning of historical records.

This chapter serves to show that the getting of food by agriculture, by the use of domesticated animals, or even by hunting, has had profound consequences on human behaviour. Food-production has enabled mankind to multiply enormously. It has involved men in all sorts of new activities. Many important

[1] Reinach, S., i. Vol. 37, 244 e.s. ; Vol. 38, 31 e.s. ; Vol. 39, 9 e.s.
[2] Evans, Sir A.
[3] Erman i. 489; Howard Carter, Vol. II. Pl. 3, p. 18.
[4] Howard Carter, Vol. II. 269, Pl. LXXXVIII. Maspero in his Manual of Egyptian Archaeology describes a poignard found in the coffin of Aahotep, the wife of Kames, a king of the seventeenth Dynasty, and probably the mother of Aames I, the founder of the eighteenth Dynasty (323). This poignard has a golden sheath and a wooden hilt inlaid with triangular mosaics of cornelian, lapis lazuli, felspar and gold. ' Four female heads in gold *repoussé* form the pommel ; and a bull's head reversed covers the junction of blade and hilt. The edges of the blade are of massive gold ; the centre of black bronze damascened with gold. On one side is the solar cartouche of Aames, below which a lion pursues a bull, the remaining space being filled in with four grasshoppers in a row. On the other side we have the family name of Aames and a series of full-blown flowers issuing one from another and diminishing towards the point. The poignard found at Mycenae by Dr. Schliemann is similarly decorated ; the Phoenicians, who were industrious copyists of Egyptian models, probably introduced this pattern into Greece ' (p. 328).

social institutions have been based upon it, or greatly influenced by it. The organization of the state, the functions of the kingship, religious ceremonial, magic, all these have become associated with the great food quest. Much of what I have said in this chapter is obvious. It is only necessary to take thought on the subject to realize how fundamentally the getting of food must necessarily have exercised man's activities.

I must, however, in conclusion, stress one important point. It is obvious that the adoption of agriculture and the domestication of animals was the result of rational reasoning based upon a recognition of reality. Early man learned that certain activities, such as the digging of irrigation canals and the sowing of seed, would procure food for him. He also argued, for some reason or other, that it was necessary to perform certain ceremonials in order to secure his crops. It is quite easy to understand the foundation of the early kingship on a basis of utility. We know, for example, that the earliest known kings possessed a knowledge of the calendar, and were concerned with the administration of the irrigation system. That is perfectly natural. But why should the same people imagine that the marriage of this same king could have any positive influence on the crops ? Why should they kill the king when he was getting old, for fear of disaster ? Such reasoning is not based upon the recognition of reality, but on a misapprehension of it. The explanation of this failure of the human mind to base all its actions on logic is one of the most formidable tasks awaiting the historian of culture.

CHAPTER VIII

THE FAMILY

THE great stability displayed by the family among food-gatherers leads us to expect this fundamental grouping to exert a powerful influence in the food-producing stage of culture. Although we do not as yet know exactly how the transition to food-production took place, we may be certain that the first step was small, and did not at once influence the structure of society. The family persisted with all its inborn characters and tendencies. It was a self-perpetuating grouping in food-gathering societies, and did not display any obvious tendency to transform itself in any way.

Savage society often displays obvious signs of the influence of the family. For instance, anyone who travels through the native reservations in eastern Cape Colony will observe groups of native huts, termed kraals, scattered here and there on the hill-sides. These groups usually consist of not more than a few huts, together with an enclosure for cattle. These kraals, as they are termed, are each occupied by a family group ; it may be it contains parents, children and grand-children, or just parents and children, or two or more brothers, but the inhabitants are almost invariably all related. Occasionally there is a larger settlement, as, for example, that of Queen's Mercy among the Bakwena Basuto of East Griqualand, just below the border of Basutoland proper. Such larger groups are the villages of Chiefs. That is to say, if we abstract the Chiefs, the family grouping reigns supreme. With the exception of the Chiefs no tendency appears for individual families to group together. The economic and local unit is the family.

Students of peoples of the lower culture are familiar with the form of social grouping known as the Dual organization. This is found throughout the greater part of North America, Oceania, Australia, and in other parts of the world.[1]

---

[1] See Rivers v. Chap. II ; Hocart iv. Chap. XX ; Perry vi. Chaps. XVIII–XX ; Olson. A recent study carried out by my pupil, Dr. M. I. Machin, has revealed the widespread existence of the Dual Organization in Greece and Rome.

The usual rule is for a group of people to be divided into two distinct divisions, called moieties. These two groups, though distinct, have mutual associations of various kinds. They officiate at each other's funerals; they play on opposite sides in ceremonial games; they usually intermarry.

The dual organization has the remarkable characteristic of being associated with various social groupings. A tribe, a village, an island, a territorial division of a tribe, may all be divided into intermarrying moieties. Membership of the moiety is through the father or the mother.

These intermarrying doublets usually possess the so-called Classificatory System of Relationship. This means that a member of either division groups all other members of his division under the terms brother, sister, father, mother, son and daughter and so on. That is to say, his moiety is theoretically his family, in the narrow sense of the term. The other moiety is that of his cousins, his potential wives and ' in-laws '.[1] Thus the tribes of Australia, the tribes of North America, the tribes and villages of Fiji, have acquired a social convention based on the theory that they form two intermarrying families. For example, the Huron Indians of the United States relate that when their tribe was organized in the past a dual grouping was set up. All the members of one group were ' brothers '; at the same time they were ' cousins ' to those of the other side. These two groups had to intermarry.[2]

In this instance, as in all the others, it does not follow that genealogical relationship can be traced between two men who call each other ' brother '. Their use of the term is traditional; but it is obvious that this system of kinship terms has received its impress from the family in the strict sense of the word.

The organization into two intermarrying divisions has another interesting characteristic. Although the two groups intermarry, yet the choice of a wife is usually restricted. The structure of the dual organization is such that children of two brothers or two sisters belong to the same group, and are therefore ' brothers ' and ' sisters ' to each other. On the other hand, children of brother and sister are called ' cross-cousins ', and belong to opposite groups, and therefore may marry. That is to say, a man classes as potential wives a group of women, with some of whom he cannot trace relationship.

That is the theory. But in practice it is different. For instance, many Australian tribes require a man to marry the daughter

---

[1] Rivers iii. I. 400; Radcliffe-Brown iii. 112–14.
[2] Barbeau 82–9.

of the actual brother of his mother, not the classificatory brother.[1]

The dual organization therefore has the following significant characteristics.

(1) Membership follows the father or the mother.
(2) The members of each moiety regard themselves as a large family.
(3) In certain instances the usual form of marriage is between cross-cousins in the strict sense of the term.

It may thus be concluded that the dual organization, wherever found, bears the unmistakable imprint of the family. It must be remembered, however, that the dual organization is something more than a grouping of relatives. It has political, social, economic, and ceremonial characters as well. It is only necessary to note here that this social institution bears the imprint of the family writ large across it.

The clan is another important social grouping. As in the case of the moiety of the dual organization, membership is through one or other of the parents. There is also a claim to common ancestry, often undemonstrable, as in the case of the moiety. The group regards itself as a large family, and uses classificatory terms of kinship; consequently marriage is forbidden between its members.

The characteristics of the clan reveal once more the influence of the family on social structure. It must be remembered, once again, that the group has other characteristics. Clans are often associated with animal, plant, or other emblems, with which kinship is sometimes claimed. Clans have various aspects, and are not merely groups of persons claiming relationship through common ancestry.[2] It is therefore only possible, at this point, to note, as in the case of the moiety, that the group bears the imprint of the family.

The tribes of Australia provide a remarkable instance of the effects of the family on social structure. These tribes are divided into dual divisions, called moieties, and also into clans, as well as local groupings termed ' hordes ' by Professor Radcliffe-Brown. There is a vast amount of ceremonial activity, and stereotyped modes of behaviour towards other members of social groups.

' In a typical Australian tribe it is found that a man can define his relation to every person with whom he has any social dealings whatever, whether of his own or of another tribe, by means of the terms of relationship. In other words, it is impossible for an

---

[1] Radcliffe-Brown i. 156.
[2] See, for example, Chaps. XXI–XXII of ' The Children of the Sun '.

Australian native to have anything whatsoever to do with anyone who is not his relative, of one kind or another, near or distant.' [1]

The structure of the state or tribe reveals the influence of the family. China provides an instance. ' It has . . . always been a political principle in China that every state, and above all the Empire itself, is to be regarded as the extension of one family, and the authority of its ruler as the extension of the authority of a paterfamilias.' [2]

This example is interesting because it is based on a fiction. The Emperor of China cannot possibly be the ancestor of all his subjects. This technicality of relationship is undoubtedly a means of expression of the unity of the state, particularly as regards its administration, both secular and religious.

Peru under the Incas provides a somewhat similar example. The high offices of the state were held by members of royal blood. The Inca and his wife were regarded as ' father ' and ' mother ' to all their relatives and vassals.[3]

Japan provides another example. The hereditary principle is strong. The highest offices of the state, civil and religious, including the kingship, were hereditary in certain families. These corporations included the Nakatomi, the Court priests, who recited the Purification Rituals ; the Imibe or Imbe, who were concerned with mourning and funerals ; the Sarume, Court dancers and mediums ; the Otomo, the Commander-in-Chief ; the Kumebe, the Royal Guards.[4]

These offices have been hereditary since the beginning of Japanese history. The families of their holders are the aristocracy of Japan, intermarrying among themselves, and filling the highest offices from generation to generation.[5]

The population of Japan is divided into descent groups called Uji, sometimes ruled over by hereditary chiefs drawn from the leading family. There were a certain number of great Uji composed of a number of smaller Uji. Nearly every Uji had a hereditary occupation, the name of which formed part of the name of the Uji. For instance, the gem polishers' Uji was named Tamatsukuri-Uji, and that of the boat builders, Fune-Uji.[6]

Egypt supplies a remarkable instance of the influence of the family. From the earliest historical times to the end of its independence the ruling power displays but little alteration. The earliest known kings had Horus for their official title, and this persisted for thousands of years.[7]

[1] Radcliffe-Brown iii. 13–14.   [2] de Groot II. 509.
[3] Vega I. 96, 132.   [4] Brinkley 33.
[5] Op. cit., 62.   [6] Op. cit., 93.   [7] Perry vi. 430.

During the first four Dynasties the highest official positions
were held by members of the royal family.   For example, Egypt
was divided into territorial divisions, called Nomes by the Greeks.
The earliest nome rulers, or nomarchs, were relatives of the king.
This system was altered at the beginning of the Fifth Dynasty.
For some reason or other the nomarchs then became independent,
and made their offices hereditary.[1]   This is an interesting example
of the working of family sentiments.   It would appear that the
nomarchs were more intent on seeing their sons succeed them
in their office than on allowing the royal family to retain its
domination.

This is a constant characteristic of ruling groups.   The royal
family itself strives to control the whole organization of the state.
If, for any reason, the power of the ruling family weakens, holders
of minor offices, such as the nomarchs in Egypt, tend to assert
their independence, and establish a hereditary succession to their
office.   At the same time, they will, if possible, claim a connexion
with the royal family.

The Egyptian royal family, from beginning to end, was closely
associated with incestuous marriages, usually between brother
and sister.[2]   The reason for this is unknown.   It is interesting
to note, however, that this, the earliest ruling group of which
we have detailed knowledge, was as close knit as it is possible
to be.   Marriage literally in the family ; the concentration of
power within a group of brothers and sisters ; this comprises the
utmost limit to which the ruling function could hope to attain.

Many theories have been put forward to account for the origin
of magic and religion.   Some students believe that religious ideas
and practices are the outcome of the speculations of early man.
They would urge that the idea of a supreme god originated in
this way.   Others place great emphasis upon the influence of
dream experiences, as evidence of the continued existence of
human personality after death.   Others, again, believe in an
innate tendency on the part of man to explain striking natural
phenomena as the result of the workings of spiritual beings.

I do not intend to discuss these theories, for I simply wish to
show that the development of religion and magic, and particularly
religion, has been influenced by the family.

If we begin as near to the beginning as possible, and ask in
what respects the family displays its influence on the development
of culture, it seems certain that the ritual connected with the
dead should take a prominent place.   From early times it has
been customary to bury the dead with some sort of ritual.   The

[1] Perry vi. 450–5.   [2] Murray, M. A. 309–10.

ceremonial burials of the Aurignacian caves of the Upper Palaeolithic Age in Europe are witnesses to the presence of definite
desires on the part of the living. They placed with the dead
various substances, such as red ochre, cowrie and other shells,
which, as we know from the study of the funeral customs of
the Chinese and others, were presumably placed with the body
with the aim of restoring life, as it were, to the dead.[1] This
act has been interpreted as a manifestation of the instinct of
self-preservation, or the desire to retain life. But it can hardly
be said that the dead person placed these substances in the
grave with himself. Surely it must be admitted that the
family sentiments were at work, and that the living wished to
help the dead as best they could, and that they used certain
' givers of life ' for this purpose ? They, after all, were the
active agents in the matter, and it must have been as the
result of the promptings of affection that they performed such
acts. It is common to say that fear was the great factor
inducing men to initiate funeral rites, but there is a vast array
of evidence telling against that point of view.

It is possible to show by example what an important part has
been played by the family sentiments and emotions in the building
up of the ritual of the dead and of the cult of the dead generally.
We find in pre-Dynastic Egypt, that is, in Egypt before the
foundation of the First Dynasty, which on the most conservative
estimate happened about 3300 $\pm$ 100 B.C., that the dead were
invariably provided in their graves with food, and with domestic
and other objects. Food was placed regularly on the little mound
of sand that was made over the grave. To this day the Egyptian
and Nubian peasantry perform ceremonies in memory of departed
members of their own families. Indeed it is rare, if not unknown,
for rites to be performed on behalf of members of other family
groups.

The development of the royal mortuary ritual in historical
times was evidently based, in part, on the family affections. The
Egyptian rulers began to practise mummification about the time
of the First Dynasty.

The first man to be mummified was remembered by the
Egyptians as Osiris. Osiris was killed by his brother Set. His
body was recovered by his wife Isis and his son Horus, together
with Nephthys, his sister, Anubis and Thoth. They mummified
him, and brought him to life by certain magical ceremonies.
The whole drama of the death, the finding, and the reconstitution
of Osiris was performed every time anyone was mummified.

[1] Perry vii. 6, 7.

During the ritual of mummification Isis and Nephthys weep for Osiris. ' The Het-bird comes, the falcon comes ; they are Isis and Nephthys, they come embracing their brother Osiris. . . . Weep for thy brother, Isis ! Weep for thy brother, Nephthys ! Weep for thy brother ! Isis sits, her arms upon her head ; Nephthys has seized the tips of her breasts (in mourning) because of her brother.' ¹

The author goes on to say that ' the lamentations of Isis and Nephthys became the most sacred expression of sorrow known to the heart of the Egyptian, and many were the varied forms which they took until they emerged in the Osirian mysteries in Europe, three thousand years later.' ²

The son of Osiris was Horus, and his filial piety was a theme which the Egyptians never tired of contemplating.³

We are told by Breasted that ' the Osiris myth expressed those hopes and aspirations and ideals which were closest to the life and affections of this great people. Isis was the noblest embodiment of wifely fidelity and maternal solicitude, while the highest ideals of filial devotion found expression in the story of Horus. About this group of father, mother and son the affectionate fancy of the common folk wove a fair fabric of family ideals which rise high above such conceptions elsewhere. In the Osiris myth the institution of the family found its earliest and most exalted expression in religion, a glorified reflection of earthly ties among the gods. The catastrophe and the ultimate triumph of the righteous cause introduced here in a nature-myth are an impressive revelation of the profoundly moral consciousness with which the Egyptian at a remote age contemplated the world. When we consider, furthermore, that Osiris was the kindly dispenser of plenty, from whose prodigal hand king and peasant alike received their daily bounty, that he was waiting over yonder behind the shadow of death to waken all who have fallen asleep to a blessed hereafter with him, and that in every family group the same affections and emotions which had found expression in the beautiful myth were daily and hourly experiences, we shall understand something of the reason for the universal devotion which was ultimately paid to the dead god.' ⁴ The same authority says in another place, ' Among the people the most common virtue discernible by us is filial piety. Over and over again we find the massive tombs of the Pyramid Age erected by the son for the departed father, as well as a splendid interment arranged by the son.' ⁵

¹ Breasted iii. 27.   ² *Id.*, 27.   ³ *Id.*, 29.
⁴ *Id.*, 37.   ⁵ *Id.*, 167.

The influence of the family emotions and sentiments is clearly shown in the fact that after a few generations the old shrines were neglected.   Much more attention was paid to the recent dead, to parents, and perhaps also the grandparents, all of whom had been known in the flesh.   Beyond that degree but little interest was taken in the dead, and it was common for the Egyptian king to divert to the tomb of some favoured nobleman the endowments of other tombs, the occupants of which had almost been forgotten.

The family nature of the Osirian rites is shown again in the fact that the parts of Horus, Isis, Nephthys, Anubis and Thoth in the drama of the death and resurrection of Osiris were played by the royal family, the king himself playing the part of Horus, the queen that of Isis, and so on.   The king was Horus, because the kings of Egypt had that title.   Horus was the living king, while Osiris was the dead king, the king who had been mummified.   The Horus of the drama of Osiris, who fought Set the king's brother, and who played so prominent a part in the first mummification, was thus the king of Egypt, the son of the dead king.   So throughout the history of the Egyptian religion, the family of the deceased personated Horus, Isis and Nephthys, and acted the drama of the death and resurrection of Osiris.

Thus, as the drama of history slowly unfolds itself, as men acquire new thoughts, and proceed to act upon them, the old family sentiments and emotions, which presumably acted powerfully throughout the time when men were simply food-gatherers, are still potent.   The funeral ceremonies associated with Osiris show the continued working of the same feelings, of the desire to retain the dead with the living, to hold continued intercourse with them.   The family is thus at work powerfully as a factor to maintain certain rites in existence.

It must not be thought, however, that the family sentiments were the only ones at work stimulating men to develop their mortuary customs.   There was the personal element, the desire of every one for life, the hatred of death.   The living no more wish to depart from the company of loved ones than the survivors wish to see them go—except when stresses and strains of life cause upheavals in the usual feelings towards one another in a family.   The wish of every man is to survive as long as possible, and in good health, hence the immense popularity throughout the ages of devices for the prolongation of life, for the attainment of perpetual youth, from the 'fountains of youth' of ancient times to the use of monkey glands of the present day.

The instinct of self-preservation is constantly ready to take advantage of every opportunity for the advancement of personal interests, so it is to be expected that the theory that accompanied the practice of mummification, the theory that the dead might be made to live again, found an immense popularity awaiting itself once it became known.   Thus we find that the doctrine of the resurrection of the body, the idea of conscious life in the hereafter, ultimately enjoyed a wide vogue in Greece, Rome, and elsewhere in the ancient empires.   It finally caused the drama of the death and resurrection of a man to be the symbol of the gift of eternal life to every one who went through the same process of death and rebirth.   The family aspect became somewhat pushed into the background, and the main interest centred on the belief in a future life beyond the grave, a life far different from the miserable existence pictured in the underworld of Babylonia, the Jews, Greece and Rome.

Although the family element became somewhat detached in time from the idea of immortality, yet it was potent in the further developments of thought that characterized the Pyramid Age of Egypt, which ultimately led up to the triumph of the solar theology of the Fifth Dynasty.   In the earlier dynasties of Egypt there is but little trace of the sun-god, who was so prominent a feature of the state theology after the foundation of the Fifth Dynasty.

The most that can be detected is the use of the name of the sun-god Re in the royal names of certain kings of the Second to the Fourth Dynasties.   But with the foundation of the Fifth Dynasty (*circa* 2750–2625 B.C.) the name of Re, the sun-god of Heliopolis, enters into the royal name, and the eighth king of the same dynasty, Dedkere-Isesi, called himself the *Son of the Sun*.   Henceforth the king of Egypt used this title.[1]

It is worthy of note that the solar cult became the state cult of Egypt when the kings were beginning to call themselves Sons of the Sun.   There is an oft-quoted tale of the announcement to Khufu of the Fourth Dynasty of the impending birth of the Children of the Sun, the sons of Re (the sun-god), and of the wife of the high priest of Heliopolis.   This story was to the effect that the sun-god would be the father of certain sons who would sit on the throne of Egypt.[2]

It is certainly suggestive to find that the sun-god could only be the state god of Egypt when he was the father of the king. As a converse to this we find that, in outlying parts of the world, such as Polynesia, India and so forth, the sun-god only lasted

---

[1] This statement is based on Chapter 26 of ' The Children of the Sun '.
[2] Erman (-Blackman) ii. 36.

as the state god so long as his presumed descendants lasted on
the earth. Once they disappeared, so did his cult.[1]

It is practically certain that the idea of the sun-god was not
formulated under the direct stimulus of the family feelings.
Rather does it appear that it was the result of certain circumstances associated with the getting of food. For it is a remarkable
coincidence that Heliopolis should have been the home of the sun
cult in Egypt and also, in the opinion of Eduard Meyer, Borchardt
and Sethe, three eminent German authorities on Egyptology, of
the solar calendar which supplanted the older lunar calendar.
Re, the sun-god, seems to betray his origin in the fact that he
was born on the Egyptian New Year's Day, the day of the beginning of the Nile flood, which was closely bound up with the
Egyptian calendar.[2]

But once this new theory had come into existence it would find
itself taken up by the royal family for more than one reason. It
offered to the king a glorious life in the hereafter in the world
of the sky, as an alternative to the older land of the dead. The
new cult reached its final success when the king became an incarnate deity on earth. This added glory to the king, and was thus
an additional reason why he should adopt the new title.

In dealing with this situation it is evident that other factors
than the simple emotional innate ones associated with the family,
food, and self-protection come in. The royal family exists, and
uses any and every possible device to enhance its position. Not
only does the mutual affection of its members keep it together,
but the desire for power and glory urges it to buttress its position
by every available means.

There is ample evidence to show that the cult of the sun was
confined to the royal family. The rest of the people, nobles
included, adopted the rites associated with Osiris, if they did not
retain rites dating back to times before the invention of mummification. The later mortuary texts reveal the progressive decline
of the influence of the solar theology in the royal funerary ritual
itself, and the progressive enhancement of the Osirian ritual.[3]

The Book of the Dead, the great collection of funeral texts that
date from times subsequent to the composition of the Pyramid
Texts, reveals the working of this process.

Only those who are descended, in theory, from the sun-god
can be expected to pay much attention to him. The ordinary
folk practically ignore him. Only the Son of the Sun can approach

---

[1] More will be said later on this point. See p. 198.
[2] See Perry vi. Chap. XXVI, for a discussion of these matters.
[3] Breasted iii. 142, e.s. 276.

the sun ; ordinary people have to be content with their own dead, and to appeal to them for help and advice.

It must not be imagined that the quotations from the writings of Professor Breasted, based on the Pyramid Texts, give a complete picture of the attitude of the various members of the royal family of Egypt towards one another.   The quotations given refer to the sentiments of Isis, the wife of Osiris, and Horus his son towards the dead king.   These and other members of the family express their sentiments of grief and affection towards the dead king.

Another personage played an important part in the drama of the death and resurrection of Osiris.   This was Set, his brother, who killed him.   Set and his followers are prominent in the ritual of mummification.   Horus and his four sons prevent Set and his followers from obtaining possession of the body of the dead Osiris.   The walls of the temple at Edfu, for example, depict several scenes in the running warfare between these two groups.   Osiris is mentioned frequently as having conquered Set.[1]   The royal family of Egypt in the days of Osiris was thus divided into two warring factions.

It is not possible, in the existing state of knowledge, to formulate any reason for the murder of Osiris by Set.   But certain texts suggest that Set was dispossessed of his kingdom, which was given to Horus.[2]

The incident of Set and Osiris suggests that political motives can so override family sentiments as to produce internecine strife within the royal family itself.   Indeed, history abounds in such examples.   Palace intrigue has been a constant feature of royalty throughout the ages.   When it is realized that a king has numerous relatives plotting to depose him, it is hardly surprising that he begins his reign by eliminating as much of the potential opposition as possible.   The temptation to plotters is so strong, the prize is so great, that it cannot be surprising that royal families throughout the ages have often exhibited violent and brutal behaviour.

It has already been stated that the ancient kingship was intimately bound up with the performance of ceremonials on behalf of the State as a whole.   The king was the high priest of the national cult.   He was intermediary between earth and heaven.   He was usually closely related to the gods.   One or two instances will make this clear.

The State cult of the Chinese was that of Heaven, and this cult was in the hands of the members of the ruling group, par-

[1] Naville, E. ii.   See also Breasted iii. 40.
[2] Perry vi. 273.   See p. 255 for a further discussion of this topic.

THE FAMILY

ticularly of the Emperor himself. Père de son peuple, l'empereur est aussi son pontife. C'est pour le bien du peuple, qu'il honore le Ciel, le Souverain d'en haut. C'est pour le bien du peuple, qu'il invoque les Génies des monts et des fleuves. C'est pour le bien du peuple, qu'il salue les Génies des localités. Culte officiel, auquel les seigneurs avaient une part subordonnée, chacun dans son ressort et dans une certaine mesure. Le peuple, il était spectateur de ce culte officiel ; mais il n'avait pas droit d'y participer, sous peine de lèse-majeste.[1]

The reason why the emperor alone was able to approach the Heaven and perform cults associated with it, is given in the story of the birth of Sie, the ancestor of the Chang Dynasty (1687 B.C.). ' A swallow let an egg fall into the mouth of his mother and she conceived.' This was the beginning of the use of the royal title of Son of Heaven.[2] The ruler henceforth acted as intermediary between the sky and his people because he was the son of heaven in the literal sense.

The state cult in Japan displays the same characteristics. As a member of the solar family, the Mikado is the High Priest of the national cult of Shinto. In this he is simply one of a long line, descended from the Sun-goddess Hirume, or Amaterasu, as she is also called.[3]

The Japanese cult differed profoundly from the Egyptian—I speak, of course, of the royal families—in that it included no well-marked belief in immortality. ' Like the Old Testament the ancient Japanese records afford but few and uncertain glimpses of the condition of the dead. The doctrine of the immortality of the soul is nowhere taught explicitly ! ' There are no prayers for the dead or for happiness in a future life.[4] The Japanese, indeed, only seem to have believed in an underground land of the dead.

The examples of Egypt, China, and Japan show that the ruler carried on the state cult because he was related to the gods. The family principle is of extreme importance in connexion with cults of gods. It can, indeed, be laid down as a general principle that cults of gods are, in early religious systems, in the hands of hereditary priesthoods who claim relationship with the gods. Apart from this relationship such cults do not appear to exist in a developed form.[5]

The Zuñi Indians of New Mexico in the United States may be chosen for this purpose. They provide a good example of the

[1] Wieger 11–12. [2] *Id.*, 21, 22.
[3] Aston 201. [4] Aston 53.
[5] Perry v. Chap. 18.

religious systems of peoples of the lower culture who have no
hereditary ruling group. As we have seen, they have an extensive
ritual, centred mainly round their food supply. Although they
have creation myths associated with the Sun-Father ; although
they call themselves the Children of the Sun ; although they tell of
the twin Children of the Sun who brought them out of the Underworld, yet they have no cults of the sun-god such as are found
in Egypt, no daily ritual toilet of the image of the sun-god. They
certainly offer prayers to the Sun-Father, but little else attaches
to him in the way of cult.

All their ceremonial is bound up with priesthoods and fraternities. There is a Sun priesthood, the high priest of which is
responsible for the calendar.[1] The chief priesthood, however,
is that of the Rain Priests. ' This priesthood is confined to
families, the rule being that each member of a division of the
priesthood must be of the clan or a child of the clan of the shi'wanni
(priest) of the division. The son or brother of the shi'wanni
fills a vacancy, preference being given to the eldest son.'

Thus even where there is no direct cult of gods, no daily feeding
and clothing of the image the fraternities tend to be hereditary.
But associations of such a kind are often perpetuated because
they serve certain functions such as those connected with food-
getting, medicine, death and so forth, which are of direct interest
to everybody. The Rain Priesthood of the Zuñi has a sacred
object which is supposed to have been handed down from the
priest who brought it out of the ancestral underworld. Part of
this sacred object consists of all the kinds of edible seeds known
to the Zuñi. This sacred object is in the care of a woman of the
clan, the office passing from mother to daughter or from sister
to sister.[2]

In general among the Zuñi ' the clan plays an important part
in ceremonials. Many ceremonial offices are filled either by a
member of a given clan or by a " child " of the clan—that is,
either the mother or the father must belong to the particular clan.
In some cases offices are filled annually, in rotation, first by a
member of a particular clan and secondly by a " child " of the
specified clan. Some offices are always filled by a particular
clan ; in other cases the offices must be filled only by a " child "
of a designated clan.'[3] Thus once again is the family seen at
work.

Many peoples of the lower culture practise what is called an
' ancestor cult '. But this cult usually extends no further back

[1] Stevenson 175–6.   [2] *Id.*, 163, 164.
                [3] *Id.*, 291.

than the grandparents. That is to say, it concerns only those who have been known in the flesh. Earlier generations are forgotten, except when there is reason to remember them.

The corollary to this is that no attention is paid to the ghosts of other people. We find also that the ghosts of ordinary people are sometimes supposed to live in the house they built : in like manner the ghosts of chiefs live in the village temple.[1]

There is a common tendency throughout the world for property to be owned or transmitted among families. In certain cases territory is owned by clans, and not by the tribe as a whole. This land is not used by the clan as a whole. Agricultural peoples usually divide the clan lands among groups of relatives, who work their portion in common, and share its produce.

This common ownership by a group of relatives may perhaps be termed ' communism ' ; but care must be taken not to import into the term the concepts of the modern economic theory of Communism. The essential characteristic of the common ownership of property among savages is that it is confined to groups of relatives, and does not tend to be extended to wider groups.

Many peoples are divided, more or less completely, into hereditary occupations. We have already seen this in the case of Japan, and innumerable other instances could be quoted. The caste system of India is a classic example. Kings, priests, nobles, merchants, skilled craftsmen, farmers, scavengers, are all controlled, more or less strictly by the rules of caste.

Knowledge was originally accumulated and handed down in families. The convenience of this method among illiterate people is obvious. Young people learn the family craft at an early age, and acquire the hereditary skill almost intuitively.

These few examples show that the family is associated with a large number of social institutions. The state with its ruler and nobility ; the tribal organization, including its sub-divisions, such as moiety, clan, etc. ; religious belief and practice ; kinship organization and marriage regulations ; these, and other forms of social behaviour, depend largely on the family for their form and expression.

It is not surprising that membership of social groupings, other than the family, should depend upon the family. Savage life is lived in the society of relatives. Contacts with other groups of relatives are comparatively rare. Each boy and girl would readily conform to the type of behaviour of their near relatives. The clans they belong to, the moiety, the age-grade and so on, would

---

[1] Kruyt, A. C., i. 390–1, 405.

7

follow the family tradition.   Thus social behaviour, once anchored in family groups, would tend to persist indefinitely.

I do not propose at this stage to enter into more detail concerning the rôle of the family in human society.   This topic will be constantly under discussion ;   it is one of the major themes of this book.

CHAPTER IX

ACQUISITION

IT is now time to give a new direction to the argument, and to consider some modifications of human behaviour which are the outcome of the working of certain institutions. In the series of chapters that have preceded this it has been shown that the fundamental innate tendencies that were so patently at work in primitive society, continued to exert a powerful influence in moulding the behaviour of mankind in food-producing communities. In the course of the working-out of the historical process they have been constantly active, causing men to adhere to one set of beliefs rather than another, and to form certain definite patterns of behaviour. It is safe to predict that the family will, throughout the length and breadth of any society, play an important part in the social life. It is easy to predict that the getting of food will be of great importance, and that much ritual, in early societies, will be directed towards this end, that the gods will be importuned for food and wealth. It is easy to assert that men will usually seek their own interests, and will try always to avert or to avoid danger. These are fundamental forms of activity of behaviour which, as we have seen, can be predicted of any form of human society.

In addition to these fundamental innate tendencies of men, there are forms of behaviour that can be shown to have been mainly, if not entirely, the outcome of social institutions.

Once institutions come into existence they interact one on another, and tend to produce new forms of behaviour which were not manifested, or but rarely manifested, by peoples of a simpler form of culture. In this and the following chapters instances of this process will be brought forward. It will be shown how the development of civilization, with its concomitant formation of new social institutions, has produced a complicated interlacing of institutions with corresponding complexities in human behaviour.

The common tendency to credit any widespread form of human activity to an instinctive tendency is dangerous. It has well been said that if you once start multiplying instincts you can go on indefinitely. A gregarious instinct would imply one of solitude, and an instinct of pugnacity requires one of pacifism, and so on. Whatever contrasted modes of behaviour are found, if one is chosen as instinctive, it is possible to argue that the other is also.

It has often been said that man has an Instinct of Acquisition. McDougall says : ' The impulse to collect and hoard various objects is displayed in one way or another by almost all human beings, and seems to be due to a true instinct. . . .' ` He goes on to say that this instinct seems to be deficient among peoples of the food-gathering stage of culture. ' Or perhaps it is that it never is able to determine the formation of a corresponding habit owing to their wandering mode of life. Among pastoral nomads, the working of the instinct is manifested in the vast herds sometimes accumulated by a single patriarchal family. But it was only when agriculture began to be extensively practised that the instinct could produce its greatest social effects. For grain of all sorts lends itself especially well to hoarding as a form of wealth.' [1] He then states that the motives leading to accumulation of wealth in highly organized societies are complex.

If by ' acquisition ' is meant the mere act of ' getting ', then this activity is present in many forms. It is a common element in the getting of food, the collecting of stamps and cigarette cards, the hoarding of precious metals, the adding of field to field and house to house, the cold storage of beef and the freezing of credits. All these involve ' getting ', but this does not explain them.

Such a definition as ' the impulse to collect and hoard ' is even less adequate. It does not recognize the basic distinction that some of these activities are founded on primal biological needs, whilst others are more directly due to the existence of social institutions.

This distinction can readily be made if we examine the behaviour of food-gatherers. Their culture is obviously most closely related to biological needs, and is not canalized by complex social institutions.

What part does acquisition—in any meaning of the term— play in these groups ? The food-gatherer certainly ' gets ' food and a mate. But this is surely the satisfaction of hunger and sex impulses, rather than acquisition *per se* ? No acquisitive instinct need be postulated. Food, moreover, is usually shared out amongst the family groups ; there is not exclusive individual

[1] McDougall 87–8, 322–3. Rivers also discusses the problem of instinctive acquisition. Rivers iv. Appendix VIII, pp. 260 ff.

appropriation or hoarding. Children and old people are often
fed before the strong. Food-gatherers are usually improvident,
living from hand to mouth. Stores of food, as among the Eskimo,
are for family consumption. Instruments used in the getting
or preparation of food are personal property through personal
use and familiarity. It appears that even the wife is not
normally the mere property of her mate ; affection, help, and
children form the link.

Food-gatherers, therefore, fail to yield evidence for a sort of
inchoate instinctive impulse towards acquisition for its own sake.
Their personal possessions are what they use in everyday life.
They do not accumulate for accumulation's sake.

When we turn to food-producing peoples, the evidence strongly
suggests that, throughout the whole range of human society, the
possession of property objects is influenced by other motives
than that of the mere desire to possess. This complexity of
motives becomes clear when actual examples are analysed.

It can readily be shown, for instance, that family sentiments
strongly influence the distribution of property. Rivers has
pointed out that in speaking of ' communism ' in property, we
usually mean common possession by a group of relatives. In
Eddystone Island in the western British Solomons, property of
various sorts, especially land, is vested in a group called the
Taviti, consisting of relatives reckoned on either side. When
a member of such a *Taviti* group has individual rights in his land
or other property, these are subject to many claims on the part
of other members of the group. Again, in the Island of Ambrym
in the New Hebrides, land was the property of the clan as a whole,
a clan being a group of people claiming common ancestry. But
actually a kindred group called *Vantimbul* possessed any land
that they have cleared and brought under cultivation. ' A man
might clear a piece of ground entirely by his own labour, and
might plant and tend it without help from any one, but any
member of his *Vantimbul* could nevertheless help himself to
any of its produce without asking leave or informing the cultivator. Inhabitants of the village belonging to a *Vantimbul*
other than that of the cultivator might also take produce, but
had to ask leave. Since such permission, however, was never
refused, the communism extended in practice to the whole
clan.' [1]

Rivers has made it quite clear that the family has the important
function of giving status to the individuals belonging to it.[2]
Thus the family and relationship systems functioning within an

[1] Rivers v. 104, 105, 106.   [2] *Id.*, 125–6.

hierarchic social structure largely determine the distribution of property, whether in Melanesia or the Western World. The complexity of sentiment and motive resulting from these social institutions is well illustrated from the Banks Islands in Melanesia. These have secret societies, the membership of which is highly prized. Entrance is by the payment of strings of shell discs. Admission to the higher degrees in the society is also the occasion for additional payments.[1] The accumulation of property thus has a definite institutional incentive, namely, the social privileges and prestige attaching to membership of such a society, and especially of its higher ranks. But the family sentiments are actively at work. Thus Rivers : ' A man who has spent large sums of money in order to rise high in the *Sukwe* (a secret society of the Banks Islands) does so partly in order that by receiving money from those initiated later he may acquire wealth which will enable him to help his children and other relatives to follow in his footsteps. That such an idea is clearly present in the minds of the people is shown by the reasons given for the gift of the *Tamate worawora* by Gapal to his niece. I think there can be no doubt that one of the motives which leads a man to advance in the *Sukwe* or to enter his children is an idea corresponding very closely to that which underlies our practice of investment of capital.'

Other forces are at work tending to the accumulation of wealth. Rivers proceeds to say : ' From one point of view, then, the *Sukwe* and *Tamate* societies and other associated institutions form a complex organization by means of which wealth is acquired, and since it is only the rich or those with rich friends who can advance far in these bodies, the organization is a means for the perpetuation and even the accentuation of differences of social rank in so far as this rank is dependent on the possession of ' wealth '.

The secret societies form practically the only institution in these islands with which the use of money is concerned ; so that any one who wishes to stand well with his fellows has to accumulate wealth by some means or other.

Rivers goes on to say : ' It is, however, clear that there are other deeply seated ideas in the minds of the people which prevent wealth from becoming the chief means of social differentiation. The mere acquisition of wealth for its own sake is probably wholly foreign to the ideas of the people. The wealth derived from a high position in the *Sukwe* is probably regarded merely as a means to still further advance. It has been seen that the

[1] Rivers v. 124.

highest ranks in the *Sukwe* are often without members, and there is always the possibility of further advance with the great expense which such a step would involve. There are also the elaborate *kolekole* performances . . . which are the recognized means of further advance in social estimation.'

' A man, however high in the *Sukwe* he may be, will suffer social depreciation if he does not undertake such expense. Mr. Durrad was told that when a man reaches high rank in the *Sukwe* and has thereby the power of amassing wealth, he would be considered unworthy of respect and honour if he hoarded his gains. To retain his influence and glory, he must distribute his money by paying people to work for him in his gardens and by giving splendid *kolekole* performances. The Banks Islanders seem to have developed a sentiment which has removed a social danger to which the organization of the *Sukwe* standing alone would have exposed them.'

' Though there are thus social factors which have prevented the *Sukwe* and *Tamate* societies from becoming too exclusively the means for the acquisition of wealth, there can be no doubt that the high development of these bodies has brought in its train so complicated a mass of vested interests that their disappearance would produce very great confusion in social values.' [1]

Thus the secret societies constitute a constant stimulus to the accumulation of property, not for its own sake, but because thereby advancement in the society may be effected. To account completely for this form of activity it would be necessary to explain how and where such societies came into existence.

Strong though this evidence is, it is equalled by the facts brought to light by Malinowski during his stay in the Trobriands. He there shows that the accumulation of property is controlled and stimulated by certain social processes, among which rank in society is predominant. He recounts how much time is spent by the Trobrianders in their gardens, and stresses the great care they take to make them neat and tidy.[2] He then goes on to say of the Trobriander that : ' He works prompted by motives of a highly complex, social and traditional nature, and towards aims which are certainly not directed towards the satisfaction of present wants, or to the direct achievement of utilitarian purposes. Thus, in the first place, . . . work is not carried out on the principle of the least effort. On the contrary, much time and energy is spent on wholly unnecessary effort, that is, from the utilitarian point of view. Again, work and effort, instead of being merely a means to an end, are, in a way an end themselves.

[1] Rivers iii. I. 140–1.   [2] Malinowski ii. 58–9.

A good garden worker in the Trobriands derives a direct prestige from the amount of labour he can do, and the size of the garden he can till. The title *tokwaybagula*, which means " good " or " efficient gardener ", is bestowed with discrimination, and borne with pride. Several of my friends, renowned as *tokwaybagula*, would boast to me how long they worked, how much ground they tilled, and would compare their efforts with those of less efficient men. When the labour, some of which is done communally, is actually being carried out, a good deal of competition goes on. Men vie with one another in their speed, in their thoroughness, and in the weights they can lift, when bringing big poles to the garden, or in carrying away the harvested yams.' [1] That is to say, the spirit of emulation is responsible for the production of wealth as a by-product of their activities in the gardens. The motive is not acquisitiveness, but self-esteem, the desire to do better than any one else, a very common trait amongst human beings.

Malinowski stresses this fact. He says : ' The most important point about this is, however, that all, or almost all the fruits of his work, and certainly any surplus which he can achieve by extra effort goes not to the man himself, but to his relatives-in-law . . . it may be said that about three-quarters of a man's crops go partly as a tribute to the chief, partly as his due to his sister's (or mother's) husband and family.' [2] The fruits of his efforts therefore are not intended for his own material satisfaction. He heaps up food not for himself, but for others. His own satisfaction lies in another direction. Thus Malinowski : ' But although he thus derives practically no personal benefit in the utilitarian sense from his harvest, the gardener receives much praise and renown from its size and quality, and that in a direct and circumstantial manner. For all the crops, after being harvested, are displayed for some time afterwards in the gardens, piled up in neat, conical heaps under small shelters made of yam vine. Each man's harvest is thus exhibited for criticism in his own plot, and parties of natives walk about from garden to garden, admiring, comparing and praising the best results. The importance of the food display can be gauged by the fact that in olden days, when the chief's power was much more considerable than now, it was dangerous for a man, who was not either of high rank himself or working for such a one, to show crops which might compare too favourably with those of the chief.

' In years when the harvest promises to be plentiful, the chief will proclaim a *kayasa* harvest, that is to say, a ceremonial com-

---

[1] Malinowski ii. 60–1. [2] *Ibid.*, 61.

petitive display of food, and then the straining for good results
and the interest taken in them are still higher.' [1]

The magic associated with food also shows the same complexity
of motive, especially the desire for distinction. The magic performed over crops is not designed to cause them to increase, but
rather to make people inclined to eat less yams and to desire
jungle fruit more. Thus half the yams will lie rotting, to be
eventually thrown away. ' Here again we meet the typical idea
that the main aim of accumulating food is to keep it exhibited
in yam houses till it rots, and then can be replaced by a new
etalage.' Distributions and displays of food form part of most
ceremonial. For instance, mortuary ceremonial consists largely
in the distribution of an enormous display of food. ' In fact one
could almost speak of a " cult of food " among these natives, in
so far as food is the central object of most of their public
ceremonies.' [2]

In general, ' The Trobriander works in a roundabout way, to
a large extent for the sake of the work itself, and puts a great
deal of aesthetic polish on the arrangement and general appearance
of his garden. He is not guided primarily by the desire to satisfy
his wants, but by a very complex set of traditional forces, duties
and obligations, beliefs in magic, social ambitions and vanities.
He wants, if he is a *man*, to achieve social distinction as a *good
gardener* and a good worker in general.' Again, ' These natives
are industrious, and keen workers. They do not work under
the spur of necessity, or to gain their living, but on the impulse
of talent and fancy, with a high sense and enjoyment of their
art, which they often conceive as the result of magical inspiration.
This refers especially to those who produce objects of high value,
and who are always good craftsmen and are fond of their workman-
ship. . . .' [3]

It should be plain, therefore, that the acquisition of property
in these instances is not the direct result of an instinctive process.
It is rather the outcome of social processes which cause men to
follow certain lines of activity. The individual is born into this
social heritage, and tends to adjust himself to it. Thus his family
grouping will determine much of his property relationships. And
since this is usually part of a larger social structure, so rank
and status play their parts in inducing acquisition and exchange.
Prestige may be purchased, wealth may be a sign of rank. But
so equally may be generosity—generosity on a seemingly excessive
scale.

This adjustment of the individual to his social environment

[1] Malinowski, op. cit., 61.   [2] *Id.*, 169, 170.   [3] *Id.*, 62, 172.

also brings into play the element of self-esteem, of competition. It stimulates the desire to excel, in giving as in taking. This is put very clearly by Malinowski, who says that : ' The view that the native can live in a state of individual search for food, catering for his own household only, in isolation from any interchange of goods, implies a calculating cold egotism, the possibility of enjoyment by man of utilities for their own sake. This view, and all the previously criticized assumptions, ignore the fundamental human impulse to display, to share, to bestow. They ignore the deep tendency to create social ties through exchange of gifts. Apart from any consideration as to whether the gifts are necessary or even useful, giving for the sake of giving is one of the most important features of Trobriand sociology, and, from its very general and fundamental nature, I submit that it is a universal feature of all primitive societies.' The whole tribal life is permeated by constant give and take, so that ' wealth, given and taken, is one of the main instruments of social organization, of the power of the chief, of the bonds of kinship, and of relationship in law '.[1]

Can it be said that these instances show the dominance of the ' impulse to collect and hoard ' ? Such an explanation has frequently been advanced when the collection has consisted of objects for which the Westerner has no value—shells, teeth, metals, ornaments, etc. But these are not valueless to the owner. They are usually of magical importance. They are ' life givers.' Many are heirlooms. Much prestige may be associated with them.

Magical traditions may yield other results curious to the acquisitive Westerner. Sometimes property objects are inalienable because of their alleged associations with the personality of the owner and his well-being. Their exchange would be useless or dangerous. And many such objects may be destroyed at death of the owner.

It is interesting to note that in many psychological studies it has been common to correlate the behaviour of the savage with that of abnormal Europeans and of children. Today it should be unnecessary to combat such a curious misconception. A savage is neither a baby nor a pathological specimen. He is a normal member of a community whose customs differ, superficially perhaps, from that of the Westerners who write about him. But he is a man, no less.

Certainly so far as the ' collecting impulse ' is concerned, the instances quoted above make it difficult to correlate the savage

[1] Malinowski, op. cit., 175, 167.

with the miser or kleptomaniac.   These manifestations are often
assumed to throw light on the problem of acquisition.   The
assumption is that their apparently unreasonable nature betrays
a fundamental instinctive basis for the activity.   But abnormality
may be simply the result of maladjustment to the traditional
behaviour of the group.   The adjustment of the individual must
surely be a difficult process ; and it is surprising how little the
misfit comes to the surface.   Pathological stealing, therefore, can
legitimately be regarded as a channel of discharge for some inner
conflict.   The literature of psychoanalytic practice abounds in
such cases.   This discharge, this relief, may seem more or less
haphazard.   But usually it is shown to be associative, and the
specific selection is of objects of emotional value to the subject.

   In short, the activity is an outlet for internal conflict, and the
collecting of certain objects brings relief.   It is not a manifestation
of acquisitiveness, any more than suicide is a manifestation of
' the instinct of pugnacity '.   It is an escape.

   The behaviour of children is also used as evidence for instinctive
acquisition.   They are often great collectors of trifles.   Moreover,
young children especially appear to be very possessive.   It may,
however, be pointed out that if the abnormal person is possibly
the result of maladjustment, on the other hand there is no doubt
whatever that the child is in the very process of adjustment.
And this means, *inter alia*, a growing acquaintance with the
complicated system of property rights around him.   For example,
a young child is given food.   The food is his, in his plate.   He
wears his clothes, sleeps in his bed.   He probably appropriates
any bright-looking article that attracts him ; though sometimes
he is deprived of the object he is about to swallow, because he is
yet unable to assimilate explanatory homilies.   He thus builds
up an attitude to objects.   They are his because he uses them,
subject only to apparently arbitrary prohibitions.   Without
much warning he is introduced to articles which are common to
a group, in a nursery school, for instance.   He picks up a toy,
etc. (i.e. if he isn't shy, and so keeps away).   He plays with it.
He uses it.   It is his.   Teacher, nurse, gave it him.   He will
later, and with difficulty, have to extend his concept of property
to include common group property.   Finally he will have to
respect the rights of others, reasonable and unreasonable, over
what they own, whether they use it or not.   So well is this
achieved, that in his early teens the child has become a respectable
conservative, and a nice discrimination in social observances
earns the approval of adults.   Does any one doubt that the education of the child in our property rights is at least as difficult as

its education in arithmetic or spelling ? Can we expect no difficulties, conflicts and mistakes ?

Collecting is certainly a common habit with most children, but it is not universal. Very young ones are not interested in collection, they too soon lose interest in things A little later, especially when they learn to play games and share group excitements and stimuli, many children become collectors. Observation shows that the extent of the habit varies with local fashion. It appears to vary with the provision of alternative amusements.[1] Fundamentally it is an activity which is pleasurable according to the competition of others, the thrill of achieving distinction and consequent social approval. It helps to satisfy, in a harmless way, self-esteem, the desire to excel, to be conspicuous. Other thrills may come by handling and arranging the specimens—the achievement of a ' set ' is very satisfying, for instance. And finally, the objects are rarely without some specific interest : pretty, brightly coloured eggs or shells, rock crystal, etc., are prized, and but little interest is taken in mere winkles or limestone.

Childhood's collections are soon forgotten. The earlier interests and values give way to others, and such collecting rarely survives.

The habit does remain significantly, however, if the specific interest survives. This is fundamental. Collecting is specific, it depends on some set of specific values and satisfactions. If the youthful interests are not replaced by others, then the ' hobby ' continues. If something tends to further the supposed interests of the individual, then that object may be acquired, and in appropriate cases hoarded. Behind the problem of acquisition therefore lies the problem of value, of interests.

Men's interests are limited by the nature of their knowledge, i.e. by their culture, their social heritage. Primitive man, the food-gatherer, has but few interests, and they are close to primal biological satisfactions. He is not a collector, for he has no incentives. Such values do not exist in his simple cultural environment. And, since he is a normal human being, he is not a pathological hoarder of unconsidered trifles.

On the other hand, food-producing man, with his complex social structure, may find that acquisition and collecting yield many values. They may mean security, rank, status, personal success and other socially desirable results. These apparently new acquisitive activities are the product of civilization. They are related to some historical process, to some theory, to some social institution. Civilization breeds new habits and interests, but it does not invent instincts.

[1] Lehman and Witty 49–56.

CHAPTER X

VIOLENCE

ONE of the best instances of the effect of social institutions on human behaviour is afforded by warfare and other forms of violent behaviour displayed by men. Warfare is a form of violence, and can best be treated as part of the general problem pertaining thereto.

There are two aspects under which violence can conveniently be considered. There may be conflict between members of the same community, or between two communities, usually manifested by more than one member from each community. These two forms of violent behaviour can well be treated apart. For even if it be admitted, as it is by many, that physical conflict between communities is an organized form of behaviour that may not be deeply rooted in human nature, it may be contended that some form of violent behaviour occurs in all societies. Therefore it will be well to study first of all the question of violence within the bounds of a community, and then to go on to the more general question of warfare between communities.

Before embarking on this enterprise, it may be well to insist upon one point. At the beginning of this study it was pointed out that the actions of individuals in highly developed societies such as our own are not necessarily an index of the innate fundamental tendencies of mankind as a whole. When any one asserts that the spiteful behaviour of civilized children is an index of the nature of human behaviour, he is entirely ignoring the influence of institutions upon behaviour; and, as I shall hope to show before long, this influence has been tremendous. All such statements really amount to is this—that violent behaviour is sometimes displayed in our society by children. If it is desired to make a general statement with regard to human behaviour as a whole, if what is 'natural' is sought, then the study must embrace a wide range of human societies, and then only can such wide generalizations be made. It is possible to retort to such an observation, that this form of behaviour may simply be the reaction to the conditions under which a particular child was brought up. All children are not rough and cruel: some are gentle. Who, then, is to say that the one or the other is the normal, and the other the abnormal, type of behaviour ?

It is only necessary to think for a moment of the conditions of the upbringing of a child, to realize that a naturally peaceful and gentle creature can be made violent and cruel. The upbringing of many children is violent to an extreme, and punishment, often cruel, or the fear of punishment, is all too frequently the mode by which a child is brought up to be a ' decent ' member of society. Every one who has associated with children must realize that their dispositions are moulded almost entirely upon their surroundings. For the first few years it is hardly possible to detect any really original thoughts or actions. Play is imitative ; so is talk and general behaviour. When, therefore, a tired mother slaps her young child she is probably teaching it a lesson that it will never forget. The tremendous prestige of the parent will endow violence with a definite sanction, and this form of behaviour will tend to be accepted by the child as natural and reasonable. ' If you do that again, I will slap you,' is a common expression. The consequences are all too well known. A struggle develops between the adult and the child, and divers types of behaviour are engendered. Resentment, the desire for revenge, hatred of the tyrant, stubbornness, all appear, to the great detriment of the character of the child, and, as is well known from the modern study of psychology, of the adult. Therefore so long as adults continue, in this and other countries, to ill-treat children in their desire to train them, or, what is more common, in exasperation at their behaviour, it will be unscientific to maintain that the violent behaviour of children has any reference to any other society than our own. Only the wider study of other communities will settle that point.

An excellent illustration of the tendency to erect comprehensive systems on the basis of the study of civilized children, is afforded by Pierre Bovet's work on the ' Fighting Instinct '. He opens with the sentences : ' Children fight. . . . The study of it offers no difficulty. Events in school playgrounds, in the street, and in the home circles, are directly accessible to our observation, and have often been described.' [1] Such statements may be accepted as true of European children. But the question is—Do children the world over habitually fight ? Is violent behaviour present everywhere ? It is all very well to analyse such behaviour into its elements, but it is not proper to claim that it is ' instinctive ', except in a very loose sense of the term, which renders it valueless.

[1] Bovet, P., 15.

Another consideration must be brought to mind. It may be true that children are prone to occasional forms of violent behaviour as part of their play activities. But that does not mean necessarily that the adult normally indulges in such forms of behaviour. It may be said that play is a preparation for adult life, so that the fact that boys fight shows that they are preparing to fight in adult life. On the other hand, it may be urged that play among children is an imitation of the activities of their elders, so that the fighting of boys may be nothing more than the imitation of the fighting activities of adults which have come to their knowledge through the intermediary of schools, where they are taught of the battles in which our country has been engaged in the past, together with discourses on the glory of fighting in a just cause and the necessity of defending one's country against aggression. Therefore any discussion of the behaviour of children which has not previously discounted such possible influences is founded on sand, and may crumble away at the first contact with wider knowledge.

As an instance of the danger inherent in the reasoning indulged in by thinkers who confine themselves to modern warlike societies, with a long history of violence, I may cite the instance of the Cheyenne Indians of North America, studied by George Bird Grinnell, who has lived among them for many years. He speaks of the behaviour of the children of this tribe when at play. ' Children seldom or never quarrelled or fought among themselves, and though, as they grew older, continually engaging in contests of strength, such as wrestling and kicking matches, and games somewhat like football, they rarely lost their temper. Two boys might be seen swaying to and fro in a wrestling bout, each encouraged by the shouts of his partisans among the on-lookers, and each doing his best. When finally one was thrown all the spectators raised a great shout of laughter, but he who had been overcome arose laughing too, for he realized that the others were not ridiculing him, but were showing their enjoyment of the contest they had witnessed. The Cheyenne boys are naturally good-natured and pleasant, and the importance of living on good terms with their fellows having been drilled into them from earliest childhood, they accept defeat and success with equal cheerfulness. Among a group of white children there would be much more bickering.' [1]

This statement is in flat contradiction to that of M. Bovet, and it follows that no generalization can be laid down as to the behaviour of children. It varies from community to community.

[1] Grinnell ii. I. 122–3.

I do not wish to urge any positive conclusions at this point. I wish, however, to insist that the accounts of behaviour of children that are given to us by people who have studied the food-gatherers do not afford any substantial evidence of an innate tendency to violence among human beings, that is as obtrusive as the innate tendency to eat when one is hungry. If such a claim is made, then it simply follows that every form of human activity whatever must be put down as instinctive, and the term thereby loses its meaning. The fact that certain communities, and, indeed, certain individuals, do not display violent behaviour on any considerable scale, goes to support the theory that man is not possessed of an innate tendency to react violently to certain situations.

If we assert that there is an instinct of pugnacity, then we have just as much reason to assert the existence of an instinct of pacifism. We can only speak of an instinct of pugnacity as a result of an ignorance of facts and an unwillingness to take into consideration the behaviour of people in all stages of civilization.

It is important, when speaking of violent behaviour, to be careful how we define the term pugnacity. It is often asserted that the striving for superiority over another man in some form of contest is evidence of a pugnacious instinct. Such an assertion has even been made in regard to the game of chess.[1] It is said that the delight that we take in watching boxing contests shows that we have an instinct of pugnacity ; but surely this pleasure is in the skill displayed by the combatants, for we are just as pleased to witness skilled play at billiards, where the element of triumph does not enter to anything like the same extent.

It is certain that in games of skill we like to win. But surely that is simply associated with the element of self-esteem, which makes us pleased when we do anything better than our fellows, from gardening to fighting. The self-esteem of men is active in anything that they do in competition with their fellows, and is an integral part of the self-regarding sentiment. So whether it be wrestling, tennis, golf, or chess, the aim is to be superior to the opponent, and thus to satisfy the feeling of self-esteem.

With regard to the satisfaction of the spectator of the game, it may likewise be said that the pleasure is not due to an instinctive desire to fight, but to a pleasure in witnessing things well done, and, perhaps, in watching one's friends overcoming strangers, and thus again satisfying the feelings of self-esteem that belong to a man as a member of a group. Every one likes to feel that the group of which he is a member is better than others, and likes to satisfy that feeling by demonstration.

[1] Bovet 103.

It may be claimed, with much justice, that frequent individual violence may, after all, be but a repercussion of organized violence between communities.   The habit of violent behaviour, learned by fighting in the army, may cause an increase in the violent behaviour of individuals.   Habits learned during warfare often are carried into civil life, and behaviour becomes altered to an appreciable extent.   Who is warranted in denying the statement that perhaps the greater part of the violent behaviour in society may be the result of such experiences repeated over generations, the sentiments being handed on from parent to child in continuous succession, until this type of behaviour appears to be an ingredient of human nature ?   It is only necessary to reflect for a moment on this matter to see how vital it is to use extreme caution when discussing violence.   When behaviour in a country such as ours is reviewed over long periods, it is evidently subject to considerable modifications.   Our treatment of boys in schools is not so severe as it was fifty years ago, or even less.   More humanitarian ideals are at work.   We have a society for the prevention of cruelty to children.   Behaviour constantly alters under pressure from social institutions :   it is not fixed.   Therefore what warrant is there for taking one particular form of behaviour in one particular society, or even in a given range of societies, and generalizing it to apply to the whole of mankind ?

In food-gathering society as a whole there is but little occasion for speaking at all of violent behaviour within the community. On the contrary, there is much more justification for taking the happy relations that exist in these communities as the normal form of activity, and for treating the other as abnormal.   At the same time, there is no doubt that a certain amount of violence must have characterized the relations between individuals ; but as to the extent of this it is difficult to make any direct statements.   This violence was, however, rare, and thus abnormal as a form of behaviour.   It was due, perhaps, in many cases, to accidental circumstances, such as insanity, for instance, and not to the orderly functioning of a process such as that associated with the sexual life of the community.

Grinnell gives, in his work on the Cheyenne Indians, an account of murders committed within that tribe during a long period— about forty-three years.   In that time, he says, only five or six cases of murder took place, a remarkable record for a tribe that spent so much time in fighting.[1]   From this it appears that any theories of violence starting from the small group and extending outwards to the larger units have little substance.   For, in

[1] Op. cit. I. 358.

8

the case of the tribe in question, fighting with other tribes was a common occurrence, parties continually going off on the war-path, certainly in later years.

In setting out to discuss the violence of food-gathering peoples, it must first of all be agreed that any form of behaviour other than peaceable is unusual among them. The testimony of the accounts of the great majority of these peoples is witness enough to that conclusion. There is, in their case, no fundamental tendency to quarrel over certain things, not even over women. I know of no account of such a community in which it is stated that males fight for their mates as do some animals ; so that violence does not even appear as a secondary manifestation of the sex instinct.

Certain food-gatherers show signs of more or less organized violence, sometimes within the community, sometimes between communities, and these instances will have to be explained if the general principle is to hold, namely, that violence is largely absent from the behaviour of food-gatherers. The three cases that must be treated are those of the Eskimo, the Andamanese and the Australian natives. I shall take them in the order given.

We have already learned that the behaviour of the Eskimo differed markedly ; the Eskimo of Greenland being peaceful, and those of Alaska, violent (see p. 42). It is not possible to call in racial or climatic factors to explain this marked difference, for the Eskimo are uniform throughout the whole of the vast area occupied by them.

Throughout the Eskimo area there is mention of individual violence, murders being committed, which are avenged sometimes by the family of the victim. The usual rule is that public opinion sanctions the revenge, so that the family of the murderer does not retaliate. Such happenings occasionally lead to feuds, some-times handed down from generation to generation which, in some cases, according to Boas, are settled eventually by mutual agreement.

The accounts given by Boas, Hawkes, Nelson and others do not make it possible to estimate the frequency of these family feuds resulting from murders (see pp. 40 e.s.). Evidently they form part of an organized mode of behaviour among these people. In any case they do not seem to have been common in occurrence, for all writers agree as to the great degree of friendliness and unanimity characteristic of Eskimo society.

In the case of warfare between communities the evidence is clear. It is practically unknown among the Greenland, Central and Labrador Eskimo, but is found in Alaska.

What is the reason for this extraordinary contrast between the
Eskimo of Bering Strait and those of the other parts of North
America ?   The answer to this question evidently lies in the fact
that the fighting Eskimo use plate armour, as do the peoples of
north-eastern Asia and north-western America.[1] The peaceful
Eskimo lack it.   The possession of this form of armour suggests
that these Eskimo have been influenced by peoples among whom
fighting was a regular procedure, and therefore a ready explanation
is forthcoming for the contrast between their behaviour and,
say, that of the Eskimo of Greenland.

With regard to the question of feuds, I cannot say anything,
for I am unaware of their frequency.   Were the Eskimo in the
habit of murdering one another frequently, and was this practice
the result of their wretched surroundings, as is suggested by
Hawkes ?   It seems to me that the accounts given of the Eskimo
tend, as a whole, to suggest that violence was rare ; otherwise
how is the universal testimony as to their harmonious mode of
living to be accounted for ?   In any case it is, to my mind, impossible to explain how the feuds of the Eskimo can have developed
into the regular warfare of the Bering Straits group.   They are
sporadic in the first place, and are usually merely the concern of
two families.

The next food-gatherers with a certain degree of organized
violence are the Andamanese, who belong to the Negrito stock
(see p. 12).   Radcliffe-Brown states that murder is extremely
rare among them, so this form of violence can at once be put on
one side as negligible.

A certain amount of fighting takes place in the Andamans.
Radcliffe-Brown speaks of the meetings between local groups
that were organized by the more prominent men.   These meetings
were occasionally the cause of quarrels, which might lead to feuds.[2]
' Quarrels between individuals were often taken up by friends on
each side.   This was particularly the case when the opponents
belonged to different local groups.   Before the days of the settlement of the islands there often arose in this way petty quarrels
between neighbouring local groups.   In some instances there
appear to have been feuds of long standing ; in others there was
a quarrel, a fight or two, and the enemies made peace one with another, until a fresh cause of disagreement should arise.'   In the case
of such differences it would happen that ' after one or two fights
peace would be made '.   He then goes on to give important
information.   ' An example of a long continued feud, which, to
all appearances, has been in existence for several centuries, is

_____

[1] Ratzel.   [2] Radcliffe-Brown ii. 83, 84.

THE PRIMORDIAL OCEAN

that between the Aka-Bea and the Jarawa of the South Andaman.
The Jarawa have the advantage over the Aka-Bea in that their
camps are situated in the dense forest and are difficult to find,
while the camps of thç Aka-Bea are mostly along the sea-coast.
. . . The Aka-Bea and the Jarawa were inveterate enemies.
Whenever two parties of them met by chance or came into the
neighbourhood of one another, the larger party would attack the
other. When the Settlement of Port Blair was established,
friendly relations were set up with the Aka-Bea, and since that
time the hostility of the Jarawa has been directed not only against
the friendly Andamanese (Aka-Bea, etc.) but also against the
inhabitants of the Settlement.' [1]

This quotation touches the fringe of a great problem, that of
organized hostility between communities ; a problem that cannot
be settled within the limits of the Andaman Islands. The problem
of such hostility is important. For its offers the choice of two
opposite explanations of the warlike behaviour of the Andamanese. This behaviour may be divided into two parts. In
the first place small feuds arise between different local groups.
Professor Radcliffe-Brown, it must be noted, is particularly
careful to note that these quarrels arise especially in this way,
and not within the group itself. Therefore there is something
in the relationships between different groups which produces
friction. What a field for speculation ! But let us proceed
cautiously. It must be noted that feuds between communities
are usually of short duration, one or two fights ending them. So
one would expect to find that the Andamanese were often starting
feuds of short duration. But what are we to make of the age-
long feud between the Jarawa and the Aka-Bea ? How is it to
be compared with those which arise at the meetings between
groups ? That is the question which will have to be answered
definitely. Has the small feud gradually crystallized into a
permanent hostility, or has the permanent induced the small
feud ? Here is a beautiful instance of the difficulty, if not of the
impossibility, of discovering, in the compass of one community,
the relationship between cause and effect in behaviour. Are we
to believe that the society of the Andamanese has spontaneously
developed a sort of perpetual hostility between two great divisions,
or has some irritant been introduced into the body politic from
without ?

We are now brought up against the great problem of the culture
of any community, that of determining how much has originated
within the community itself, and how much has come in from

[1] Radcliffe-Brown ii. 84–6.

outside. Allied to that problem is that of the effects of the introduced culture upon the behaviour of the members of that community. In this particular case we are to ask ourselves whether, in the life of the community itself, there has gradually developed a systematic type of violent behaviour, whereby the members of two groups regard one another as enemies without, in most cases, any just cause, or whether this sentiment of hostility has been imported from elsewhere. It is not saying too much to assert that the solution of this problem involves the whole theory of society, and that according as the answer is given one way or the other, so will the answer to a multitude of other questions be given. Much hinges on this apparently simple problem, at first sight capable of being settled on the spot.

One point must be noted about the feuds of the Andamanese. The standing feud between the Aka-Bea and the Jarawa is between coast-dwellers and forest-dwellers. We are told by Portman that, in the parts of the Andaman group treated of by him, tribes are divided into ' coast-dwellers ' and ' forest-dwellers '. In his own words, ' Fights take place between sub-divisions of the same tribe, and between *Aryauto* and *Eremtaga* of the same tribe (i.e. coast-dwellers and forest-dwellers respectively), who do not mix much together. Eremtaga and Aryauto of the same tribe are allowed to intermarry. Many of the tribes have both these divisions.' [1] From this we learn the important fact that the fights in certain Andaman tribes are actually between two divisions of the same tribe, and not necessarily between members of different tribes.

The statements of Portman suggest that fighting is principally between subdivisions of tribes. This apparently is in line with the information of Radcliffe-Brown, who states that the standing feud is between coast-dwellers and forest-dwellers, Aka-Bea and Jarawa. It would be interesting if they formed one group, and if the designation of Aryauto and Eremtaga held in their case. This designation holds apparently throughout the Andamans, but it is not certain whether every tribe is divided in such a manner.[2] It is possible that the Aka-Bea and Jarawa do form such a grouping. ' The Aka-Bea tribe was in an abnormal position as there was no recognized boundary between them and the Jarawa.' [3] This evidence, such as it is, therefore suggests that the fighting of the Andamanese has something to do with the organization into coast-dwellers and forest-dwellers, which is bound up with the tribal organization. But Radcliffe-Brown's evidence suggests the need for caution in accepting Aka-Bea and

[1] Portman i. 364–5.   [2] Radcliffe-Brown ii. 23 seq.   [3] *Id.*, 25.

Jarawa as forming one community. The Jarawa differ markedly in language and culture from the Aka-Bea and other people of Great Andaman, so that, to quote Brown, ' There can be no doubt that the Jarawa are the descendants of emigrants who at one time in the past made their way across from the Little Andaman and thrust themselves in upon the inhabitants of Rutland Island and the South Andaman, maintaining their footing in the new country by force of arms.' The Jarawa, he says in another place, have lived in a state of constant warfare with their neighbours.[1]

It might be thought that the mere act of migration into a new territory would account without further ado for the hostility between the tribes. But the question is not settled so easily as that. In the case of the Eskimo, for instance, there is positive evidence that tribes of Indian stock have lived as their neighbours without any resultant fighting. On the other hand, once there is a tradition of fighting between any peoples, the occasions for violence will soon multiply, as we shall have reason to see later on. The only positive information, therefore, with regard to the Andamans, is that of Portman. The rest is entirely inconclusive, one way or the other. It is necessary to turn to other directions for more specific evidence.

The violent behaviour of the Australian natives is largely bound up with the dual organization and its attendant marriage regulations, as well as with the theory of causation of death held by these peoples (see pp. 37 e.s.).

The Australians resemble the Andamanese in that feuds occur between the dual divisions of tribes, rather than between tribes themselves.[2]

Australian tribes usually practise marriage between the moieties into which they are subdivided. The usual rule is for a man to marry the daughter of his mother's brother, or else his mother's mother's brother's daughter's daughter.[3] Infringements of these marriage regulations bring about quarrels between moieties.

The spontaneous expression of violence seems to be largely absent from Australian behaviour. The fighting is often of a ceremonial nature, combat by ordeal being frequent. There appears to be little trace of pugnacious emotion.

Whence did the Australian aborigines get the dual grouping of their tribes ? They are quite clear about it. In every case this form of society dates from the beginning of the tribe, and was instituted, either by the ancestors of the tribe, or by some being whom they recognize as superior to themselves. One

[1] Radcliffe-Brown ii. 13, 14.   [2] *Ibid.*, i. 144–5 ; Elkin, 62.   [3] *Ibid.*, 147–9.

typical example will show how they speak of their origin, and particularly of their marriage customs, and of the dual organization which is so closely bound up with them. The Kulin speak of Bunjil as their great teacher. ' *Bunjil* taught the Kulin the arts of life, and one legend states that in that time the Kulin married without any regard for kinship. Two medicine-men (Wirrarap) went up to him in the *Tharangalk-bek*, and he said in reply to their request that the Kulin should divide themselves into two parts—*Bunjil* on this side and *Weang* on that side, and *Bunjil* shall marry *Weang* and *Weang* marry *Bunjil*.' Many of the tribes ascribe their beginnings, in the cultural sense, to such a being, who is supposed to have retired to the sky.[1] They do not say that they instituted such rites themselves, nor do they claim any responsibility whatever for the dual grouping of tribes with its attendant hostility.

If it so happens that the Australian violence is associated with institutions they have not originated, then the origin of that violence will probably have to be sought elsewhere. Where is it to be sought ? Australia is ringed with islands in which the dual organization is the basic form of society. It is not present everywhere today, but it can be shown to have been the original form of society in Indonesia, Melanesia, Micronesia, and Polynesia alike. That has already been shown in ' The Children of the Sun '.[2] Some communities have lost it, but it is probable that the original communities all had it. Therefore, in asserting that their social organization and marriage rules were brought to them from elsewhere, the Australians may well be stating the literal truth. For it is known that large movements of peoples, and consequently of culture, have taken place in this surrounding region, and it is hardly possible that these movements failed to affect Australia. It is known that the Polynesians, for instance, came into the Pacific from the West, and most probably from India, having passed through the East Indian Archipelago on their way.[3] If men could wander so far, it would have been easy for them to touch at such places as Australia. Indeed we know that some outside influence must have percolated into Australia. For in North Queensland mummification is practised, and the technique is similar to that of Torres Straits, between Queensland and New Guinea. This technique again is similar to that of Egypt in the Twenty-first Dynasty.[4]

These facts open up entrancing vistas of inquiry, but we cannot follow them now in details. More facts could be added to make

---

[1] Howitt 491, 500.   [2] Chaps. XIX, XX.   [3] Smith, S. Percy, 108.
[4] Elliot Smith i. 21 et seq.

it impossible to think that Australia had remained entirely untouched while such intercourse was going on in the Pacific, particularly as this intercourse must have lasted for many centuries.   If men could colonize New Caledonia, as they certainly did, surely they could, and did, land in Australia ?   They would, in that case, introduce some practices that would reveal their presence.   Since wherever they went they established a dual organization of society (see ' The Children of the Sun ' for details, Chaps. 18–20), it is only to be expected that they would have established it in Australia.[1]

Even if this explanation is not accepted, it is certain that the assumption that the Australian dual organization is indigenous cannot be made until it is proved that no outside influence could have caused it.   Consequently, it follows that the specialized violence of the Australians cannot be claimed as manifesting an inborn tendency to fight until this external influence has definitely been disproved.

In ' The Children of the Sun ', I have already collected several instances, throughout a region extending from India to America, of the existence of standing feuds between the two sides of communities possessing the dual organization.   The following are examples.

The Sema Naga of Assam were probably once organized on the dual system.   Some villages have two divisions with distinct chiefs, and in one case mention is made of ' an ancient and abiding feud ' between them.[2]   The castes of southern India are organized on the dual basis, and between them is a permanent hostility.[3] In the Moluccas the two sides of the dual divisions that are so prominent there are hostile to one another.   In Halmahera, of this area, the Tobelo and Tobaru, evidently forming a dual grouping, are hereditary enemies.   Among the Tobelo the two most important clans are likewise hereditary enemies.[4]   The same is found in Micronesia.   In Yap, for instance, the people are divided into

[1] Rivers, in his ' History of Melanesian Society ' (Vol. II. 559 e.s.), was of the opinion that the dual organization was the result of the fusion of peoples of two different stocks and cultures. That may be partly true. But it is certain, on the evidence gained from a wide survey of the facts, that the idea was carried about. It might well happen that a light-skinned ruling group arriving in Melanesia with a following of commoners would incorporate the black aboriginal population into the scheme, and make them part of their subjects, thus producing the colour difference. But the fact that the two sides of the dual organization had different colours to begin with, usually red and white, makes it more probable that the colour idea arose from this source. It is not possible to explain great dual settlements like Ponape on the basis of culture mixture.

[2] Hutton ii. 121, 125.   [3] Perry vi. 280.   [4] Hueting 220 seq.

two groups hostile to each other, between which groups fighting takes place.[1] In the Pelews the same hostility occurs between dual groups.[2] A clan can divide into two parts, and between them will be hostility.

In New Guinea hostility exists between the two divisions of the Koita. In the words of Professor Seligman : ' It is obvious that a line joining the island Lolorua to Pyramid Hill divided the Koita settlements into eastern and western moieties, which correspond geographically as closely as possible with the distribution of the sections at enmity. Although nothing was said by my informants to show that they recognized such a dual grouping, the enmity between eastern and western sections was so constant, that I have found it convenient to regard the Koita as consisting of eastern and western moieties.' [3] The Mekeo tribe likewise consists of two divisions, Biofa and Vee, between whom there has been ' chronic warfare '. The Torres Straits folk also have hostility between moieties of dual groupings.[4]

Dr. C. E. Fox's work on ' The Threshold of the Pacific ', dealing with the island of San Cristoval in the Solomons, makes it possible to amplify my account. In his first statements on the subject he says, speaking of a district of the island where the dual organization was prominent, Bauro by name, that ' the real division of society in Bauro is into Atawa and Amwea . . . and between these two divisions there was constant fighting '.[5] In his book he goes further. ' There were two kinds of fighting in Arosi, the *heremœ*, a traditional state of war between two villages or two districts, each containing a number of villages ; and the *surumœ* or *uraimœ*, a sudden temporary war between two places. Many villages or districts lived always in a normal state of war with others ; there was a regular fighting ground called *bwaonga*, where they met from time to time after regular and formal notice had been given. . . . In Bauro Atawa and Amwea [dual divisions] have traditions of such a normal state of war, and these two clans had regular places for fighting one another. Though war was the normal state between such places, and its cause often forgotten, the people were not always fighting, as is generally imagined. When they fought it was arranged by some one on each side standing near the *bwaonga* on their respective sides of it, and calling out to one another, arranging the day when they would meet. Or a regular herald was sent, usually the chief's son, to the enemy, and his person was sacred

[1] Müller (Wismar) 169, 242–3, 234.   [2] Kubary 46, 69–70.
[3] Seligman i. 42.   [4] Torres Straits Report V. 172 e.s.
                    [5] Fox i. 122–5, 160.

so that he was never in any danger.'[1]   Therefore the dual grouping
of society was bound up with a regular institution of fighting.
I shall call attention later to the other form of fighting, that named
surumœ, and shall show that it, in its turn, manifests the working
of a definite social institution.

Mr. Handy's recent work on the Marquesas states that in several
islands there were two main territorial divisions, the inhabitants
of which were in a state of chronic hostility.   In the great island
of Hiva Oa, for instance, there were two main divisions, Nuku
and Pepane.   ' All the inhabitants of the Nuku side of Hiva
Oa were the irreconcilable enemies of all the inhabitants of
Pepane.'   All through this island we find various tribes linked
together as hereditary friends, or opposed to other tribes as
hereditary enemies.   On the large island of Nuku Hiva, again,
the two large divisions ' were bitter enemies as were Nuku and
Pepane on Hiva Oa '.   The smaller divisions on either side had
their hereditary feuds also.   In general, ' In connexion with war
the most important matter . . . is the dual division of Hiva Oa
and Nuku Hiva, the eastern and western sections of these
respective islands being in a continual state of enmity with
each other.' [2]

Enough has been said to show that the dual division of society
is accompanied from India to eastern Polynesia by a continued
hostility between moieties.   I do not mean to assert that there
was no other sort of fighting, but simply to point out that a social
institution carried with it a definite obligation to be quarrelsome.
We know that this dual grouping of society was carried about
the Pacific from one island group to another, and presumably
with it went the sentiments of hostility between the moieties.
We have the spectacle of communities thousands of miles apart
fighting for reasons of which they themselves know nothing.
They are simply maintaining an hereditary feud, and carry it on
because it has always been so.   This is the most impressive
instance that I know in which sentiments have been transmitted
through many generations and across great stretches of the
earth's surface.

With the knowledge that the early communities of the islands
ringing Australia had a similar social grouping of moieties, between
which there were constant hostilities, we can approach the fighting
of that continent in a new light.   The fact brought to light by
Radcliffe-Brown, that fighting in West Australia takes place
between moieties of tribes, and not between tribes as a whole, is
seen in its real perspective.   This quarrelling is simply what

[1] Fox ii. 305.   [2] Handy 27, 31, 123.

would be expected of a people with the dual grouping.   Everywhere else fighting and hostility are the rule, so why not here ?
There is thus no reason for believing that the fighting of the
Australian natives is the result of the working of an inborn
tendency to violence.   On the contrary, all the facts associated
with it suggest strongly that it is directly the outcome of a social
institution, the dual organization, so that in order to understand
why Australian natives fight, or the natives of so many other
places, for that matter, the origin of the hostility in the dual
organization must first be ascertained.   We are therefore dealing
with the working of a complicated social process, and not with
the simple primitive behaviour of food-gatherers.   Only when
this process is better understood can we hope to understand the
ultimate reason why the Australian natives fight.

The case of the Andamanese is similar.   They lie right in the
track of migration from India into the Pacific.   The division
of the tribes into coastal and forest groups suggests that a like
foreign influence has caused them to indulge in continual feuds.

To turn to another form of violent behaviour.   In the account
of the warfare of the natives of the Marquesas Mr. Handy states
that ' there were two basic causes of all wars.   The first was
the necessity of securing human sacrifices at certain times for
offerings to the tribal god, such sacrifices being always obtained
from an enemy tribe.   The second cause was revenge, the occasion
being frequently the killing or stealing of men, women, or children
for sacrifices on the part of another tribe, or possibly the necessity
or demand for revenge growing out of an insult to the tribe.
If one tribe that went to visit another was received in an unfriendly
and inhospitable spirit, the visiting tribe, thus insulted by not
being offered the usual courtesies, would return home and prepare
for war.   War has even been made by one chief on another to
avenge personal slights or insults.' [1]

We can leave the topic of revenge on one side for the time being,
and consider the first cause, namely, the procuring of victims for
human sacrifice.   In this case again we find that warfare is bound
up with a definite social institution.

Were it not for the necessity for human victims, it is safe to
say that the Marquesans would not indulge in so much fighting,
even though they have the dual divisions with their concomitant
hostility.

Human sacrifice was formerly widespread in the Pacific, and,
if the case of the Marquesans can be taken as typical, must have
been responsible for much of the fighting that took place there.

[1] Handy, op. cit., 123.

The warfare of the peoples of Indonesia has some interesting characteristics. We may begin with the description of the warlike habits of the Kayan of Borneo given by Hose and McDougall. Kayan warfare centres round head-hunting, and does not display much pugnacity. 'The Kayans are perhaps less aggressive than any other of the interior peoples with the exception of the Punans.'[1] . . . 'It may be said generally that Kayans seldom or never wage war on Kayans, and seldom attack others merely to secure heads or in sheer vainglory, as the Ibans [Sea-Dyaks] not infrequently do. Nor do they attack others merely in order to sustain their prestige, as is sometimes done by the Kenyahs, who in this respect carry to an extreme the principle that attack is the most effective form of defence.

'War is generally undertaken by the Kayans very deliberately, after much preparation and in well-organized parties, ranging in numbers from fifty to a thousand or more warriors, made up in many cases from several neighbouring villages, and under the supreme command of one chief of acknowledged eminence.' . . . 'The avenging of injuries and the necessity of possessing heads for use in the funeral rites are for them the principal grounds of warfare : and these are generally combined, the avenging of injuries being generally postponed, sometimes for many years, until the need for new heads arises.'[2]

Head-hunting is the main form of warfare among the Kayan. It is a deliberate matter, and not an affair of anger, though revenge, long delayed, may play its part. Other tribes are more given to violent forms of behaviour, but their case may be deferred for a while.

Head-hunting is the means of getting human victims for various purposes. It is allied to the practice of getting prisoners of war and of killing them on certain occasions. Many of the peoples of Indonesia practise, or formerly practised, this form of warfare.[3]

This hunting of heads is part of a widespread social system, which is deeply rooted in the life of the peoples who practise it. The motive for the practice, the attendant circumstances, and the disposal of the skull, are the same from one end of this great region to the other. In certain instances people 'head-hunt' regularly at definite times of the year. The Bontoc of Luzon in the Philippines are head-hunters. One of their words for war means 'Take-heads'. Heads taken on raids are brought back and placed in the council house of the particular division of the village to which the slayer belongs.[4] The Ilongots and the

[1] Hose and McDougall I. 158.   [2] *Ibid.*, 159.   [3] Pleyte.
[4] Jenks 172, 180.

Kalingas of the same island take heads in order that their rice crops may succeed.[1]

The main interest of this evidence lies in the fact that it reveals warfare among certain peoples as the outcome of certain social institutions, and not as the manifestation of a pugnacious instinct. We find that the necessity of victims for agriculture, for funerals of chiefs, for the building of houses, for the launching of canoes, or for marriage ceremonies, causes men to set out, sometimes at definite seasons of the year, to get heads. There is good reason to believe that this form of warlike activity, together with the fighting caused by the hostility of the dual groupings, constituted the first forms of warfare in Indonesia and Oceania in general. That is to say, the warfare of these two great regions seems to be definitely bound up with social institutions. Consequently its real meaning can only be understood in terms of these institutions.

Fighting between two sides of the dual organization and fighting for human sacrifice, whether in the form of victims for sacrifice, or of heads taken during raids, does not account for the whole of warlike behaviour. It must be remembered that this practice has a history, and therefore that it is likely that the later developments of the practice may have been very different from its beginnings. In the Pacific it is probable that warfare was formerly largely centred round the dual grouping and human sacrifice : indeed, in the Marquesas the two coincided, victims for sacrifice being got from the hereditary enemies. But once the practice of fighting has crept in, it is likely that other institutions may be involved, so that the animosities engendered will accentuate the fighting, and thus set up a vicious system of retaliation between communities.

There are other definite causes of fighting between communities than those already mentioned. It will be remembered that Australian tribes often ascribe death to the evil magic of some member of another community, and send an expedition to kill the offender. In other places it is likewise believed that sorcery can kill a man, so that vengeance is called for. This is the case in San Cristoval.[2] The Australian custom therefore does not stand alone. It is bound up with a definite theory of magic, and consequently must be explained in terms of it.

In considering the warfare of savage peoples, it must be realized that, so far as I know, it is usually organized and accompanied by definite ceremonial. There is usually a complete equipment for the warrior ; he is trained from his youth up ; he is provided

---

[1] Worcester 816, 824.   [2] Fox ii. 306.

with a proper dress and ornaments ; and the whole of his activities are regulated by definite customs. When military organization is considered, it is found that it is closely bound up with the institution of the chieftainship. Usually there is a definite chief who leads the warriors, and he often is hereditary. Indeed it is impossible to conceive of a warlike organization in any part of the world apart from the institution of the chieftainship. Only, as a rule, in places where there is a definite hereditary chieftainship, or in communities directly derived from others with hereditary chiefs, can the warlike machine and definite warlike behaviour be witnessed. As Basuto and Pondo men have said to me, ' We only go to war when the chief orders us.'

The warlike behaviour of a tribe is often of a complicated nature. The different institutions involved act and react on one another, and often produce new social values. We may take for an example the Jibaro Indians, who live in the forests around the great rivers Pastaza, Morona, Upano-Santiago and their affluents, on the borders of Ecuador and Peru.[1] These people are divided into a number of tribes ' generally hostile to each other '.

' The Jibaros no doubt at present are the most warlike of all the Indian tribes in South America. The wars, the blood-feuds within the tribes, and the wars of extermination between the different tribes are continuous, being nourished by their superstitious belief in witchcraft. These wars are the greatest curse of the Jibaros and are felt to be so even by themselves, at least so far as the feuds within the tribes are concerned. On the other hand, the wars are to such a degree one with their whole life and essence that only powerful pressure from outside or a radical change of their whole character and moral views could make them abstain from them. This one may judge even from the fact that from a victory over his enemies the Jibaro warrior not only expects honour and fame in the ordinary sense of the word, but also certain material benefits. The head trophy which he takes from his slain enemy is not merely a token of victory, but becomes a fetish charged with supernatural power, and the great victory feast itself with its many mysterious ceremonies, in fact, forms a part of the practical religion or cult of the Jibaros.' That is to say, the warfare of the Jibaros is a highly organized system.

The boys are educated to fight. ' The education of the boys among the Jibaros first of all aims at making them brave and skilful warriors. When a Jibaro has enemies on whom he wants to take revenge for offences and outrages, perhaps committed

[1] Karsten i.

long ago, but despairs of being able to do it himself, he systematically tries to awaken and maintain hatred against them in his
young sons by discourses directed to them every day. . . . This
discourse is, at times, repeated every morning when the house
father gets up, and with about the same words ; and, of course,
cannot fail to make an impression upon the minds of the young
ones.' When a boy reaches the age of puberty he is received
among the grown men, and undergoes an initiation ceremony.
In it he is instructed. ' They speak to the young Jibaro and advise
and teach him in all kinds of manly businesses, but first of all
in warlike deeds.' [1]

' Between the different tribes in the regions inhabited by the
Jibaros there exists almost perpetual enmity, and destructive
wars are often carried out, especially between neighbouring tribes.
. . . It is not easy to state what originally has been the cause
of this enmity. Generally speaking, one may say that it has
originated in the jealousy and rivalry existing between the different
tribes, a rivalry personalized in the proud and ambitious chiefs
who stand at the head of the different tribes. One chief tries
to surpass another in warlike deeds and cannot endure seeing
his rival increase in wealth, power, and influence. . . . But in
addition to this, even with regard to the hostility reigning between
the different tribes, superstition—the belief in witchcraft—plays
its fatal part, this being nearly always the principal cause of the
wars. The rival chiefs combat each other not merely by natural
means, but also with the supernatural weapon which is called
tunchi (in Quichua *chunta*), for a great Jibaro chief is as skilled
in witchcraft as a professional sorcerer. . . . If, in a tribe and
especially within the family of the chief, in a short time various
cases of disease, death or accidents of other kinds occur, these
are generally set down to the evil machinations of the sorcerers
in a hostile neighbouring tribe. Thus, for instance, the Jibaro
chief Nayapi on the Pastaza, and the old Canelos chief Palati on
the Bobonanza, have for many years been enemies and have sent
menacing messages to each other. In the family of Nayapi
within a comparatively short time several deaths took place—
two of his sons, one daughter, and his son-in-law dying from
mysterious diseases or through accidents. Nayapi said that his
enemy Palati was the cause of all these deaths by systematically
letting off his witchery arrows against Nayapi and his family.
Palati, again, by no means denied that this was so, but, on the
contrary, confirmed it, menacingly announcing that he would,
by and by, exterminate Nayapi's whole family. The latter was

[1] Karsten i. 1–2, 3.

seized with wrath and desire for revenge, and certainly would have wreaked a terrible vengeance upon his enemy if regard for the Catholic monks, under whose protection Palati stood, had not made him abstain from carrying it out.'

Heads are only taken in the case of fights between different tribes : the Jibaro never take the head of a fellow tribesman. ' The making of a *tsantsa* of an enemy's head, and especially the feast which follows the acquiring of such a trophy, implies the grossest insult, not only to the murdered person himself and his family, but to his whole tribe.' [1]

The complete analysis of Jibaro warlike behaviour would be a complicated enterprise. It involves, for example, tribal organization, chieftainship, head-hunting, witchcraft and other social institutions. Warfare is part of the education of the young man. The element of self-esteem is involved, the warriors striving to outshine one another in bravery and skill. Animosities are aroused, particularly among chiefs, as the result of raids of one tribe on another. Karsten himself ascribes much of the inter-tribal warfare to the jealousy and rivalry of chiefs. It is far more likely, however, that head-hunting and the belief in witchcraft were the more likely aggravating causes, as, indeed, Karsten himself suggests. The factor of glory, the desire to shine as a warrior, can easily have been just the reaction to the organized warfare of the tribe. Indeed, it is evident that once warfare has become habitual in a community, it will soon react upon the social values in that community. For instance, ' The motives which led the Cheyennes to go to war were . . . a desire for glory, a wish to add to their possessions, or eagerness for revenge, but the chief motive was love of fighting, which was instilled into them from early youth. From their earliest days boys were taught to long for the approbation of their elders, and this approbation was most readily to be earned by success in war. The applause of their public was the highest reward they knew.' [2]

It must not be thought that the desire for glory and for the approbation of elders was the cause of Cheyenne warfare. Grinnell is very emphatic on this point. For he states clearly that the beginnings were quite otherwise. ' The Cheyennes have a tradition of a golden age when war was unknown and universal peace prevailed. All strangers met in friendship and parted on good terms. Such a far-off time, when hostile encounters were unknown, is told of by many of the tribes of the northern plains.

' No doubt there were fightings and wars long before the coming of the white man, but these were probably the result of more or

[1] Karsten i. 14–15.   [2] Grinnell ii. II. 7.

less temporary quarrels, and were not bloody. The only incentive likely to have caused such fightings was the desire for revenge, and this desire, unless promptly gratified, was apt soon to be forgotten. The introduction of the horse, however, furnished to all the plains tribes a new and strong motive for war, for by war men might acquire something of very great value.' [1] In the beginning the warfare was mostly centred round horse-stealing, and the killing of men was not common.[2] Therefore, when we read that, in later times, men went to fight for the sake of the social status it gave them, we are clearly dealing with another instance of the effect of a social institution upon the behaviour of a community. The calling of the fighter requires special qualities of virility and courage, and the successful warrior reveals them all. Hence, when a community is warlike, courageous men are the most highly honoured. But the instance of the Cheyenne shows clearly that this high estimation of the warrior, with the desire to shine in fighting, is but a secondary manifestation of the military system itself, and may, and probably does, have nothing whatever to do with its inception. Warfare on a serious scale probably began as the result of the aggression of the Assiniboine, who had got guns from the French and were making good use of them. The Assiniboine, in their turn, may have learned much of fighting from the French and English, and have passed it on to the Cheyenne.[3]

The case of San Cristoval of the Solomon Islands is interesting in this connexion. We have already seen from Dr. Fox's work that in the district of Bauro there was constant fighting between the two divisions of the dual organization. He states further that a similar condition of hostility existed in the district of Arosi. He says in one place ' the causes of war were numerous, but the most common was a woman. Other causes were the death of some man who had been killed, it was believed, by a spell from some one in another village ; or from unfair distribution of property among relatives after a man's death ; or from land quarrels, a man of another place making a garden on land which did not belong to him ; or from a woman stepping over a tree leaning over, so that subsequently a man walking under the tree became degraded ; or from breaking a chief's taboo (beri tongo) ; or from the desire of a chief to possess some famous weapon or ornament.' [4]

This suggests that a traditional hostility, of unknown origin, may manifest itself in many ways. The two sides of the dual organization have hostile sentiments towards one another ready

[1] Grinnell ii. II. 1. [2] *Ibid.*, 2. [3] *Ibid.*, 3-6. See also Friederici 256-7.
[4] Fox ii. 306.

9

to burst out into violence. That is to say, a fundamental social institution, such as the dual organization, may have profound effects on behaviour.

A good example of the effects of warlike institutions on behaviour is afforded by the peoples of Borneo. The inland tribes of this island may be divided into four groups. First there are the Punan, peaceful food-gatherers of the interior.

In the same part of the island live the Kayan, already mentioned (p. 112), the most highly civilized of the native tribes. Between them and the coast, in Sarawak, come the Kenyah and Klemantan tribes, similar in culture to the Kayan, but on a lower level. Finally on the coast come the Iban, or Sea-Dyaks. Kayan warfare, as has already been observed, is synonymous with head-hunting. It is a highly regularized mode of behaviour.

The Kenyah come next to the Kayan in culture, and have probably acquired their culture from them. ' Kenyah warfare is very similar to Kayan, save in so far as their more impetuous temper renders their tactics more dashing. While the Kayans endeavour to make as many captives as possible, the Kenyahs attach little value to them. While Kayans never attack communities of their own tribe, such " civil war " is not unknown among the Kenyahs, whose tribal cohesion is less intimate in many respects.' [1]

This grading of behaviour can be followed still more clearly in the case of the Iban, or Sea-Dyak. ' The Ibans conduct their warfare less systematically, and with far less discipline than the Kayans and Kenyahs. . . . They seek above all things to take heads, to which they attach an extravagant value, unlike the Kayans and Kenyahs, who seek heads primarily for the service of their funeral rites ; and they not infrequently attack a house and kill a large number of its inmates in a perfectly wanton manner, and for no other motive than the desire to obtain heads. This passion for heads leads them sometimes into acts of gross treachery and brutality. The Ibans being great wanderers, small parties of them, engaged perhaps in working jungle produce, will settle for some weeks in a household of Klementans, and, after being received hospitably, and sometimes even after contracting marriages with members of the household, will seize an opportunity, when most of the men are away from home, to take the heads of all the men, women and children who remain, and to flee with them to their own distant homes.' . . . ' The Iban women urge on the men to the taking of heads ; they make much of those who bring them home, and sometimes a girl will

[1] Hose and McDougall I. 184.

taunt her suitor by saying that he has not been brave enough
to take a head ; and in some cases of murder by Sea-Dyaks, the
murderer has no doubt been egged on in this way.' [1]

The Klemantans constitute an intermediate group. They are
on the whole far less warlike than the Kayan, Kenyah and Iban.
They seek heads for the termination of a period of mourning.
' Their offensive warfare is usually on a small scale, and is undertaken primarily for revenge.' [2]

The differences between the tribes of Borneo are illuminating.
The Kayan practice is regularized, and there is little sign of
sporadic violence. The Kayan do not fight among themselves,
but confine their raids to peoples of other tribes. Kayan head-
hunting is associated with funerals of chiefs, and thus is bound
up with a definite social institution. What is more, the behaviour
of the Kayan is more definitely regularized than that, say, of
the Iban ; they have more discipline, so to speak. The contrast
offered by the Iban is remarkable. The taking of heads is a
passion ; they get heads in order to satisfy their self-esteem, to
gain the applause of their fellow-tribesmen. How is this difference
in behaviour to be explained ?

The explanation is forthcoming. ' From what we have said
above it is clear that the Ibans are the only tribe to which one
can apply the epithet head-hunters with the usual connotation
of the word, namely, that head-hunting is pursued as a form of
sport. But although the Ibans are the most inveterate head-
hunters, it is probable that they adopted the practice some few
generations ago only (perhaps a century and a half or even less)
in imitation of Kayans and other tribes among whom it had
been established for a longer period. The rapid growth of the
practice among the Ibans was no doubt largely due to the influence of the Malays, who had been taught by the Arabs and others
the arts of piracy, and with whom the Ibans were associated in
the piratical enterprises that gave the waters around Borneo
a sinister notoriety during the eighteenth and first half of the
nineteenth centuries. Until the middle of the nineteenth century,
the settlements of the Ibans were practically confined to the rivers
of the southern part of Sarawak ; and there the Malays of Bruni
and other coast settlements enlisted them as crews for their pirate
ships. In these piratical expeditions the Malays assigned the
heads of their victims as the booty of their Iban allies, while they
kept for themselves the forms of property of greater cash value.
The Malays were thus interested in encouraging in the Ibans the
passion for head-hunting which, since the suppression of piracy,

[1] *Id.*, 186-7.   [2] *Id.*, 187.

has found vent in the irregular warfare and treacherous acts described above. It was through their association with the Malays in these piratical expeditions that the Ibans became known to Europeans as the Sea-Dayaks.' [1]

The story of Iban head-hunting opens up an interesting vista. It reveals to us the working of processes over vast stretches of the earth's surface. It is suggestive to think that the Arabs could ultimately be the cause of the intensification of head-hunting in Borneo, yet such is the case. The Arabs influenced the Malays, who, in their turn, influenced the Iban.

Their deadly work was not yet finished ; for the Malays stirred up strife in other parts of the Archipelago. For many years the Andamanese did their best to exterminate any strangers who landed on their shores. Many a shipwrecked crew has been done to death by these pygmy folk. We have seen that they are not usually given to ferocious behaviour, but their ferocity towards strangers can well be explained. It was the outcome of a long series of piratical raids by the Malays.[2] The Andamanese were simply seeking revenge, and the innocent suffered for the guilty. The Malays, so Professor A. P. Elkin informs me, also raided certain parts of the northern coast of Australia. The Australian natives usually received strangers peacefully, but those who have been subjected to the attentions of the Malay pirates form an exception. Like the Andamanese, they have attacked strangers.

This story can be repeated in every part of the world. In Asia, Africa, and America it can be shown, in like manner, that the intensified warfare of peoples of low culture has been the result of contact with civilized people. This, indeed, is part of the general proposition that, throughout the ages, peoples of lower culture have learned their violent habits from contact with peoples of higher culture,[3] so that the incessant fighting of certain savage communities is the outcome of a long historical process. In this case the intensified fighting habits of the Iban are undoubtedly the outcome of their contact with the Malays, which historical experience has had great effect upon them, and has induced them to allot great prestige to the getting of heads. Instead of the getting of heads now being a necessity solely for funerals of chiefs, it has become a matter of personal pride and prowess. The social value of the practice has therefore altered. The reason for this is undoubtedly to be found in the association

---

[1] Hose and McDougall I. 187–8.   [2] Portman i. 369.

[3] See Perry viii. Chap. 7, for a discussion of this process. See also Sir E. im Thurm.

with the Malays of Bruni and elsewhere.   It has become a matter of pride to be associated with these great men, and thus the desire to be prominent has come into play to cause men to follow this honourable pursuit.

The Kenyah and other tribes differ from the Kayan in that they often attack other people in order to satisfy their self-esteem. It is practically certain that these other peoples derived their warfare from one source, presumably, in the case of Borneo, the Kayan.   For not only do they all seek heads, but they have similar weapons and war-dress.[1]   There is thus no reason to believe that they have come to fight independently of one another.   Agreeing that the practice came in with the Kayan, as Messrs. Hose and McDougall believe, it follows that the Kenyah and other tribes have got their weapons, head-hunting, and thus their fighting habits from that source.   The Kayan are the principal tribe and the most powerful tribe, and thus the Kenyah regard them as superiors.   May it not, therefore, be that when the Kenyah fight to maintain their prestige, they are suffering from what the psychologists would term an ' inferiority complex ' that causes them to satisfy their self-esteem.   Thus it is seen that, as the practice of fighting and the warlike organization is handed on from one community to another, it sometimes breaks up and becomes diffuse, so that fighting now takes place, not for definite purposes as among the Kayan, but simply to satisfy a frame of mind.

This conclusion may be applied to the cases of the Marquesas and to the people of San Cristoval studied by Dr. Fox.   The Kayan practise head-hunting, but know nothing of the dual organization. That is to say, while they were constantly making raids for heads on other tribes, they were free from the constant irritation of the hostility of the dual grouping ; thus there was but little internecine struggle among them.

On the other hand, the people of San Cristoval had their villages and districts divided into two moieties.   There was a definite system of fighting between hostile districts, with boundaries where the fighting took place.   The system was highly organized and part of the traditional life of the people, sanctioned by the traditions of the foundations of the culture by divine or semi-divine beings.   I suggest that the increased violence, as compared with that of the Kayan, is to be ascribed to the presence of this constant irritant.   There may indeed be other factors in the process, but that alone would account for a considerable difference in social behaviour.

If we compare the behaviour of the Kayan of Borneo with

[1] Hose and McDougall I. 159.

that of the Marquesans, we find that both groups make raids for
sacrificial victims.   In addition, however, the Marquesans have
a more diffused sort of fighting.   This may be accounted for by
the persistence of the dual organization with its hereditary sentiments of hatred between its two parts.

The evidence adduced in this chapter shows that a large amount
of the violent behaviour of any savage society is canalized by the
action of certain social institutions.   If we abstract head-hunting,
human sacrifice, witchcraft, dual organization and chieftainship,
and military organization in general, what would be left of violent
behaviour ?   Very little, it would seem.   That is to say, if we
strip off social institutions, we at the same time strip off social
behaviour.   We arrive at the food-gatherers with their lack of
social institutions and their peaceful behaviour.   Apart from the
food-gatherers, without violent behaviour and without military
organization, there are certain peaceful food-producing peoples.
The Todas of the Nilgiri Hills in southern India may be mentioned.
According to Rivers : ' At the present time it cannot be said that
the Todas use any weapons, but they retain in their ceremonies
weapons which were, no doubt, formerly in use.   These are the
club and the bow and arrow.' . . .   ' The use of the bow and
arrow and the club in ceremonial furnishes us with another
example of material objects which have wholly disappeared from
the active life of the Todas, and here again it is easy to see why
the disappearance has taken place, for on the Nilgiris the Todas
have no enemies, either human or feral.' [1]

The Todas have no organization for warfare, and they do not
manifest any warlike behaviour.   It is not strictly accurate to
state that the Todas have no enemies, so that they have ceased
to fight.   They certainly are surrounded by other peoples, but
they do not fight them.

Cases such as this constitute negative evidence.   They suggest
that peoples without warlike institutions are not warlike.   In
other words, these cases suggest that warlike behaviour is the
result of social institutions, causing men to commit violent deeds
for certain definite purposes.   In no way can the head-hunting
of the Kayan of Borneo be explained as resulting from the workings
of innate violence.

The evidence suggests that the earliest form of violence was
sporadic in nature.   The food-gatherers only manifest it rarely.
They have no military organization, no training of the young in
military ideals.

The evidence suggests, further, that the earliest food-producing

---

[1] Rivers i. 586, 715–16.

communities had their violent forms of behaviour strictly canalized. This violence is centred round the ruling groups, human sacrifice and associated institutions. The head-hunting expeditions of various peoples, such, for instance, as the Kayan, would produce in their victims feelings of revenge, and thus retaliations would take place. So the constant irritant of human sacrifice can easily produce in time a situation of intense hostility. The cases of the Iban and the Andamanese show clearly that animosity can exist as the result of harsh treatment on the part of more highly civilized peoples, e.g. the Malays, who in their turn learned their violence from the Arabs, and so on backwards into the higher civilizations of antiquity. The contact between civilized peoples and savages shows that the aggression has almost invariably been on the part of civilized men. The evidence suggests that the diffused violence found among so many peoples is the result of the existence of military institutions among them.

CHAPTER XI

THE THEORY OF THE SOCIAL INSTITUTION

THE argument has now reached a stage when it is necessary to try to understand the meaning of the process at work in the development of civilization from the earliest times to the present day. The discussion of man's behaviour in society, so far as it has gone, shows that, so far as can be told, the fundamental innate need of food, and the group of sentiments and emotions centred round the family, have persisted throughout the whole development of society, and have formed much of the bases upon which society itself has been built. Moreover, it can be shown that each social institution in turn, be it religion, the class-system, warfare, dress or any other form of organized activity, has been profoundly influenced by the fundamental tendencies.[1]

Not only have the fundamental tendencies continued to mould human society, but a secondary process has been set up. Each social institution has been modified by others. Religion, compounded of divers elements, now serves many purposes other than those which it first fulfilled. Thus, by reason of this secondary elaboration of culture, great complexities have been set up, which it will take long to unravel. Nevertheless it seems possible to resolve any social institution or group of institutions ultimately into simple elements, resting directly upon the fundamental innate behaviour of mankind.

A comparative study of any social institution shows that its distribution is usually limited, and often discontinuous. It can be shown, for example, that peoples living in close proximity may have markedly different institutions. For instance, the Californian Indians lack much that is found among the Pueblo Indians of New Mexico and Arizona. The Pueblo Indians make pottery, the Californian Indians do not; the Pueblo Indians live in houses, the Californian Indians do not; the Pueblo Indians have an elaborate system of agriculture, the Californian Indians

---

[1] It need hardly be recalled that ' food ' and ' family ' do not comprise the whole of the innate tendencies. The ' danger ' instinct, in its varying manifestations, and ' self-esteem ' are also constantly at work. Others could be mentioned.

have none. A similar gap exists between the Kayan of Borneo and their food-gathering neighbours the Punan. The Kayan live in large wooden houses; they work iron; they practise agriculture; and in many other ways possess institutions and knowledge that the Punan lack.

These examples show that social institutions are specific in nature. They differ from modes of behaviour based directly on the innate tendencies, which are exhibited by every normal human being. Therefore, the process of elaboration of social institutions must itself be specific. It must differ somewhat in nature from the more general biological processes.

The study of the growth and development of social institutions has long occupied the attention of students. Attempts have been made from various directions to account for the rise and fall of civilizations. It will be interesting to glance at some of these theories.

The climatic factor has long been a favourite explanation for the rise and falls of civilizations. In this way Huntington reckoned to account for the various phases of the Mayan civilization in America. His work ' The Pulse of Asia ', also based on the hypothesis of climatic cycles, was at one time widely accepted.[1] It is so easy to account for the various incursions of nomadic tribes or the more advanced civilizations as the outcome of a sort of climatic pulsation. Alternate periods of heavy rainfall and drought seem to account for the facts. The wet period would cause a large increase in population, and the drought would bring about starvation, and cause a migration of hungry hordes into more fortunate lands.

It only needs but a modicum of historical knowledge to realize that these so-called ' tribal ' migrations were really the warlike incursions of military geniuses. The desire for power and not food was the motive that led Genghis Khan, Tamerlaine, Attila and others to found great empires.[2] This sort of theorization that makes man the creature of climatic cycles, of shifting cyclonic belts, is now out of favour, and need not detain us.

Other schools of thinkers ascribe much weight to the racial factor. It is assumed that each racial type is capable of a certain form of culture. Races are divided into superior and inferior. Some thinkers argue that a dying culture is due to a kind of racial decay; the corollary being that cultural advance can only take place as the result of racial mixture.

[1] Huntington i. and ii.
[2] See Perry viii. Chap. VII, for a discussion of this topic. See also E. H. Parker.

These two modes of explanation express cultural development and decay in terms of something that is not directly human and cultural, something that cannot be put in terms of the relations between men.   Both explanations assume that social institutions have been elaborated by men in all parts of the world in isolation from one another.   It is rather suggestive of ' Hamlet ' without the Prince of Denmark.   A specific process is held to be the outcome of general tendencies.   No inquiry is made into the essential nature of civilization.   It is obvious that climate and race have played their part in human history, but what we have to do in the present circumstances is to account for certain specific social phenomena.   We want to know why the Kayan of Borneo make iron swords, while their immediate neighbours, of the same racial type, and living under identical climatic conditions, do not work iron.   We want to know why the Pueblo Indians make pottery, while the Californian Indians on the other side of the River Colorado do not, although both groups are identical in race, and are living in similar climatic circumstances.   Thousands of other instances could be adduced to show that the facts of human culture cannot be deduced from *a priori* generalizations.   Cultural facts are specific, and need specific explanations.

Another school of thought looks at human culture from a severely biological standpoint.   Human culture certainly is the outcome of biological processes ; but it is rash to assume that close parallels can be drawn between a civilization and a living organism.   It is often argued that civilizations come into being, mature, and finally decay.   This reasoning is based upon a hypothesis of the organic nature of human culture.

This method of interpretation, like those based on race and climate, seeks to explain the facts of human culture as the working of a process above and beyond culture itself.

It would be possible to spend much time examining and ex-pounding these views.   At the same time there is always a line of escape.   We may ignore environmental, racial, and other extra-social factors for the moment, and think of the life of society itself.   It will be remembered that it was possible to adopt this device in the case of the food-gatherers ; for their social life, the relationship between members of each community, as well as between different communities, appears to be rooted in society itself, and not dependent upon external factors.

It needs but little reflection to realize that what we term ' civilization ' is simply a grouping of social institutions of varied sorts.   These institutions have come into being for the most varied of reasons, and therefore it is difficult to form any concept of them as a whole at this stage of the analysis. The word simply covers a vast process, the nature of which it is necessary here to interpret, so far as that is possible. Therefore it is advisable to confine attention in the first place to specific institutions, to subject them to examination, and thus to reach, from the study of particular instances, some notion as to the meaning of the general process by which they came into being.

I propose to begin with the study of the practice of human sacrifice.[1] There are several reasons for this choice. In the first place it has definite modes of occurrence among mankind; its limits in time and space can readily be determined; its objects are usually specifically defined; and, what is still more important, it can be shown to have been repugnant to the innate sentiments of mankind throughout the ages.

Human sacrifice has already been mentioned in the chapter on Violence. The food-gatherers rarely or never practise it. Therefore it is a form of behaviour that is determined by other processes than the fundamental innate tendencies of mankind. It must consequently come into the category of institutional forms of behaviour, forms that originally were unknown, but that have come into being as the result of the working of the social process.

One of the most remarkable characteristics of human sacrifice is its rejection by peoples of low culture, as well as by highly civilized peoples. The best known instance of such a change is that of Abraham and Isaac, where a ram was substituted for the human victim. In the story of the foundation of Samoa, it is said that Ui, the ancestress of the first royal house, came from across the sea. Her former countrymen offered human sacrifices to the sun-god. She had persuaded the sun-god to give up the practice, and had then left the country, presumably in consequence.[2] In like manner certain members of the ruling group of the Natchez of Louisiana, who called themselves Children of the Sun, left the country because they disapproved of the practice.[3]

Other peoples had the same repugnance to the practice. Here is an extract from the Nihongi of Japan.[4] In the year 2 B.C. the following incident is said to have occurred:

' 10th month, 5th day. Yamato-hiko, the Mikado's younger brother by the mother's side, died.

' 11th month, 2nd day. Yamato-hiko was buried at Tsuki-

---

[1] I include cannibalism in this term.   [2] Pratt 121–2.
[3] Du Pratz 314.
[4] The Nihongi is a legendary text compiled about A.D. 720.

zaka in Musa.   Thereupon his personal attendants were assembled, and were all buried alive upright in the precinct of the tomb.   For several days they died not, but wept and wailed day and night. At last they died and rotted.   Dogs and crows gathered and ate them.

'The Emperor, hearing the sound of their weeping and wailing, was grieved at heart, and commanded his high officers, saying: "It is a very painful thing to force those whom one has loved in life to follow him in death.   Though it be an ancient custom, why follow it if it is bad?   From this time forward, take counsel so as to put a stop to the following of the dead."

'A.D. 3.   7th month, 6th day.   The Empress Hibasu-hime no Mikoto died.   Some time before the burial the Emperor commanded his Ministers, saying : "We have already recognized that the practice of following the dead is not good.   What should now be done in performing this burial ? "   Thereupon Nomi no Sukune came forward and said : "It is not good to bury living men upright at the tumulus of a prince.   How can such a practice be handed down to posterity ?   I beg leave to propose an expedient which I will submit to Your Majesty."   So he sent messengers to summon up from the Land of Idzumo a hundred men of the clay-workers' Be.   He himself directed the men of the clay-workers' Be to take clay and form therewith shapes of men, horses, and various objects, which he presented to the Emperor, saying : "Henceforward let it be the law for future ages to substitute things of clay for living men, and to set them up at tumuli." Then the Emperor was greatly rejoiced, and commanded Nomi no Sukune, saying : "Thy expedient hath greatly pleased Our heart."   So the things of clay were first set up at the tomb of Hibasu-hime no Mikoto.   And a name was given to these clay objects.   They were called haniwa, or clay rings.' [1]

It seems certain that human sacrifice was practised in the earliest civilizations of both North and South America.   Readers of Prescott's ' Conquest of Mexico ' will remember his account of the extent to which human sacrifice was practised.   Moreover, the Mexicans added cannibalism to human sacrifice.   When the victim had had his heart cut out and offered to the sun-god, his body was taken home and eaten by his captor as part of a banquet.   Cannibalism never found any firm footing in the United States, except round the shores of the Gulf of Mexico, and to a certain extent among the coastal tribes of British Columbia.[2]   It cannot therefore be asserted that these cruel

[1] Aston 56–7.
[2] 'Handbook of American Indians.'   Art. ' Cannibalism '.

habits arose in a lower stage of development of culture, and survived to a higher. Such an argument would ignore the patent facts of degradation of culture, and turn the process backwards. For it must be remembered that the earliest known civilization in America, both North and South, was the most highly developed in the arts and crafts.[1]

If we follow the track of civilization westwards from America, we find that human sacrifice characterized the earliest known settlements in the Pacific, in Indonesia, and probably also in India. It was a common characteristic of that civilization which I have termed the Archaic Civilization, and is found, speaking generally, wherever that civilization can be detected in its more or less pure form. In many parts of the region just indicated it dies out, or is replaced by head-hunting or the sacrifice of animals.[2]

Why had these communities the custom of offering human sacrifices ? The answer is simple. It is because they believed that they would benefit by it in some way or other. In Dravidian India, as elsewhere, human sacrifice for agriculture was supposed to be necessary in order that the crops might be good. If victims were not offered the crops would fail. Offerings had to be made to certain snake-gods in order that they might give good harvests.

This brings us to a crucial point in the argument. People with a highly developed civilization are incited, by virtue of certain theories, to a loathsome form of activity. The mainspring of the practice of human sacrifice is the possession of a theory concerning the need of human blood, or parts of the human body, for the success of crops, for funerals of chiefs, for the foundations of buildings, for the making of canoes and other social purposes. It is accepted as a practice because it fulfils this fundamental need. It must be remembered, however, that people who practise agriculture do not always consider it necessary to fertilize their fields with the blood of human victims. The matter is much more complicated than that. All we can say at the present moment is that certain peoples possess a theory that human sacrifice is necessary for certain social purposes, and this has caused them to seek victims in order to ensure the well-being of the community.

It is not necessary, at this moment, to inquire how these peoples have come into possession of such a theory : the point is that, once they have it, they act on it, and perform deeds that are

[1] Perry vi. 17.
[2] See Perry vi. Chap. XV. for evidence on this point.

clearly repugnant to the bulk of mankind. Therefore when people kill a victim for agriculture they are actuated not by any innate desire to perform an act of cruelty, but simply by the belief that they are thus ensuring their food supply. When we remember the ease with which the practice dies out, it is evident that the theoretical basis must be very strongly supported to cause it to produce such terrific results. But once firmly established, it would seem that it can become hypertrophied, as in the case of the Aztecs of Mexico, who sacrificed victims by the thousand.

It is therefore possible to assert that this particular form of cruel behaviour is directly the outcome of the social process, that it is not innate in mankind and manifested in every member of the race. It is an ' institutional ' form of behaviour, and only exists in specific circumstances that can readily be defined. And the motive that leads to it is supplied by the theory that human victims are necessary for agriculture, funerals, house building and so forth.

Innumerable other instances could be discussed, with similar results. For instance, the initiation of youths, so widely practised throughout the world, yet not universal among mankind, is bound up with certain definite theories. The initiation of boys among the Bakwena Basuto, for example, ensures them a conscious life in the hereafter. Those who are not initiated are said to ' die like dogs '. This initiation includes the operation of circumcision. It is not easy to see the connexion between circumcision and immortality, yet such is the conviction of the Basuto. In like manner the Mystery Religions of Greece and Rome had as their main object the attainment of immortality.[1] This boon was gained by undergoing a complex ritualistic performance. The same might be said of even Christianity itself, particularly with regard to the more ritualistic branches of the Church.

Such institutions as these differ profoundly from the biological grouping of the family. The family needs no interpretation, no justification ; its appeal is innate. The social institutions just mentioned have as their justification an appeal to events beyond the ken of individual experience. They are the outcome of a social process of which the ordinary man may be ignorant.

---

[1] Reitzenstein 1910. ' Osiris, Attis and Adonis were men ; they died and rose again as gods ' (p. 6). ' When we become united with them, absorb or attract them into ourselves, we have the certitude, as solid as a rock, of our own immortality, nay our own divinity ' (p. 7). Men expected also safety from danger, success in business, and protection from illness—(a comprehensive insurance policy), 17.

The study of these and other social institutions suggests that, in many instances, they are the outcome of the impact of a body of knowledge or theory on human society. In other words, social institutions possess a core of theory or knowledge.

This proposition, of course, is evident in the case of arts and crafts. It is obvious that pottery is only made by those who know how to make it. Pottery can, of course, be used by those who cannot make it. Pottery is useful, but that does not ensure pottery-making throughout the world. On the contrary, the craft has disappeared more than once; for example in the island of Pentecost of the New Hebrides,[1] and in the United States, in the case of the Pawnee.[2] It is indeed likely that the use of pottery, or even its manufacture is, in the vast majority of cases, the result of a process of transmission. It may well be that this craft took shape in one community and spread throughout the world. Even if this were not true, it is nevertheless demonstrable that the craft of the potter has been handed on from one region to another over vast areas of the earth's surface. Pottery may be made by certain communities because the craft is hereditary among them. Similarly, other communities may acquire it by barter.

Pottery is useful; it supplies a need; but its use is not universal. That is to say, the need for containing liquids for cooking and other domestic purposes does not necessarily give rise to the craft of pottery-making. Food-gatherers usually do without it; food-producers can lose the craft. It is therefore not surprising that no one has yet succeeded in formulating the exact steps by which men were first led to construct clay pots. They may have based them on basketry; they may have derived the idea from the use of gourds or ostrich shells, or bamboo tubes. We do not know. All we can postulate is some situation that aroused their interest and produced a fruitful idea. In order to discover the exact origin of pottery we must be able to formulate the precise situation that gave rise to this fruitful idea. The invention of pottery, once made, would awaken an instant appeal.

It does not follow that a craft is necessarily adopted because it is useful. Food-gatherers live in close proximity to food-producers and fail to practise their crafts, or even to acquire their products. It does not follow, therefore, that because we have ascertained, in broad terms, the reason for the origin of an art or craft in some obvious need, that we can account for the presence of that art or craft in any particular case. The need for pottery is latent everywhere, but this need is not everywhere effective. As we have already seen, certain peoples make pottery; others merely

[1] Rivers vi. 193–4.   [2] Grinnell i. 255.

use it, while others do not use it, even though they have the
opportunity.

It is possible to formulate three propositions regarding a social
institution :
(1) It comes into being for some definite reason.
(2) It persists for reasons that may be quite different.
(3) Once in existence a process of action and interaction is set
up between it and other social institutions.

The wearing of dress may be taken as another example. The
practice of wearing clothes by modern peoples does not give in
itself any unmistakable clue to its origin. The fact that certain
savage tribes habitually go about stark-naked without exhibiting
any traces of shame suggests that modesty was not the reason why
our ancestors began to wear clothes. Protection from the weather
hardly suffices as an argument, when we consider that civilization
originated in warmer climates than ours. It cannot be urged
that clothing was first worn to distinguish the sexes, to denote
differences of rank or profession, or for other social purposes.
On the contrary, it would appear that the earliest ' clothing '
worn by man had a ' magical ' purpose. Necklaces, girdles, and
other forms of ornamentation were made up of magical substances, and were used for such purposes as the ensuring of
fertility in women, protection from illness and so forth.[1] We may
therefore say of the practice of wearing dress, that :
(1) Its original aim was to benefit its wearer in some way
or other.
(2) Once in being it created new needs. Feelings of modesty
developed ; clothes became necessary to protect the body
from extremes of heat and cold. The sexual appeal of
clothes became developed. The original magical character of clothes receded.
(3) Clothes became a means of indicating class distinctions,
trades, professions and so forth.

The institution of dress thus illustrates the working of the
hypothetical social process just outlined. An institution takes
its birth under the influence of certain theories formed by man
to enable him to control birth, death, illness and other happenings
of life. This new addition to his equipment reacts upon his
behaviour, and produces feelings of self-consciousness with regard
to sex and climate that he probably had not before experienced.
Vanity certainly came to play its part. As time went on and
life became more complicated, the original meaning of dress

[1] Elliot Smith iv. 377 ; Perry vii. 14–15.

receded more and more into the background.   A series of ramifications grew up that would take a book to describe.

Most of us spend our days entirely ignorant of the working of this process.   We interpret the secondary feelings associated with dress as the original causes of the adoption of the practice itself.   In so far as we accept these secondary accompaniments to dress as fundamental, we are living in a world of illusion. What appears to us to be so natural and simple may well have a long and complicated history.

The possession of knowledge or theories, therefore, by any community is not to be assumed as self-evident.   It is usually the outcome of some social process, and, in most cases, is not shared by all members of the community.   There is thus a social process at work over and above any individual member of the community, and it is to this process that the acquisition of knowledge is ultimately to be referred.   It is indeed not too much to say that the great bulk of humanity goes through life largely dominated by this process.   The child is educated and receives knowledge from the society in which he lives.   He often contributes nothing whatever to the common store of culture.

Dr. Lowie gives an excellent summary of the working of this process in the case of the Crow Indians :

' The individual Crow is indeed free from the dictates of a priesthood, but he is in the grip of a more potent, precisely because it is a more subtle, leadership.   The stock of ideas and emotions characteristic of his social group fashions his whole cosmic outlook as it fashions the very pattern of his vision.   There are certain conceptions which from a child he receives as unchallengeable, even though they are not formulated as so many propositions ; and while they may in themselves be completely devoid of religious value they inevitably frame and tincture whatever acquires such value.   To give a positive definition of what Dr. Thurnwald calls the primitive *Denkart* (mode of thinking) or *Geistesverfassung* (mental constitution) is not so easy as to sense it from such concrete exhibitions as are yielded by the visionary experiences. Negatively, it seems easy enough to contrast it with our modern world-view, to define it as an eminently irrational one, that is, one that does not involve the checking of associations by the spirit of critical inquiry.   No woman has ever been known to handle a Sun Dance doll, hence Pretty-enemy, who disobeyed the rule, must die or suffer the loss of some dear relative as an automatic punishment.   A horseman seen in a vision escapes from the enemy, hence the visionary will be invulnerable.   To draw a representation of one's enemy and puncture the heart is to

10

injure the man figured.   These are all actual illustrations of how
the Crow mind applies the principle of causality.   The implicit
philosophy of reality, imbibed with the mother's milk, limits and
predetermines the individual's religious views, just as the social
standards current in his community predetermine his life-values
and the wishes he seeks to fulfil through religion.   In contrast
with this body of received notions and ideals the scope for individual creativeness seems, from an outsider's point of view,
pitiably meagre.   Thus even the most extreme subjectivism may
merge in abject servility, not to the authority of a personal
dictatorship, but to the impersonal, though none the less real,
dominance of folk-belief and folk-usage.' [1]

The words of Dr. Lowie suggest that the thoughts and actions
of the Crow Indians, so far at least as their ritual and ceremonial
is concerned, are largely determined for them by their institutions.
Each boy or girl, therefore, finds himself or herself born into a
community that from the time of birth exercises a potent influence
upon him or her.   The social environment constitutes the concrete
experience of each child, and on it as basis behaviour is built
up.   The only question that can be asked in this connexion is,
where does this process end ?   How much of the religion or
ceremonial of such a people is autogenous, and how much has
been introduced ?

The evidence given by Dr. Lowie concerning the Crow Indians
illustrates the positive action of society on the individual.   The
beliefs and practices of a tribe exert their influence upon its
members.   On the other hand, where there is a dearth of social
institutions, there does not seem to be any attempt to fill the
gap.   Even in so universal a phenomenon as children's games
there is little or no sign of originality.   As an example of this,
I was struck by the behaviour of boys in Pondoland.   They
begin to help tending the cattle at the age of six, and continue
to do so until the age of sixteen or more.   Boys from neighbouring
kraals usually band themselves together to spend the day in
looking after the herds.   They have ample spare time on their
hands, for their duties are light.   They seem to have, however,
practically no games or amusements to help them pass the long
hours.   They cook food, and occasionally make small models of
cattle or sleds.   They seem to be able to pass hours doing nothing,
and do not show the slightest tendency to invent any means of
spending their time.

It is worthy of mention, perhaps, that the society of savages,
so far as I have enjoyed it, is more restful than that of the super-

[1] Lowie 31–2.

civilized. It is possible to spend hours in a savage kraal, leaning against the side of a hut, surrounded by children, dogs, fowls, pigs, and grown-ups, without experiencing the slightest degree of boredom. The savage seems content with his lot, provided he is not interfered with too much. The civilized man is brought up in an environment where knowledge has been stored for generations, and this knowledge influences him from birth. The small boy knows all about aeroplanes, motor-cars and bicycles, and his great ambition is to scour the countryside at as rapid a pace as possible. The mechanically propelled vehicle has produced a profound unrest in civilized countries, causing people to wish to visit the most widely separated places, in contrast to the condition of things centuries ago in the same countries, when most folk stayed at home for the whole of their lives.

The dynamic effects of the impact of culture upon a people is illustrated in the classical example of Japan. This country throughout the ages has been largely dependent on China and other Asiatic countries for its cultural inspiration. Certainly it is difficult to trace any real originality in early Japanese culture.

The Japanese continued as a race of barbarians, living more or less in isolation from the western world, until the middle of last century. It was then decided to welcome western civilization. Foreign experts were attracted to the country, and the effects of their teaching have in the course of half a century worked great changes. The Japanese are now in the first rank in more than one branch of science ; and they are now able to compete on equal terms with European manufacturers.

Japan affords one example of the working of a general process, namely, the reorganization of the whole world on the basis of the civilization of western Europe. The vast majority of peoples are passive agents in this process. The number of men whose brains are responsible for this modern development of civilization in western Europe is small. The industrial revolution, based upon the invention of the steam-engine, is transforming the world. We owe the steam-engine to a small group of men. The rest of mankind benefits by their originality.

We may therefore assume a large amount of passiveness with regard to social institutions. In most instances they produce their own needs and induce their own specific types of behaviour. Human material under their influence is as clay in the hands of the potter. There does not seem, moreover, to be any inherent reason, in the vast majority of instances, why any particular social institution should be possessed by any particular community. On the contrary, the community usually receives its specific character from such social institutions as have come to it from without. Most human societies are like mosaics, made up of variegated items derived from many sources, but contributing little or nothing themselves. They are the outcome of the workings of the social process that fashions these institutions.

CHAPTER XII

TRADITION

THE argument of the last chapter has taken us one stage further. Evidence has been adduced to show that a community owes some of its activity to the influence of social institutions of various sorts, each with a kernel of theory or knowledge. These institutions act as dynamic agents, causing the people to adopt definite types of behaviour. That is to say, we explain the witch-burning of Europe as the result of the theory of witchcraft held by the people of that time. We recognize that they were men and women as ourselves, but that they had come into possession of certain theories that forced them to action. If we have any candour and insight, we recognize that had we lived in those days, we should have acted in a precisely similar manner. We recognize thus the potent effect of society on the individual.

Realizing how powerfully society can influence the behaviour of its members, as the result of the action on each person of its accumulated knowledge or theories, manifested in the shape of institutions, it is now time to turn to the next question, and to inquire how a community usually comes by its store of institutions.

We can well say, with Dr. Lowie, that the Crow Indian is largely influenced in thought and behaviour by the society in which he finds himself. What we have then to ask ourselves is, how did the Crow society, or any other society, come to possess its institutions ?

This presents us with a serious dilemma. If human beings throughout the ages, and in all parts of the earth, are at all comparable to the Crow, how comes it that originality has ever found expression on a large scale ? Human society consists of individuals, and ultimately, individuals must have made social institutions. The question is, how did it happen ?

It is evident that minor variations of custom can and do arise. No two communities are identical in their culture ; they always present a definite character of their own. The student of arts and crafts can usually tell, if he has the requisite knowledge, the provenance of any pot, any carved image, and so forth, with a great degree of certainty. But these characteristic features appear to be but variations on a theme ; they do not usually constitute specific differences. In spite of minor differences we find great groups of communities resembling one another in their important cultural characteristics. The difficulty is to discover the sources of important social institutions. We want to know how ruling classes arise ; the same with agriculture, pottery-making, metal-working and so forth ; but as soon as we start making these inquiries we meet with a blank wall ; usually nothing is known in a particular community.

It is interesting to consider the attitude of men towards their social institutions, and particularly people of the lower culture. We may begin with Australia, the natives of which are in a simple stage of culture. They present, moreover, characteristics that are of great use at this juncture. They are still food-gatherers, but at the same time, as has been seen already (see p. 74), they possess certain cultural characteristics, such as the dual organization, in common with the neighbouring food-producing peoples.

It is therefore interesting to try to see what is the real meaning of the possession of these seemingly more advanced forms of social structures by food-gathering peoples.

It is agreed that the Australian natives are very conservative and unoriginal. For instance, Messrs. Horne and Aiston say : ' The old habits and the old thoughts cling very firmly, and, after all, it is on the surface that the change is greatest. Behind the real inward beliefs and feelings the weight of centuries presses heavily.' [1]

Some initiative might be expected in the case of weapons, but there is little or no trace of improvement. ' It must be always remembered that the peculiar intelligence of the black fellow deprives him of the capacity of estimating anything complicated, and also prevents initiative in throwing. He throws a weapon as his father has taught him, and is afraid to initiate an improvement for fear that he may be deemed *kootchi* (uncanny). He will develop wonderful skill in the use of things that were used by his father and his father's father, but never attempts to get out of the groove. If they get white men's tools they use them as nearly as possible in the same way as they used their stone tools.' And again, ' " We do it because our fathers did it " is the usual cry when asked the reason for a custom or a performance.' [2] The authors go on to say that such an innovation as the introduction of marriage classes ' seems to be quite beyond the ideas or capabilities of the present-day aborigines or even their immediate ancestors. This would presuppose them a

[1] Horne and Aiston, 15.　　[2] *Ibid.*, 82–3, 123.

mentally depreciated race.' [1] The same resistance to change is
stressed by the late Sir Baldwin Spencer in his work on the Arunta.
He says that ' the Australian native is bound hand and foot by
custom. What his father did before him, that he must do. If
during the performance of a ceremony his ancestors painted a
white line across their fore-heads, that line he must paint. Any
infringement of custom, within certain limitations, is visited with
sure and often very severe punishment.'

Sir Baldwin Spencer speaks, in the same work, of the possibility
of innovation of custom : ' At the same time, rigidly conservative
as the native is, it is yet possible for changes to be introduced. . . .
It must, however, be understood that we have no definite proof
to bring forward of the actual introduction by this means of any
fundamental change of custom. . . . That changes have been
introduced—in fact, are still being introduced—is a matter of
certainty ; the difficulty to be explained is how, in the face of
the rigid conservatism of the native, which may be said to be
one of his leading features, such changes can possibly even be
mooted.' [2]

Mr. John Layard has given an example of the introduction of
minor changes. He has described what he calls ' degree-taking '
ceremonies in certain parts of the New Hebrides in southern
Melanesia. These ceremonies are acquired by purchase, and
thus are transferred from village to village. They are all more
or less similar, and only differ in minor details. [3]

Examples such as these are of importance. It must be clearly
understood, however, that this is but a secondary process, working
within a larger orbit. The transference of a ' degree-taking '
ceremony is one thing ; the origin of such ceremonies is another.
Much ground will have to be cleared before we can approach
this problem with any degree of confidence. In some cases
modifications of practices are easily introduced ; in others it
appears to be a matter of extreme difficulty. For instance, it is
almost impossible to persuade the native Australian to take up
agriculture or cattle-rearing, in spite of the obvious advantage
that would accrue from their adoption. Similarly with the
Negritos of Luzon in the Philippines. Mr. Raven of the Natural
History Museum at New York tells me that some years ago he
visited a part of Borneo where food-gathering Punan were living
near to tribes who cultivated rice. When asked why they did
not adopt rice-growing, these Punan said, ' What is the use ? If
we planted crops and went off hunting, the animals would eat
them all up before we returned.'

[1] *Ibid.*, 123.   [2] Spencer ii. 11, 12.   [3] Layard 139 e.s.

The incentive to change must be extremely powerful to over-come habitual modes of life, even where the change is obviously advantageous.   Certain tribes of South Africa cultivate maize and also grow tobacco.   They do not manure the fields for their maize crops, although they have ample supplies from their cattle. At the same time they are well aware of the value of manure, and use it for their tobacco crop.   When questioned why they do not manure their maize crops, they reply that it is not the custom.   Such a breach of tradition could only take place as the result of a strong incentive—such, for example, as the orders of a chief.

Vested interests offer resistance to change.   For example, the cattle of the Pondo are poor creatures, a herd of seven or eight cows in full milk only yields about a gallon of milk a day.   The Government is trying, through its agricultural institutions, to induce the natives to breed better stock, so as to improve the supply of beef and of milk ; but the native is so ingrained in his traditional ways that he pays little attention to the wiles of the White Man.   Indeed, when I told a Pondo that cows in England gave four or more gallons of milk a day he refused to believe me, thinking it utterly preposterous.   The life of the natives of South Africa, whether Pondo, Tembu, or Xosa, is so bound up with cattle that it is hard to see how they can be induced to alter their ways.

For instance, when a marriage takes place cattle, usually eight or ten head, are paid over by the family of the husband to the family of the bride.   It seems to be a matter of indifference whether the cattle paid are heifers, milch cows, oxen or bulls. The affair is settled by arbitration between the two groups, long and elaborate discussions taking place before a decision is reached. The cattle are valued at a flat rate of £5 per head, irrespective of quality.   The bride's family usually receive part of the cattle at the time of the marriage, and the rest in instalments.   Each family group has a complicated system of accounts, cattle being owed to other groups, and vice versa.   Imagine the complications set up by the introduction of cattle of good breed, in which the cows are valued at, say, £30 each.   It almost defies reason to picture the muddle.   That is why these natives stick to their accustomed ways.

This example shows that certain social institutions are so woven into the fabric of their lives as to make it very difficult for people to change.[1]

---

[1] This point has already been stressed in Chapter IX on Acquisition. See p. 91.

An excellent example of a failure to adopt new practices is afforded by the Nubians. They have lived in close contiguity to Egypt for thousands of years. At the beginning of the pre-dynastic period Nubia and Egypt were culturally one, but after the middle pre-dynastic period Egyptian civilization moved forward and ultimately achieved the triumphs of the Pyramid Age. The Nubians, on the other hand, have remained as they were fifty-five centuries ago and more.[1]

When we ask a native the meaning of his customs we get a variety of answers. The Pondo have very little ceremonial, but they still celebrate the Ntonjane, a puberty ceremonial for girls. Mr. J. E. S. Griffiths and I attended several of these ceremonials in 1930. On one occasion I teased one of the women who were taking part in the ceremonies as to what was the meaning and reason of what they were doing. 'Just custom,' she answered. 'That is a poor reason for keeping on a ceremonial,' I replied. She at once flashed round on me. 'Why do you have parties in your country?' I had weakly to admit, 'It is just a custom.' She immediately retorted, 'Ours is a custom too, and we keep it up because we like it.'

She was right. Such gatherings are pleasant. People come from the countryside to spend a pleasant time. The women dance in the open space in front of the huts singing their traditional ditties. Occasionally a local comedienne performs a *pas seul*. The men meanwhile are assembling for the great event of the day, the killing of the ox. They take their place on the outskirts of the cattle kraal, and sit in the South African sunshine smoking and talking. The ox is killed, divided out, cooked and eaten, the whole company partaking. This is one of the rare occasions on which meat is eaten, so no wonder the good old custom is kept up. It must be remembered, however, that this has nothing whatever to do with the origin of the Ntonjane ceremony, or its introduction among the Pondos. We are simply witnessing a social institution in decay; it has lost much of its original meaning, and survives mainly as a jollification.

In certain instances it would seem that something more than tradition is causing the retention of social institutions. This may be observed among more highly developed civilizations, such as that of India. The great rituals of the Brahmanas have as their deliberate aim the faithful re-enactment of certain events supposed to have happened in the past, in the age of the gods. Throughout the whole of these rituals it is expressly stated that the priest is doing what the gods did in the past. For instance,

[1] Firth i. ; ii.

in certain ceremonials the king has to create men. The text says, ' Therewith the gods came by men, and in like manner does this [king] now thereby come by men.' In the introduction to the ceremony of consecrating a king it says, ' The gods now desired, " May we be consecrated even on this occasion with all the rites of consecration." They were indeed consecrated on this occasion by all the rites of consecration ; and in like manner is the Sacrificer [that is the king], on this occasion consecrated by all the rites of consecration.' [1] Throughout the vast range of these ceremonials this fidelity to tradition is continually reiterated to a wearisome degree. As these ceremonials have a definite purpose, namely the securing of life, health, prosperity and happiness for the community, this persistence is readily understood.

Mankind, therefore, appears to act differently with regard to traditional and non-traditional social institutions. His mind is a kind of filter, allowing some things to pass, but preventing others. His interest seems to be centred mainly on traditional lore. This interest, of course, is not based entirely on the traditional nature of the lore. There are other reasons for its persistence. For example, native medicine is almost entirely traditional in its nature, but that is not the sole reason for its existence. Mankind always has been, and always will be, interested in illness and its cure, for illness is always with us. Medicine arose as a result of the desire to cure illness. We need not inquire at this point what led to the origin of any particular form of treatment ; but this treatment, once in existence, usually becomes part of the traditional lore of the community, and is handed on simply because it is traditional, while its real origin may be forgotten.

Some notion of the factors controlling the acceptance or rejection of new ideas may be gathered from evidence collected by Mr. J. E. S. Griffiths and myself among the Pondo of South Africa in 1930. We spent some months in almost daily intercourse with a remarkable old man named Mtandama. One morning we determined to try to find out whether he had any ideas concerning supposed relations between men and animals. I had in mind, for instance, the case of the Bakongo, which I had heard of from Mr. Torday.[2] They believe that Kongo, the great ancestor of their chiefs, had a leopard as his twin-brother. The Bakongo also confuse the after-birth with a leopard. I remembered also that the natives of widespread areas of Africa associated leopards with chiefs, that they alone were entitled to wear leopard skins. Pondo custom required that leopards could only be killed, in

---

[1] Satapatha-Brahmana V. 2, 5, 1 ; IX. 3, 4, 6.   [2] Torday 237.

the course of a hunt, by members of the chief's clan. I therefore
felt certain that I should be able to extract some information from
Mtandama concerning the supposed relationship between men and
animals ; so I asked him whether he had ever heard of a man
changing into a leopard.

The result was emphatic and surprising. He refused to believe
that such a thing could happen. It was just a story, made up
to amuse. The Bakongo might believe in such things. It was
no concern of his. Try as I would, I was unable to persuade the
old man that men could change into leopards. I cited also the
birth of leopards from women. To that he replied, ' Cows give
birth to calves, women give birth to children, leopards give birth
to leopards. Whoever heard of a woman giving birth to a leopard.
It is a story.' The old man chuckled. He felt himself much too
smart to be made a fool of by me. He was amused.

This robust, sceptical, concrete, matter-of-fact attitude towards
the beliefs of other peoples took me by surprise. Nothing in our
previous intercourse had suggested the possession of this attitude
of mind. I therefore proceeded to exploit the situation, to see
how the old man would react. I tried him with as accurate a
version of the Huron creation story as I could remember at the
time. Once upon a time there only was a world in the sky and
an expanse of ocean underneath. There was no land for people
to dwell in. The people in the sky decided to create land. They
sent down the otter, who dived down into the depths and brought
up some earth. Then they sent down some of their people to
inhabit it. The old man was equally emphatic in this case.
My assertion that the Huron believed in a sky-world made no
impression whatever on him. ' It was just a story.'

I pursued this topic with the old man on several occasions, and
failed to find any trace of anything but a matter-of-fact attitude
towards other people's abstract ideas. In his mind the sun was
just the sun, and the moon the moon. He had been accustomed
to them since childhood, and had never taken any notice of them.
I asked him if he would like to go up and see the Victoria Falls.
He replied, ' Why should I ? It's only a lot of water, and there's
plenty down here to look at.'

This is simply the attitude of mind stressed in the preceding
chapter ; namely, the failure on the part of savages to originate
new ideas except to a very limited extent.

A great surprise, however, awaited me. One day we were
talking about magic. Mtandama was describing the doings of
the Lightning Bird, the Mpondulu. In the course of his account
he mentioned that the Mpondulu could change into a man and

have intercourse with a woman. I at once demanded why he was so inconsistent; why he now believed that an animal could become a human being.

His answer was intriguing. He believed it because the doctors said it was so. We argued the matter backwards and forwards for the rest of the morning, but I utterly failed to get him to see his inconsistency. He insisted all the time that the belief of the Bakongo about men and leopards was their concern, but was none of his.

I received a further shock. Speaking of the Lightning Bird, he mentioned that the woman with whom he had intercourse became a doctor. She learned her craft in the course of a visit to the sky-world.

I immediately jumped in with a reference to the Huron story of beginnings. Here again he was in nowise dismayed. It was their concern, not his. He was willing to take my word for it if I had been there; for his part he would have none of it. His sky-world was a different thing altogether. He knew about that from the doctors.

These and other similar conversations led me to conclude that Mtandama's attitude towards ideas depended entirely upon their manner of presentation to him. Evidently seeing was believing, so to speak, in his mind. An abstract idea, presented in a traditional setting, was accepted without question. The same abstract idea, coming from a non-traditional source, practically unconnected with any concrete basis, was unhesitatingly rejected. I must mention that its rejection was not entirely unconditional. Mtandama insisted that he would accept the fact if I sponsored it, because I was his friend.

The attitude of mind of my Pondo friend Mtandama is similar to that of natives of the Purari Delta of New Guinea, as described by Mr. Williams. Mr. Williams speaks of ' the general intellectual complacency, the absence of any inquiring spirit—a negative quality which the Purari, no doubt, share with most other primitive peoples. It is not in a state of philosophic unrest, but of thorough animal contentment that the native chews his betel. He is not revolving hypotheses in his head, and does not allow a problem unsolved to be a worry to him. He is inclined to be impatient with a man who asks him : " What of the wind ? Where does it come from ? What causes it to blow ? " And will answer : " I have no idea where it comes from, and it blows by itself." *U e'e* is the final explanation—" himself ". It is the nature of the wind to blow, and of the sun to rise and set. No one thinks to inquire further into the matter.

' To one who is for ever pestering the natives with questions about their ideas of things it is a little surprising and disappointing that they never rejoin by asking him for his own ideas. One individual asked me once whether the white men could tell me what made the thunder, and on another occasion the same individual asked if they could tell what became of a man's soul after his death. But in the course of seven or eight months in the Delta I do not recollect any other question of a similar nature. Thirdly, one may detect in natural philosophy, as far as it goes, a generally rational trend. Ideas are sensible rather than fanciful, and formed under the limitation that " seeing is believing ".

' The sun passed across the sky, but whether the sun that rose this morning were the sun that set last night or a new one, it is impossible to say, because a man could not watch it during the night. The water in the River Urika, came from the River Purari. But where did the water in the River Purari come from ? That a man could not say, because he had not been far enough upstream to see. Informants are curiously reluctant to guess or to express an opinion on a matter which they have hitherto taken for granted. Thus, seeking to learn something of native geography, I asked where a man would finally come to if he took his canoe and paddled away and away to the south. No one knew, and no one would venture a suggestion, until finally some more nimble spirit answered the question very sensibly and unimaginatively by saying that the canoe would be swamped.

' As an instance of the absence of speculation concerning natural objects, it is said that " altogether the moon was regarded with favour, but did not seem to fill a place of any consequence whatever in the religion of the people . . . it has apparently no religious import ".' [1]

Professor Malinowski has given a parallel instance from the Trobriands. He says that ' the periodicity of the solar movements, the double yearly passage of the sun overhead—its southerly path in winter, northerly in summer—are all known to the natives, but never used in framing the idea of a solar year ; in fact, there is in the native remarkably little interest in all these established facts about the main heavenly body and the relation of its warmth to fertility. When pressed, the native will say that the sun walks or moves across the sky ; that it dips down at sunset ; that afterwards it moves round under the rim of the earth, from the west along the southern horizon to the east and there rises again in the morning. But even this theory would be advanced by the most intelligent natives only, and that without

[1] Williams 230, 231.

the least enthusiasm or interest. Any other question would be answered by an *ayseki* (" I don't know ").' Again, he says, ' The moon plays a far greater part in the life of the natives than either the sun or the stars. But here also there are no traces of the pseudo-scientific curiosity frequently ascribed to the natives.' [1]

These examples serve to disallow the assumption of a wholesale accumulation by men of ideas, or formulation of theories concerning the world around us. The sun, for example, is not always included in the native pantheon. In fact, on the contrary, it has but rarely been an object of ceremonial. We hear of a god associated with the sun in some way, but not of the sun as a god, The sun-worship of Akhenaten in Egypt is almost the only example of pure solar worship. In short, natural phenomena, such as the heavenly bodies, rivers, volcanoes, and so forth, seem to have interested mankind very little during the ages. Man prefers to live as regards his thoughts in a traditional and social *milieu*. He prefers to do what his forefathers did.

Pure intelligence, of course, is used in certain activities by the whole of mankind. The procuring of food, for example, is obviously dominated by intelligence. Men have long since learned what is good to eat, and what is harmful, or else they would long ago have died of food poisoning. But it would appear that the activities of mankind are usually dominated by tradition. Social institutions are handed on from generation to generation, and are usually preserved for the simple reason that they have been handed on. It does not seem to occur to mankind as a whole to inquire into the reasons for social institutions, even those which are farthest away from reality. The pressure of tradition often blinds men to the obvious, it perverts their intelligence. At the same time it must not be forgotten that the failure of men to allow their minds to work freely is not confined to food-producers. Food-gatherers, with their almost total lack of social institutions, are even less original. This suggests that the factors controlling the free use of intelligence are complicated. The food-producer has to break with tradition ; the food-gatherer has to have his intelligence awakened. He has not even got so far as the elaboration of social institutions. In a sense, of course, the food-gatherer is dominated by tradition, but this tradition is mainly negative, except in so far as it concerns food.

Even our own modern society fails in that respect. Our thoughts and actions are largely traditional, even when we think we are masters of the facts. Social institutions act upon us and mould us into their ways of behaviour. We are often unable,

[1] Malinowski iii. 204–5.

when challenged, to account for much of our behaviour. The Victorian English thought well of themselves. We of a later generation can understand the reason for much of this behaviour, and often like to pour ridicule on it. We forget, however, that our grandsons will do exactly the same thing to our age. Each one of us is walking about in a mental fog. We voice opinions simply because we hear them spoken around us. Our minds are partly divorced from reality. The history of science has shown that tradition plays a large part in moulding thought. The voice of authority is ever at work charming the listener, and saving him the necessity for hard thought. Scientific views are often accepted because they come from a trusted source. It requires a stubborn spirit to maintain intellectual integrity.

CHAPTER XIII

CONTINUITY

THE chief characteristic of communities of the lower culture is an apparent lack of any signs of the elaboration by them of fresh elements of culture. The most that can happen is, as in the case of the North American Indians, the reshuffling of existing elements of thought. This conservatism can well account for a paucity of advance among the food-gatherers as a whole. Evidently they have led uneventful lives, and nothing has occurred to cause them to come into possession of various institutions that can cause them to become more active.

It is now time to turn to the positive aspect of the question, and to inquire in such societies themselves the nature of the process whereby they have acquired their various social institutions.

I shall begin with the Australian natives. As we have already seen, they are more complicated in their culture than most other peoples of the food-gathering stage. They have the dual organization, with a definite totemic clan system ; they have elaborate initiation ceremonies ; and thus are more complicated in their lives than, say, the Punan of Borneo.

What is the real meaning of the possession of these institutions that certainly do not seem to belong as a rule to the food-gathering stage of civilization ? The Australians are themselves very conservative and lacking in initiative, so much so that those who have lived with them doubt whether they could have been capable of elaborating their culture. That this doubt is well founded is shown by the natives themselves.

As an instance, I may take the accounts of rain-making given by Horne and Aiston in their work. They say that every man who has the power of making rain has his own method of working this particular form of magic. But the method is always acquired. ' Some claim that the method was shown them by the moora in a dream, others depend on legends, and some on traditional happenings.' [1] That is to say, the natives themselves do not believe that they have any power over rain. They can only

[1] Horne and Aiston 110.

148

obtain it by the aid of procedures communicated to them by
beings whom they believe to be more powerful than themselves.

The Wonkonguru group of tribes round Lake Eyre, which
includes the Dieri, Yaurorka and Ngameni, call these beings
mooras. 'A moora sometimes appears to have been a master-
mind who was the first to discover anything, or through whom
anything was first discovered or done. They were the first to
fashion human beings out of lizards, and they formed the sun.
To them is attributed the making of *murdus* or totems, and
ceremonies or corroborees invariably have the moora behind
them, instigating or appointing, and thus giving them authority.
The old men maintain their influence partly by receiving com-
munications in dreams from the mooras. They thus tell where
to sink for water and where game may be found.' [1] The moora
are responsible for the ceremonial and marriage rules of this group
of Australian natives.

One interesting feature of the initiation ceremonies of these
peoples is worthy of notice, for it has a direct bearing on the general
question of the origin of native custom. When a boy has been
initiated, he is allowed to wear a mussel-shell (*Unio*). 'There
does not seem to be any recognized place to wear this. Some tie
it on the end of the beard, others hang it around the neck, and
others hang it from their waist cord in front. They do not like
parting with these shells until they are certain that they will not
have a son to hand them on to, and some of those in use are yellow
with age. The shells came from the sea originally, but no one
knows how they were first brought into the country, and now
fresh-water mussel-shells are substituted.' [2]

There are thus two distinct links with the past. The people
not only claim that the mooras began their social organization,
but also lay great stress on a shell that originally was derived
from the sea, and later, in default of sea-shells, replaced by similar
varieties coming from the rivers. Therefore, not only do the
natives assert that they were taught their ceremonies by wonderful
beings at some distant time in the past, but they also strive to
maintain continuity with the past by means of shells originally
coming from the sea. They rely on tradition and on continuity.

Howitt gives instances of the acquisition of cultural capital
from beings of the same order as those who equipped the Wonkonguru. For instance, the Yuin say that Daramulun, their

---

[1] *Ibid.*, 125. It will be seen later on in this book that these mooras,
even in their creative aspects, are not products of the imagination of the
Australian natives.

[2] *Ibid.*, 160–1.

'All-Father', invented all their weapons and implements and gave them to them. After the initiation ceremony—*Kuringal* —the boys were told all about him and of his powers. 'When a man died he met him and took care of him. It was he who first made the *Kuringal*, and taught it to their fathers, and he taught them also to make weapons, and all that they know. . . . He is the great *Biamban* who can do anything and go anywhere, and he gave the tribal laws to their fathers, who have handed them down from father to son until now.' [1]

In like manner the Kurnai owed everything to a similar being. 'Long ago there was a great Being, called *Mungan-ngaua*, who lived on the earth, and who taught the Kurnai of that time to make implements, nets, canoes, weapons—in fact, all the arts they know. He also gave them the personal names they bear, such as Tulaba. *Mungan-ngaua* had a son named *Tundun*, who was married, and who is the direct ancestor—(the *Wehntwin*, or father's father)—of the Kurnai. *Mungan-ngaua* instituted the *Jeraeil* [initiation ceremony], which was conducted by *Tundun*, who made the instruments which bear the names of himself and of his wife.' [2]

These facts, taken together, suggest that communities such as those of Australia received a primordial impulse from without, and that they have continued ever since to live on their capital, sometimes dissipating it to a certain extent. They conduct their ceremonies, and regulate their marriages, according to these prescriptions. They make their emblems of initiation nowadays of fresh-water mussels, instead of, as formerly, marine shells (*Unio*). All over Australia the pearl-shells that they use have a similar type of curious zig-zag ornamentation, which is suggestive of a common origin for the use of these shells. They likewise make their churinga of wood instead of, as formerly, of stone.[3]

These few quotations, taken at random, show that the Australian natives ascribe their cultural beginnings to the agency of certain beings whom they regard as superior to themselves in many ways, but particularly in knowledge. They are not unique in

---

[1] Howitt 543.   [2] *Ibid.*, 630.

[3] In 'The Children of the Sun' I stated, erroneously, that the Australian natives did not use stone in their magic, with the exception of quartz. The fact that they formerly made their *churinga* of stone, and have now substituted wood is a point in favour of the thesis I supported there. I regret much that I overlooked this important piece of evidence. Miss McConnel has published some descriptions of circles of stones, of standing stones and so forth, in connexion with the totem centres of the local groups of certain tribes of North Queensland. This is important evidence for the understanding of Australian totemism. See *Oceania* II. No. 3, 1932, pp. 292 e.s.

this desire to maintain continuity with the past. A detailed
study reveals the same process at work throughout the length
and breadth of savage society, as well as among more advanced
societies. It is impossible, so far as I am aware, to point to any
savage society in which all ceremonial and social institutions are
claimed to have been originated by the members of that society.
Indeed, it is possible to go further, as we have seen already, and
to suggest that no savage society ever lays claim to the origination
of a cultural element of major importance.

The workings of the strivings after continuity with the past
are various. We find families, villages, clans, tribes, states, all
possess traditions and customs linking them with the past. I
shall give a selection of examples of the working of this process
in Indonesia, Oceania, and America.

About the year 1912 I began to collect information concerning
the burial of the dead, the destination of the ghost, and kindred
topics. My aim was to correlate, if possible, this material with
the results obtained by Rivers in his work on the ' History of
Melanesian Society ', which was then passing through the press.
Although the results obtained by me did not tally closely with
those of Rivers, the inquiry owes its inception to his stimulation.
Among other things I became interested in the mode of orientation
of the dead. It became obvious that in many places the dead
were placed in a position of definite relationship to some particular
direction; that is to say, they were orientated.[1] The definition
is vague for good reasons. It is possible to ' orient ' a body in
many ways. It may be placed, sitting or standing, to face some
particular direction ; or it may be lying on its side, in an extended
or a contracted position, facing any particular direction ; it may
be placed, say, south of a village.

Investigation showed that there was some meaning in this
practice. The dead were being orientated towards the land of
the dead. This may be seen by reference to the table on page
152.

Further inquiry revealed other cases of orientation. For
example, certain people built their houses with reference to certain
directions. In the majority of instances this direction was that
of the land of the dead. Certain people possess carved stone
images, which face towards the land of the dead.

Then came the revelation of the meaning of these acts of
orientation. The study of native tradition showed that the land
of the dead was in the direction whence the forefathers of the
people in question had come. The dead were being returned to

[1] Perry i.

	Orientation of Dead.	Orientation of House.	Orientation of Images.	Direction of Land of Dead.	Direction of Land of Forefathers.
Kachari . . .	S.	—	—	—	S. or E.
Khasi. . . .	E.	—	—	—	E.
Kuki-kom . .	S.	—	—	S.	S.
Ronte . . .	S.–W.–E.	—	—	—	—
Musho or Lahu.	—	E.	—	—	E.
Karo	W.	E.–W. ; N.–S.	—	W.	—
Angkola . . .	E.–W.	—	—	—	—
Andaman . .	E.	—	—	E.	—
Mentawi . . .	E.	—	—	—	E.
Mantra . . .	E.–W.	—	—	—	W.
Badoej . . .	S.	N.–S.	—	S.	S.
Olo Ngadjoe .	Orient their dead to land of dead and land of forefathers.				
Olo Dusun . .	E.–W.	—	—	E.	—
Pangin . . .	E.	—	—	E.	E.
Posso-Todjo To-radja . . .	W.	W.	—	W.	N.
To-napoe. . .	—	E.	E.	E.	E.
To-bada . . .	—	N.–S.	N.	N.	N.
Minahassa . .	—	N.–S.	—	N.	N.
Toumbulu . .	—	E.	—	—	N.
Toumpakewa .	—	E.	—	—	N.
Nuforeeze . .	Men's balcony of house apparently orientated to land of dead.				
Galelareeze . .	W.	—	—	W.–E.	N.–W.
Seranglao . .	N.	—	—	N.	N.
Kei	N.	—	—	N.	N.
Timor Laut . .	W.–E.	—	—	W.	W.
Babar . . .	W.	—	—	W.	W.
Leti, Moa, Lakor	E.	E.–S. ?	—	E.–S.	E.–S.
Beloe . . .	Orient graves and houses to land of dead.				
S.W. Timor . .	E.	—	—	—	E.
Savoe. . . .	W.	—	—	W.	W.
Tenggerese . .	Orient dead to holy mountain.				

the land of their forefathers. For example, the people of Minahassa in Celebes claim to have come from the north ; they place their land of the dead in the north ; they build their houses in a north-south direction ; and they also make an offering place in the north-east corner of their garden huts.[1]

The Beloe district of Timor furnishes another good example. Houses are often built with a veranda in the direction of the land of the dead, or of the places where the first chiefs procured their wives : these directions correspond with those of the graves.

[1] Op. cit., 290.

Another example is that of the Kom clan of the Kuki-Kom of Manipur. The dead are interred on the south side of the village; the land of the dead is situated in the south; and they believe themselves to have come from the south.[1]

These few examples illustrate the general principle, the validity of which is established by the table.

It became apparent, on further inquiry, that the mode of disposal of the dead had, in many cases, direct reference to the land of the dead, and, consequently, to the land of the forefathers.[2] For instance, those who interred their dead often believed that the dead went to an underground world, whence their forefathers had emerged. People who claimed descent from a world in the sky believed that they went to the sky after death. Sometimes they are interred lying on their backs, so as to face the land of the dead. A curious instance of the same group of these beliefs is afforded by the people of the Beloe district of Timor, already mentioned. Their land of the dead is on a certain mountain, where their ancestors emerged from an underground world.

Two remarkable instances of the belief that the dead return to the home of the ancestors turned up in the course of the inquiry. The Olo Ngadjoe of south-eastern Borneo believe that the land of the dead is situated up the river on the banks of which they live. The dead are placed in canoe coffins. These are placed parallel to the river, and are left there for two years, when a big ceremony is held, during which the bones are placed in their final resting-place. In the course of this ceremony a litany is chanted by a priest. This litany describes the journey of the ghost, guided by the priest, to the land of the dead. It was formerly thought that this chant was purely imaginative, but the researches of Heer Braches showed that this people originally came from the direction of Central Borneo, and must have descended the river to their present home. It is probable that formerly, just after the migration, they actually took the dead back to the home of their fathers. Certain spots mentioned in the story have actually been identified. Moreover, the boats used in the last part of the journey are much smaller than those used farther down. This strongly suggests that the people actually came from the central part of the island, where the rivers are much shallower.[3]

Another like case is that of the Karen of southern Burma. At certain intervals they endeavour to transfer the bones of the dead to the tribal burial-place, situated in Upper Burma, at the source of the people.[4]

[1] Op. cit., 288.   [2] Perry ii.   [3] Kruyt, A., i. 345.
[4] Forbes, C. J. F., 252; Carey and Tuck 191.

This association between the land of the dead and the home of the forefathers expresses itself in an interesting manner in certain cases.   In parts of south-west Timor the ruling class is descended from the people of the sky-world, and its members are supposed to go there at death.   On the other hand, the commoners are interred and supposed to go underground, whence their ancestors came.[1]   The island of Nias affords a parallel example. The chiefs, who are ' sky-born ', go to the sky, while the commoners go to their ancestral home underground.[2]

These two examples are of considerable theoretical importance. They reveal the fundamental difference between these two classes. The commoner, after death, has to dispense with his chief. This raises the important question of the origin of this social dichotomy.

Another interesting problem arises out of the consideration of the belief in an underworld of the dead.   We find, in south-west Timor, as has been seen, tribes with sky-born chiefs, and ' underworld ' commoners.   Interment is the general rule throughout the vast area reaching from Sumba by way of Timor to Timor Laut. Therefore one would expect that the land of the dead would be underground.[3]   The only places, however, throughout this great region where, so far as I am aware, commoners go to an underground world, are those ruled over by chiefs calling themselves the Children of the Sun.   The other peoples, particularly those in the islands east of Timor, believe that their dead go back to the home whence their ancestors came, which is often in Timor itself.   It would, therefore, appear as though the underground land of the dead had been displaced by one in the direction of migration.   The belief of the people of Beloe, in Central Timor, already mentioned, appears to show this process of supplantation at work.   People of the Fialarang district believe that they are descended from ancestors who came out of Mt. Lekaan.   The ghosts of the dead go to Mt. Lekaan at death, but it is not clear whether they go underground or not.[4]

The evidence collected in ' The Megalithic Culture of Indonesia ', and in ' The Children of the Sun ', suggests strongly that the peoples of the islands in the east end of the Timor region have originated in communities with sky-born chiefs.   Their belief in a land of the dead located in the home of the ancestors, instead of in the underworld, suggests that in their ancestral home they were ruled over by the Children of the Sun, who went directly to the sky-world, while the commoners went underground.

[1] Bastian II. 8   [2] de Zwaan 237.   [3] Perry vi. 260.
[4] Gryzen 46.

Another example will serve to impress this point. The Toradja of Central Celebes are divided into certain groups, among them those of Lake Posso, and the so-called mountain Toradja. The Posso Toradja, who all go underground at death, say that they were visited in the past by a sky-born being, who married one of their women, but did not stay among them.[1] The sons of the stranger migrated and became the ancestors of the chiefs of the mountain Toradja. These mountain Toradja, as may be seen from the table on page 152, believe that their dead go overland to the home of the dead. This apparently, therefore, is another case of the same kind. The people who had direct contact with these sky-born rulers go underground after death; while those who have traditions of migration return to the land of their fore-fathers, presumably to some community originally ruled over by the Children of the Sun.

The Winnebago Indians of North America provide an illuminating example of the desire of men to maintain continuity with their forbears. In the course of the Bear Clan feast, the host says to the guests, ' Let us send, on this occasion, to the place at which we all originated, whatever we possess of wealth. This is what the spirits asked of old. . . . We were told that at the place where we originated our ancestors now remain, regarding it as their home. There they expectantly await us.' [2]

The desire to maintain continuity with the past expresses itself in many ways. The examples just given show the desire to reunite the individual, chief and commoner, with his ancestors. The maintenance of continuity can be detected also in the case of larger agglomerations, such as villages that contain more than one family. The great chain of islands running eastwards from Timor reveal clearly the working of the principle of continuity in village structure. Village temples are mentioned in certain of the islands. These temples are served by a priest and a priestess, of chiefly rank, who are the direct descendants of the original founders of the village.[3] The temples contain certain stones, said to have been brought from Timor, whence these ancestors came.[4]

A similar process is at work in Minahassa. A Tontemboan story recounts how a man took a piece of the holy stone of Kema and planted it in the ground at Ka'kas. This man disappeared into a tree, and while there told his son to come and cultivate the land at Ka'kas. The son did so, but was only successful when he had obeyed the instructions of his parent : ' You, my son,

[1] Kruyt and Adriani I. 268. [2] Radin, P., ii. 322, 323.
[3] Perry v. 141 e.s. [4] Op. cit., 57 e.s.

must go to the east and fetch a piece of the stone which I have planted in the ground, a heritage of your forefathers.' [1] Evidently the people of Minahassa believed that the preservation of continuity with the past was essential for success in agriculture. Another Tontemboan story shows that people in the past were in the habit of transporting stones to be placed in new villages.[2] Each village had to have a sacred stone structure, to be the residence of the guardian spirits, who were usually, so far as can be told, the ghosts of the founders of the village.[3]

The island of Nias, west of Sumatra, affords another example of this process. When a village is moved, the stones of the ceremonial stone circle and the stones of honour erected in memory of the common ancestor, are taken to the new site.[4]

The evidence just cited reveals the desire of certain groups of people to maintain contact with the past. Members of single families, as well as of larger groups such as villages, have been considered. Certain evidence discussed in ' The Megalithic Culture of Indonesia ' bears on this point. A study originally intended to deal with the distribution and functions of typical ' megalithic monuments ', led to the generalization that the uses of stone for graves, offering-places, seats, memorials, walls round villages and houses, were usually connected with chiefs or villages as a whole, and not with commoners. For example, I found records of stone offering-places among twenty-eight groups of peoples in that great archipelago. These offering-places were recorded in or near a commoner's house in three instances only ; offering-places were associated with chiefs in eight cases ; while village offering-places occurred in twenty-five instances.[5] I found records of stone seats in fourteen cases ; in eleven cases they were associated with chiefs ; in eight cases with villages ; while in no case were they associated with private people.[6] Stone graves were widely used both for chiefs and commoners, but those made for chiefs were the more elaborate.[7]

Memorial stones and stone structures are usually associated with villages and chiefs, but not with commoners.[8] In many cases villages have sacred stones, tended by the village priest. These stones are tenanted by the guardian spirits of the village, who are the ancestors of the priests, but not of the commoners.

The hereditary priest of the island group which I have termed for convenience the ' Timor region ', carry on a cult directly associated with fertility. An annual ceremony is held, in which

[1] Schwarz 79, 273.   [2] Ibid., 352.   [3] Perry v. 64.   [4] Ibid., 48.
[5] Perry v. See table, p. 31.   [6] Op. cit. See table, p. 37.
[7] Ibid., table, p. 25.   [8] Ibid., Chap. VIII.

the ' sun-lord ' is supposed to descend and fructify the ' earth-mother '.[1]

Phallic ornamentation also suggests the same conclusion. I found mention of it in thirteen groups of people : in one case it was associated with a stone urn ; in another a sacred phallic image is associated with villages ; it was reported on five village temples, on three village offering-places, and at the entrance to three villages ; but it was never mentioned in connexion with ordinary houses.[2]

About twenty years ago I began, under the inspiration of Rivers, to undertake an inquiry into the head-hunting of Indonesian peoples. I had not gone far before an interesting generalization began to emerge. In all the cases examined by me, heads taken on raids were placed in village temples, in sacred village groves, on special structures, but never in ordinary houses. Only skulls of members of families were placed in ordinary houses.

These examples show a practically complete break between the private individual and the village as a whole. They give no reason to assume that the village cults have developed out of private cults. The evidence collected in ' The Megalithic Culture of Indonesia ' appears to suggest that the chiefly classes are more closely associated than the commoners with beliefs concerning the relationship between men and animals, some of which beliefs would be called ' totemic '.[3]

There is a widespread occurrence throughout Indonesia, as well as in many other regions, of sacred trees. These are usually associated with villages and with chiefs. These trees are usually some sort of Ficus.

The sacred trees of the Batak of Sumatra may be taken as an example. Each sacred tree is planted at a burial site, and is associated with the chiefly family. Each tree is grown from a cutting from the sacred tree of some earlier burial-place of the family. This series of trees is derived in continuous progression from the original tree of the founder of the particular chiefly group. The line of descent of the sacred trees is as well known as the line of descent of the chiefs buried beneath them.[4]

The conclusion is that the village structure has been carried about the Archipelago by people of chiefly class, who founded priesthoods wherever they went to carry on the cults of the village that they founded. The ghosts of these founders protect the village, residing, for that purpose, in stones, carved or plain,

[1] Perry v. 87, 105-6, Chap. XVIII.   [2] *Ibid.*, table, p. 110.
[3] Op. cit., Chaps. XVI, XIX, XX.   [4] Bartlett, H. H., Pl. XXII.

associated with the village.   The evidence leaves us no alternative to the conclusion that Indonesian peoples, as a whole, owe their stone offering-places, stone seats, and other uses of stone, as well as their phallic ornamentation and head-hunting, to these wanderers.

These people in certain cases called themselves the Children of the Sun.   They brought with them beliefs concerning a sky-world, from which they held themselves to be descended.   The people over whom they ruled, on the other hand, knew little or nothing of this sky-world.[1]

These sky-born strangers exerted their influence in different ways, according to local circumstance.   In certain places they founded lines of chiefs ; for example in Timor and Nias.   In other places, for example in Minahassa of north-eastern Celebes, tradition tells of their arrival in a ship.[2]   I know of no definite evidence of the foundation of a chiefly class by them, but we have seen that stories are told of the foundation of villages by people wandering south from Minahassa subsequent to the implantation of this culture.   Certain tribes living in the Naga Hills of Assam, for example the Tangkhul and Kabui Naga, apparently migrated after acquiring the use of stone.   Other peoples, for instance the Bontoc and associated tribes of northern Luzon in the Philippines, have stories of sky-born strangers who brought to them the use of stone and its associated culture. These strangers failed to establish lines of chiefs.[3]

These peoples possess origin stories that all refer back, directly or indirectly, to the sky-born strangers.   The chiefs of South Nias, for example, who are sky-born, state that their ancestors were a brother and sister.[4]

This opens up an important topic, which will receive attention later, namely, the incestuous marriages of the Children of the Sun (see pp. 200 e.s.).   It may be of interest to mention here what is recorded of these exalted beings among the Tontemboan of Minahassa in north-eastern Celebes.   The ' ancestress ' of this people, Lumimu'ut, is said to have been born out of a stone.   Her son To'ar, a Son of the Sun, married her.   Their son, Si Marendor, another son of the sun, married his sister Lintjambene.   Lintjambene also married her son Muntu'untu, who again was a son of the sun.[5]   This family practised incest on a comprehensive scale !   A story told by a cognate tribe, the Toumpakewa, says

[1] Bartlett, H. H., Chap. XXI.   [2] Schwarz II. 97.
[3] Details will be found in ' The Megalithic Culture of Indonesia ', particularly in Chapters VI, VIII, IX, XI.
[4] Wilken I. 459.   [5] Schwarz I. 240 e.s.

that Lumimu'ut and To'ar changed into two stone images, on a hill named Tonderukan, where the ancestors of the tribes of Minahassa assembled to divide up the land.

The origin stories of other peoples serve to illuminate this seemingly contradictory series of beliefs. We find the belief in an origin from a split stone among the Tangkhul and Kabui Naga, who have migrated after acquiring the use of stone.[1] This belief harmonizes with that of the Tontemboan, who date their history back to the meeting on Mt. Tonderukan, where the chiefs sat round on stone seats and divided out the ground. For some reason or other, the tradition of the Children of the Sun has persisted in Minahassa, but they have no direct descendants, so far as I know. The belief that ancestors changed into stone images is evidently the result of closer contact with the strangers than the belief in an origin from a split stone ; for the two Naga tribes already mentioned make no mention of the Children of the Sun in their origin stories, but simply state that they migrated from a place where their ancestors came out of a split stone.

The statement that the ancestors of the Tontemboan changed into two stone images can be compared with a Toradja story that their ancestors were created by sky-beings in the form of two stone images.[2] This belief, which is held by the Toradja round Lake Posso, has definite historical support : for the sky-beings did not stay among them, but went elsewhere to found chiefly houses, particularly in Bada, Besoa and Napu, the home of the so-called mountain Toradja. Certain villages of this group of Toradja possess stone images, which certainly were the work of the stone-using immigrants.[3] It may be, therefore, that the belief in an origin from a split stone is in some way due to a confusion of beliefs associated with the stone images carved by these stone-using people.

Another group of peoples, the Bontoc and other tribes of Luzon in the Philippines, who state that sky-beings came among them and gave them all their culture, but did not found a chiefly class, make considerable use of stone. They have an interesting story of origin.

Once there was a great flood, and a brother and sister were the only people left alive. They were given permission by the sky-beings to marry, and thus became the ancestors of the peoples.[4] The Toradja of Central Celebes have an origin story which states that the first pair of human beings descended from the sky. The son and daughter of this couple were given permission to marry by the sun-god. A story of a flood, and an incestuous union,

[1] Perry v. 79.   [2] Loc. cit.   [3] Ibid., 69.   [4] Ibid., 66, 96–7.

allowed by the gods, between its survivors, is told by the Mao Naga of Assam.[1]

It will be remembered that lines of chiefs claiming descent from the sky said that their ancestors were a brother and sister. We now find that peoples among whom these sky-born strangers settled, but did not found a line of chiefs, also claim descent from incestuous unions, but with this difference, that the ancestors were the survivors of a flood, and were given permission by the sky-people to unite.

It is not necessary to go into further detail. Enough has been said to show that peoples whose culture is obviously to be ascribed to an external source, preserve traditions which vary in accordance with their past history. The implantation of a chiefly house; a temporary sojourn by culture heroes; a migration after acquiring the use of stone; all have their characteristic effects. Native traditions bear witness to the desire of the present generation to maintain contact with the past. They bear witness, moreover, to the consciousness on the part of the peoples themselves that they were in no way responsible for the elaboration of their culture, or, at any rate, a considerable portion of it.

It is evident that Indonesian peoples have not retained the whole of the culture introduced by the chiefly wanderers. The crafts of agriculture and metal-working serve to illustrate this process.

The sky-born strangers brought with them the custom of cultivation by means of terraced irrigation. The following table shows a close correlation between the erection of megalithic monuments and this form of agriculture.

	Terraced Irrigation.	Megalithic Monuments.
Sumba	+	+
Roti	+	?
Kei		+
Seran		+
Halmahera		+
Bontoc ⎫ . .	+	
Igorot ⎬ Philippines .	+	
Ifugao ⎭ . . .	+	
Formosa	+	?
Minahassa	+	+
Mountain Toradja ⎫ .	+	+
Sadang Toradja ⎬ Celebes		
Dusun, Borneo . . .	+	+
Nias	+	+
Khasi, Assam . . .	+	+
Naga ,, . . .	+	+
Karen, Burma . . .	+	?

[1] Perry v. 98.

This table shows that terraced irrigation is closely associated with those parts of Indonesia where the influence of the stone-using immigrants has been strongest. Those places where the influence has obviously been weaker have failed to acquire this form of agriculture.

One of the most interesting problems is to account for the movements of the introducers of the use of stone. There seems to be little doubt that the presence of gold induced them to settle in certain places. The Children of the Sun formerly ruled over Sonabait in Timor, and dominated the whole of the island. Sonabait contains, or contained, the richest alluvial gold-workings of Timor. Gold was sacred in Timor, and therefore connected with the rulers. Mr. H. O. Forbes has described a ceremonial gold-washing in Central Timor, presided over by the chief, which leaves no room for doubt as to the association between chiefs and gold. This ceremony took place on Mt. Fatunarak, where was the most sacred stone offering-place in the kingdom. This suggests that the Children of the Sun had definite ideas about settlement. They visited Central Celebes. Heer Kruijt informed me in a letter that the distribution of metal-workings in Central Celebes coincided with that of stonework. This stonework is associated with gold; for when people visit certain memorial stones erected at a place where the Sun-lord is said to have lived for a time, they strew gold on these stones. We are told of one district, Bada by name, where these strangers settled, that gold-washing is one of the most profitable occupations of the people.

Northern Luzon of the Philippines is occupied by tribes who certainly have been largely influenced by the sky-born strangers. These tribes, the Bontoc, Ifugao and Igorot, work extensive gold and copper mines. I am informed by Mr. Robertson that, so far as he knows, the distribution of gold and copper mines in Luzon is the same as that of the immigrants.

I must mention one curious fact that I have not been able to explain. The evidence just cited suggests that the original wanderers settled in places where there was gold, with which they were associated in a magical way, and possibly also copper and iron. Two places where alluvial workings or mines would be expected are Nias and Sumba, both of which islands show strong signs of the influence of the wanderers. Both these islands are known as Islands of Gold, but I have no reason to assume that gold existed there in natural state. At the same time the name given to these islands is very significant.

The evidence concerning the use of metals in Indonesia as a whole, goes to show that the working of gold, copper, and iron was brought in by the strangers whose activities have just been considered. These people have only succeeded in implanting gold-working in places where their influence has been most notice-able. Where the influence of the strangers has been weaker, only iron-working has been retained. Other places, where the influence has been weaker still, have no metal-working at all.[1] For example, a certain group of islands, called Luang-Sermata, east of Timor, was for some reason or other particularly favoured by the stone-workers. They are said to have come there from the west, and to have brought with them the sun-cult, which was spread thence throughout the neighbouring archipelagos. The Luang-Sermata group is particularly noteworthy for its goldsmiths and ironsmiths. Other islands east of Timor, such as Wetar, have no metal-working.

These examples are enough to indicate the widespread practice of referring social institutions of the most diverse kinds to some extra-tribal source. The interest of the people appears to lie back and beyond their present setting. The dead often go back to ancestors, who live in another place, situated over the sea, or over the land. The result of migration has not, in such cases, led to a breaking of continuity between the generations. Villages owe their structure to certain people of the past, with whom con-tact is maintained through their descendants, as well as through certain material objects such as stone images. The chiefly founders of such villages made their impress upon them to such an extent that those who have come after them preserve, as faith-fully as they can, the institutions of the past. Whatever may be the aim of those alive to-day in preserving these institutions, whatever satisfaction they may derive from them, the explanation of the institutions themselves must be sought in the past. The transportation of stone from one village site to another is the sure and certain expression of the conviction that by preserving continuity between village site and village site something is to be gained. These stones are the outward and visible signs of an inward and spiritual theory. The village is a social institution. Its structure and its continuity with the past, with the ghosts of the chiefs who founded it, reveals more than the mere blind work-ings of an innate tendency of people to agglomerate themselves into groups of non-related families. The cardinal feature of the structure of such a social group is, of course, its ruling family. It did not spring out of the structure of the village itself, but, we

[1] A detailed discussion of the evidence will be found in ' The Megalithic Culture of Indonesia ', 176 e.s.

are told in all cases, it came from the outside, and brought the village into being. The explanation of the village, therefore, as a social institution, lies in the past. Fundamentally it is, in a sense, an expression of its chiefs.

The study of ruling groups of larger units, such as we call tribes or states, reveals a similar process at work. In no case is it claimed that the tribal structure was the work of the tribe itself. In all instances quoted here and, so far as I am aware, throughout the whole range of human society, with one or more exceptions, of course, peoples assert that their social institutions, from their tribal structure downwards, came to them from elsewhere.

We may, therefore, conceive of some process at work that, in all parts of the world, has given rise to societies of greater or less complexity. These societies differ from those of the food-gatherers, in possessing a more or less highly organized culture from their very inception. They do not reveal any process of evolution. On the contrary. An example cited by Mr. John Layard shows the native attitude towards this process. Speaking of the island of Vao, on the north-eastern coast of Malekula, he tells us that all the villages derive from one parent village, which is the most complicated of them all. This village was founded by a sky-being named Tagar, obviously a member of the great sky-family who ranged so far throughout the Pacific. This village is said to be the only one that is ' straight ', that is to say, perfectly organized. At the beginning of Samoan history we likewise have a more complicated condition of affairs than later on. The organization of the colonies in Savai'i, Upolu and Tutuila shows a progressive simplification of the original complexity of the settlements of the Children of the Sun in Manu'a. For the Samoans, as for the people of Malekula, the most exalted form of human society was at the beginning. As in the case of the Australians, the peoples of Celebes, Luzon and Samoa, and Malekula, the beginnings were due to the sudden appearance of a complicated form of civilization which provided cultural capital. This capital almost immediately begins to crumble away, and is not replaced. The Children of the Sun disappear from Central Celebes, Luzon, Samoa and Malekula, never to return. The people of these places are incapable of replacing the loss. They have come into possession of something that they do not properly understand. They have only imperfectly comprehended the teaching of their sky-born overlords, but they are anxious to remember, in every possible way, how they acquired their institutions. The past alone gives them stability.

CHAPTER XIV

SOCIAL UNITY

THE series of beliefs and practices discussed in the last chapter were associated both with individuals and social groupings. It was found that social groupings were formed at some time in the past, and owed their persistence to a desire to maintain contact with the past. The social groupings involved may be arranged in a kind of hierarchy. We may speak, in considering the life of any given community, of simple families, of larger groups of kindred, of clans, of moieties, and other minor groups, as well as of tribes and states. The family groupings, as we have already seen, do not come under the heading of social institutions. The larger groupings, clans, moieties and so forth, are social institutions. They have a definite meaning in the society which possesses them. They embody a theory, they have a personality of their own.

In setting out to try to understand the ultimate meaning of these social groupings, it is as well to repeat that there is probably no inherent necessity in any of them. We have failed to find anything but simple family groupings among the food-gatherers as a whole. In this they differ profoundly from the majority of food-producers. Is there any inherent reason for this contrast ? Does it necessarily follow that human beings, once practising agriculture and the domestication of animals, should inaugurate clans, moieties, age-grades, and so forth ? It does not appear to be so. Consider the Toradja people of Central Celebes. They are, as we have seen, divided into various groups, based on a geographical scheme. So we speak of the Lake Posso Toradja, the Mountain Toradja, and the Sadang Toradja, in addition to others. Confining ourselves to the Lake Posso Toradja, we find ourselves confronted with a democratic society, whose social relationships are based entirely upon kinship. There is no trace among them of any attempt to form a complicated tribal organization with social classes. They are agriculturalists, who also rear buffaloes ; they live in well-built houses ; they are metal-workers ; they wear clothes of bark-cloth ; they make baskets. They therefore possess a complicated form of culture. But they have no trace of any comprehensive tribal organization. The villages are small and consist of groups of relatives. These are grouped together into small ' tribes ', consisting always of people related to one another. No traces are to be found of a wider organization. These villages and tribes have been formed by a continuous process of budding-off, village giving rise to village. Yet all the ' tribes ' remember that their ancestors were once grouped together at Pamona, a village on the banks of Lake Posso, where important events happened in the past. This grouping by relationship is the only one that plays any part in warfare.[1] Therefore it is possible for a people to have acquired a fair degree of culture and to remain simple in their social organization.

The Bontoc of Luzon in the Philippines illustrate the same principle, but with the difference that they have a somewhat more elaborate grouping than the Toradja of Lake Posso. They have several villages, but there is no central organization for the people as a whole. The village consists of a number of independent groups, based, it would seem, entirely upon kinship, and not subordinated to any superior authority. Each of these groups manages its own affairs by means of a council of old men. This council is self-elective, invitations being issued to those who are considered by the existing council to be mature enough to join it.[2] There is no corresponding body for the village as a whole. The Bontoc lack the office of head-man found among other tribes of northern Luzon. Their social organization is, in fact, simple to a degree. ' The Bontoc Igorot has not even a clan organization, to say nothing of a tribal organization. I fail to find a trace of matriarchy or patriarchy, or any mark of a kinship group which traces relationship farther than first cousins.'[3]

This simplicity of social organization is the more remarkable when it is remembered that the Bontoc are remarkably high in culture. They are skilful agriculturalists, who construct terraces up the sides of their mountains, and irrigate them by water brought by canals, often from a long distance. They grow rice on these terraces. They build good houses, they make pottery and baskets, they work iron, they weave. They are, in fact, highly civilized, and yet their social organization is simple.

These two peoples, the Toradja and the Bontoc, evidently have little notion of social unity, so far as political organization is concerned.

The statement concerning the limitation of the Bontoc of Luzon as regards kinship is illuminating. It shows how confined is the

[1] Kruyt ii. I. 117 e.s.   [2] Jenks 32–3, 49, 166.   [3] *Ibid.*, 167.

12

acquaintance of the average savage with his fellows. The Bontoc man evidently does not find it necessary to remember vast genealogical tables—he only remembers in a limited circle of kinship.

This limitation of knowledge of relationship is not surprising in the case of the Bontoc and other peoples who lack more complicated social groupings. But it is disturbing, at first sight, to encounter a like limitation among peoples with, say, the clan organization. Such a limitation occurs among the tribes of the Transkei Territory of South Africa. I collected a number of genealogical trees from members of the Tembu, Fingo, Pondo and other tribes, as well as the Bakwena Basuto of East Griqualand.

All these tribes have a clan organization involving the belief in a common ancestry. Marriage is theoretically forbidden between clan members for this reason.

These peoples are all strongly patrilineal, so that they have little to do with their mother's family. All my informants knew the names of their father's brothers and sisters, and their families. Some of them knew the names of their father's father, but usually no more of that generation on the male side. They knew practically nothing about their mother's brothers and sisters, and still less about their mother's parents and their families.

The sole exception was a Basuto, Joseph Phaaroe, who traced back his descent in the male line for several generations, until it reached an ancestor who belonged to the ruling family.

This limitation of knowledge of kindred reflects the narrowness of the lives of these peoples. Each child is brought up in its father's kraal, and does not habitually associate with its maternal relatives.

Dr. Paul Radin makes a similar comment as regards the Winnebago tribe. There are a number of clans, associated with animals. Dr. Radin says that the clan was called ' those-who-are-relatives-to-one-another '. Nevertheless, kinship was only reckoned to four, or even three, generations.[1]

These examples show that a definite gap may exist between the family and the clan. All members of the clan are technically related, and yet the ordinary member of the clan cannot demonstrate that relationship. That is to say, the members of a clan may bear to each other a dual relationship, based partly on real kinship, and partly on a fictitious kinship that, nevertheless, is bound up with the actual family, in that membership of the clan descends through one of the parents.

It is agreed that the family is based on innate tendencies of

[1] Radin i. 27–8.

a general character. Family life is the common experience of humanity. But when we consider such an institution as the clan, which is not universal in human society, and also possesses characteristics not directly attributable to the family group, it is obvious that we are dealing with a specific social phenomenon. The clan must be the result of experience of a particular group or groups, and not of the working of generalized impulses characteristic of all mankind.[1]

In attempting to understand the social hierarchy of tribes, etc., we are thus met at the outset with a gap that will have to be bridged. This gap recalls that revealed, in the last chapter, between the village and its constituent families in many parts of Indonesia. We found there that a complicated grouping of social institutions clustered round the village itself, and had no direct association with the individual families living in it. In such cases the ceremonial of the village was carried on by members of the chiefly family who were descended from the founders of the village. That is to say, there was a gap between the ruling group and the rest of the village. This gap, as we have already seen, was still more complete after death; for these sky-descended rulers went to the sky at death, while the ordinary folk went to an underworld, or to the mountains.

The social unity of the village, in the places under consideration, therefore consists of a number of social institutions carried down from generation to generation through a chiefly family. This suggests that the ordinary people may be left on one side so far as the inception of social institutions such as we have just studied is concerned. We have to deal with isolated family groups that have become superposed on other family groups. These special family groups are the product of a social process yet to be defined.

A similar conclusion is suggested by the study of peoples with complicated organization of tribe, moiety, clan, age-grade, and so forth.

An example may be taken from the great Siouan group of tribes of the United States, which includes the Dakota, Assiniboin, Omaha, Ponca, Osage, Kansas, Kwapa, Iowa, Oto, Missouri, Winnebago, Mandan, Hidatsa, Crow, Tutelo, Biloxi, Catawba, and Sapona. All these tribes are allied in language, and possess cultures so similar that their derivation from a common source cannot be doubted.[2]

[1] I gather from his remarks in 'Man' 1930, 17, that Professor Malinowski would agree with this statement, and not with that of his pupil Dr. Richards, which asserts that ' the clan grows out of the family '. Op. cit., 180.

[2] Fletcher and la Flèsche 34–5.

A beginning may be made with the Winnebago. This tribe is divided into two divisions : ' those who are above ', connected with the sky ; and ' those who are on earth ', connected with the earth.[1] These divisions play an important part in the life of the tribe, in connexion, for instance, with marriage, funeral ceremonies, ball games, feasts, war, and village organization. Each division has to marry into the other.[2]

Each dual division of the Winnebago has certain subdivisions, in the form of clans. The Sky division is divided into Thunder-bird, War-people, Eagle and Pigeon clans. The Earth division is divided into Bear, Wolf, Water-spirit, Deer, Elk, Buffalo, Fish and Snake clans.[3] These divisions form an integral part of the ceremonial life of the tribe. The Thunder-bird is the chief clan, and in addition to the fact that the chief of the tribe is selected from it, has important functions connected with the preservation of peace. The Warrior clan has functions connected with war ; the Bear clan, those relating to policeing and discipline, both within the village and while on the hunt ; the Buffalo clan, those relating to the office of public crier and intermediary between the chief and his people. The Wolf, Water-spirit, and Elk clans seem also to have possessed minor political-social functions. Thus the Wolf people are regarded as ' minor ' soldiers ; the Water-spirit people are connected with the passage of streams, etc. ; and the Elk are connected with the care of the fire-places while on the hunt and warpath.[4]

The Omaha, who also had the dual organization, had a tribal camping circle in connexion with the annual tribal buffalo hunt. At night the tribe camped in a circle opening to the east. The Sky part of the tribe camped to the north of the circle, and the Earth part to the south.

The southern portion of the tribe, consisting of five clans, had charge of the physical welfare of the people. The Elk clan had charge of the Sacred Tent of War and its duties, and also of the rites connected with the first thunder of the spring. The other four clans were charged with duties and rites connected with the food supply, and were under the direction of the Honga, the ' leader ' or ' first ' clan. This clan had charge of the two sacred tents. One contained the White Buffalo Hide, the keeper of which conducted the rites attending the planting of maize and the hunting of the buffalo. The other tent contained the Sacred Pole. Its keepers were the custodians of the rites concerned with the maintenance of the authority of the chiefs in the government

---

[1] Radin i. 185.   [2] Ibid., 187–9.   [3] Ibid., 190–1.
[4] Ibid., 200.

of the tribe. This half of the tribe, in short, was supposed to look after protection from without, the preservation of peace within the tribe, and the obtaining of food and clothing.

The clans of the ' sky ' side of the tribe, on the other hand, were ' the custodians of the rites that related to the creation, the stars, the manifestations of the cosmic forces that pertain to life '. Most of these rites have become obsolete, except those by which the child was inducted into its place and duty in the tribe ; and the ritual required when the two tribal pipes were filled for use on solemn tribal occasions.[1]

The examples just quoted show that the moiety and the clan are not independent groupings, but are constituent parts of the wider unity, the tribe. Each moiety and each clan has its individuality ; but that does not permit us to study it in isolation.

There is no reason to assume that these minor groupings have given rise to the tribe ; on the contrary, the available evidence suggests that the members of each tribe are unaware of the real origin and meaning of their tribal organization.

The Siouan tribes of the Plains are all convinced of the importance and necessity of their dual divisions, but there is a diversity of interpretation of the meaning of the moieties. They are named Sky people and Leaders ; Thunder and Earth ; Sky and Earth ; Right and Left Hand, while some of the tribes have no names for them.[2] The fact that these tribes differ in their interpretation of a common feature of their social organization shows that the original nature of the tribal unity has become partially obscured. The organization has become largely traditional, it has deviated from its original form and has lost its original meaning.

The clan organization, in like manner, varies from tribe to tribe. Each tribe of the group under examination has its moieties divided up into clans. As we have seen, clans of each moiety have characteristics consonant with that of the moiety ; and each clan of a moiety has its own characteristics. The number of clans in a tribe is not constant ; nor are their emblems. It is only possible to state that the clan is an essential part of the structure of certain tribes. This does not mean, of course, that the tribe cannot persist should it lose one or more of its clans. The Omaha have lost certain clans, and yet still exist as a tribe. It simply means that the clan organization is traditional, and is preserved as far as is possible.

An instance of this kind is provided by the Huron tribe, who have a tradition that the chiefs originally chose names for the

[1] Fletcher and la Flèsche 194–5. [2] Radin i. 181.

clans of the two sides of the tribe.[1] They were re-constituting, to the best of their endeavour, the traditional tribal organization.

The Omaha, as we have seen, lost some of their rites, and have not replaced them. They formerly had hereditary chiefs, but have lost them, and have to be content with elected chiefs.

These facts concerning chiefs, moieties, and clans all point to the same conclusion; namely, that the organization of these tribes is, to a great extent at least, if not wholly, traditional. Once the hereditary chiefs have gone, the tribe has to be content with elected chiefs; once certain rites have died out, they are lost for ever. The original organization of the Siouan tribes can now only be inferred. Were these social institutions an inevitable product of human society, were they produced to satisfy immediate social needs, we should expect something more constructive in the attitude of the tribes towards them.

This conclusion agrees with that derived from the study of ordinary family groupings, namely, that the clan and moiety organization was superposed upon groups of families, and not evolved independently.

The tribe therefore may be looked upon as a complicated social institution, incorporating an indefinite number of subsidiary institutions. It is a hierarchy, comprising individual families, as well as other groups such as we have already studied.

The tribe has many aspects—territorial, linguistic, ceremonial and so forth. Which of the social institutions it comprises expresses this unity most completely? There is little doubt that tribal unity is most closely bound up with the kingship. The king is the high-priest of the state, who carries on the cult of his divine ancestors, the gods, on behalf of the people as a whole.

The Chinese and Peruvians expressed the relationship between the kingship and the state by calling the kings and queens 'fathers' and 'mothers' of their subjects. This of course is not strictly true, but it may be nearer the truth than appears at first sight.

Let us consider how far the social hierarchy of the state or tribe can be expressed in terms of kinship, how far the king can really be regarded as the 'father' of his people.

We may begin with the clan organization. We have already seen that there is a gap between the clan kinship and the actual genealogical knowledge of its individual members. What is the real reason why members of a clan claim a relationship with all other members of the clan, even when they cannot prove it?

[1] Barbeau 82–9.

This difficulty is partly removed when we realize that clans are often grouped round a family of hereditary chiefs, who represent it in the wider political and ceremonial life of the tribe.

Lewis H. Morgan shows that this is so in North America. He states that those Indian tribes of North America that possess the clan system usually have hereditary chiefs in each clan. These hereditary clan chiefs form the tribal council. Thus the clans of the Plains Indians of North America resemble the villages of Indonesia, in that they form political and ceremonial units centred round certain families that provided the rulers.[1]

If we agree that clans should have hereditary chiefs, a further difficulty arises. A clan cannot be isolated; it is always associated with other clans, more or less independently, as part of a tribe. That leaves us to explain how the hereditary kingship became associated with a hereditary nobility of clan-chiefs.

We are told that in Aana, a district of Upolu, one of the islands of the Samoan group, the most important council chiefs, who were said to be the heads of clans, were often connected by marriage with the ruler of the district.[2]

This suggests that the fundamental form of social structure of tribes and states was one in which the nobility was derived from the royal family itself; that is to say, the ruling function was in the hands of a group of relatives.

The study of the hereditary ruling families of Japan suggests the same conclusions. We have seen that their Ujis (hereditary groups) were ruled over by hereditary chiefs.

We have seen likewise that the five followers of Ninigi, the descendant of the sun-goddess, were the ancestors of the great hereditary corporations. We are told, further, that Ninigi and these five Kami, as they were called, traced their ancestry back to the primal trinity comprising the Central Master, who was the ancestor of the rulers, and the two constructive chiefs, who gave rise to the noble and official classes.

We may go further, as is shown by the following quotation. ' Further, they hold that whereas Ninigi and his five adjunct *Kami* all traced their lineage to the two producing *Kami* of the primal trinity, the special title of sovereignty conferred originally on the sun-goddess was transmitted by her to the *Tenson* (heavenly grandchild), Ninigi, the distinction of ruler and ruled being thus clearly defined. Finally they hold that Ninigi and these five adjunct *Kami*, though occupying different places in the national

---

[1] See Perry vi. 352. Much more evidence on this point will be found in Chaps. XXI and XXII of ' The Children of the Sun '.

[2] Perry vi. 348.

polity, had a common ancestor whom they jointly worshipped, thus forming an eternal union.' [1]

If we go back for a moment to the Pondo of South Africa, it may be possible to illustrate the nature of this process. The Pondo, we found, have a chiefly group superimposed upon the mass of the people. Kraals split off from kraals, as the population increases ; this is true both of chiefs and commoners. Jobs must be found for younger sons of chiefs. New local groupings arise ; the commoners contribute themselves, so to speak, while the chiefs control the ceremonial organization. For instance, any one may give a beer-drink at any time, but this has to be subject to the permission of the local chief. The government of the Bakwena Basuto of East Griqualand in South Africa is based on this principle. The ruling chief is Jeremiah Moshesh, a member of the royal family of Basutoland proper. He carries on the administration of his territory with the aid of his numerous relatives. This great family group fill most of the administrative posts except that of head-man.

The case of Egypt may be cited in this connexion. The royal family had the whole of the administration of the country in its hands from the earliest historical times to the beginning of the Fifth Dynasty. The country was divided into divisions that bear a strong resemblance to the clans of the tribes already studied. Each Nome had its characteristic emblem, its characteristic ceremonial, and its own ruler. These rulers became somewhat independent at the end of the Fourth Dynasty, and made their offices hereditary.

It is therefore possible to argue that the social hierarchy of rank and office has in many parts of the world developed out an administration carried on by groups of relatives. We can watch the process of the family principle breaking down, so that the ruler has to deal with a hereditary nobility ; but we do not meet with the opposite process often, if at all. It is significant that the earliest ruling family known to us, that of Egypt, should display such a complete dominance of all aspects of the state.

This topic will be discussed in later chapters, for example in that entitled ' The Age of the Gods '.

The tribe or state is a social institution. The ruling group of any community is the first approximation to the expression of its unity.

The ruling group is something more than a family. It is a connecting-link between men and gods. The kingship is associated

---

[1] Brinkley 33.

with the community of divine beings, usually living in a sky-world, from whom the community acquired their initial store of culture. We have seen how societies endeavour to maintain intact the traditional lore that they acquired from this source. That is to say, the earthly society seemingly has to be interpreted through the heavenly society.

Japan provides an excellent example of this process. It will be remembered that an account was given, in the chapter on ' The Family ' (see p. 75), of the five great hereditary corporations : the Nakatomi, the Imbe, the Sarume, the Otomo, and the Kumebe. These five great families were descended from Koyane, Futodama, Usume, Oshihi and Kume, who were associated with Ninigi, the ancestor of the royal family, when he conquered Japan and founded the dynasty.

These five attendants consisted of four men and a woman (Usume). They were sent by Amaterasu, the sun-goddess, and ancestress of Ninigi, and were ordered to discharge at his Court the same duties as those which they had performed in the country of their origin.[1]

It must be remembered, however, that this heavenly source of culture is not always apparent in the beliefs of peoples. We have found, for example, that certain tribes that lack hereditary rulers only know that their ancestors came from elsewhere (see p. 154). There is no reasonable doubt that they originally received their culture from a group of sky-born rulers ; but that has all been forgotten. Their beliefs concerning origins are but fragments of what they must formerly have possessed. For the present purpose, tribes such as these may be left on one side.

The account given of the grouping of the Lake Posso Toradja of Central Celebes is interesting in this connexion. These people have no social hierarchy—they are not ruled over by chiefs. At the same time, however, they retain the memory of the sojourn of a sky-born culture-hero who lived at Pamona on Lake Posso. The account given at the beginning of the chapter mentions only families and small ' tribes ' consisting of relatives.

These so-called ' tribes ' place their ancestral home at Pamona, the spot where Lasaeo, the sun-lord, lived. That is to say, the ' tribal ' grouping of the Toradja is the result of a social experience at some time in the past.

The Toradja and the Bontoc, quoted at the beginning of this chapter, both lack a definite social hierarchy, and both have received their culture from beings of the sky-world, who would

[1] Op. cit., 98.

be expected to have left descendants to rule. In neither case have they done so, and the reason given is interesting.

The sons of Lasaeo went elsewhere to rule, and the people likewise migrated and erected seven stones in memory of the event.

The Bontoc culture-hero had sons. They were killed, and thus no line of chiefs was established.

A wide survey of origin stories, particularly those connected with sky-beings, reveals signs of a fundamental unity.

The existence of a fundamental unity of mythology has struck many observers. They agree upon the fact of unity, but differ as to its nature. The tendency has been to choose out a certain theme to express this unity. The key to all mythologies has taken the form of symbolism connected with the sun, with phallic ideas, the serpent, the pole-star, the moon, not to mention the typical symbols of the psycho-analyst. The similarities between mythologies of all sources are so great that the phrase ' the similarity of the working of the human mind ' has been invented to account for them. These interpretations all suffer from the weakness inherent in simplifications. While it stands beyond any reasonable doubt that mythology is specific in nature, it is at the same time extremely complicated. It contains solar, lunar, phallic, and other ideas, often intricately woven together.

This common agreement as to the fundamental unity of mythology, makes it necessary to endeavour to detect the underlying process of which it is the expression. Mythology is a social institution ; [1] it therefore presumably has an inner core of fact and theory, of which its various features are but the expression.

If a survey be made of origin stories, it is often found that the history of a tribe begins with an act of creation. The story usually runs as follows :

In the beginning inhabited land did not exist ; there was only a world in the sky, with an expanse of water beneath it. The community in the sky decided to make habitable land. They caused one of their number to produce land from the bottom of the ocean. They then sent down some of their number to people the earth. They provided them with plants and animals on which to live ; they gave them all their different social institutions, among them certain ceremonials.

That is the story in its bare outlines. In one or other of its

---

[1] Malinowski argues this theme in his ' Myth in Primitive Psychology '.

versions, this creation story is possessed by the vast majority of
the mythologies of North America ; it is widespread in Polynesia
and Melanesia ; it is found in Japan and in many parts of north-
east Asia ; it occurs in the sacred books of India and Babylonia,
not to speak of West Africa and Europe.[1]

This story has many versions. The Japanese, for example,
say that Izanagi and Izanami, brother and sister, were commanded
by the gods to create firm land. They stood on the bridge of
heaven and fished about in the waters beneath, ultimately bringing
up the island of Onogoro. There they lived, and all the other
islands were born to them as children.[2]

These stories, with their fundamental similarity, serve to link
together vast chains of human societies. They serve to establish,
more or less loosely, the fundamental unity of mythology throughout the world. It will be useful, before passing on, to glance for
a moment at this interesting creation story. We are confronted
in it with a situation that certainly does not belong to normal
human experience. It is not unreasonable for any man to dismiss
the incidents contained in these stories as entirely fanciful, or at
least as a gross perversion of actual happenings. The mere fact,
however, that so many peoples have found it necessary to preserve
such a story among their most treasured possessions demands our
respect. There is certainly some unifying process at work, and
this process must be understood before we can hope to understand
such social institutions as the sky-born kingship, tribal organization, and, above all, ceremonial activities.

I have chosen a central incident of this characteristic origin
story as the title of this book. The term The Primordial Ocean
thus stands as an expression of the essential unity of culture
throughout the ages. This theme of cultural unity will be
developed systematically in the chapters that are to follow. The
meaning of the term will become evident in due course.

The discussion on which we are at present engaged is part of
the general examination of the theory of the Social Institution.
The study of the beliefs and practices of mankind shows them
to contain both concrete and abstract elements. For example,

[1] Lowie in his ' Primitive Religion ', p. 180, mentions ' the remarkable
recurrence among the Chukchi, Yukaghir, Mongolic, Turkic, and Finnic
tribes of the widespread North American " earth diver " motive, viz. the
diving into water for mud from which the earth is created '. He could have
added Japan (Aston 87), India (Satapatha-Brahmana, in the Introduction
to the great ' Ritual of the Fire Altar ' (see pp. 222–4 of this book), as well as
Egypt (see p. 250).
[2] Aston 87.

certain tribes of Assam assert that their ancestors emerged from a stone in a given place.   This stone is a concrete enough object ; but the act of emergence is irrational.   That is to say, the tradition of origin of these tribes appears to be partly historical and partly fictitious.   Again, we have found that many villages of Indonesia have a hereditary priest who is in charge of the sacred stones of the village.   These stones, or stone images, are supposed to be tenanted, temporarily at least, by the ghosts of his ancestors, the founders of the village.   This situation, again, contains both concrete and abstract elements.   The priesthood is concrete enough, and so are the stone images ;   but the ghosts of his ancestors are objects of belief, not of demonstration.   Their occupation of the stone images is purely imaginative, and it is usually the outcome of a ritual performance.

It must be noted that beliefs such as these vary in their degree of concreteness.   For if we arrange, wherever possible, origin stories in historical sequence, we find them becoming increasingly logical and concrete, as we go back in the past.   In the group of beliefs discussed in the last chapter, we find that the belief in an origin from a split stone is probably a traditional misunderstanding of beliefs connected with carved stone images made by certain people who brought the use of stone to the archipelago.   The beliefs held by chiefs descended from these strangers are still more concrete.   These chiefs claim to have been descended from a brother and sister.   This belief, as we saw, was probably correct.[1] It is concrete in so far as the ancestors were a man and a woman. Its concreteness is not complete ;   for we are not told why the union should have been incestuous.

Another example of the interaction between the concrete and the abstract is furnished by the belief concerning the home of the dead.   We have seen that the home of the dead is often situated in some other place, sometimes across the sea.   This place is the traditional home of the ancestors, and is therefore real enough.   But once again, why should it be considered necessary to go back to this home ?   The father of a Pondo kraal sleeps his long sleep in a grave just outside the entrance to his cattle kraal. His ghost watches over his descendants ;   it has nothing to do with his remote ancestors.   Given the belief in a ghost, the Pondo belief is in a more concrete social setting than the Indonesian belief in a journey to the land of the dead.

We have therefore to ask ourselves why certain social situations should be chosen out for special attention.   Why do certain chiefs practise marriage between brother and sister, and do not

[1] See pp. 76, 158.

leave their marital unions to chance ? We must ask ourselves why there is such an interest in an origin from a certain split stone ; why the dead should necessarily go back somewhere else. We must inquire why concrete and abstract ideas are found intermingled.

CHAPTER XV

THE GETTING OF LIFE

ENOUGH has been said to show that people in all stages of culture try to maintain continuity with the past. The individual returns to his ancestors when he dies. Village priests are descended from the founders of villages. Tribes were founded in the past by gods or by culture-heroes. Ruling groups trace their ancestry back to the past. All this points to a continuous process running down through the generations, knitting past and present together into one continuous whole.

We must now inquire into the meaning of this desire to maintain continuity with the past. In searching for the reasons for this great interest in the past it will be useful to begin with the initiated priesthood of the Lake Posso Toradja of Celebes. This priesthood constitutes what was left after the departure of the sky-born rulers from the Posso Toradja to found ruling houses elsewhere. This priesthood is concerned with the cure of disease, the building of houses, the burial of the dead, and agriculture. Its craft was taught by the beings of the sky-world, that is to say, by some external agency.[1] The Toradja believe that each person is animated by something which we may call his 'life'. They are rather vague as to its nature. Some of them identify it with the breath. Others say they do not know. But they possess a creation story which makes it quite clear that originally life was the breath. This story tells how the sky-people, whom we should term 'gods', made two stone images, of a man and a woman. They went back to the sky to get the breath of eternal life to animate these images. A wind blew while they were absent, and animated the images, but they were mortal instead of immortal. This suggests that 'life' was originally the breath. It also shows that the Toradja attribute to the sky-beings the power of bestowing immortality. More has to be said on this topic later on [2] (see p. 225).

The sky-beings of the Toradja have a direct relationship to each member of the tribe. It is believed that the sun-god has a smithy up in the sky in which he fashions each child, and then

[1] Perry v. 144 e.s.   [2] *Ibid.*, Chap. XIX, 79, 152.

places it in its mother to be born, but I am not aware that it is said that the breath of life is imparted to each child.[1] The belief in Nias, an island west of Sumatra, is that the ' breath of life ' is given at birth to each child by a sky-being who lives in the sun. It returns to the sky at death.[2] We can therefore assume confidently that the Toradja ' life ' is the breath.

When a Toradja falls ill he is thought to have had his life abstracted. The possible agencies are evil spirits, ghosts of the dead, and sky-beings, or gods, as we usually call them. It is the business of the priestess to determine which of these three groups is responsible, and to act accordingly. She is able to recover the life from evil spirits or the ghosts of the dead, and so can always cure the disease when caused by these agents. When the sky-gods have abstracted the life, she is not so competent to cure. She goes up to the sky in a trance, accompanied by her familiar sky-spirit, and asks the sky-god for a return of the life. If he consents, she returns to earth with it, and the patient recovers. If he refuses, the patient dies, and the life remains on high.[3]

The motive for the retention of the initiated priesthood is therefore clear. The Toradja possess the theory that the sky-people have the gift of life. It is a theory which naturally would arouse the interest of everybody, for it appeals to the fundamental, innate tendency to preserve life by all possible means. That interest is not in itself enough to cause the acceptance of any theory of life. It must have been embodied in such a form as to carry conviction to those who had nothing to do with its formulation. The initiated priesthood of Indonesian peoples, such as we find it in Celebes and Borneo, is also concerned with funeral ceremonies. We have already found that the Toradja priestesses learned their craft from the people of the sky-world. These priestesses conduct the ghost to the land of the dead. It would therefore appear that these sky-people have also introduced certain theories respecting life after death, seeing that they taught the priestesses the way to the home of the forefathers. This suggests an explanation of certain instances already considered, in which the dead, instead of going underground, go across the sea, up a river, or over land, to their ancestral home.[4] The explanation may be that migrations may have broken the connexions with the sky-world, thus necessitating a return to the original home in order to regain contact with the source of life.

An example will illustrate my meaning. Certain Australian peoples, such as the Urabunna, have a belief in spirit children.

---

[1] *Ibid.*, vi. 207. [2] *Ibid.*, v. 152. [3] *Ibid.*, 151.
[4] See p. 153.

They believe that the people to whom they owe all their social organization made a certain number of spirit children, of which each member of the tribe is a reincarnation. The process is as follows. When any one dies he goes back in spirit form to a certain spot whence the original spirit child came. He there awaits the passing by of a woman who is entitled by the rules of their social organization to become his mother.[1] In this way there is a perpetual coming and going throughout the generations of spirit children to and from certain spots where life was first given to the tribe.

If this case be applied to those already cited in Indonesia, it will appear that the dead are returning back to the place where they can become individuals again, where they can be reborn on earth. This surmise is supported by the Toradja belief that the sky-god, already mentioned, makes each child and places it in its mother. This sky-god therefore corresponds to the people of old in Australia who made the spirit children. So those who migrated from this spot where the original sky-people lived may have become cut off from the source of life, and consequently return there after death, guided by the priestesses who have learnt the way from the sky-people themselves.

A great amount of information exists to show that the sky-world and its denizens are believed to be the supreme sources of life to men. This statement may be made without hesitation in respect of those communities who believe they were created by the act of sky-beings. 'The Children of the Sun' contains in Chapter XIV, entitled 'Sky-gods as Life-givers', a mass of information on this topic. We have already seen that new-born babes are animated by breath from the sky. Sky-gods also make the child and place it in its mother. The breath of life by which it is animated returns at death to the sky-world. Therefore, in some instances at least, individuals, as well as communities as a whole, owe their being to the gods in the sky.

One feature of the relations between the sky-world and the earth must be considered, namely, the priesthood. It will be remembered that the Toradja priesthood which acted as a link between the earth and the sky was not hereditary, and that its personnel was feminine. This priesthood depended upon knowledge acquired from the sky-world, for the first priestess was taken up there to learn her craft.

Communities that have derived their culture from the sky-world usually possess hereditary priesthoods. The king or the tribal chief usually acts as high-priest. He carries on rituals that were

[1] Spencer and Gillen 145–7.

handed down from the sky-world to the earth. In the case of a
king acting as high-priest, the ceremonial is carried out on behalf
of the tribe as a whole, as well as for the king's ancestors.

The essential characteristic of ritual is its abstract basis. We
apply manure to a land with the knowledge that, provided the
manure be suitable, the crops will benefit. We can prove that
they will. That is a purely practical act, resting on an objective
basis. If, on the other hand, we were to slaughter a sacred
animal, or a human being, and sprinkle some of the blood on part
of a field, in the belief that the crop would benefit, we should
be performing a ritual. (I refer, of course, in this case, to the
ceremonial sprinkling of a few drops of blood, not to the systematic
drenching of the ground with blood.) This action may be termed
' abstract ', for it bears no direct relation to reality, as it can easily
be proved to have no practical value in the raising of crops. In
this case the ritual itself fills in the gap between the intention
and its fulfilment.

One essential characteristic of ritual is the necessity of learning
it correctly. Its performance is of real or pretended use to society ;
but only certain members of that society are entitled to procure
those benefits. They usually have to undergo some process of
initiation, as a result of which they are enabled to perform their
allotted part.

Rituals are associated with all manner of social situations.
Agriculture and other food-getting activities, house building,
boat building, and many other industrial activities have, in part
at least, a ritualistic character. The disposal of the dead and the
treatment of disease are also based on ritual. That is to say,
many social situations have certain abstract characteristics that
are held to be an essential part of them.

Rituals are of many forms, but in general they conform to a
type. The more complicated are usually carried out by important
priestly corporations. A special ceremonial area or building is
set aside for the purpose. This ranges from a temple, as in India,
to a space marked out on the ground, as in Australia. The
various groups of participants in the ritual, usually priests, generally arrange themselves in particular groupings within this building. In addition to the king or high-priest, who represent the
state as a whole, there may be, as we have seen, minor priests
representing constituent parts of the state or tribe. These priests
are often supposed to represent gods, or evil spirits, or perhaps
the ghosts of the dead ; and they are sometimes dressed to represent their parts. In any case they usually wear a special dress,
of prescribed colour and ornamentation.

13

Rituals include dances, processions, songs, and invocations. Certain material objects are used : food, water, paints, plants, animals, and so forth. All these items go to make up the combined whole. Their meaning and use are usually only known in detail by the priests themselves. They learn it through their process of initiation. The ritual as a whole is a complex dramatic performance, concerned with the doings of the gods or of the ghosts of ancestors.

These dramatic performances are not an end in themselves. They are complicated religious acts, performed on behalf of the community. They bring the world of gods to earth, so to speak. They perpetuate happenings of long ago. They are supposed to be of direct benefit. Concerned, as many of them are, with the doings of sky-gods, their aim can be easily guessed. These sky-beings, as we have seen, are the creators, the givers of life, and the founders of ruling houses and priesthoods. These life-giving attributes ascribed to sky-beings, suggest that the rituals, with their dramatic performances, are the means whereby earthly communities gain life from the sky.

It would appear that these dramatic performances are essential for that purpose. They are, it might be termed, ' life-giving situations '. Their aim would seem to be to fill in the gap between abstract and concrete. They constitute, as it were, the vehicle for obtaining benefits not immediately derivable from concrete experience.

It is not necessary to speculate on these matters. It is only necessary to examine any ritual, taken at random. I have chosen for this purpose the Hako ceremony of the Pawnee Indians of Nebraska, studied in detail by Miss Alice Fletcher.[1] One reason for choosing it lies in the detailed priestly commentary that reveals the attitude of the Pawnee themselves towards it.

The main theme of the Hako is the establishment of relations between a group of people, called the Father, led by a chief, called the Father, and another group of people, called the Son, led by another chief, called the Son. The Father group journey to the place where the Son group live. They there hand on ' life ' to the Son, in the person of a little child.

The Hako ceremony is performed in a ceremonial lodge of a particular plan. Paraphernalia of various kinds are used. There are also songs and dances, and invocations and certain dramatic performances. Every item of this ritual, whether the spoken word, the gesture, the paraphernalia, the setting of the ceremonial lodge, or whatever it may be, has a bearing on the

[1] Fletcher i.

central theme of the ritual. Everything is intended to procure the ' breath of life ' from the creator, Tirawa, who lives in the world beyond the sky. This breath does not come down to earth directly from Tirawa, but through one or other of the beings associated with him. For example, the sun is not regarded as an original source of life ; it merely transmits the breath of life from Tirawa, the creator, to earth. Again, the earth gets the power of giving life from the creator. As the priest says, ' All the powers that are in heaven and all those that are upon the earth are derived from the mighty power Tirawa. He is the father of all things visible and invisible. He is the father of all the powers represented by the Hako. He is the father of all the lesser powers, those which can approach man. He is the father of all the people, and perpetuates the life of the tribe through the gift of children.' [1] . . . ' It is he who sends help to us by these lesser powers, because they alone can come to us so that we can see and feel them.' [2]

The ceremony is divided up into a number of distinct rituals, each forming an integral part of the whole. These rituals, which have a symbolical meaning, must be performed in a prescribed manner. The knowledge of the ceremonial is explicitly stated by the priests to have come down from the sky by means of visions. None of the songs of this ceremony can be changed. They must be sung accurately, just as they have been handed down. For the words speak of the powers above and their gifts to men, who must be careful of such words. The priest has received these teachings from older priests, who also received them, and so on through generations back to the time when they were revealed to the fathers through a vision from the mysterious powers above.[3]

Much of the early part of the ceremonial consists of the preparation of the necessary paraphernalia. The Hako required first of all two feathered stems of ash wood, rounded and smoothed, and hollowed as with pipe-stems to allow the breath to pass. One of these was supposed to be dark and the other light. The other requirements were an ear of white corn, two small round straight sticks from a plum tree, a crotched stick of the plum tree, feathers from the tail of an owl and from the wings and tail of an eagle, the heads of two woodpeckers, the head, neck and breast of two ducks, a wildcat skin, a shell, two wooden bowls, a braid of buffalo hair, a braid of sweet grass, blue, green and red clay, deer or buffalo fat, the nest of an oriole.[4] All these articles, together with the garments and regalia worn by the performers,

[1] *Ibid.*, 107. [2] *Ibid.*, 109. [3] *Ibid.*, 148, 149, 162.
[4] *Ibid.*, 19, 20.

had a symbolic meaning.   They could only be prepared by a man
who had been taught the sacred songs sung in the ceremony, and
been instructed as to their meaning.[1]

The ceremonial begins with invocations to the powers that
intervene between the creator and men.   These include the Winds,
the Sun, Mother Earth, Vegetation, and Water.   They are simply
the means whereby life is brought down to men from the creator.
None of them seem to act by their own virtue.   They have
different ranks, so that Vegetation and Water, for instance, are
lower than the others.

A lodge is built in which the ceremony is to take place.   It is
dome-shaped, and is approached by a passage from the east.
It is supposed to represent the earth and the dome of the sky
above it.   The long passage-way that leads to it represents the
days of man's life.   Life is given to it by the observance of the
proper rites.

The ceremonial objects are then prepared.   Mother Corn is
the most prominent.   She is the leader in the expedition that
goes to the land of the Son.   She consists of an ear of maize,
painted blue to represent the sky.   She acquires her authority
from Tirawa, the Creator, for she goes to the sky, in company with
the priest, to ask the permission of Tirawa to perform the ceremony.   This being done, the priest ties to Mother Corn a downy
feather of an eagle, which is said to be ' always moving as if
breathing '.[2]

The next stage of the ritual is the setting out to the land of
the Son.   Before starting, the various ceremonial objects are
animated with life.   This is done by a remarkable ceremony.   A
straight pole, with the articles tied to it, is set up at the entrance
to the lodge in which the ceremonial takes place, this entrance
being at the east end.   It stands where the wind of the dawn may
breathe upon the Hako, and the first rays of the sun strike the
objects and give them life.[3]

All these objects ultimately get their powers from Tirawa.
This is expressly stated to be the case.   The most important part
of the ceremony begins when the party arrives at the land of the
Son.   This group of rituals is divided into two parts, public and
secret.   The performers sleep during the night before the opening
of the ceremonial.   In the morning comes the ceremony of the
Dawn.   All are supposed to be asleep in the lodge.   Mother Corn
wakes first of all, that she may be the first to receive the breath
of the new day.   The lesser powers that act between Tirawa and
the people awake and arise, for the breath of the new dawn is

[1] Fletcher i. 26.   [2] *Ibid.*, 47.   [3] *Ibid.*, 58.

upon them. All the powers above now wake and stir, and all things below wake and stir. The breath of new life is everywhere. The new life comes with the signs in the east.

The Dawn is said to be the child of Tirawa. It gives the blessing of life; it comes to awaken man, to awaken Mother Earth and all living things, that they may receive the life, the breath of the Dawn which is born of the Night by the power of Tirawa.[1]

The Morning Star then comes and brings strength and new life to the people. He leaves with the people the gift of life which Tirawa sent him to bestow.[2]

This part of the ritual shows that the aim of the whole ceremony is to procure life. Insistence is made time after time upon the fact that life in the form of breath comes to earth from the creator god Tirawa. It is acquired by means of rituals handed down from antiquity. The songs, rituals, forms, and material objects, all contribute their parts, for all of them contain the desired breath of life.

The second day of the ceremony begins with the invocation of the Sun as the male power. The sun is said to come directly from Tirawa, and whoever is touched by the first rays of the sun in the morning receives new life and strength which have been brought straight from the power above. We are told, in another place, that the Sun breathes forth life which he has acquired from the creator himself.[3]

This again is a clear statement of the acquisition of life from the sky. The ritual quoted here explains the meaning of the practice of exposure to the first rays of the morning sun. The aim is to get life for each day.

In the later parts of the ceremony a small child has put upon it the promises of children, of increase, of long life, of plenty. The signs of these promises are put upon this little child, not merely for that particular child but for its generation, that the children already born may live, grow in strength, and in their turn increase so that the family and the tribe may continue.

A warrior and a chief touch the child on the left and right shoulders, and thus impart what they have received from the Creator. The ear of corn is held near the child, so that the powers from above and below may come near it. The child is touched with the ear of corn in order that it may receive the powers. The priest strokes the child with the ear of corn down the front, the right side, the back and the left side. The four lines stroked upon the little child make the paths and open the way for the descent of the powers upon it. Every side of the child is now

[1] *Ibid.*, 124, 127.   [2] *Ibid.*, 129.   [3] *Ibid.*, 134, 136.

said to be open to receive the powers, and as he goes through life,
wherever he may be, on every side the powers can have access
to him.   The priest touches the child with the feathered stems.
It is said that the breath of promised life has now touched the
child.

A bowl of water from a stream is then taken and set down
before an old man.   He has been chosen because of his long life,
and his having received many favours from the powers above, in
order that similar gifts might be imparted to the child.   This
water is to sustain and make strong the child.

The child is then brushed with grass and then anointed with
red clay mixed with sacred buffalo fat.[1]   When he has been
anointed, his life is consecrated to Tirawa, the father above, who
gives life to all things.   He is then painted with red and blue
pigments.   The red paint signifies the sun and its life-giving
powers, the blue represents the sky, the abode of Tirawa.

The same lines are made with the red paint, on the face of the
child, as were made with the water, the brush of grass and the
ointment.   This symbolizes the derivation from Tirawa of the
vigour of life, the power of the touch of the sun, and the new life
of the dawn.   The lines form an arch across the forehead and
down each cheek, representing the dome of the sky, the abode of
the giver of life.   A line from the middle of the forehead, the
centre of the arch, down the ridge of the nose, represents the
breath of Tirawa, which descends from the zenith, passing down
the nose to the heart, giving life to the child.

The child is then touched with down of the white eagle, ' the
father of the child '.   This down is the breath and life of the
eagle.   This soft downy feather which is ever moving, as it were
breathing, represents Tirawa who dwells beyond the blue sky,
which is above the clouds.[2]

All is now ready.   The child has been fully prepared, the sacred
symbols put upon it, the powers from above have come, and
Tirawa breathes over it.[3]   The child then looks into a bowl of
running water.   The running water symbolizes the passing on
of generations, one following another.   The little child looks on
the water and sees its own likeness, as it will see that likeness in
its children and children's children.

The study of this ritual lays bare the inner significance of
Pawnee ceremonial.   The central theme is ' Life ' and its attainment.   Tirawa in the sky is the sole source of life, and every
means is taken to obtain it from him.   The whole Pawnee symbol-

[1] Fletcher i. 201, 204, 206, 208, 216, 220, 222.
[2] Ibid., 225, 227, 229, 233, 236, 239.   [3] Ibid., 241.

ism is directed towards that end, and no means are neglected that are known to the priests. The Pawnee act on this theory in their ceremonial in order to obtain security, prosperity, and the continuance of the tribe. The life is the breath of the creator, even when it comes to man through the wands, the red paint, the shell, the ear of corn, the sun or by any other means.

Man does not get life directly from the creator. It comes to him through intermediaries. Ceremonial and myth are in agreement on this point. The wind, the sun, the feathers, all bring life from the creator to man in the ceremonial. The intermediaries perform the acts of creation. Tirawa does not act directly.

The rôle of the breath is fundamental. This is revealed by the order in which the lesser powers bring life to man during the ceremonial. The breath comes first. It is followed by the vitality or strength. Then comes the ability to conserve or use that strength. Finally come food and drink to sustain life.[1]

This indicates a highly elaborated theory based on an abstract point of view, and not on direct experience. Food and drink would surely come first in a sequence of life-givers, not the breath.

Countless instances could be given of the relationship between ritual and ' life '. The Zuñi Indians of New Mexico, for example, possess rituals the aim of which is the getting of breath, which originally came from the creator god in the sky. The creation took place by the supreme creator breathing breath from his heart and creating clouds. He is the blue vault of the firmament. ' It is not strange, therefore, that the A'shiwi [the Zuñi] cover their altars with symbols of cumulus and nimbus clouds, with " the flame of the cloud crest ", and " the blue of the deep wells of the sky ", and use all these, woven into plumes, to waft their prayers to the gods, and have as their symbol of life, embracing all the mysterious life-securing properties, including mystery medicine, an ear of corn clothed in beautiful plumage ; for the spirit of A'wonawilo'na [the creator] is " put into and upon this created form ".'

This is the most sacred fetish (sic) of the Zuñi. ' While every Zuñi is taught that in inhaling the sacred breath from his fetishes or in breathing upon the plumes he offers to the gods he is receiving from A'wonawilo'na [the creator] the breath of life or is wafting his own breath prayers to his gods, only the few have any conception of all that is implied in their observances or fully appreciate the poetic nature of their myths.'[2]

The ritual of the initiation of Zuñi children clearly bears out this aim, to get the breath of life. The society concerned with

[1] *Ibid.*, 284.   [2] Stevenson 24.

this ritual possesses a story of its inception, and this story is the basis of the ritual. The gods who brought to men the precious gift of the breath of life are impersonated by the performers. ' The body of one wearing a mask becomes the abode of the god he impersonates ; he blows from his heart the breath of A'wona-wilo'na [the creator] upon the plumes or the hand and carries these to the mouth of another, that the sacred breath may be inhaled. The breath of A'wonawilo'na is everywhere ; it is life itself.'

During the performance the god who first brought the breath of life to the people, and was responsible for the inception of the initiation, says : ' In a short time my fathers, whom I have there, will meet you on the road. You will meet together. They will come, and will give to all your children more of the great breath, the breath of A'wonawilo'na ; the breath of the light of day.' [1] The gods blow on a plume and pass it before the child's lips, ' giving to him the sacred breath of the god '.[2]

It is said, further, of this breath, that it is connected with the greatest creator of all, ' who is the breath of life and life itself '. And when the breath of the plumes, which are a part of A'wona-wilo'na, is inhaled, one receives that life which is the great mystery, which when given by the Supreme Power defies all life-destroying agencies. The Earth Mother can only yield nourishment with the all-pervading power of A'wonawilo'na.[3]

An immense range of societies in different parts of the world, in different stages of culture, could be shown to be acting under the theory that the welfare of the community depends upon the getting of life from beings whom we should term ' gods '. These beings are usually connected with the sky-world, and are usually said to be creators. They often create the first man and woman ; sometimes they create the earth and people it with animals, plants and human beings. They animate the child at birth ; they instruct mankind in all manner of ceremonials, the aim of which is to secure a continuance of that life which was bestowed by the gods in the beginning. That is to say, any such community can possess a variety of social institutions centring round this theory of life.

It is interesting to note that the gods did not give life to mankind once and for all at the creation. It has to be procured by a definite procedure handed down from one generation of priests to another. In order to ensure continuance in health and prosperity, continuity with the past must be preserved. The Hako ceremony

---

[1] Stevenson 88.   [2] *Ibid.*, 100.   [3] *Ibid.*, 416.

is carried on by those who possess the traditional lore, that is to say, who are in the direct line of continuity. It is to be noted, further, that the gods who gave life in the beginning, and who still continue to give it to individuals and groups, do so by virtue of certain ceremonial acts performed by men, and not as an act of grace. It is true, of course, as we have seen among the Toradja of Celebes, that the gods can withdraw life from men and retain it, so that men die. That appears to be an act of free will on the part of the gods ; but this is not necessarily the case, for men have to die some time or another ; and if they die by the abstraction of life that has to be returned to the sky, it is obvious that the sky-gods can well be held responsible without ascribing free will to them. In the larger ceremonials, such as the Hako of the Pawnee, the sole requisite is the exact performance of the ritual. The god has no choice in the matter, he is simply a part of the ceremonial procedure.

This opens up an interesting vista. It makes the god into a ceremonial puppet, a lay figure with little or no free will of his own. At the same time he is, according to the people, the original source of life, the great creator. This puppet, whoever he may be, is of an exalted nature, and can only be approached by intermediaries, who themselves are puppets. We have seen, in earlier chapters, that gods are not so remote from men as might be expected. We have seen that many ruling groups claim descent from the beings of the sky-world, that is, from gods. We have seen, moreover, that cults of gods are usually only carried on by their descendants. There is no need, therefore, to assume that the gods of the Pawnee ritual are the result of fantasy. We are therefore faced with the interesting problem of explaining how beings who are the ancestors of ruling groups and priesthoods are themselves merely ritual puppets. If we assume for a moment that these gods are human beings, who played their part in the creation drama as ritual puppets, only one conclusion seems to emerge. It is that human beings made themselves into gods by ritual proceedings ; for it is impossible to abstract gods from the rituals in which they figure. Tirawa, for example, the creator of the Pawnee, is, in some way or other, a product of ritual ; he is, in his creative aspect, the product of a series of ceremonials performed by human beings. As it is impossible, in any part of the world, to escape from traditional ceremonial, it follows that, as we go backwards in time, we are constantly faced with human beings performing rituals. These human beings are usually members of a priestly corporation or ruling group. Each ritual situation, therefore, involves human beings performing traditional acts. That is to say, each ritual is the ostensible reproduction of some preceding ritual situation. I mean by this that the Pawnee priests who perform the Hako ceremonies do this and that because their predecessors did so, and ultimately because the sky-beings did so. These sky-beings also procured life by means of certain ceremonial acts. Therefore, as far back as we can go, we are faced with human beings grouping themselves in situations that we may call ' life-giving '. So if we go far enough back we shall find some situation in which human beings became gods and creators, and raised themselves to a world in the sky.

All this seemingly hazardous speculation is based on the insistence of the Pawnee priest that everything in the Hako ceremonies has to be done exactly as it was handed down from the gods. If that be accepted as characteristic of all ritual, then I see no escape from the conclusions I have reached, namely, that certain events in the past caused human beings, by means of dramatic performances of an elaborate nature, to transform themselves into what we term ' gods '. Finally, we must assume that these dramatic performances were the re-enactments of certain actual events that happened in a ruling group or groups.[1]

[1] See Perry ix. for a discussion of this topic.

CHAPTER XVI

THE MYTHOLOGICAL PAST

THE next task is to understand the nature of the divine world from which so many peoples derive their culture. A good rule in such circumstances is to inquire of the people themselves what they think about it. They lack, of course, a wide comparative knowledge of the subject, but, on the other hand, they are steeped in traditional lore which has been handed on from generation to generation. When we make such an inquiry of any particular people, such as the Pawnee, we find that they usually possess a fund of stories concerning their past history, and particularly relating to beginnings. Those that refer to the gods are commonly known only to certain people who have been initiated, either into a priesthood, or into a secret society, or into some other social group.

These stories are highly prized. In the words of the late G. A. Dorsey, ' each bundle ceremony and dance was accompanied, not only by its ritual, but by its tale of origin. This tale was generally the personal property of the keeper or owner of the bundle or dance, and, as a rule, was related immediately after the recitation of the ritual or at the time of the transmission of the possession of the bundle or the ceremony to its next owner. Thus, each of these tales was esoteric, and was concerned only with that part of the origin which related directly to the bundle or the dance. Hence it is that only with the greatest difficulty can anything like an origin myth of the Skidi as a whole be obtained.

' As has been stated, these traditions, along with the ritual, are regarded as personal property. They have been paid for by the owner, and consequently, according to his belief, now form an intimate part of his life. As he tells them he gives out from himself a certain part of his life, levying a direct contribution upon its termination. Thus, as one middle-aged individual exclaimed, " I cannot tell you all that I know, for I am not yet ready to die," or, as an old priest expressed it, " I know that my days are short. My life is no longer of use. There is no reason why I should not tell you all that I know." ' [1]

[1] Dorsey i. XXII. For an explanation of the ' bundles ' mentioned here, see p. 242. The splitting-up, so to speak, of the origin story of the Pawnee into sections, has an important bearing on the discussion of Social Unity, carried on in Chapter XV.

These statements elevate the ritual story to the rank of a Social Institution. It is surprising to find that knowledge is regarded as part of the life of a person. This fact will have an important bearing on the general theory of constructive thought.

In addition to what might be termed ' myths ', the Pawnee, like many other peoples, have a collection of stories of the Brer Rabbit type, in which animals with well-defined human characteristics play tricks upon one another. A fundamental difference exists, in the minds of the Pawnee, between the Brer Rabbit stories and the myths. They say that the animal stories are fiction, and are told for amusement.

Myths, on the other hand, are taken with great seriousness. They are asserted to be literally true. Before studying the origin stories a comment must be made upon the assertion that the Brer Rabbit stories are purely imaginative, invented for amusement. I found my Pondo friends telling just such stories to while away the long evenings. If the claim of the Pawnee were true, it would be necessary to credit savage man with a measure of imaginative constructiveness that does not appear to be possessed by him. There is a possibility that this kind of story has a definite social origin, and that it was originally in no way spontaneous. That, however, is a minor matter for the present. We must return to the origin stories, and the claim of the Pawnee concerning them. This claim is that origin stories are literally true.

This claim is astonishing, and at first sight, fantastic. It runs counter to accepted conventions ; for does not the word ' myth ' convey to most of our minds the impression of unreality ? Yet it must be remembered that the study of the Hako ceremony shows that the Pawnee act up to their beliefs. They wish to retain their ritualistic equipment intact ; no conscious deviation from the prescribed ritual is allowed. They do this in the obvious belief that they are actually imitating the acts of the gods.

Let us see what is involved in this belief of the Pawnee in the truth of their origin stories. As was seen in the chapter on Social Unity (see p. 174), the Pawnee, together with many other people, say that habitable land was produced out of a ' Primordial Ocean ' by beings of the sky-world. The earth was not yet. The sky-beings created the earth, and provided it with plants and animals, and all things necessary for life. They also endowed it with life. When they had prepared everything they sent down a young man and maiden to be the first rulers of the tribe : they taught them all manner of things, from household economy to the details of the most complicated ritual ; in fact, they set

the young couple up in house-keeping, and prepared them to
be the ceremonial centre of the tribe.[1]

This sounds like a farrago of fact and fiction. Let us jot down
the chief characteristics of this story. It involves

(1) A primordial ocean.

(2) A sky-world inhabited by gods.

(3) The creation of earth out of the primordial ocean.

(4) The endowment of this earth with life.

(5) The transference of a young couple from the sky to the
earth.

(6) The endowment of this couple with knowledge of every
manner of tribal activity, including the growing of maize.

These characteristic details of the origin stories are of various
kinds. Some concern the tribe itself. For instance, we know
that the Pawnee tribe, when living in Nebraska and cultivating
maize, must have received that maize originally from Mexico.
It may therefore be perfectly true that they acquired their maize
from elsewhere.

We can likewise examine the institutions with which the sky-
people endowed the young couple on earth, and compare them
with those of other tribes. But it may not be so easy to explain
how they came from the sky-world, or what the sky-world really
means. We have, further, to explain the creative activities of
these sky-beings.

We must remember that the Pawnee accept all these details
as real. They are sure that the gods exist in the sky-world, and
on them they depend for life.

Certain origin stories describe the conditions when the tribe
was first organized. The first chief and his wife were Son of the
Sun and Daughter of the Evening Star. Shortly after their
arrival on earth a son was born to them. This son learned certain
secrets from the ' Animals ' in their ceremonial lodge. One
Animal said to him, ' My son your father and mother came from
the Heavens ; they are not to stay upon this earth for ever.' His
mother then gave birth to a girl, after that she gave birth to
another boy and another girl. The elder and younger pairs of
brothers and sisters married. The eldest son became the High-
priest. Every spring he gave out the seeds for planting to the
people, telling them how to cultivate them. When the harvest
had been gathered the people took some of the seeds to him, and
he kept them till the next spring.[2]

---

[1] See p. 212. These statements have a bearing on the theme of Social
Unity. They suggest that the tribal organization depended on the Chief.

[2] *Ibid.*, 22.

Mention is made in one story of a former society of the Children of the Sun. They were all killed because of their pugnacious habits.[1]

Another Pawnee story tells of a son of the Sun and his sister, who lived between two villages, one far in the east, the other far in the west. Nobody knew anything about them. The boy travelled far and wide. His sister made twin balls and a shinny ball.[2]

Other stories from the Pawnee and their cognates are more precise. One story starts as follows : ' Once upon a time there was a village which had two chiefs. The village was divided into two parts by a wide, street-like space which extended east and west.' [3] This village had north and south parts.

Another story describes a village with east and west parts : ' Once upon a time there was a village which was divided by a street passing through its centre from north to south. Each part of the village was ruled over by a chief. The chief who ruled the west part of the village was a good man. The chief who ruled the east side was a bad man.' [4] Certain stories told by the Wichita, a cognate tribe of the Pawnee, describe dual villages of a similar type. Each side has a chief, and the son of the chief of one side marries the daughter of the chief of the other.[5]

A Skidi-Pawnee tale tells of a young girl whose parents would not allow her to marry. They kept her under strict supervision. She slept at night at the west end of the tent opposite the door, her uncle slept on one side and her brothers on the other to protect her from other men.

One night she was taken out, and while outside a meteor passed through the heavens. Six months later she showed signs of being pregnant. The meteor was the father of the child, who was a wonderful boy. This sky-being came to live among the people, and bestowed many benefits upon them.[6]

These stories tell of a condition of affairs that is not entirely characteristic of the modern Pawnee. In the beginning, we see, the Pawnee and their cognates were ruled over by sky-born chiefs, who did not stay among them, but returned to the sky. In this family brothers married sisters. The eldest son was high-priest. He was closely connected with agriculture, having charge of the seeds of corn that his ancestress, the Evening Star, originally gave to his parents. The people lived in dual villages, each part ruled over by a chief. They played ceremonial ball games. In

---

[1] Dorsey i. XXII. 57–8.   [2] *Ibid.*, 30, 24–5.
[3] *Ibid.*, ii. 67. Cf. 199.   [4] *Ibid.*, 207.   [5] *Ibid.* 199.
[6] *Ibid.*, i. 307.

these early times girls could become mothers by supernatural means.

Mention is made, in certain stories, of shinny and other ceremonial ball games among the ancestors of the Pawnee. They still play ball games, in common with the great majority of North American tribes. Mention has already been made of these games in the chapter on Social Unity.[1] The custom dates back in American history to the Maya occupation of Yucatan.[2]

The Pawnee accounts of ceremonial ball games of the past therefore simply describe the custom they still possess in common with the majority of peoples in North and Central America.

Dual villages do not appear to exist among the Pawnee any longer, but they are mentioned among the Winnebago Indians, and other peoples of America.[3] Mention may be made of Cuzco, the capital of the Incas of Peru. When Manco Ccapac and his sister-wife Mama Ocllo founded this capital they divided it into two parts; he ruled over the north (upper) and she over the south (lower).[4]

The Skidi Pawnee, on the other hand, have a dual grouping of the tribe. Their villages are grouped respectively north and south of the Loupe River. This grouping is of fundamental importance in the ceremonial life of the tribe. We have already seen, on more than one occasion, that this dual organization is a widespread characteristic of North American civilization.[5]

The earliest Pawnee chief was, as we have seen, a son of the Sun; his father was the Sun and his mother the Moon. The story, already quoted, mentions that he did not stay long on earth, but returned to the sky-world. These beings are certainly historical. We do not have to go far, among the North American Indians, to meet them in the flesh. It is not so long ago that they were ruling over the Natchez of Louisiana, whose traditions make them come from the south-west from a land where many suns rule.[6] This land in all probability was Mexico or Central America. The Maya certainly had Children of the Sun ruling over them. Mention need only be made of the Incas of Peru, Children of the Sun, to make the historicity of the early Pawnee chiefs all the more certain. In fact it can be laid down, with confidence, that the Children of the Sun were the earliest known ruling group in America. It is only necessary to remember that Manco Ccapac married his sister, and that the Incas followed this custom to the end of their days, to make the reality of the early

[1] See p. 168.   [2] See p. 330.
[3] See p. 168. Cf. Perry vi. 324 for examples outside America.
[4] Vega I. 67.   [5] See pp. 167 e.s.   [6] Du Pratz II. 331-2.

Pawnee chiefs yet more certain. The story of the girl who was kept secluded in order that she should not have intercourse with any man, has its parallel in Inca practice. The royal princesses were kept in a convent, and one of their number was chosen as chief queen of the Inca himself. Should any one of them be found with child she and the child were killed ; though if she claimed that the sun was the father of the child, mother and infant were spared, and if it were a boy he was received among the royal princes.[1]

These facts show that the society founded by the sky-beings of the Pawnee was historical. We see that America possesses evidence of actual rulers called the Children of the Sun, who married their own sisters, lived in dual villages, kept their women-folk shut up in a convent, and believed that the sun could be the father of mortal children.

The early Pawnee organization that is ascribed to the sky-gods therefore conforms to type, and can be accepted as historical. Thus far the Pawnee are justified in their belief. There are, however, other tasks to perform. We have to rationalize the sky-world, the primordial ocean, gods, and creation, and, in particular, the creation of earth from the primordial ocean.

[1] Vega I. 132.

CHAPTER XVII

THE AGE OF THE GODS

THE Children of the Sun have played an important part in the foundation of states throughout the world during many centuries. We have already met with them in preceding chapters as the bringers of culture and the founders of ruling houses. In some parts of the world their descendants are still ruling ; in others they are historical, but have died out ; in others again, they are merely traditional.

They occur in the Pawnee origin stories. The title, Son of the Sun, was held by the first chief of the Pawnee ; but the title has long since disappeared. The importance of this ruling group makes it essential to learn about them from all points of view. In particular, it is important to study their own historical records ; the cause and manner of their migration ; the foundation of states by them ; and the manner of their disappearance.

We have already found (see p. 157) that food-producers as a whole attribute their cultural beginnings to a time in the past that might be termed The Age of the Gods. The close association of the Children of the Sun with this age makes them all the more important.

The facts at our disposal are overwhelmingly in favour of the conclusion that the Children of the Sun have spread throughout a great part of the world, and have left their impress on multitudes of communities. We can watch the progress of the Polynesians from their ancestral home, right out to the furthest confines of the Pacific, and can see that their original sky-born, divine rulers have disappeared in one place after another, leaving but their memory in mythology. Thus the Maori of New Zealand speak of Tangaroa ; while in Samoa the same name is that of the Children of the Sun, who founded the first community, and then disappeared, never to return. In the traditional lore of Tahiti and Hawaii these same wonderful beings are found, but they have long since disappeared. This is the story throughout the wide track from India to Tahiti. In all parts the Children of the Sun die out, and their place is taken by rulers, who, although in a way divine, certainly do not rank with them.[1]

[1] Perry vi. Chaps. X, XI.

Since the Children of the Sun have disappeared in so many places, and have been replaced by less divine rulers, how comes it that they continue to play so important a part in the mythology of such peoples ?   What is the thread of continuity connecting the present with the past, that has prevented these beings from being entirely forgotten ?

I believe that we have enough evidence to show, in all parts of the world, and in all ages, that ruling groups have not sprung up independently, but that they have been derived from some other ruling groups, just as each new species of animal or plant is derived from some other species in continuous progression.[1]   It can be shown that the Children of the Sun disappeared as such in certain places, and that they, as it were, became transformed somehow into kings who had not so much of the divine characteristics as they themselves possessed.   Unfortunately it is not possible to watch this disappearance everywhere, but in a few places the story is perfectly clear, and the telling of it adds greatly to the realization of the past existence of an Age of the Gods, and of the way by which men lost their touch with the divine world of the sky.

It is possible to witness in India the gradual extinction of the incarnate gods of the past, of the gradual fading away of the age of the gods.   This occurs in all parts, sometimes with our full knowledge, sometimes by the fact itself without any particulars.   But of the inevitable and continuous extinction of this wonderful family of old there can be no doubt.

The Solar race was the chief ruling race of India from Vedic times onwards.   Dynasties strove to claim descent from it, whether they were entitled to it or not.   The Epics and the Puranas are full of the doings of the Children of the Sun ; [2] and there is but little doubt that these writings contain much that is historical, mixed up, of course, with a good deal of accessory matter which is purely imaginative.

A fortunate circumstance makes it possible for us to gain light upon this royal group of solar children.   For the Buddha himself was of solar line—he belonged to the branch called the Sakhyas, ' the pure of blood '—and this circumstance made the Buddhist chroniclers careful to preserve all that they could concerning the Children of the Sun.   Thus we find that the Buddhist countries of Burma and Ceylon both possess chronicles that tell of the foundation of various kingdoms by Children of the Sun from India, and these chronicles are of great value to us, for they reveal

[1] Perry viii. See Chaps. VII and VIII for a discussion of this topic.
[2] Wilson, H. H., iii. ; Ray.

much concerning the early days in India and the surrounding countries.

The Buddhist annalists, imbued with the idea of the origin of Buddha's ancestors among the solar rulers of ancient India, spare no effort to insist on that relationship. In the ' Manual of Buddhism ' of R. Spence Hardy we read : ' In the beginning of the present *antah-kalpa*, the monarch Maha Sammata, of the race of the sun, received existence by the apparitional birth. As it was with the unanimous consent, or appointment, *sammata*, of all the beings concerned, that he was anointed king, he was called Maha Sammata. The glory proceeding from his body was like that of the sun. By the power of *Irdhi* he was able to seat himself in the air without any visible support.' [1]

This ascription of magical powers to the Children of the Sun is of great importance. There is much evidence to show that throughout the world the Children of the Sun were powerful magicians. They were accredited with the power of bringing the dead to life, of changing shape, transporting themselves to distant spots, causing plants to grow with great speed, controlling the weather, and other wonderful feats.[2] In fact, most of the magical practices of people of the lower culture can be traced back to these wonderful beings.

The chronicle then proceeds to recount the descent of this great king, down to the time of Buddha himself. The branch of the royal family to which Buddha belonged was that of Kapilavastu, and was named Sakhya, because it was of the pure solar stock. It was to this family that the royal families of Burma and Ceylon traced their origin.

The first curious thing that we learn about this family is recorded in the tale of the founding of Kapilavastu. We learn that one of the inferior queens of a king named Amba or Okkaka managed, by means of a trick, to dispossess the rightful heirs to the throne in favour of her son. The dispossessed princes went away and founded the city of Kapila or Kapilavastu. The old king said to them, on parting, ' My sons, I have thoughtlessly given to another the kingdom that of right belongs to you. These women are witches, and have overcome my better judgment by their wiles ; Janta will be my successor ; therefore take whatever treasures you wish, except the five that belong to the regalia, and as many people as will follow you, and go to some other place that you may there take up your abode.' [3] So they went.

They were not to take the regalia with them, because it was essential for the king to have certain regalia ; otherwise he could

---

[1] Hardy 125.   [2] Perry vi. 403–4.   [3] Hardy 131.

not be consecrated in the proper manner. This is a point of particular importance. They therefore went away with some of their subjects to form a new settlement elsewhere. The movement was thus that of a complete community. We are told that 84,000 people joined them in their exile, including Brahmins, and men of wealth, and thousands of merchants and writers. This great concourse went to Kapila, and founded there a city.

We are also given another important piece of information, namely, that ' When the five sisters—[there were four princes]—heard of their departure, they thought that there would be no one now to care for them, as their brothers were gone ; so they resolved to follow them and joined them, with such treasures as they could collect.' [1]

This account throws light on the history of the royal family of the Children of the Sun. For one reason or another certain members went away to some other place, there to found a kingdom for themselves. They took with them numerous followers, so as to form a complete community. Since 84,000 went with them, there would be a fairly complete transplantation of the culture, for evidently representatives of most of the arts and crafts would be included.

This is a common characteristic of the Children of the Sun, as we shall see later. They evidently, in certain instances at least, did not conquer a country, but migrated to it with numerous followers. This custom explains the similarity exhibited by states founded by them in all parts of the world. No mention is made of a pre-existing local population in this instance.

This process of transplantation helps to a better understanding of the central theme of the chapter on Social Unity. The whole economy of the State depends on the ruling family. Other examples of this process will occur later in this chapter. Further confirmation will be forthcoming when the consecration ceremonies are studied. We shall then be able to watch the king bringing the State into being (see pp. 231 e.s.).

To return to the narrative. The young princes set out to find a suitable locality for their city, and built it. Then came the question of the marriages of the princes, and this is what they said : ' If we send to any of the inferior kings to ask their daughters in marriage, it will be a dishonour to the Okkaka race ; and if we give our sisters to their princes it will be an equal dishonour ; it will therefore be better to stain the purity of our relationship than that of our race.' So they appointed the eldest sister as queen-mother, and each of the princes took one of his sisters as

[1] Hardy 131 e.s.

wife. Their father, when he heard of this action, was delighted. Thrice he exclaimed : ' The princes are skilful in preserving the purity of our race ; the princes are exceedingly skilful in preserving the purity of our race.' [1] Hence the name of Sakhya.

We have now hit upon one of the most remarkable and important characteristics of the Children of the Sun. They invariably have to marry a woman of the same royal blood. In the absence of other families of solar lineage we see that they marry their own sisters ; they do not even shrink on occasion from marrying their mothers and daughters. Anything to keep the line intact. If, on the other hand, the purity of the blood was not kept, then the solar line died out automatically.

The Buddhist annals make it clear that the extinction of the Children of the Sun is ascribed to this cause. Speaking of the descent of Maha Sammata, it is said—' The Sons of Muchalinda were sixty thousand in number, who spread themselves through the whole of Jambudwipa, and founded as many separate kingdoms ; but as they were all equally descended from Maha Sammata, they were all of the same race. In the course of time, however, their descendants neglected to keep up the purity of their blood, and other races were formed.' [2] Thus the Children of the Sun were replaced by another royal line, which was derived from them.

The Children of the Sun, therefore, wherever we find them in India, are, if we are to trust the annals, evidently descendants of the original solar family founded by Maha Sammata, who have managed to retain the purity of their blood, even by the device of marrying their sisters.

This account might suggest that the founders of Kapilavastu spontaneously adopted the device of incestuous marriages for dynastic purposes. On the contrary, evidence suggests that the marriage of brother and sister was traditional in the solar family of India.

Certain texts of the Rig Veda, the earliest Sanskrit compilation, speak of Yama, the first king to find the way to the land of the dead, and his sister Yami.

Yami desired to be the wife of Yama. ' I, Yami, am possessed by love of Yama, that I may rest on the same couch beside him. . . .'

' " I as a wife would yield me to my husband. Like car-wheels let us speed to meet each other." ' [3] Yama rejects her advances. This suggests that the solar family had once practised the brother-sister marriage, but had given it up. This suggestion is supported

---

[1] *Ibid.*, 133.   [2] *Ibid.*, 129.   [3] Rig Veda X. 10, 7.

by the corresponding tradition in the Persian Bundahis, where Yim, who corresponds in every way to Yama, marries his sister. Yim and his sister are the children of Vivanghvant, just as Yama and Yami are the children of Vivasvat, the Sun.[1]

It is well known that the sacred writings of the Persians and of the Aryan-speaking invaders of India show many traces of a common origin. The conclusion, therefore, is that the original rulers of both these peoples were Children of the Sun, who married their sisters.

Evidence comes from other directions. Manu, the survivor of the flood, the story of which is recounted in the Satapatha Brahmana, married his daughter. Prajapati, the creator, likewise had intercourse with his daughter, and had a solar king as his son (see p. 223).

It would therefore appear that the solar kings of India were marrying their sisters long before the foundation of Kapilavastu.

Let us now follow the fortunes of some branches of this family and see what happens to them. I take for my first example the branch of the solar dynasty which was responsible for the foundation of the various kingdoms of Burma, namely, Tagaung, Tharehkittara and Pagan. The foundation of these kingdoms is recorded in various native chronicles, some of which have been collected and edited by the writers of 'The Glass Palace Chronicles', who, in 1829, were commanded by King Bagyidaw of Burma to write the chronicles of the Burmese kings.

The 'Glass Palace Chronicles' recount the foundation of the kingdom of Tagaung in Burma by Abhiraja, one of the Children of the Sun, a member of the royal family of the Sakhyans. Abhiraja was driven to leave India with the whole of his army. He died, and his sons founded a dynasty which lasted until thirty-three kings had reigned in unbroken succession, all, presumably, as we shall see, of pure blood. Finally the kingdom broke up and gave rise to others.[2]   In time, however, Tagaung was restored by another solar prince, Dhajaraja, who came from India, on account of the break-up of the Sakhyan kingdom. This Dhajaraja found in Burma a princess of pure Sakhyan, that is, solar blood, and married her on that account, thus keeping the line pure. This wife was a member of the original family of the Children of the Sun who had come in with Abhiraja to found Tagaung. Having married her, the king built a palace and fortifications, and was properly installed as ruler, the queen taking her share in the ceremony.[3]

[1] Darmesteter 13 ;   West 131.   [2] 'Glass Palace Chronicles' 1–2.
[3] Ibid., 4.

It will shortly be shown that the royal line of the Children of the Sun died out because the king could only be properly consecrated when he had at his side a princess of solar blood. He had, in addition, to have the regalia, as we have already seen. Dhajaraja came to Tagaung because his line had been extinguished by a prince who was suffering from an injustice. A certain king sought the daughter of another, both of them presumably of Sakhyan race. But the other king, ' desirous of preserving the purity of the race, gave him not a princess of the blood royal but gave him a daughter by a slave woman '. The son of this union vowed vengeance, and took it; hence the flight of Dhajaraja to Burma.[1]

This royal family had other characteristics. Dhajaraja had two chief queens. ' In the reign of this king there befell four showers of gems. His two chief queens had twenty sons and twenty daughters, who intermarried.' [2] There were, of course, many ladies of the harem, but these two, the solar princess and the other, stand out above all others.

These two queens are mentioned again in the Chronicles. King Dwattabaung, for instance, had two queens, we are told, one being his sister, and the other a Naga princess named Besandi.[3] Therefore the king married one of his own family and a member of the ruling group connected with the underworld, the Nagas, who play so important a part in Indian history in conjunction with the Children of the Sun. To put the matter in other terms, the king, who belonged to the sky-world, whence his ancestors came, and whither he hoped to go after death, married a sky-born princess and an underworld princess, who were his chief queens. Unfortunately we are not told whether the two queens of Dhajaraja whose sons and daughters intermarried, were respectively of solar and Naga lineage. Nevertheless the fact that the early kings of Burma had two queens, one of whom was of the same lineage as themselves, suggests that they habitually married in addition a Naga princess. Whether their children habitually intermarried it is not possible to tell from the Burmese evidence. The royal family of Tagaung in Burma kept up the same practice of intermarriage as that of India.

The same condition of affairs occurs in Ceylon. The Singhalese chronicles, especially the Mahavamsa, contain much information about the Sakhya family. The founder of the Sakhya line in Ceylon was Vijaya, son of a brother and sister, who thus married in the usual manner of the solar line. His mother, Sihasavali, gave birth on sixteen occasions to twin children. The eldest

[1] *Ibid.*, 3.   [2] *Ibid.*, 5.   [3] *Ibid.*, 15.

was Vijaya, who was sent away because of his violent behaviour.[1] He went to Ceylon, and landed there with 700 officers of state, who proceeded to divide up his territory and to give their names to the divisions.

An interesting event is then recounted. It says in the chronicle : ' Thus these followers, having formed many settlements, giving to them their own names ; thereafter having held a consultation, they solicited their ruler to assume the office of sovereign. . . . The king, on account of his not having a queen-consort of equal rank to himself, was indifferent at that time to his inauguration.' [2] Thereupon the nobles sent a deputation to the king of southern Madhura in India, with presents, and demanded of him a daughter. They went, so it was said, ' in search of a royal virgin ', which is significant in view of the widespread custom of keeping solar princesses in convents. The king of Madhura agreed, and sent his daughter, together with eighteen officers of state, and several menial servants. Also he sent 700 daughters of his nobility to marry the nobility of Vijaya. Thereupon king Vijaya married the daughter of the king of Madhura and was duly inaugurated. When Vijaya died he left no son behind him. So they sent to his brother Sumitta, who, being old, sent his son Panduvasadeva in his stead, who came and was accepted as king. But, we are told, so long as he was without a royal consort, he abstained from solemnizing his inauguration. Finally, however, he found a consort of the solar line, and married her, afterwards solemnizing his inauguration.[3]

The stress laid in these chronicles upon the necessity for purity in the blood of the solar lineage is evident. It must clearly be realized what this means. The royal family of the Children of the Sun could only persist provided there were men and women both of the pure royal blood able to marry. If necessary, as we have seen, they did not hesitate to marry their own sisters, or even their mothers and daughters. So when a member of the royal line of the Children of the Sun went to Ceylon, it was necessary, in order that he might be consecrated in the proper manner, to find for him a wife of the same purity of blood. Otherwise the Children of the Sun would have ceased to exist.

The Singhalese chronicles actually tell us of the cessation of the pure line of the Children of the Sun. For it is said that from the time of king Vijaya there ruled sixty-three kings, all of

[1] Mahavamsa 31.
[2] *Ibid.*, 34. This account shows that the foundation of the State depended on the kingship. The King alone could provide the unifying factor.
[3] *Ibid.*, 34-7.

untainted blood. After that the untainted royal blood ended :
' the kings who followed were descended of parents, one of whom
was of the Surya Wansa, descended from the bringer of the *bo*-tree,
or of the Dalidaw Wansa, descended from the bringer of the
dhawtoo, and thus of mixed blood, and on that account there
were no longer to be found the Rahatoonsancies who could fly
to the Dewa-Loka when they pleased.' [1]

The disappearance of the royal blood of solar descent is therefore an actual process revealed to us in the native chronicles.
These chronicles, as we have seen, tell of the movements of the
original solar family, and of its final extinction in certain places.
This leads us to conclude that, wherever we find the solar family,
it represents a branch derived directly from the original pure
stock, in which the absence of a queen of the royal blood, or some
other cause, has not produced extinction. From generation to
generation each king, himself of pure descent, has been able to
find a queen of equal rank. Once she is lacking, the Children
of the Sun no longer exist in their pure form. It is particularly
interesting to note that, as in the case of Maha Sammata, the
power of flying through the air disappeared when the original
purity of the royal family became impaired. Details such as
this serve to explain the loss of magical powers in various parts
of the world, and the retention in native memory of the former
possessors of such powers. Evidently such exalted powers were
the prerogative of the most exalted ranks of incarnate gods. [2]

The failure of the solar line makes a break with the past, and
much has been lost concerning these men of old. The native
writers sometimes betray this in their comments on the original
writings. They do not understand what was meant, and instead
of trying to understand, by inquiring about the same family in
other places, they proceed to quote authority to disprove the
statements to which they object. It will be remembered that
a former king of Burma is said to have married a Naga princess,
one of that race which was connected with the underworld. The
writers of ' The Glass Palace Chronicles ' quote a story which
runs as follows : ' A female Naga called Zanthi, daughter of
Nagakyaung son of Kala, king of the Nagas, came to the world
of men in order to practise the duties of virtue. While she lived
near Mt. Mali she had intercourse with the Sun prince and became
pregnant. . . .' She finally gave birth to a boy named Pyusawhti,
who ultimately ascended the throne. The chroniclers say at
the end of the tale, ' So this story runs ; but it is at variance
with all curious and reasonable versions in the Pali commentaries

[1] Upham 239.   [2] Perry vi. 137, 403 e.s.

and sub-commentaries,' a typical appeal to authority. They say, ' It is quite clear in the books that the Sun spirit dwells only in the Sun mansion, ornament of the world. Not a shadow, not a hint appears in the books of the existence of a son of the Sun spirit.' They go on to elaborate the point. They show that human beings are born from the union of a human prince and a Naga princess, or a Naga prince from the union of a Naga prince and a human princess, but they are horrified at the thought of a human prince being the offspring of a Sun prince and a Naga princess. ' Even ', they say, ' if there were a real union between the Sun prince and the female Naga, either a spirit or a Naga should have been born after the kind either of the father or of the mother. Therefore, that a human son was born, and not a spirit nor a Naga, is contrary to reason, and this is a point of variance with the books.' [1] Indeed they wax quite eloquent about it, and devote a page or two to demonstrating that what was meant was simply that the prince in question belonged to the solar line. For the story itself really shows that the Children of the Sun of Burma and other parts of the world held similar beliefs. They believed in the doctrine of theogamy, in the possibility of the divine fatherhood of the Sun god by an earthly wife. This doctrine is characteristic of the Children of the Sun the world over, especially in those cases where contact with the past has not been broken too completely. We find the belief among the Incas of Peru, in the United States, and in many other places. In this way it can readily be seen how history can become obscured. The ruling group of Burma was derived directly from the Children of the Sun ; but, owing to certain dislocations, the original purity of blood has gone, and the resulting rulers are less sacred. When the pure solar line died out the belief in their divine birth, that characterized them the world over, disappeared also.

One of the most potent causes of the extinction of the Children of the Sun is the absence of women of the blood royal, whereby the children of the union are of a lower order, so to speak. Both in Burma and Ceylon this process of automatic extinction of members of the family of the Children of the Sun can be watched, and the exact reason assigned for the happening. This disappearance of the solar family can be exactly paralleled in Samoa, as I have already shown in ' The Children of the Sun '.[2] To all appearance the Children of the Sun in this group correspond to those of Burma and elsewhere. For it is said that the first rulers married two women, one belonging to the solar line, and the other

[1] ' The Glass Palace Chronicles ' 33–5.   [2] Perry vi. 298–304, 375–7.

to a family group connected with the underworld. This is exactly what we find said of the first kings of Burma, whose chief queens belonged to the solar and Naga dynasties. In India and Burma the Naga race was closely connected with snakes, while the Samoan equivalents were connected with the octopus.

The manner of the establishment of the first settlement in Samoa is interesting. It was made on a small island, named Tau, at the east end of the group. On this island there were two settlements, named Fitiuta and Tau. Moreover, each of these settlements were divided into seaward and landward parts,[1] a typical dual division, but the secondary division of settlements need not trouble us at present. We are concerned with the marriages of the royal family. The story runs that the Sa Tagaloa, the Children of the Sun, came down from the sky and founded Fitiuta. To all appearances the first people were of the pure solar line.

The original family of the Children of the Sun was immortal, and the first mortal king was of mixed descent.[2] This is expressly stated to be so in every variant of the Samoan tradition of origin. The most explicit version is that which recounts that the founders of Fitiuta were husband and wife, evidently of royal blood, to whose son the Tagaloa gave the highest title of sacred chief, the Galea'i title. But it became extinguished, and the reason given is that the Galea'i omitted to follow the usual rule of marrying a woman of his side of the island, in addition to one belonging to the other side of the island.

To understand the meaning of this, it must be stated that the form of society in which these events took place was matrilineal. That is to say, the children of a marriage belonged to the group of their mother; they inherited property through their mother; and they succeeded to rank through their mother. So when a ruler married women of both sides of the island, his sons ruled over the respective sides to which their mothers belonged. He married a woman who belonged to the solar side of the island, and her son was of the same group as herself—he was of pure solar blood, for he was descended from the sky-born race through his mother. On the other hand, the son of the woman from the

---

[1] It is interesting to recall the division of Andamanese tribes into seaward and landward parts.

[2] The term ' immortal ' does not appear to mean eternal life on earth, although it may have acquired the sense of ' a long life '. The real distinction between the ' immortal ' and ' mortal ' kings of early Samoa and elsewhere lies in the knowledge, that the immortal kings possessed, of rituals designed to procure for them a conscious life in the hereafter.

other side of the island, who belonged to the underground people, ruled over that side of the island, and himself belonged to the underground people. Therefore, in order that a title belonging to the solar side of the island should survive, it was necessary that the ruler of the whole island should marry a woman belonging to that side. We are told expressly that he did not do so, and that, in consequence, the title lapsed, and the chief title henceforth was that belonging to the other side of the island. This title was the *Tui* title, which is also the most sacred title in Fiji and Tonga. This is in accordance with the story from Ceylon. Owing to the lack of a marriage with a woman of the right sort of birth, the title lapses, and the original family of the Children of the Sun becomes extinct. Henceforth in the history of Samoa the ruling groups are connected with the underworld. It is possible to follow in detail the process whereby the rest of Samoa was colonized from the spot where the Children of the Sun first landed. It is a most fascinating occupation to watch the process developing under one's eyes, as it were, to see one settlement after another founded and the old order of society gradually fading into nothingness.[1] A phase of history which began with the Children of the Sun, ends with rulers who are associated exclusively with the underworld, who, nevertheless, derive their descent directly from the glorious days of old. This process of transformation can be watched from one end of the Pacific to the other. The old days of the gods have vanished, and the earth knows them no more.

It will be remembered that the Pawnee tell a story of virgin birth, the girl having been impregnated by supernatural means. It was found likewise that the Incas of Peru believed in the doctrine of theogamy, and kept their royal princesses shut up in convents.[2]

These two instances suggest an explanation of a phrase used by the Singhalese Chroniclers, when they said that Vijaya's nobles went to India ' in search of a royal virgin ' (see p. 204).

We are able also to explain the meaning of a story in the Singhalese royal chronicles, of how a princess was shut up in a tower in order to preserve her virginity. This device was in vain, for a prince of the solar line managed to gain access to her, and she bore a child of the solar line.[3] In this story the original theme has become modified, for the sun-god is replaced by a solar prince. But when it is remembered that the Burmese chroniclers were ignorant of the doctrine of theogamy, it is natural that this variation should have taken place. It therefore looks as if the

[1] Perry vi. 302 e.s.   [2] See pp. 194, 196.   [3] Mahavamsa 37.

royal princesses of the solar line in India were originally shut up in convents, as they were in Peru and elsewhere.

The same story occurs in other places, in the same setting of solar dynasties. Heer Kruyt, the son of the well-known Dutch ethnologist, has published a monograph on a people of eastern Central Celebes called the ' To Mori '. He has prefaced an account of their culture with a sketch of their history. This history is illuminating. It shows that the Children of the Sun have been of paramount importance in the foundation of ruling groups all over Celebes. The vicissitudes of the solar strangers who come among the different peoples will enable us, in time, I am convinced, to reconstruct much of the past history of the island, and to account for the varieties of political and social organization that it presents. We are told of men from the sky, and therefore of solar lineage, who came among the people and married native women. It is not difficult to predict that in such places there is no ruling group of Children of the Sun. We should expect that they only occur where the king can marry a princess of the royal blood, as actually happened in Egypt and Peru. The story of Lasaeo, the original culture-hero of the Toradja round Lake Posso, is of this type. He married a Toradja woman, and his sons went elsewhere to be chiefs, but not directly as Children of the Sun, for reasons which are now evident to us. But the story of the ruling groups of the To Mori shows that the pure-blooded marriage of people of the sky-born race was formerly practised. A child came from the sky, and, when arrived at manhood, announced that he would only marry a princess of like rank with himself, some one who had descended from the sky. There were no women of that rank in his own community. But he heard of a daughter of a sky-born chief who was kept shut up so that she might preserve her virginity. His friends thereupon went to her home and prevailed on her to elope and become his wife.[1]

This story carries us back into the atmosphere of the Children of the Sun, and opens up enticing vistas in the history of the tribes of Celebes, a fascinating island for the study of the conditions of the days of old. The examination of such stories as these will, I feel certain, ultimately lead us to understand with much greater clearness the times when the Children of the Sun walked the earth in all their glory. In other instances the continuity has been so broken that, as in the case of the Chroniclers of Burma, who rejected a story of the fatherhood of a god, students are of the opinion that an element of a myth is imaginative. A story

[1] Kruyt, J., 50.

in the Japanese Annals of Shinto recounts how Izanagi and Izanami, who fished up the islands of the archipelago, were brother and sister who married (see p. 175). The Mikado claims descent from the Sun-goddess, and therefore must rank in the solar family. But, as in India, the connexion with the past has largely been broken, and the old order of things has been forgotten. This has caused an authority on Shinto to remark as follows : ' It must not be inferred from this narrative that unions between brothers and sisters of the full blood were permitted by ancient Japanese custom. . . . It is true that marriages were allowed between a man and his sister by the father's side only, but we learn from the *Nihongi* that in the case of full brothers and sisters such connexions were considered criminal. The fact that *imo* (younger sister) is also used in addressing a wife proves no more than the " How fair is thy love, my sister, my bride " of the Song of Solomon. The author of the myth of the Sun-goddess endeavours to smooth over the difficulty of her conjugal relations with her brother Susa no wo by giving them a miraculous character.' [1] Is not, however, such a story exactly what we should expect to account for the origin of the royal family of Japan, if they really came out of the same family of the Children of the Sun as in other places, such as India, Samoa and Peru, not to speak of Egypt ?

It will be remembered that the present inquiry had as its starting-point the creation story of the Pawnee. This story, together with other origin stories, were stated by the Pawnee to be true. We have since seen that their belief is well founded. The creation story opens with an account of the beings of the sky-world, whence came their first rulers. Certain evidence exists to show that this belief in a sky-world is also well founded. The Mikado of Japan is called ' The Heavenly Grandchild ' ; his courtiers are ' men above the clouds ' ; rural districts are spoken of as ' distant from Heaven ' ; the heir to the throne was styled ' August Child of the Sun ' ; and his residence was ' . . . the august house of the Sun '.[2]

The family of the Children of the Sun, the founders of Samoa, are said to have come down from the sky and to have built their first temple called ' Shining House ', which represented the ninth heaven, whence its builders came. There was a corresponding ' Shining Heavens ' on the borders of Tahiti, belonging to a person called ' Eyeball of the Sun ', who figures in the Hawaiian romance of Laieikawai.[3]

There is much in the early traditions of Samoa and Tahiti to

[1] Aston 91.   [2] Aston, op. cit., 38.   [3] Perry vi. 138, 140.

show that the earliest ruling families resembled those of India in their possession of supernatural powers, such as the ability to fly through the air from place to place.

The solar kings of India performed rituals in a ceremonial building containing two fire-hearths, representing the earth and sky.[1] They were thus able to pass from earth to heaven. We shall see later on that these kings ascended to the sky as part of their consecration ceremony.[2] Egyptian kings likewise had the sole privilege of entering the holy of holies of their temples, which was called The Sky.

These facts all serve to substantiate the Pawnee tradition of a sky-world tenanted by divine beings. This tradition surely is a memory of the days when they were ruled over by sky-born Children of the Sun, who made ceremonial buildings called ‘ the sky ’, to which they alone had access. The Pawnee, like the Samoans and Tahitians, have lost their solar rulers, and thus the connexion with the sky-world has been broken. The truth of the Pawnee contention is, however, borne out by the Japanese, the Egyptian and Indian evidence.

We have not yet finished with the Pawnee stories. The sky-world may indeed exist. What are we to say of the beings who live in it ?

[1] S.B. II. 3, 4, 36.   [2] See p. 235.

CHAPTER XVIII

THE FOUR QUARTERS

WE now enter the world of the sky. This is the place of the gods, to which the king and the priests alone have access. In it the great act of creation takes place. From this source comes life to vivify the tribe in a multitude of ways. Life streams down from the sky to the earth. It is high time we endeavoured to ascend to its source.

A beginning may be made with the Skidi Pawnee creation story. This is told in connexion with a ceremony called the Four Pole ceremony. This story is briefly as follows :

They say that originally the earth did not exist. Alone there was a world in the sky, ruled over by Tirawa, the creator, with subordinate beings, such as Evening Star, Morning Star, the Sun, the Moon, the North Star, and the Stars of the Four Quarters.

The drama of creation began with Tirawa assigning these beings their places in the sky. The gods of the four quarters were placed in order to uphold the heavens. Tirawa said to them : ' I also give you power to create people. You shall give them the different bundles, which shall be holy bundles. Your powers will be known by the people, for you shall touch the heavens with your hands, and your feet shall touch the earth.'

These gods thereupon took up their stations, and Tirawa proceeded to the act of creation, attended by the gods of the four quarters. Clouds were created, and out of them was formed the earth, by the action of the four world-quarter gods, who struck the mass with their clubs. ' After this was all done, Tirawa was glad. Then he hid himself for a time.' [1]

When the earth had been created the sky-beings sent down two of their number to people it ; the Son of the Sun and the Moon, and the daughter of the Evening Star and the Morning Star. The man was the first chief of the Pawnee, and the woman was his wife. After they had been on earth for a while the people of the sky-world sent down to them the knowledge of ceremonials. [2]

The creation story tells how the first four-pole ceremonial was performed. Evening Star had sent down by a vision the know-

[1] Dorsey i. 3 e.s. [2] *Ibid.*, 6 e.s.

ledge of how to make a bundle called the Yellow-Calf bundle, for it was made of the skin of a yellow buffalo calf. The account proceeds : ' When the people got together, the Yellow-Calf bundle was not to be used in this ceremony, but another bundle was to be used. A man came forward, who told the chief, Closed-Man, that Bright-Star had come to him in a vision and that he had learned the different ceremonies and songs belonging to the bundles ; that the Yellow-Calf bundle was not to be used or to have anything to do with the ceremony ; that it should be hung up on a tree. So now, really, Mother Bright-Star told this man that now they were to hold a ceremony in imitation of Tirawa, when he first made up his mind to make earth, people, and animals to live on the earth ; that the gods who sat in council with him had been given certain stations in the heavens ; that each of these bundles was to be dedicated to those certain gods, stars in the heavens ; and that in this ceremony they were to have the same relative positions as the gods in the heavens, who had given them the bundles. The people made their camp around the circle where the ceremony was to be held, according to their stations,—north-west of the bundle, south-west of the bundle, etc. A day was set for the people of the four world-quarter gods to go into the timber to bring up their poles. They brought them with great rejoicing, singing, shouting, and they placed the poles upon the ground where it had been cleared for the purpose of holding the ceremony. The north-east pole was painted black ; the north-west pole was painted yellow ; the south-west pole was painted white ; the south-east pole was painted red. Each of these Four-Direction people had their ceremonies, erected their own pole, and they shouted and rejoiced at the time . . . A day was set when the priests caused the errand man to bring the water from the running stream and place it in the north of the lodge. The priest went up, dancing round the pole, and made several movements over the bowl of water, to teach the people how the gods had struck the water when the land was divided from the waters.' [1]

The Four-Pole Ceremony is performed in the usual Pawnee ceremonial ground. This consists of an enclosure open to the east, and unroofed, ringed round with a screen of green boughs.[2] In the centre of the circle is a fireplace ; this is surrounded by four poles placed respectively to the north-east, south-east, south-west, and north-west. At the west end inside the enclosure is a raised altar of earth. Outside the enclosure, at the east end,

[1] *Ibid.*, 10 e.s.
[2] It often is a circular lodge, the roof of which is supported by four posts.

15

is a mound formed of earth taken from the fireplace. The ground being set, the human participants take their places. The enclosure is divided into two equal parts by the diameter running east and west. In the northern half sit certain chiefs and priests, and others in the southern half, while yet others sit at the west end. These all play their rôles in the ceremonial. They use certain ceremonial objects, such as pipes, ears of maize, and feathers; they sing songs and perform evolutions; they act parts.

The first fact to be noted is that the priests and chiefs sit in two main groups, north and south of the enclosure. The priests and chiefs of the villages sit on the north or south side, according as their villages are situated north or south of the river.[1]

The fireplace and each of the poles have a priest associated with them. These five priests constitute the ceremonial nucleus of the tribe. The priest connected with the fireplace is the most important; he is the ceremonial head of the tribe. In the ritual he and his colleagues sit at the west end of the enclosure.

The fivefold grouping of the fireplace and poles is important in Pawnee ritual. It does not occur in every ceremonial, but it is found, for instance, in the Hako.[2] When the four poles occur in connexion with a lodge, as in the Hako ceremony, they are supposed to support the sky, which is represented by the domed roof. The poles and the central fireplace in some way symbolize the tribe as a whole. But, so far as I am aware, there does not appear to be any corresponding grouping of villages similar to that which is found in the case of the north and south grouping of the villages. The village of the priest of the fireplace is called the ' centre village ', but it is not said that this village actually is in the centre of the tribal grouping.[3] Again, the four priests of the poles all live in one village, so there can be no question in their case of a territorial grouping of villages at the intermediate cardinal points, corresponding to the setting of the poles in the ritual enclosure.[4] Nevertheless, the grouping of the fireplace and poles is dramatic, for it corresponds, the Pawnee say, to that of the community in the sky, the world of the gods. The priests of the four poles sit at the west end of the enclosure, because the corresponding gods sit at the west of the sky.[5]

[1] Murie 551.   [2] A. Fletcher, op. cit.
[3] J. R. Murie, op. cit., pp. 550–1.
[4] Except, however, that the story relates that the official sent out to announce the ceremonial found in the West a village of four large houses situated, like the posts in the Four-Pole Ceremony, at the intermediate cardinal points. Dorsey i. 10.
[5] J. R. Murie, op. cit., p. 551, n. 1.

The arrangement of the Pawnee ritual thus is dramatic, and in a twofold manner; it represents both the tribe on earth and also the world of the gods in the sky.

It is now possible to understand more clearly why the Pawnee lay such stress upon the truth of their stories of the gods. They give us detailed accounts of the creative activities of the gods in the sky-world because they themselves repeat them on certain occasions. It might be thought that the Pawnee were merely imitating some imaginary event in the past, but the study of their mythology will not admit of this point of view.

The Four-Pole Ceremony of the Pawnee reproduces in the lodge certain spatial arrangements characteristic of the sky-world people. If, therefore, we turn to other societies, such, for example, as those ruled over by the Children of the Sun, we should expect to find the same arrangement either in ritual, or actual life, or both. We may for this purpose fix our attention upon the central feature of the Four-Pole Ceremony, namely, the fire in the centre of the lodge, and the four poles that surround it. The fire represents Tirawa, who was said to be in the centre; the four poles represent the gods of the four quarters. The priests of these five gods constitute the ceremonial nucleus of the tribe.

We have already discovered that peoples, such as those of Mexico, Peru and elsewhere, possessed social organizations similar to those described in the origin stories of the Pawnee. Certain tribes of the United States of about the same cultural level as the Pawnee also exhibit these characteristics. If we turn to such communities we find arrangements similar to those of the Four-Pole Ceremony of the Pawnee.

A beginning may be made with the Zuñi Indians of New Mexico. The late Frank Cushing made a remarkable discovery concerning them, which is best stated in his words. He says, ' The Zuñi of to-day number scarcely 1,700 and, as is well known, they inhabit only a single large pueblo,—single in more senses than one, for it is not a village of separate houses, but a village of six or seven separate parts in which the houses are mere apartments or divisions, so to say. This pueblo, however, is divided, not always clearly to the eye, but very clearly in the estimation of the people themselves, into seven parts, corresponding, not perhaps in arrangement topographically, but in sequence, to their subdivisions of the " worlds " or world-quarters of this world. Thus, one division of the town is supposed to be related to the north and to be centred round its kiva or estufa,[1] which may or may not be, however, in its centre; another division

[1] Ceremonial building.

represents the west, another the south, another the east, yet another the upper world and another the lower world, while a final division represents the middle or mother and synthetic combination of them all in this world.

' By reference to the early Spanish history of the pueblo it may be seen that when discovered, the Ashiwi or Zuñis were living in seven quite widely separated towns, the celebrated Seven Cities of Cibola, and that this theoretic subdivision of the only one of these towns now remaining is in some measure a survival of the original subdivision of the tribe into seven sub-tribes inhabiting as many separate towns. It is evident that in both cases, however, the arrangement was, and is, if we may call it such, a mythic organization ; hence my use of the term the mytho-sociologic organization of the tribe. At any rate, this is the key to their sociology as well as their mythic conceptions of space and the universe.' [1]

The Zuñi and the other peoples of the Pueblo region also have a dual arrangement of society. They thus actually live in a grouping that is partly ritual among the Pawnee.

Further evidence of the same kind can be found among the peoples further south, for instance, in Mexico. The city of Mexico was arranged with regard to the four cardinal points. This is shown by a quotation from Motolinia, given by Bandelier. He is speaking of the great pyramids of Mexico. ' They called these temples " teocalli ", and we found all over the land that in the best part of the settlement they made a great quadrangular court, which, in the largest pueblo, was one cross-bow shot from one corner to another, while in the smaller places it is not so large. This court they enclosed by a wall, many of which enclosures were with battlements ; the entrances looked towards the chief highways and streets, which all terminated at the court, and even, to still more honour their temples, they led their roads up to these in a straight line from two and three leagues distance. It was a wonderful aspect, to witness from the top of the chief temple, how from all the quarters and the minor places, the road-ways all led up in a straight line to the courts of the teocallis . . . the devil did not content himself with the aforesaid teocallis, but in each pueblo and in each quarter, as far as a quarter of a league off, there were other small courts containing, sometimes only one, sometimes three or four teocallis.' [2] The great temple was, therefore, in the centre, with four roads leading out towards the four cardinal points. The city was divided into four quarters, with a ceremonial centre. The chief rulers of the city belonged

[1] F. H. Cushing 367.　　　　[2] Bandelier 104.

to the four quarters, each of which had a civil chief and a war chief. This arrangement was said to have been ordered by Huitzilopochtli, the great god of the Aztecs, the founder of Mexico city. Huitzilopochtli was a chief who died, and whose body was wrapped up as a bundle and taken by the Aztecs with them on their travels. When the Aztecs had arrived at the site of Mexico city, Huitzilopochtli said : ' Say to the congregation of Mexico that the chiefs, each one with his relatives, friends, and connexions, shall divide themselves into four principal quarters, my house being in the centre among them, so that each cluster may build in its quarter as it pleases.' The original band of the Mexicans was divided into two groups, as in the case of the Pawnee, but we do not know much about this division.[1]

This arrangement appears to have been traditional in Mexico. ' If the ancient traditions may be believed, the Toltec monarchs built as magnificent palaces as their Aztec successors. The sacred palace of that mysterious Toltec priest-king, Quetzalcoatl, had four principal halls, facing the four cardinal points. That on the east was called the Hall of Gold, because its walls were ornamented with plates of that metal, delicately chased and finished ; the apartment lying toward the west was named the Hall of Emeralds and Turquoises, and its walls were profusely adorned with all kinds of precious stones ; the hall facing the south was decorated with plates of silver and with brilliant-coloured sea-shells which were fitted together with great skill. The walls of the fourth hall, which was on the north, were red jasper, covered with carving and ornamented with shells. Another of these palaces or temples, for it is not clear which they were, had also four principal halls, decorated entirely with feather-work tapestry. In the eastern division the feathers were yellow ; in the western they were blue, taken from a bird called Xiuhtototl ; in the southern hall the feathers were white ; and in that on the north they were red.' [2]

The Peruvian empire under the Incas had an arrangement recalling that of Mexico. The origin story told by the people of Colla-suyu and Cunti-suyu, south of Cuzco, the capital of Peru, was that there was a flood. ' After this a man appeared at Tiahu-anacu to the southward of Cuzco, who was so powerful that he divided the world into four parts, and gave them to four men who were called kings. The first was called Manco Ccapac, the second Collà, the third Tocay, and the fourth Pinahua. They

[1] Ad. F. Bandelier, pp. 104, 401, 584. This information serves to throw light on the structure of the divisions of a tribe or State. See pp. 169 e.s.
[2] Bancroft II. 173–4.

say that he gave the northern part to Manco Ccapac, the southern to Collà . . . the eastern to Tocay, and the western to Pinahua. He ordered each to repair to his district, to conquer it, and to govern the people he might find there. . . . They say that from this division of the world afterwards arose that which the Incas made of their kingdom, called Ttahuantin-suyu.' [1] This means ' the four quarters of the world,' [2] and refers to the fact that the empire consisted of four provinces, called ' the four parts of the empire '.[3] The capital, Cuzco, was supposed to be the navel, the centre of the earth. It was divided into four quarters corresponding to the divisions of the empire, and four roads led out from it, north, east, south, and west, to the provinces.[4] The city of Cuzco was also divided into two parts, north and south, upper and lower.

The story is that Manco Ccapac and his wife were brother and sister ; Manco Ccapac was one of the Children of the Sun, so this form of union would be expected. The account runs as follows : ' In this manner he began to settle this our imperial city, dividing it into two parts, called *Hanan Cuzco*, which, as you know, means Upper Cuzco, and *Hurin Cuzco*, which is Lower Cuzco. The people who followed the king wished to settle in Hanan Cuzco, and for that reason it received the name ; and those who were gathered together by the queen settled in Hurin Cuzco, and it was therefore called the lower town. . . . In imitation of this division a similar arrangement was made in all the towns, large or small, of our empire, which were separated into wards according to the lineages of the families, which were called *Hanan Ayllu* and *Hurin Ayllu*, that is, the upper and lower lineage ; or *Hanan-suyu* and *Hurin-suyu*, or the upper and lower provinces.' [5]

The Peruvian empire provides us with a complete parallel to the mythological community of the Pawnee. The ruler is the Son of the Sun ; each settlement is on a dual basis ; and the empire is divided into four quarters, with the capital, also divided into four quarters, in the centre. The king lives in the centre of the capital, and thus at the centre of all. The dual division of Cuzco is more definite than that of the Skidi. For the northern half of Cuzco is connected with the king, and the southern half with the queen ; that is to say, with the male and female principles. While this is not found, so far as I am aware, among the Pawnee, perhaps a trace of the grouping may be retained in the series of Wichita tales of the marriage between the son of the

[1] Vega I. 71.   [2] *Ibid.*, 142.   [3] *Ibid.*, 35.   [4] *Ibid.*, 143, 234.
[5] *Ibid.*, 67.

chief of the northern half of the village and the daughter of the chief of the southern half of the village.[1]

The situation of the Peruvian king, the Son of the Sun, in the centre of the state, surrounded by the four quarters, ruled over by high officials, suggests that Tirawa of the Pawnee was really the king of the mythological community. But the conditions in Mexico, where the body of a dead leader is in the centre, makes it uncertain whether he represented a live or a dead king. The difficulty, however, can be considerably reduced when it is stated that the Peruvians preserved the bodies of their dead kings as national possessions. When Manco Ccapac, the founder of Cuzco, died, his body was mummified. We are told that ' The vassals mourned for the Ynca Manco Ccapac, with great sorrow, and the obsequies and mourning lasted for many months. They embalmed this body so as to keep it with them, and not to lose sight of it. They worshipped it as a God, the child of the Sun, and offered up to it many sacrifices of sheep, lambs, wild rabbits, birds, maize and pulses ; confessing it to be lord of all things here below.' [2]

The arrangement of the state just described in Peru was to be found in China under the Chou dynasty (twelfth–third centuries B.C.), if not earlier. The Chou Li, the Book of Rites of the Chou Dynasty, is full of the symbolism of the four quarters. It opens by saying that ' The sovereign alone constitutes the realm ; he determines the four quarters and fixes the principal positions. He traces the plan of the capital and of the provinces. He creates the ministers and distinguishes their functions, so as to form the administrative centre of the people.' The capital has four suburbs. The royal palace is in the centre, not only of the capital, but of the realm. The capital is the navel of the earth, and its position is determined by astronomical observation.[3]

This extraordinary arrangement of society was found in Java of former days. Settlements were supposed to be arranged in groups of five, one in the centre and one at each cardinal point. The administration was formed on this pattern. Each chief ruler was surrounded at the cardinal points by four lesser rulers, the group constituting the ' Holy Five '.[4]

As this form of grouping is found in Java it is certain to be present in India. It is found in Burma. ' The modern town of Mandalay, the Burmese capital city, is likewise walled square, a mile and an eighth long on every face, and there are twelve gates, three on every side. The palace is in the midst, and in

[1] Dorsey ii. 199.   [2] Vega I. 93. See also Acosta I. 313.
[3] Biot I. 1, 2, 27 (note).   [4] Ossenbruggen 3, 4.

the exact centre of the palace and of the city rises the seven-roofed spire, which the Burmese look upon as the centre of Burma, and therefore of creation.' [1]

The ceremonial of the kingdoms of ancient India, Burma, Siam, Cambodia and Java reveals similar arrangements. The king was supposed to represent the centre of the earth where he lived surrounded by the four quarters. His capital usually had a rectangular wall surrounding it. This wall was pierced with gates, one in each side.[2]

These examples are taken at random from a vast mass that could be brought forward to show that sky-born kings are intimately associated with the symbolism of the four quarters. This gives us still more reason to believe with the Pawnee in the truth of their origin stories. Evidently the four quarters were an essential part of the life-giving situation connected with the creation of land from the depths of the primordial ocean, together with the endowment of this created land with life. The original four quarters, whatever their significance may be, have been carried along in the train of ceremonials, and appear, in America for example, in connexion with gods, stars, poles, colours, seasons, animals, and so forth.

[1] Lethaby i. 63.   [2] Hocart ii. 105.

CHAPTER XIX

THE CREATION

THE sky-world, as we have seen, was a ceremonial building to which, as a rule, the sky-born alone had entry. Let us follow in the train of these great ones, and observe what happened in their holy of holies.

The ceremonial of India will supply us with ample material for this purpose. We are coming to realize the outstanding importance of the study of Indian ritual to students of the development of civilization. We are beginning to see, moreover, that the early Sanskrit texts, such as we find them in the Rig Veda, had a ceremonial meaning, and were not merely the result of poetic fancy. The available literature is enormous, but certain of its features make it comparatively easy of manipulation.

The rituals are many in number. Those included in the ' Satapatha Brahmana ', as translated by Julius Eggeling, for example, include the Morning and Evening Sacrifices, the Seasonal Sacrifices, the New Moon and Full Moon Sacrifice, the Soma Sacrifice, the Fire Altar, the Consecration ceremonies and the Horse Sacrifice.

These rituals are all associated with the kingship. They were originally performed on behalf of the king, the Brahmin acting as officiant. These rituals, diverse as they may be in outward form, were part of a whole. They were all based upon the deeds of the gods, and ultimately upon those of a primordial being named Prajapati. The rituals themselves are strewn with reminders that what is being done is what was done in the past. Each ritual, therefore, is simply a mosaic built up out of certain incidents in a primordial drama. Each separate ritual has its own characteristics, due to the influence of the priestly schools ; but, in spite of this diversity, the priests have not departed from the correspondence between ritual and story. They cling with tenacity to the mythical foundation of their ceremonials.

The building of the Fire Altar is one of the most important of these rituals ; for it contains an account of the creation. The Fire Altar is an enormous brick structure shaped like a falcon. It contains a clay hearth holding a fire, in the midst of which is placed a ' golden man ' which will provide for the king an immortal body in the hereafter beyond the skies.

This ceremony starts with ' Verily in the beginning there was here the non-existent '. Only the ' vital airs ' existed in the form of the ' Rishis '. These ' Rishis ' were ancient priests who compiled many of these rituals. The ' vital airs ' were seven in number. Out of them was generated a being named Prajapati. The story really begins with him. He was the Great Creator, and he is the centre of the drama which is enacted in every ritual. The creation of Prajapati by the ' Rishis ' out of the ' vital airs ' appears to be unintelligible ; [1] but it is important in making the ' vital airs ', usually identified with the breath, the fundamental element of creative activity.

I shall now quote a series of texts from the ritual, and shall begin with the creative activities of Prajapati.

Prajapati, having been brought into existence, proceeds to create the universe. He said, ' " May I be more than one, may I be reproduced ! " ' He thereupon created the waters out of speech ; and then entered the waters. Thence an egg arose, from which Brahman was first created. Out of the eggshell the earth was created. ' He desired, " May I generate this (earth) from these waters ! " ' The juice which flowed from the egg became a tortoise ; and that which was spirted upwards became dissolved over the water, so that, as the text says, ' all this (universe) appeared as one form only, namely water '. Then Prajapati created foam. ' Worn out with toil and austerity, he created clay, mud, saline, soil and sand, gravel (pebble), rock, ore, gold, plants and trees : therewith he clothed this earth.' He then created the earth and spread it out.[2]

Prajapati then entered into union with the earth, and thus produced the wind. Part of the egg produced by this union became the air. From union with the air he produced the sun, while from the egg produced by the union arose the sky. By means of the sun he entered into union with the sky and produced yet another egg. Thence came the moon, the stars, and the points of the compass.

Prajapati then entered into union with speech, and created thence the gods, such as the Vasus, the gods of the earth ; the Rudras, the gods of the air ; and the Adityas, the gods of the sky. The All-gods he placed in the quarters.

Prajapati created gods and mortal creatures. Having eaten

---

[1] See pp. 261–2.
[2] ' Satapatha Brahmana ' VI. 1, 1, 8–15. The ' Satapatha Brahmana ' will henceforth be referred to as S.B.

plants he became pregnant, and gave birth to the gods and to mortals. 'From the upper vital airs he created the gods, and from the lower vital airs the mortal creatures.'

Finally, having done all this, Prajapati fell asunder. 'Having created creatures he, having run the whole race, became relaxed; and therefore even now he who runs the whole race becomes indeed relaxed. From him being thus relaxed, the vital air went out from within. When it had gone out of him the gods left him.' [1]

Prajapati conceived a passion for his daughter Ushas. From the union a son was born, who had several names, Rudra, Surya, Ugra, and others. The last name was that of Isana the Ruler. 'And because he gave him that name, the Sun became suchlike, for Isana is the Sun, since the Sun rules over this All. He said, "So great indeed I am : give me no other name after that ".' [2]

The similarity between this story and that of the Pawnee is evident. Prajapati, having come into being as the embodiment of the 'vital airs', proceeds to create the gods and to give them their stations in the universe. This is what Tirawa did, though we are not told that he created the gods. The All-gods, whom Prajapati placed in their stations, correspond to the four-quarter gods of the Pawnee.

It is important to emphasize the greater knowledge of the creator possessed by the Indian priests. The Indian texts carry the act of creation a stage further back. Prajapati actually created the gods. He is, as it were, a super-god, who lived alone before the gods. The activities in the sky-world therefore promise to be highly interesting.

The story of creation having been told, the priest then proceeds to perform a series of rites illustrating the various acts of Prajapati. Part of the ceremony consists in the making of a clay fire-pan. Each detail is carefully compared to the creative act which it repeats.

The fire-pan is made of clay, which is worked up with water. 'He then produces foam and puts it thereto : the second form which was created (in the shape of) foam, that form he thus makes it. And the clay he now mixes is that very clay which was created as the third form. It was from these forms that he (Agni) was created at the beginning, and from them he now produces him.' This is in direct imitation of the creation, where the earth was made out of foam produced from the waters.

The creative act then goes on. 'Then there are these three

[1] S.B., VI. 1, 2, 3–12.   [2] Ibid., 1, 3, 8–17.

kinds of powder (dust) (sand or) gravel, stone, and iron-rust therewith he mixes (the clay), just for firmness. And as to why (it is mixed) therewith, it is because thereof this (earth) consisted when it was created in the beginning : thus what like this (earth) was created in the beginning, such he now makes it (the earth, or fire-pan).' [1]

After a time the fire-pan is spread out, just as the earth was spread out. A blessing is called upon it. ' " Establish in me offspring, increase of wealth, lordship of cattle, manhood, clansmen for the Sacrificer ! " ' This is in imitation of the creation. ' For the Vasus, having fashioned this (terrestrial) world, invoked this blessing thereon ; and in like manner does the Sacrificer, having fashioned this world, now invoke this blessing thereon.' Similarly he fashions the air and the sky, and endows them with offspring, wealth, cattle, men, with a complete community. He finally completes it by putting the quarters into the world, in connexion with the All-gods, the gods of the four quarters. Then he endows it once more with animals and so forth.

The fire-pan is made in every way to symbolize birth, for out of it a child is to be born. It is provided with nipples, like the udder of a cow [2]

The Sacrificer. then makes the gods, Agni, Vayu, Aditya from the same clay. ' He thus produces these gods from these worlds.' He then causes children to be generated from himself by means of certain bricks. ' The Sacrificer makes them : the Sacrificer thus produces offspring from his own self. He makes them without interruption : he thus produces uninterrupted offspring from his own self.'

The fire-pan is then fumigated in order to put breath into the head.[3]

The Sacrificer now proceeds to build up the altar itself, in imitation of what happened at the creation. The universe first of all consisted of waters, so a lotus leaf is put down. The lotus leaf also stands for a womb ; ' he thereby establishes this earth on the truth '.[4]

The Fire Altar as a whole stands for the universe. As it says, ' Verily, this (brick-) built Fire Altar (Agni) is this terrestrial world : the waters (of the encircling ocean) are its (circle of) enclosing stones ; the men its Yagushmatis (bricks with special formulas) ; the cattle its Sudadohas ; the plants and trees its earth-fillings (between the layers of bricks), its oblations and fire-logs : Agni (the terrestrial fire) its Lokamprina (space-filling

[1] S.B., VI. 5, 1, 1–6.   [2] Ibid., 5, 2, 3–18.   [3] Ibid., 5, 3, 3–8.
[4] Ibid., VII. 4, 1, 6–8.

brick);—thus this comes to make up the whole Agni and the whole Agni comes to be the space-filler; and, verily, whosoever knows this, thus comes to be that whole (Agni) who is the space-filler.' [1]

This fire-altar has layers of brick with fillings of earth between them. This is what is said concerning these layers.

'The first layer is this (terrestrial) world; and the filling of soil means cattle: thus, in covering the first layer with a filling of soil, he covers this (terrestrial) world with cattle.

'The second layer is the air, and the filling of soil means birds: thus, in covering the second layer with a filling of soil, he covers (fills) the air with birds.

'The third layer is the sky, and the filling of soil means stars; thus, in covering the third layer with a filling of soil, he covers the sky with stars.

'The fourth layer is the sacrifice, and the filling of soil means sacrificial gifts: thus, in covering the fourth layer with a filling of soil, he covers the sacrifice with sacrificial gifts (to the priests).

'The fifth layer is the Sacrificer, and the filling of soil means progeny (or subjects); thus, in covering the fifth layer with a filling of soil, he covers (abundantly supplies) the Sacrificer with progeny (or subjects).

'The sixth layer is the heavenly world, and the filling of soil means the gods: thus, in covering the sixth layer with a filling of soil, he fills the heavenly world with gods.

'The seventh layer is immortality,—that is the last (layer) he lays down, and thus bestows immortality as the highest thing of all this (universe): therefore immortality is the highest thing of all this (universe); therefore the gods are not separated therefrom; and therefore they are immortal.' [2]

This long series of quotations reveals much concerning the creative activities of the sky-beings. We find the creator in India, as among the Pawnee, setting himself in the centre and surrounding himself with the gods of the four quarters. He then proceeds to diverse creative acts. Prajapati creates the primordial ocean. This is also mentioned by the Pawnee as one of Tirawa's acts. Prajapati also creates the gods; which shows that in Indian thought there was a time before the gods, when only Prajapati existed. It is interesting to note that Prajapati had incestuous intercourse with his daughter, after which a son was born, called Isana, the Ruler. The texts referring to this episode suggest the inception of the solar kingship (see p. 223).

[1] *Ibid.*, X. 5, 4, 1.   [2] *Ibid.*, VIII. 7, 4, 12–18.

We have also found the Children of the Sun throughout the world practising incestuous unions. This incident therefore seems to bring Prajapati within that group. There are differences however; for, in this case, we are not told that Prajapati was a son of the sun; on the contrary, he is said to be his father. It is to be remembered that Tirawa among the Pawnee set the sun in his place, and that the son of the sun was the first Pawnee chief; that is to say, both in America and in India, the Children of the Sun originally carried out ceremonials in imitation of a being whose relationship to them has yet to be defined.

The consideration of the Hako ceremony of the Pawnee led us to conclude that the gods of the sky-world, in their creative activity, were intimately associated with ritual. We found that an essential feature of the long chain of rituals reaching back to the original creation by the sky-beings, was the purely human element. The securance of life needed the correct performance of ritual. The gods, from Tirawa downwards, were lay figures with no free will. We now learn from the Brahmana ritual that these gods were created by Prajapati and by the king himself. That is to say, the creation of gods is part of the ritual connected with the Children of the Sun. It is to be noted further, that the sky-world is likewise their creation. That is easy to understand; for we have seen that they carried their sky-worlds about the earth with them (see p. 210).

The ritual of the Fire Altar shows the king imitating the creation of the universe by Prajapati. It is interesting to note that the king creates the heavenly world and peoples it with gods, whereas he had previously created the sky and filled it with stars. This is an interesting point, for among the Pawnee Tirawa lives in the land beyond the sky. Most interesting of all is the seventh layer of the Fire Altar. This layer, we are told, is immortality, the highest thing of all this universe. This privilege is associated with the gods. This is the culminating act of the great Fire Altar ritual. Prajapati by his act of creation produces the gods, the sky-world, the earth and all the inhabitants thereof. Finally, he produces immortality. By carrying out the same procedure the king procures immortality for himself.

CHAPTER XX

THE IMMORTAL GODS

THE Brahmana rituals of India have revealed the fact that immortality is believed to be procured by certain ceremonial means. The king enters the world of the gods to perform his ceremonies, in the sure and certain hope of a glorious life in the hereafter. He apparently does not believe that he has an immortal soul, ensuring him a conscious survival after death; he is convinced that he can obtain this privilege by imitating his ancestor, the creator of the gods, the giver of life who himself first achieved immortality.

The Pawnee know that the sky-beings are able to become immortal. They tell a story about a being named Lightning, who was sent by Mother Bright Star down to earth. She gave Lightning a sack, and Great-Star filled it with people. Lightning came down to earth with the sack, and went about the world. He opened the sack from time to time, and let the people out to form the camp circle and hunt buffalo. After a time Fool-Coyote sent to the earth the Wolf, who was finally killed by the people. Lightning then said to the men that they had lost immortality because of their act.

A remarkable ceremony followed. 'After Lightning had said these things, the priests took buffalo fat and rubbed it over Lightning's body. Then they rubbed over him hair from the buffalo. Next, the priests smeared Lightning's body with red clay and fat, mixed. That made Lightning happy again. Then Lightning told them to get sweet grass, and put it on the southwest of the lodge. Then Lightning turned over where he sat, and smoke began to rise from the sweet grass. Then the priest removed his robe, and bathed it in the smoke of the sweet grass, and put it upon his back. They then bathed in the smoke his moccasins, his feather, and all other things which he wore, shaking them first, before they put them over the incense. Thus these cloud-beings were to learn what they should do in a future state.'

Lightning met his brother Ready-to-Give, who lives in the north. They never died, ' and thus they show that the gods in

227

the heavens were never to die; but people, like wolves, were to grow sick and die.'[1]

This story shows that the people from the sky who came to the earth in the beginning, knew how to become immortal. Presumably the procedure adopted in the case of Lightning was the one necessary for the purpose; for Lightning himself was immortal, and he went through a ritual performance that was supposed to be done by the sky-beings in a future state.[2] The Pawnee themselves lost this precious gift, as they lost so many other things.

We have already had reason to believe that the nature of the gods was the outcome of ritual procedures. We now find that the sky-beings themselves are able to acquire immortality as the result of certain mechanical procedures, again by means of ritual. The Pawnee have lost the gift, presumably because they are no longer able to perform the necessary ceremony.

Stories of the loss of immortality are widespread, but they are essentially similar, in that they attribute this loss to a break in continuity with the source of life. The best known story is that of Gilgamesh, the Babylonian hero.

The Posso-Toradja likewise say that the sky-beings possess the breath of eternal life. It was intended to animate two stone images with this breath, but, owing to an unfortunate incident, they were animated as mortal.[3] The royal annals of the Bugi of Southern Celebes speak of 'the first mortal king' of Gowa.[4] In Samoa we hear likewise of immortal kings being replaced by mortals.[5] There is little doubt that the failure of the pure-bred line of the Children of the Sun was responsible for this loss of immortality.

The Pawnee story suggests that by the term 'immortality' they really mean 'conscious survival after death'. We have already seen that much confusion is involved in the use of the word 'immortality'. It may refer to immunity from death, or it may refer to a conscious survival after death, not necessarily of indefinite duration.

Confusion has also been caused by the application of our own phraseology referring to the spiritual nature of men, to the supposed beliefs of people of alien cultures. I have long suspected that throughout the whole range of human society, not even excluding certain branches of the Christian Church, the privilege of life hereafter was reserved for those who had been through certain ceremonies. My reasons have been many, prominent

[1] Dorsey i. 14–20.   [2] *Ibid.*, 19.   [3] Kruyt and Adriani I. 245–6.
[4] Erkelens 81.   [5] Krämer 8, 382, 385 n. 7, 393.

among them is the growing conviction that all initiation ceremonies
are originally based upon the ritual connected with death.   The
Mystery Religions of Greece and Rome ; the Initiation Ceremonies
of the Australian natives ; the Secret Societies of North American
Indians, such as the Mide' Wiwin of the Ojibway ; the Secret
Societies of the New Hebrides ; and countless other instances,
force me to this conclusion.[1]

The Aurignacian people of southern Europe show by their
burial ceremonies that they had ideas concerning the nature of
death ; but it does not follow that they believed in conscious
survival after death.   It is more likely that they looked upon death
as a sleep, and that their practices had relation to that belief.   There
is much reason to suppose that early man had no definite conception of a soul, but regarded death as the cessation of consciousness.   This was certainly the belief of the Babylonians, whose
dead slumbered in the underworld.   The Egyptians originally
had the belief that the dead were asleep in their graves, and only
could live again after certain rituals had been performed.

I am not aware that any inquirers have paid attention in the
field to the supposed fate of individuals after death.   In 1930
I began an inquiry into the initiation ceremonies of the Bakwena
branch of the Basuto living in East Griqualand under Chief
Jeremiah Moshesh.   I was informed that only those men who
had been through this initiation lived after death ; the others
' died like dogs '.   I had no opportunity of testing the matter
in detail.

I was, however, able to do so among the Pondo.   Inquiry
there showed that the fate of young children and of unmarried
men and women was not known.   They were just buried anywhere, and then forgotten : so far as was known they simply
ceased to exist.   On the other hand, I found that those who
survived after death had what was termed a ' name '.   This
means that they were occupying a hut of their own that had been
named.   When a son of a kraal marries, he builds himself a hut,
either in his father's kraal or on a site that has been granted
by the chief.   After a time he gives a ' beer-drink ', and the hut
is then named.   He then is assured of survival after death.[2]

The Pondo whom I questioned on this topic were unable to
give me any reason why only those who had names could survive
after death.   The reason may lie in the fact that they have dis-

[1] See Perry vii. 134 e.s. for a discussion of this topic.   See also pp. 249 e.s.
of this book.
[2] The Pondo ' beer-drinks ' attended by Mr. J. E. S. Griffiths and myself
were almost devoid of their former ceremonial accompaniments.

16

continued the practice of initiating boys, and with it have lost
the knowledge of the life after death that usually forms part of
this ritual.   When I asked what evidence they had of the survival
of these people with names, they said that they had none.   The
doctors told them.   For instance, a member of a kraal might
fall ill ; if the illness was serious the doctor might say that it
was caused by the ghosts of the dead, whom he would mention
by name, who desired meat.   The owner of the kraal thereupon
killed one of the cattle in the hope of securing a cure.   I was
told that those who had died without a ' name ' were never
mentioned by the doctor.

It is obviously useless to inquire of the Pawnee, the Samoans,
the Pondo or any other such people concerning the attainment
of immortality, using that term in the sense of a conscious survival
after death.   These peoples merely know that sky-beings could
become immortal.   They may therefore be left on one side, but
before doing so it is worthy of note that, although they know about
immortality, they are unable themselves to attain it.   On the
other hand, the ancient kings of India could secure it by imitating
the acts of creation of Prajapati.   The people of India had knowledge that was lacking in the others.   Therefore if we wish to
understand more concerning the sky-world, gods, kingship, and
immortality we turn towards India.

It is curious, and somewhat confusing, to contemplate the
general features of the ceremonial connected with the great Fire
Altar.   We have already learned that to acquire immortality
the whole history of the world, from the creation of the primordial
ocean to the making of the world beyond the sky, had to be
enacted.   It is difficult to imagine the meaning of this seemingly
incongruous medley of ideas and events.   Yet we find that the
creation by Prajapati was the source and fount of the whole of
the Indian ritual as set out in the Brahmanas.

There seem to be two fixed points in the situation.   Throughout
the whole of the series of ceremonials contained in the Brahmana
we have at one end Prajapati the creator, and at the other the
living king who imitates him.   The king likewise imitates the
gods.   If, therefore, we can determine the nature of Prajapati,
his relationship to the king, and the relationship of the king to
the gods, we shall be well on our way to the final solution of the
problem set by the Pawnee ritual.   Evidently much must lie
behind the quotations made from the Fire Altar ritual.   We are
simply told that certain results follow from certain procedures,
but no explanation is as yet forthcoming to account for the
meaning of these details.   In order to understand these matters

more fully, I propose to consider briefly some of the ceremonials connected with the consecration of the king.[1]

In these ceremonials the king imitates the gods. In the introduction to a consecration ceremony, it says : ' the gods now desired, " May we be consecrated even on this occasion with all the rites of consecration ! " They were indeed consecrated on this occasion by all the rites of consecration ; and in like manner is the Sacrificer [that is, the king] on this occasion consecrated by all the rites of consecration.' [2] It says, in another place : ' These deities, indeed, have been consecrated by this same consecration ceremony by which he (the Sacrificer) is now to be consecrated : it is them he gratifies, and thus gratified by offering, they grant him permission (to perform) this consecration ceremony, and, permitted by them, he is consecrated ; for only he becomes king whom the (other) kings allow (to assume) the royal dignity, but not he whom they do not (allow to do it).[3]

The king imitates the gods in his consecration ceremony ; for the early kingship claims direct connexion with the gods. The king's consecration consists partly of a re-enactment of the creation drama, partly of an identification of the king with the gods themselves.

The creation story recounts how the earth was formed out of the primordial ocean, and supplied with all manner of living things. The king, in his consecration, repeats the process of creation. We find him saying, ' May I be consecrated, after creating abundance and creatures.' . . . ' May I be consecrated for healthy, faultless creatures.' . . . ' May I be consecrated, when safety and security are gained.' . . . ' May I be consecrated, having encompassed both essences.' [4]

The king produces these effects by various ceremonial procedures that are supposed to follow the example of the gods when they were consecrated in the beginning. One of these ceremonial performances is called the Trishamuykta offering, ' the triply connected '.[5] This offering is made up of three rounds, each of three separate oblations. It is said of this offering, ' Therewith the gods came by men, and in like manner does this (king) now thereby come by men.' [6] That is to say, the king creates men at his consecration.

The whole realm depends upon the king. ' " This is thy realm ; a supporter and sustainer art thou for the friend : for

[1] Particularly the Ragasuya and the Vagapeya. See S.B., V.
[2] S.B., IX. 3, 4, 6.   [3] Ibid., IX. 4, 1, 1.
[4] Ibid., V. 2, 4, 1 ; V. 2, 4, 2 ; V. 2, 4, 7, 12.
[5] Part III. 54 n. 1.   [6] S.B., V. 2, 5, 1.

sustenance, for rain, for the lordship of creatures (do I consecrate
thee) " . . . that is to say, " This is thy kingdom; thou art
consecrated (anointed)!   Thou art thy friend's supporter and
sustainer: for our sustenance art thou; for rain unto us art
thou, for our lordship of creatures art thou!" They thereby
entreat him, " For all this thou art unto us: for all this we have
consecrated thee!"   And therefore people thus entreat a human
king who has been consecrated.' [1]

The king in his consecration sets in order the whole of the
community.   He is responsible for the crops.

' It is for the plants that he who is consecrated, is consecrated;
therefore he now makes the plants healthy and faultless, thinking,
" May I be consecrated for (the obtainment of) healthy, faultless
plants (crops) ".' [2]

The king supplied strength to the community.   ' Yea, the
impulse of strength prevailed over all these worlds, on every
side; from days of yore the king goeth about knowing, increasing
the people, and the well-being amongst us . . . with the remaining
(offering material) he sprinkles him (the Sacrificer); he thereby
sprinkles him with food, bestows food upon him.' [3]

When the king is consecrated he is endowed with all manner
of qualities by those gods with whom the kingship is especially
associated.   He is supplied with ' life ':

' " May Savitri quicken thee for (powers of) quickening (ruling),
Agni for householders, Soma for trees, Brihaspati for speech,
Indra for lordship, Rudra for cattle, Mitra for truth, Varuna for
the lord of the law." . . .   " Quicken him, O gods, to be un-
rivalled ".' [4]

And again, ' " with Soma's glory I sprinkle thee," . . . " with
vigour," he thereby says; " . . . with Agni's glow . . ." " with
vigour " he thereby says . . . " with Surya's splendour " . . .
" with vigour " he thereby says; " be thou chieftain of chiefs!"
. . .[5] " be thou the supreme king of kings " he thereby says.'

The king is the supreme upholder of the law.   ' The king is
the upholder of the sacred law, for he is not capable of all and
every speech, nor of all and every deed; but that he should
speak only what is right, and do what is right, of that he " . . . is
capable ".' [6]

The king establishes the social order of the community in his
consecration.   He goes on a ceremonial visit to the Commander
of the Army, to the Court Chaplain, to the Queen, to the Court
Minstrel and Chronicler, to the Headman, to the Chamberlain,

[1] S.B., IX. 3, 3, 11.   [2] Ibid., V. 2, 3, 9.   [3] Ibid., 2, 2, 7, 12.
[4] Ibid., 3, 3, 11–12.   [5] Ibid., 4, 3, 2.   [6] Ibid., 4, 4, 5.

to the Charioteer, to the Carver, to the Keeper of the Dice, to the Huntsman, to the Courier, and finally to a discarded wife, one who has not borne a child to him. . . . ' These are the eleven jewels he completes . . . it is for the sake of vigour that he completes the eleven jewels . . . it is their king he becomes ; it is for them that he thereby is consecrated, and it is them he makes his own faithful followers.' [1]

The king institutes his officers and his followers in yet another way. At the end of the consecration ceremony he is handed a wooden sword by the priest, the Brahmin. ' " Indra's thunderbolt thou art : therewith serve me ".' The king then hands the wooden sword on to his brother. ' Thereby the king makes his brother to be weaker than himself.' The king's brother in his turn hands the wooden sword to the governor, in order to make him weaker than himself. Similarly the governor hands it on to the village headman, who hands it to a tribesman. ' And as to why they mutually hand it on in this way, they do so lest there should be a confusion of classes, and in order that (society) may be in the proper order.' [2]

We learn from these quotations that ancient society was a unity, based on a regular hierarchy, which was instituted by the king at his consecration. Each group had its proper place in the scheme, and was supposed to maintain that place. The king was above all, the source and fount of the community. He fulfilled the same function with regard to the community as the gods themselves. He created everything, including the earth. He was godlike in his activities. He was endowed at his consecration with magical force that enabled him to maintain the activity of everything within the realm.

These texts once again reveal to us a knowledge of the sky-world that the Pawnee do not possess. The king in India was an active source of life to the community over which he ruled. He delegates this life down through a hierarchy of officers. He is enabled to do this by virtue of his consecration ceremony, by means of which he is endowed with life. This is all done in imitation of the past, when the gods themselves were consecrated, and, ultimately, in imitation of Prajapati, the creator of all things.

It will be remembered that it was found in the chapter on Social Unity, that certain tribes formed great ceremonial complexes. Moreover, the principal ruler of the tribe or state was the personage round whom everything revolved. The chief was the ceremonial centre of the tribe. We now see that there is a reason for this. The sky-born chief acts as a connecting-link between sky and

---

[1] *Ibid.*, 3, 1, 1–12.   [2] *Ibid.*, 4, 4, 15 e.s.

earth. He lives on the earth, but also, as we have seen, in a 'sky-world' of his own. He and his office therefore constitute the expression of an all-embracing theory, that life comes from the sky. We are thus able to understand more clearly why such efforts are made to preserve continuity with the past. It is to keep in touch, by whatever means possible, with the primordial source of life. We have, however, much to learn about the source of this life. It comes, in India, as we have seen, from Prajapati. He acquired it in the form of 'vital airs' from seven priests; and there we must leave the matter for the present.

The king, in the ritual of the Fire Altar, created the gods, raised them to the sky-world, and made them immortal, just as Prajapati did in the beginning. This is a constant and necessary feature of the king's consecration ceremony.

It is a commonplace in the Brahmanas that the gods were once men. 'Now, indeed, the gods were at first mortal; and only when they had gained the year they were immortal; for the year is everything, and the imperishable means everything.' [1]

The gods that live in the sky had to learn their way to Heaven. The texts state that 'it was after making the sacrifice . . . that the gods seated themselves on that firmament, in the world of heaven; and in like manner does this Sacrificer now, after making the sacrifice his own self, seat himself on that firmament, in the world of heaven.' [2]

The Indian king does not merely make the gods. He also makes himself into a god. 'He who is consecrated indeed becomes both Vishnu and a sacrificer; for when he is consecrated, he is Vishnu; and when he sacrifices, he is the sacrificer.' [3] The consecration of the king makes him identical with the gods Brahman, Varuna, Indra, and Rudra.[4] He is also identified in the course of the great Horse Sacrifice, with Agni, Savitri, and others.

The king is identified with several gods, because they are the personifications of certain aspects of the kingship. The king is the maintainer of law and order; he is Varuna. He is the gainer of victory, and as such takes the form of Indra. As the upholder of truth he is Mitra. As the giver of life to the community he is Savitri. These deities play their fixed rôle in the consecration ceremony, and as such are personified by the king. Vishnu conquered by his three strides the three worlds, of the earth, the air and the sky. In the ritual the king does the same. Vishnu, therefore, is nothing more than the king performing the three

[1] S.B., XI. 1, 2, 12.   [2] Ibid., VIII. 6, 1, 10.
[3] Ibid., III. 2, 1, 17.   [4] Ibid., V. 4, 4.

ritual strides. Indra fights Vritra the serpent, and kills him. The king fights the enemies. The king is Indra, and Indra is the king. But the king is greater than Indra. He is at one and the same time Varuna, Indra, Vishnu, Mitra, Savitri and the rest.

These gods, so closely connected with the kingship, form a definite group. They are called the Adityas, after their common mother Aditi. They are all solar gods. Prajapati does not appear to occur among them. He is their originator.

As we have seen repeatedly, the king imitates Prajapati in every ceremony. He does not identify himself with him, although he identifies himself with the solar gods. Prajapati occupies a unique position. He is, as it were, over and above all other gods, human and celestial.

It is interesting to note also that the king does not identify himself with the gods of the four quarters, the All gods, as they are called in the Indian texts. Prajapati creates them, and places them in their position, as did Tirawa in the case of the Pawnee. This introduces a further complexity into the situation; for the king creates two different kinds of gods, and identifies himself with one group and not with the other.

There is a further complication. Prajapati created beings called Asuras. These beings perpetually try to prevent the gods from carrying out their ceremonials. Apparently they are equal in rank with the gods. The king does not identify himself with them. On the contrary, as he plays his part in the rituals, they are his ceremonial enemies, who try to impede him.

We may safely leave the gods on one side, as being the by-products, as it were, of the ritual, and turn to the problem of the attainment of immortality. The king makes himself immortal when he is consecrated. He is thereby raised to the world of the immortal gods beyond the sky. He acquires the greatest thing that he can obtain; for the texts say that ' immortality is the highest thing of all this universe '. [1]

The raising of the king to the sky, in order to attain immortality, is carried out in realistic fashion in the Vagapeya consecration ceremony. Part of the ceremony consists of the erection of what is called the Sacrificial Stake. It is eight-cornered, and is wrapped round with seventeen cloths, in imitation of Pragapati, the creator, who is said to be seventeen-fold. The stake has a wheaten head-piece, and it is hollow at the top. The king and his wife ascend this post.

' Being about to ascend, he (the Sacrificer) addresses his wife,

[1] *Ibid.*, IX. 1, 2, 43. This has already been made clear in the last chapter. (See p. 225.)

" Come, wife, ascend we the sky ! " " Ascend we ! " says the wife . . . he ascends with, " we have become Prajapati's children " ; . . . He then touches the wheat (top-piece) with, " We have gone to the light, O ye gods ! " . . . He then rises by (the measure of) his head over the post, with, " We have become immortal ! " whereby he wins the world of the gods.' [1]

These utterances show that the idea in the minds of the compilers of the Brahmanas is that the king, when he goes to the world beyond the sky, gets immortality and becomes a child of Prajapati.

This reveals to us a fact of the utmost importance. The great creator of all things, Prajapati, is the father of the king, and of the gods. We have already seen that the persons of Tirawa and Prajapati were associated with the Children of the Sun, but we were unable to define the relationship between them. The texts just quoted make it clear that the earthly king has two fathers, the sun and the great creator. They show, moreover, that, in the Divine hierarchy, Tirawa and Prajapati rank above the sun.

The texts show clearly that the attainment of immortality and godhead is, as it were, mechanical. This exalted privilege can only be gained by those who have gone through the proper ritual performance. The association of the queen with the king in the consecration ritual has a bearing on the principal topics of the chapter on the Age of the Gods. It was found that the Children of the Sun disappeared because of the lack of suitable queens. We have seen that immortality was also lost. We now learn that the king and queen both ascend into the sky-world, there to become divine and immortal.

It is not obvious why the queen should be so necessary, but necessary she was. Failing her, the king must be content with a less exalted title.

Pawnee ritual is shot through and through with the notion of the ' breath of life ', that comes solely from Tirawa the creator. We do not know from the texts why this breath gave eternal life to sky-beings. There is no mention of the breath of life in the story of Lightning already quoted at the beginning of this chapter.

There is much concerning breath in the Brahmanas. Prajapati himself was made out of the ' vital airs ', which were identified with the breath. The Brahmanas say, ' breath is the fundamental thing in the universe '.

' Who is the one god ? . . . Breath.' Again, ' The sky, doubtless, is the breath,' and ' Breath is necessary for this entire universe.' [2]

[1] S.B., V. 2, 1, 10–14.   [2] Ibid., XI. 6, 3, 10 ; VI. 7, 4, 3 ; VII. 4, 2, 28.

Prajapati created and was created by means of breath. He ' laid the power of reproduction into his own self. By (the breath of) his mouth he created the gods ; the gods were created on entering the sky '.[1] Prajapati is therefore once more equated to Tirawa, for both of them possessed the breath of life.

Breath is immortal life. The Brahmana texts speak of ' his immortal element the breath '.[2] Breath is equated to the ' vital airs '. Prajapati in the beginning was animated by the vital airs. Again, ' The prospering (libations) are vital airs, and the vital airs are the immortal element ; with the immortal element he thus consecrates him.' [3] That is to say, the king is made immortal by means of the breath.

The priests of ancient India went further than their Pawnee colleagues. The Indian priest can use his own breath as a life-giving agency. We read of the rite called Agni Pavamana, ' the Blowing '. ' Now the blowing one is the breath, so that he thereby puts breath into him (the Sacrificer).' This breath is given to the new-born child. ' Now the reason why he makes offering to Agni Pavamana is that the blowing one is the breath. When (the child) is born, then there is breath. And as long as it is not born, it breathes in accord with the mother's breath ; but when it is born, then he thereby puts breath into it.' [4] The Brahmin therefore does what the gods of other peoples are sup-posed to do. He animates children. His powers are godlike.

This widespread association of breath with the sky calls for comment. Why, we may ask, should the whole of a ceremony like the Pawnee Hako centre round the getting of breath from a being in the sky ? The theory of breath involves the Pawnee priest in a logical absurdity, in which values are transferred. Food and drink, for example, rank after the wind in importance. It would appear more natural to assume that the breath of the priest could be used. The quotation from the Brahmanas concerning the animation of the new-born child bears out this suggestion, for the priest himself breathes the breath of life into the new-born child. It must not be forgotten that the priest probably went through some ceremony himself before animating the child. He would be like Prajapati, who was animated by breath before he could create. In both cases life has to be imparted to the life-giving agent.

We have now seen that the solar king in India was able, in his ceremonies, to ascend to the sky and to become divine and im-mortal. In the course of the consecration ceremony the solar

[1] *Ibid.*, XI. 1, 6, 7.   [2] *Ibid.*, X. 2, 6, 18.   [3] *Ibid.*, IX. 3, 3, 13.
[4] *Ibid.*, II. 2, 1, 10.

king was endowed with various qualities that belong to his royal functions. He had to sustain and support the realm, and to keep subjects, crops and cattle in good health.

The Brahmana texts give precise information concerning immortality.

We read such phrases as, ' May I gain immortality '. . . . ' By this sacrificial performance, and by this order of proceeding he makes his body uniformly undecaying and immortal.' [1] It is laid down that the attainment of immortality is the result of a ceremonial performance. ' Now, at the beginning, Prajapati was (composed of) both these, the mortal and the immortal ; . . . by this sacrificial performance, and by this order of proceeding, he made his body uniformly undecaying and immortal. And in like manner . . . the sacrificer . . . makes his body uniformly undecaying and immortal.' [2]

The king attains immortality by imitating what happened to Prajapati in the beginning. Prajapati created the world and peopled it. The king does likewise in his consecration. Prajapati fell to pieces when he had accomplished his creative act. ' Having created creatures he, having run the whole race, became relaxed (literally he fell asunder, or to pieces, became disjointed). From him being thus relaxed, the vital air went out from within.' . . . ' Prajapati, when relaxed, said to the gods, " Restore me ! " The gods said to Agni (the Fire Altar), " In thee we will heal this our father Prajapati." ' [3]

The meaning of these texts is clear. The being whom we know as Prajapati, the father of the king, and of the gods, had to be reconstituted, and his body made whole. He thereby became immortal. The king, in his turn, can attain to immortality by building up for himself an immortal, undecaying body. This he does by means of the Fire Altar. He does it also in his consecration. The Râgasûya, for instance, the consecration of a king, is said to be the consecration of Varuna, who is the personification of one of the aspects of the kingship.[4]

The process of consecration of the king is long and complicated. Cakes are made, of various sorts, for the different gods who take part in the ceremony. Water, taken from all manner of sources, is procured in wooden vessels made from certain trees. It says in the texts that, ' he who performs the Râgasûya [the consecration ceremony for a king] is indeed a child of the waters '.[5] A curious saying.

[1] S.B., X. 1, 4, 1.   [2] Ibid.
[3] Ibid., VI. 1, 2, 12 ; VII. 1, 2, 21.   [4] Ibid., V. 4, 3, 2.
                    [5] Ibid., 3, 5, 19.

The real consecration then follows. Just before it begins reference is made yet again to the fact that Prajapati's body is being reconstituted. A tiger's skin is spread out in front of the sacred hearth. Then six oblations are performed. Four consecration vessels stand in front of the hearth, made of wood of various sacred trees. Two strainers are made with golden threads woven into them; these are used for the purification of the consecration waters.

The king is then purified with the waters. During the purification the priest says, ' " By the impulse of Savitri I purify you with a flawless purifier, with the rays of the sun." ' This is because the threads of the strainer are of gold, which is connected with the sun and with immortality (see p. 241).[1]

The king is then made to assume garments representing the fœtal membranes, the amnion and the chorion, as well as the womb itself, while a head-band represents the navel.[2] This symbolizes the process of ritual rebirth that he has to undergo in this and every consecration ceremony.

The ritual of death and rebirth is the central feature of consecration and initiation ceremonies the world over. It is symbolized in dramatic and concrete fashion in the Brahmanas, by making the king into an embryo. The symbolism of the embryo is certainly present in the minds of the compilers of these books, for they constantly refer to the king in this way while he is being consecrated. This rebirth ritual, therefore, has a deep-seated symbolical meaning, for it is the central part of the ceremonials connected with the Indian kingship.

The priest then puts a piece of copper into the mouth of a long-haired man, that is, an eunuch. The king is now made to ' ascend the regions ', in order that he may be high above everything on earth, particularly his subjects. He then steps on the tiger's skin, on which a gold plate has been placed to symbolize immortality. Another gold plate is placed on his head with the phrase, ' Might thou art, victory thou art, immortality thou art.' His arms are then uplifted, and he is sprinkled with water. This identifies him with the gods Mitra and Varuna.[3] The king rubs water over himself with the horn of a black antelope.[4] On some occasions the king is anointed with fresh butter. He is also purified with a cleanser of sacred grass.[5]

In the Sautramani, another consecration ceremony, the king is anointed with gravy from the sacrificial animals. He is also sprinkled with water contained in a reed bowl. ' The bowl is made

[1] *Ibid.*, 3, 5, 3–16.   [2] *Ibid.*, 4, 1, 1–16.   [3] *Ibid.*, 3, 5, 20 e.s.
[4] *Ibid.*, 4, 2, 4.   [5] *Ibid.*, III. 1, 3, 7, 18.

of reed, for the reed has its birthplace in the waters, and the waters are all the deities : by means of all the deities he thus consecrates him.'

Then follows a remarkable episode. ' A rubbing down (of the Sacrificer) with all manner of sweet-smelling substances takes place (before sprinkling him with fat), for such a rubbing down with all manner of sweet-smelling substances means supreme fragrance : with fragrance he thus consecrates (anoints) him.' [1]

He then makes the three strides called Vishnu steps, which take him over the earth, air, and sky and land him in the heavenly world.[2]

A chariot race follows, the king racing against a rival.[3]

The king mounts a throne after the race. This places him above his subjects. It symbolizes a womb, and the king is provided with the skin of a black antelope to emphasize the symbolism. The king is then given five dice, probably in the form of gold cowries, with which he plays. These dice are supposed to represent the four quarters and the sky.

The end of the ceremonial is now near. The king is struck on the back by the priests, and is afterwards identified with certain gods, Savitri, Varuna, Indra, Rudra, and Brahman, who, as seems certain, are personifications of different attributes of the kingship.[4]

The definition of immortality in the Brahmanas has now become clearer. Its concept is expressed in definite terms of a corporeal body. A great creator, Prajapati, had his body reconstituted, revitalized, and made incorruptible.

It is interesting to note that there is only one Prajapati. He is the father of every king who is consecrated. We do not find that each successive king becomes identified in the ritual with his own father. Each successive king, on the contrary, acquires the sonship of the great creator. His kingship thus is based upon a unique series of events that happened to the person of one man. In this individual are centred the creation of the primordial ocean, and of the earth out of that ocean ; the peopling of the earth ; the provision of food ; as well as the acquisition of immortality, godhead, and access to the sky. The central episode of the events that happened to this primordial personage was the reconstitution of his body. This body was reconstituted by the priests, the Rishis, and thereby became the great source of life.

The ritual procedure carried out in the various consecration

[1] S.B., XII. 8, 3, 12–16.   [2] *Ibid.*, V. 4, 2, 6.   [3] *Ibid.*, 4, 3.
[4] *Ibid.*, 4, 4, 1 e.s.

ceremonies that have just been described involve, as we have
seen, certain processes of treatment of the body of the king. He
is treated like a new-born babe ; he is anointed with water, gravy
and fat, and his body is treated with sweet-smelling grass. We
are told that this procedure causes the body to become undecaying
and immortal.

The obvious interpretation of these facts is that Prajapati's
body was mummified. The king, as the descendant of Prajapati,
goes through a ritual which is a mimetic performance of the
original incidents centring round his primordial ancestor. This
ritual is based on mummification.

This conclusion is confirmed by the accounts given of the
treatment of the body of a dead king who had qualified for immortality by performing the necessary ceremonies. The body
was ultimately cremated ; but not before it had undergone a
ceremonial preparation. This preparation was in imitation of
the treatment of the body of Prajapati. The description of this
treatment is so important that I give the text in full.

' Now, in the first place, he cleanses it of all foul matter, and
causes the foul matter to settle on this (earth) ; for this (earth)
is indeed foul matter ; he thus consigns foul matter to foul matter.
For indeed, from that intestine of his, filled with foul matter,
when it is burnt, a jackal is produced ; (hence he removes it),
lest a jackal be produced.

' But let him not do this, or his family will be liable to starve.
Having washed him out inside, he anoints him with ghee, and
thus makes it (the body) sacrificially pure.

' He then inserts seven chips of gold in the seven seats of his
vital airs, for gold is light and immortality ; he thus bestows
light and immortality upon him.

' Having then built a pile for him in the midst of his fires and
spread out a black antelope skin with the hairy side upwards,
and the neck-part towards the east, he lays him down thereon
with the face looking upwards. . . .

' Thus supplied with the sacrificial weapons (implements), that
Sacrificer passes on to that place which has been won for him
in heaven. . . .

' This, then, is that offering of the Sacrificer's body which he
performs at the end ; from out of that place which has been won
by him in heaven he rises immortal in the form of an oblation.' [1]

These texts show that, in spite of the fact that the body of the
dead king is ultimately burned, it is previously made immortal
by being embalmed. There is no need to discuss this point,

[1] S.B., XII. 5, 2, 5–13.

for this has been done by the late Miss Mary Levin with great detail.[1] The point to be emphasized is that the king in India was embalmed before cremation, in imitation of his primordial ancestor. We are told that the gods performed this ceremony for Prajapati. The gods being the sons of Prajapati, and the king being also, by virtue of his consecration, the son of Prajapati, it follows that Prajapati was embalmed by his son the king. Again, as the king imitated, in his consecration ceremonies, the events centring around Prajapati, and as he thereby becomes a god, it follows that the godhead came into existence by the process of embalming. That is to say, Prajapati, the first man to be embalmed, was, at the same time, the first god ; and the attainment of immortality is only secured by the performance of the rites connected with mummification.

If we turn back to the creation story of the Pawnee we shall now find certain statements made clearer. It will be remembered that Tirawa gave various powers to the gods of the four quarters.

' I also give you power to create people. You shall give them the different bundles, which shall be holy bundles.'

These bundles play an important part in the ceremonial life of the Pawnee. Dorsey says that 'the bundles and their accompanying ceremonies collectively regulate and make provision for all the necessities of life during the calendar year '. He goes on to say : ' In each of the nineteen villages of the Skidi . . . was a bundle received by the village direct from its god. The arrangement of the Skidi villages when they came together for certain purposes, as for instance in a great ceremony, was based upon the relationship in space which the gods or stars, the givers of the bundles, sustained in the heavens.' [2]

These bundles consist usually of a buffalo skin, containing various objects of ceremonial importance. They included, for instance, pipes, paints, feathers of certain birds, bits of flint, and so on.

The study of the contents of the existing Pawnee bundles does not lead us far ; but the origin stories of the tribe give us one important piece of information. We are told that the skull of the Son of the Sun, the first chief of the Pawnee, who came down from the sky, was placed on a bundle in the ceremonial enclosure. This bundle belonged to the tribe as a whole, as did also those connected with the central fireplace and the four posts. This fact is significant. It suggests that the bundles were originally associated with human remains.

This supposition is strengthened by the fact already mentioned

[1] Levin 18, 32, 48.   [2] Dorsey i. XX.

(see p. 217), that the great god of the Aztecs, Huitzilopochtli, was formerly a man whose remains were preserved by them on the top of a pyramid in the centre of the city of Mexico.

Acosta describes him : ' The chiefest idol of Mexico was, as I have said, Vitzilipuztli. It was an image of wood, like to a man, set upon a stool of the colour of azure, in a brankard or litter ; at every corner was a piece of wood in the form of a Serpent's head. The stool signified that he was set in heaven : this idol had all the forehead azure, and had a band of azure under the nose from one ear to another : upon his head he had a rich plume of feathers like to the beak of a small bird, the which was covered on the top with gold burnished very brown : he had in his left hand a white target, with the figures of five pineapples made of white feathers, set in a cross : and from above issued forth a crest of gold, and at his side he had four darts, which (the Mexicans say) had been sent down from heaven. . . . In his right hand he had an azured staff, cut in the fashion of a waving snake.' [1]

It will be remembered also that Manco Ccapac, the founder of the Inca Dynasty of Peru, was mummified and regarded as a god.[2] The fact that the supreme beings of the more advanced peoples of America were mummified men, usually Children of the Sun, suggests that the use by the Pawnee of the skull of their first chief in connexion with the bundle was a survival of a former practice of preserving the bodies of dead chiefs, so that the existing bundles would represent a further process of degradation. This is borne out further by the fact that certain tribes of the United States, for instance, the Sauk (or Sac) and Fox, treat their bundles as human beings, although they contain no human remains. The Sauk and Fox bundles ' are thought to have a consciousness of their own, to understand what is said to them, and to enjoy offerings '.[3]

It will be remembered that, in the Pawnee story of Lightning, already quoted at the beginning of this chapter, Lightning's body is subjected to certain treatments. It was rubbed with fat and red clay, it was fumigated with the smoke of sweet-smelling grasses. This procedure, it was stated, had relation to a future state ; it obviously referred to a life after death. A similar treatment of the body occurs in the Hako ceremony, where the

---

[1] Acosta I. 319. Note the connexion between the stool and the sky.

[2] Saintyves remarks concerning the dead, ' Toutes les practiques antiques semblent concourir au même but, la divinisation du mort ', 65, n. 1. Truly a clear-headed generalization.

[3] Harrington 128. The Toradja tribe of the To Napoe keep the body of their first chief, Goema ngkoana, in a temple. Kruyt (i) 421.

child is painted red and blue ; brushed with water and sweet-smelling grass ; and anointed with red clay united with sacred buffalo-fat.

The king in India is subjected to similar procedures in the course of consecration ceremonies. He is sprinkled with water ; rubbed down with sweet-smelling grasses and other sweet-smelling substances ; he is anointed with butter and gravy and fat.

These parallels serve still further to emphasize the unity of ritual throughout the world. It is well known that the ritual of mummification included a ceremonial lustration, anointing, painting, and censing of the body. We thus have yet more reason to conclude that mummification has played a part of the utmost importance in the development of ritual.[1]

The evidence at our disposal from America therefore leads us to assume that national gods were mummified human beings, usually of the family of the Children of the Sun. Their bodies were preserved to become the centre of ritual, and the great source of life to the State.

It must, however, be remembered, in this connexion, that it does not follow that a being such as Tirawa ever actually ruled over the Pawnee. If we refer back to India for a moment, and consider the relationship between the king and Prajapati, we shall see that quite clearly. It has already been pointed out that Prajapati is the man who acquired immortality, and produced the gods.

It is quite easy to conceive the Children of the Sun entering India with a ceremonial organization harking back to some time in the past before they entered that country. In like manner Tirawa may simply be a ceremonial figure whose personality is unknown to the American people. In that case all we have in America is a series of dead kings, who have acquired godhead and assimilation to the original creator by virtue of the process of mummification, carried out symbolically at their consecration, and actually at their death. The evidence from America suggests, moreover, that the rites associated with the reconstitution of the body of Prajapati were those connected with embalming.

A serious difficulty arises here. It does not appear that the royal ceremonial in India depended upon the possession of the body of the mummified king. Although the body of Prajapati was embalmed, it does not appear to have been used as a national talisman, as was the body of Manco Ccapac in Peru.

I do not propose to discuss this matter in detail here. It is worthy of note, however, that the priests in India evidently were

[1] See, for example, Elliot Smith i. ; Elliot Smith and Dawson iv. ; Budge.

aware of the physical basis of the ritual ; for in the building of
the Fire Altar an image of a man, the Divine Man, is made of
gold. This image is incorporated in the Fire Altar that had the
form of a hawk, which was supposed to fly with it to the sky.
Gold was highly regarded in India, as is shown by the following
quotations from the Satapatha Brahmana :

' " Thou art pure, thou art shining, thou art immortal, thou art
sacred to all the gods." . . . " gold means light " . . . " gold means
immortal life." . . . " that (gold man) is his (the sacrificer's)
divine body." . . . " As to that gold man, that is his immortal
form, his divine form, gold being immortal." ' [1]

We may argue from this that the compilers of this particular
ritual overcame the difficulty with which they were faced, that
of making the body of the king uniformly undecaying and immortal, by the expedient of using gold, the incorruptible, immortal
metal of the sun, to take the place of the body that was about
to be destroyed.

[1] S.B., III. 2, 4, 14 ; X. 4, 1, 6 ; VII. 4, 2, 17.

CHAPTER XXI

THE PRIMORDIAL OCEAN

THE study of the ceremonials of various peoples reveals one important fact. In spite of the immense diversity of detail, the result of centuries of work on the part of priests of different schools and countries, those who conducted these ceremonials never swerved from their original aim. The constant reiteration of the statement that every ceremonial is a re-enactment of a great creation drama, or part of it, reveals the faith of the performers of these ceremonials. In India the consecration of the king; his attainment to immortality and godhead; his creative acts, are all recapitulations of some primordial events. So with the Pawnee rituals. In both cases, the events of the creation are as real as the rites of the ceremonial. The Pawnee priests perform the creation ceremonial in direct imitation of a continuous line of predecessors. In their minds Tirawa and his followers are as concrete as themselves. In India, likewise, the king and his priests are the successors of a long line of previous sacrificers.

We began by accepting the Pawnee statement that their creation story represented an historical fact. The result has been to show that they were substantially correct. It is necessary, however, to insist upon one point. The Pawnee assert that the creation began with Tirawa and his followers in a sky-world, with the primordial ocean beneath, out of which ocean land was produced. The most we can say about this story, so far, is that it is a record of rituals performed in the past in a ceremonial building, part of which, at least, was called the sky-world, by kings who had the privilege of attaining to godhead by ceremonial means. It has been possible to rationalize the Pawnee story to a great extent. We have discovered real societies where the kings live in the sky-world, and are able to become divine.

Thus far the Pawnee are justified in their beliefs; but we are still confined to the world of ritual, even in those countries, such as India, where we can watch these exalted kings; for we find that they, in their turn, have to rely on the past for the sanction for their rituals. Indeed, although we have obtained new light on the original creative society of the Pawnee ritual, fresh problems are opened up. We have learned from India that the great creator was the father of the king and of the gods, and that his body was embalmed. The king in India has to imitate this process of embalming in the course of many ceremonials in which he takes part. But in this instance again he only does this in the course of a ritual that re-enacts certain events that happened in the past. We have seen likewise that in America there is a close connexion between ritual and mummification.

The study of ritual, therefore, forces us continually back into the past. We are assured by priests, from one end of the world to the other, that what they do in their ceremonials actually happened in the past. By this they mean that their rituals are based ultimately on historical happenings.

This may be true ; but there are many facts yet to be explained. In the creation stories which have so far been considered, in the vast range from America to India, the creation of land from the primordial ocean, by beings of the sky-world, is the first known event. Actually it occurs only in ritual. In no place as yet have we seen this act of creation actually performed in the sight of the whole world. Yet it is imperative for the substantiation of the beliefs of priests all over the world that it should be a public event ; that is to say, there should be a country in which the primordial ocean is a well-known physical fact. The kingship of this country should be associated in some way with this ocean, and should be believed to be able to create land out of it. I say ' believed ', for it is obvious that no king ever performed such an act. All we can hope to find is an association of the king with the primordial ocean that has been accepted as causative by the people. That is to say, it is believed that this king brought up land from the ocean. This king, the prototype of Prajapati and Tirawa, died and was embalmed, thereby becoming immortal. He was the first of the gods ; or rather, was the creator of the gods. Presumably he came before the gods. His son, known in India and elsewhere as ' the Son of the Sun ', embalmed him, while, in Indian ceremonial at least, certain enemies tried to prevent him. This is the primordial situation that we have outlined in discussing the ritual of the Brahmanas.

Before seeking the solution of these problems it may be well to consider once again the long chain of societies that possess the story of creation out of the primordial ocean. One and all assert that this event actually happened, and place the event at the beginning of the foundation of their society. For instance, the Samoan Archipelago was fished up from beneath the waters by sky-beings, who therefore preceded the Samoan people. That is to say, such a community as Samoa is a link in a chain. We may ask how many of these chains there are. There may be more than one, though this is doubtful. One reason for this lies in the close association between the Primordial Ocean and the Children of the Sun. Throughout America, Oceania and Asia we find solar families constantly associated with this mythological incident. They are credited, likewise, with the organization of society, as among the Pawnee, in Peru, Japan, Burma, Ceylon and elsewhere. As their marriage regulations and other practices suggest, there is good reason to believe in the continuity of this great group of families from one end of the earth to another. The probability is that the original creation of land out of the Primordial Ocean happened in one place only. It is well known that the title ' Son of the Sun ' was assumed by the kings of Egypt during the Fifth Dynasty.[1] There is no reason to believe that any other people was responsible for a like innovation. In the present state of our knowledge Egypt has the sole claim to be the home of the ' Children of the Sun '. Therefore it is in Egypt that we should first seek the Primordial Ocean.

The rituals of the Brahmanas in India centred round the ruling group. The unanimous testimony of the Egyptian texts also shows that the religious ceremonial centred round the kingship. The ruler was closely associated with the gods.

The late Edouard Naville is very clear on this point. He says that ' the apotheosis of himself, the putting himself among the gods, is always one of the chief objects of a Pharaoh, whoever is the god in whose honour he celebrates a festival '.[2] The king was closely intimate with the gods. ' The first ceremony performed in a temple or in a sanctuary was always the introduction of the king by the gods. They take him by the hand and lead him themselves to the place where he is to act as their priest.' [3] The identification of kings with gods went so far as acting as priest to his own person considered as that of a god.[4]

Naville comments on a certain ritual scene in the following terms : ' Here it is not the god only to whom it [a clypsydra or water clock] is offered, it is the king who is the god, and he raises it in his hand in the presence of a numerous train of priests.' [5]

These quotations show that the intimacy between the king and the gods could go no further.

This intimacy has its counterpart in the case of the ordinary people. ' They had no right of direct intercourse with the god.' [6]

[1] Breasted ii. 123 e.s.   [2] Naville iii. 18.   [3] *Ibid.*, i. II. 8.
[4] *Ibid.*, V. 8.   [5] *Ibid.*, iii. 24.
[6] Maspero iii. 94. The royal cult in China was forbidden to the commoners. Wieger 16.

This bears out directly what we have seen to be the case in Indonesia and elsewhere (see p. 154). Kings and gods form a group apart from the people. Only the sky-born can have direct communication with the sky. Tirawa only deals with mortals by means of intermediaries. Initiated priestesses in Indonesia have no right of direct access to the sky-world.[1] This place is the concern of the sky-born and of them alone.

Let us examine this exalted society in Egypt.

We have already learned that the Egyptian king bore the name of Horus from the earliest known times down to the extinction of the royal family. Horus is the name of the consecrated living king.

The Egyptian king was closely associated, in ritual at least, with Osiris, and, to a lesser extent, with Re, the sun-god, each of whom was his ' father '. He was, at one and the same time, the son of a king who died and was brought to life again, and of a living god. His royal office included the duty of carrying on the cults of these divine beings. It would appear, however, that the living king ranked after his parents, particularly Osiris, in his godhead. He addresses Osiris thus : ' Thou art more divine than I.' [2]

Good reason exists for concluding that the Egyptians themselves regarded Osiris as the prototype of their gods. ' The Tanis Sign Papyrus ', published by Sir Flinders Petrie and the late F. Ll. Griffith, is a dictionary written by the Egyptians themselves, and therefore authoritative. It tells us that the word for ' god ', ntr, means ' embalmed '. Professor Griffith adds a note saying that this means ' duly buried and therefore deified, being assimilated to Osiris '.[3]

The Pyramid Texts, which date from the Fifth and Sixth Dynasties, have some remarkable statements bearing on this point. They contain such phrases as ' the gods serve (the dead king), for he is older than the Old One ' (i.e. Re—Atum) (PT. 306, b, d) : ' [the dead king] is He—who—is—upon—his—Single —Nome, the oldest of the gods ' (PT. 309, e) : ' This [dead king] has been given birth to [fashioned] by his father Atum, (c) before the sky existed, before earth existed, before men existed, before the gods were fashioned [or " given birth to "], before death existed ' (PT. 1466, b, c).[4] These texts place the matter beyond all doubt. In the person of Osiris the world beholds the first man who was awakened from the sleep of death to enjoy a glorious resurrection, of the mind as well as of the body, to enjoy a life

[1] Perry v. 147.   [2] Sethe ii. 240.   [3] Griffith and Petrie iii. 16.
[4] The numbers in brackets refer to Sethe's arrangement of the texts. See Sethe iii. I owe the translation of these texts to Professor Blackman.

that was a continuation of this. Osiris stands for a new epoch in human history.

Osiris was a creator. An Eighteenth Dynasty text speaks of him as follows: ' *The Nile issueth* (?) from the sweat of thine hands. Thou spittest out the air which is in thy throat into men's noses. . . . Trees and herbs, reeds and . . . , barley, wheat, and fruit tree. . . . Thou art the father and mother of mankind. They live on thy breath, and they (eat) of the flesh of thy body. Primordial God is thy name.' [1]

This text shows that a close connexion existed between Osiris and the Nile. This is also shown in the Pyramid Texts, written more than a thousand years before. ' The lakes fill, the canals are inundated, by the purifications that came forth from Osiris ' (PT. 848). . . . ' Ho, this Osiris, king Mernere, thy water, the libation is the great inundation that came forth from thee ' (868). . . . ' Horus comes, he recognizes his father in thee, youthful in thy name of fresh water ' (PT. 589). . . . ' It is Unis who inundates the land ' (PT. 388). . . . ' Unis comes hither up stream when the flood inundates. . . . Unis comes to his pools that are in the region of the flood, . . . to the place of peace, with green fields, that is in the horizon. Unis makes the verdure to flourish in the region of the horizon ' (PT. 507–8).[2]

It will be noted that these texts refer by name, not only to Osiris, but to certain kings, such as Unis, in whose pyramids they were inscribed. Throughout the Pyramid Texts constant reference is made by name to dead kings as being identified with Osiris and Re, the sun-god.

The close association between kings and gods runs, as we have seen, through the whole of Egyptian ritual, whether of gods or of the dead. This matter will be discussed later on.

Attention meanwhile must be paid to the creative activities of Osiris and other gods.

The Nile flood is the great source of life to Egypt.[3] It is not surprising, therefore, that it should be of fundamental importance in every aspect of Egyptian life.

The ancient Egyptians called the annual inundation by the name of Nun. It was the Primordial Ocean.[4]

We have now reached the end of another stage on our journey. The Primordial Ocean was to the Ancient Egyptians a palpable fact. It could not escape their attention, and thus formed a solid foundation for their accounts of beginnings.

[1] Erman ii. 304.   [2] Breasted iii. 18, 19.
[3] ' Father of the gods.' Budge ii. cvii.
[4] See, for example, Budge ii. cvii.

This concrete notion places the Egyptians in marked contrast to the peoples of Asia, Oceania, and America whose ideas about beginnings have been studied. The nearest approach in this respect to Egypt is Mesopotamia. The late L. W. King tells us that the Euphrates was always regarded by the Sumerians and Babylonians as the source of life and the creator of all things. He quotes the following late Babylonian copy of an early incantation:

> ' O thou River, who didst create all things,
> When the great gods dug thee out,
> They set prosperity upon thy banks.
> Within thee Ea, the King of the Deep, created his dwelling.
> The deluge they sent not before thou wert.' [1]

This concreteness of ideas concerning the Primordial Ocean in Egypt and Mesopotamia constitutes yet another instance of the cultural similarities between the two peoples. I do not propose to discuss the significance of this similarity in this place. I have already shown that the evidence is wholly in favour of Egyptian priority over Sumer, particularly as regards the early settlement of Ur.[2]

To return to Egypt. The association between the inundation and Osiris, a dead king who has been reanimated, is remarkable. It is not easy, indeed, it is very difficult, to suggest why a dead king should be accredited with this remarkable power. Even the great creator-god, Re, the sun-god, father of kings, does not seem to have created the Primordial Ocean. This may be seen from the following texts: ' I am he who evolved himself under the form of the god Chepera. . . . There was no heaven, there was no earth, ground-animals and reptiles were not then in existence. I constructed their forms out of the inert mass of watery matter, I found no place there upon which I could stand, . . . I was quite alone, . . . there existed none other who worked with me.' [3]

There may, of course, be texts that ascribe to the sun-god the act of creating Nun, or of producing the annual inundation. I have likewise failed to trace any texts to show that the living king, or his prototype Horus, was supposed to control the inundation, or to create Nun, the Primordial Ocean. One possible exception is that of Rameses II, of the Nineteenth Dynasty, who used, on the first day of the inundation, to throw a written order into the Nile, commanding it to do its duty.[4] This is all the more surprising, when it is remembered that the earliest annals, recorded

---

[1] King 129.   [2] Perry x.   [3] Budge iii. 440–1.
[4] Moret ii. 180.

on the so-called Palermo Stone, regularly note the annual height of the inundation.[1] The installation of a series of Nilometers from the Delta to the First Cataract also reveals the vital interest taken in the Nile flood.[2]

If we assume, for a moment, that Osiris was more fundamental as a creator than Re, we have a parallel to Prajapati and the sun-god in India, and Tirawa and the sun-god among the Pawnee, in both of which cases the sun-god was of secondary rank compared with the great creator.

It will be remembered that the stories of creation of the Pawnee and other peoples assert that habitable land was brought up from the bottom of the Primordial Ocean. A similar notion occurs in Egyptian belief. The great temples of Memphis, Hermopolis, Heliopolis, Thebes, and elsewhere, were built on mounds representing the land that first emerged from the Primordial Ocean.[3] For example, an inscription in the temple of Hatshepsut, of the Eighteenth Dynasty, speaks of ' my temple, which arose in the beginning '.[4] It thus dates from the time when the first land was made. Another inscription made on one of the obelisks of the same queen says, ' I know that Karnak is the horizon on earth, the holy hill of the beginning.' [5]

De Buck has collected several texts claiming that the sacred mound of Thebes was not only the first to emerge from the waters, but also gave rise to others. ' Thou art the primordial mound, which was placed in Nun in the beginning, of whose earth all lands were made.' And again, ' Thou art " the City " with whose name the cities are made, out of whose soil the Nomes arose.' [6]

Another remarkable text states, ' Thou art the sand . . . of which men have taken to establish the two lands.' [7]

These quotations suggest that the Egyptian priests were convinced that the holy places of Egypt were linked together, and that they were derived from one common prototype. This is in accordance with the practices discussed in the chapter on Continuity, where it was shown that vast chains of settlements are linked together by physical ties, sacred stones, earth, and so forth (see p. 155).

One series of texts asserts that the mound was brought up from the ocean by Ptah, the god of Memphis, who is also known under the name of Tatenen. ' Thou hast formed the land . . . when thou wast in thy activity as Tatenen, in thy manifestation as the

[1] Breasted i. 51 e.s.   [2] Borchardt i. 41.
[3] A collection of these texts will be found in de Buck 72 e.s.
[4] Op. cit., 72.   [5] De Buck 43.   [6] Id., 46.
[7] De Buck 47.

uniter of both lands . . . thou hast drawn it (the land) from out the waters of Nun.' [1]

We have already seen that the dead king Osiris was especially associated with the Nile flood. It is therefore important to learn that Ptah, the god of Memphis, was represented as a mummy, and was therefore a form of Osiris.

Much discussion might be devoted to the problem of priority in Egyptian temples. That, however, need not detain us at present. The important point to appreciate is that the rituals of the various temples in Egypt certainly differed in detail, but were formed on one vast ground plan. They were always associated with the royal family.

This association has already been stressed. But it must be further emphasized that this association between kings and gods is, in all cases, a dramatization of a unique series of events that took place within the narrow circle of the Egyptian royal family at some date in the past. These events provided the framework on which the variant local temple rituals were hung. So although we hear of the temple of Min at Coptos, of Ptah at Memphis, and so forth, yet these gods only find their expressions in their association with the ruling group.

It would appear, thus, that each temple ritual formed part of the great national cycle, somewhat on the plan of the distribution of rituals among the Pawnee and other peoples.

The words of Erman on this subject are illuminating. He says, in commenting on the temple rituals, ' Would that there had been in these long speeches some trace of feeling for the sacredness of the place, the majesty of the god ; but all personal feeling had long since disappeared from this ritual, and it was celebrated in a way that could not well have been more absurd, as though the whole religion in every temple consisted only of the history of Horus and Set, and that of Osiris.' [2]

These words, coming, as they do, from an eminent authority on Egyptian religion, are significant for more than one reason. They emphasize the entirely matter-of-fact character of Egyptian ritual from beginning to end. But they illuminate still further the frame of mind of Erman himself, and of the many students who would agree with him. Erman obviously expected to find some strong emotional tone, of the nature of awe and wonder, exhibited by the compilers of the ritual. The average text-book on comparative religion speaks confidently of the ' worship ' of gods, both among savages and civilized men, as if that were a universal feature of early religion. Erman's reaction to the dis-

[1] De Buck 56.   [2] Erman iii. 45.

covery of the essentially human aspect of early Egyptian religion led him to characterize their ritual as ' absurd '. He looks upon it as the bare survival of a former system of religious practices in which men actually ' worshipped ' their gods, in the usual sense of that term. The evidence already considered suggests that Erman was completely wrong in his assumption.

Some idea of the varied nature of the temple rituals of Egypt may be gained from Dr. A. M. Blackman's contribution to the collection of essays on ' Myth and Ritual ' edited by Professor S. H. Hooke. He deals with the national festivals in honour of Osiris in the month called Khoiakh ; the harvest festival of Min of Coptos ; the coronation dramas described in the so-called Ramesseum Papyrus, and on the Schabako Stone in the British Museum ; [1] the marriage festival of Horus and Hathor at Edfu ; and the great Theban festival of Ōpet.[2]

These ceremonies, as may be seen, vary greatly in details ; but they are all concerned with the kingship, and they are mostly consecration festivals. They are all dramatic ; they are the re-enactments of some of the events associated with Osiris and his relatives.

It is not known, so far as I am aware, how this distribution of temple rituals took place ; why, for example, the temple of Min was at Coptos, with its special royal ritual. It has already been mentioned that the eminent German Egyptologist, Sethe, has recently published a translation, accompanied by a detailed commentary, of certain texts inscribed on a stone known as the Schabako Stone, now in the British Museum. This document is of great importance, for, according to Sethe, it must originally have been compiled about the time of the First Dynasty in Egypt.[3] The modern version was made by the command of King Schabako of the Twenty-fifth Dynasty, as an act of respect for the ancients.

The scene of the events recorded in this inscription is Memphis, the Great White Wall, which was built at the junction of the two kingdoms at the beginning of the First Dynasty. It became the capital of Egypt in the Third Dynasty, at the beginning of the Pyramid Age. For this reason I shall refer to this text as the *Memphis Text*.

These facts lend peculiar importance to these inscriptions. Memphis was, at the time of their compilation, a place of unique importance to the whole of Egypt. It symbolized the unification

[1] See Sethe ii. for these two texts.
[2] ' Myth and Ritual ', 19, 26. See also Junker, Schaefer.
[3] Sethe ii. 4–8.

of the country, and, from the Third Dynasty onwards at least, must have been the administrative centre of the country.

The text is, of course, dramatic. Its ceremonial occasion is the king's consecration. It is divided into two parts. The first opens with an account of the political manœuvrings at the time of the unification of Upper and Lower Egypt. Then follows the consecration of Horus as the ruler over united Egypt. Memphis is built, and there is buried Osiris, his father, who had been found drowned in the water. The second part of the text likewise ends with the drowning and burial of Osiris, as well as the consecration of Horus. The earlier portion contains an account of the creative activities of Ptah.

This bald summary shows that this text conforms to a general type. In both parts the consecration of the king, as Horus, is intimately associated with the death and burial of Osiris.

The Ramesseum Papyrus, also edited by Sethe, has a similar structure. A series of ritual events is followed by the consecration of the king, and also by certain ceremonials associated with the body of Osiris.

The opening scenes in these two rituals are concerned with the foundation of the Egyptian State as we know it. The Memphis text deals with the foundation of the historical monarchy, and thus takes us a step further back than was reached in India and elsewhere. In the beginning Set was king of Upper Egypt, and Horus was king of Lower Egypt. Set was dispossessed of his kingdom, and Horus became king of United Egypt.

We are told that the former division of the kingship between Horus and Set took place to avoid quarrelling. Set was made king of Upper Egypt ' in the place where he was born ' ; while Horus was made king of Lower Egypt ' in the place where his father was drowned '.[1]

This division of the kingship was the work of Geb, the grand-father of Horus. We are then told that Geb could not tolerate this arrangement, and so gave the whole kingdom to Horus, ' the son of his son, his first-born ' (11c 12 c).

Horus was consecrated, and ruled over the united kingdom, the two parts being united in the ' Wall-Nome ', that is Memphis, at the point of junction of the two lands. Here was ' the house of Ptah ', the ' balance of the two lands ', in which the Upper Egyptian and the Lower Egyptian lands were balanced (13–16).

A remarkable episode now follows. Isis and Nephthys, sisters of Osiris, and wives of Osiris and Set, saw Osiris in the water.

[1] The numbers in brackets in the text refer to the sections in Sethe's arrangement. See Sethe, op. cit.

Horus told them to seize him before he drowned (or sank) (18, 19). They brought his body and buried it in the 'royal city' (21B) which was built at that time (21–23).

The body of Osiris thus appears to have played a part similar to that played by the mummified body of Manco Ccapac in Peru, or the 'bundles' of North American peoples.

The second part of the Memphis text opens with the creation of the gods by Ptah. The gods all acquire their power from him (48–53).

Ptah created by means of his heart and tongue (56). The heart conceived the ideas, and the tongue gave expression and shape to them (53–56). Ptah is in the body of every god, man, cattle, every worm and all that lives, in the shape of the heart and tongue (54). Ptah also created certain 'spirits', male and female, 'who made all nourishment and all food' (57).

The text says that Ptah, as creator of gods, and as provider of nourishment and food, surpasses the other gods in strength (58). He made the cities and founded the nomes (58, 59). He placed the gods in their shrines (Kultstatte), and allotted their revenue. He made bodies for the gods out of appropriate substances (59–60). In this way, we are told, all the gods and their Ka-spirits assembled round Ptah, the lord of the two lands. Memphis became the granary of Egypt. This, we are told, greatly pleased the gods in the 'house of Ptah', the lords of all life. By means of this granary the life of the two lands was maintained (61).[1]

The Memphis text then turns abruptly to the incident of the drowned Osiris and his burial in Memphis. He entered the city as the lord of Eternity, and lived in the company of the gods of Ptah, the lords of the year (63, 64).

His son Horus then 'appeared' as king of Upper and Lower Egypt, 'in the arms of his father Osiris amidst the gods who were in front of him and the gods who were behind him' (64).

Much could be said about the details of this text, but we shall have to be content, for the present, to consider its general characteristics. Some of these have been already noted : the dramatic nature of the texts ; the consecration of the king in the guise of Horus, son of Osiris ; the death and burial of Osiris, closely associated with the consecration of Horus ; the political events centring round the unification of the kingship, an episode in the enigmatic relationship between Horus and Set, friends and enemies, collaborators and adversaries.

Ptah, the great creator, who is Osiris, created the gods, and

---

[1] According to Erman and Sethe the old name for Memphis meant 'the two lands live', or 'the life of the two lands'. Sethe, op. cit., 72.

established them. He provides every living being with life ; his city is the source of all life for Egypt, and is its granary as well. His creative activities also include, as we have seen, the making of the primordial mound in the primordial ocean, which in its turn was produced by Osiris.

The Ramesseum Papyrus agrees with the text of the Memphis text, in that it opens with certain dramatic episodes, and leads up to the consecration of the king as Horus, son of Osiris, this ceremonial being closely associated with the finding of the body of Osiris.

The opening scenes depict the building and equipping of a ship to convey the royal party to their various destinations (1–7). All manner of food and drink is prepared; a bull is slaughtered (8–10) ; spelt is threshed (15–16) ; cakes are made (18–20) ; barley is threshed on the threshing-floor, male cattle being used to tread it down (29–33) ; goats and geese are killed (46) ; and other preparations are made.

The heads of the slaughtered goats and geese are presented before the mysterious d e d pillar, that plays so important a part in Egyptian ritual. The pillar is raised up, and the royal party embarks on the two ships that have been built (46–54).

A fighting scene follows, based on the struggles between Horus and Set. It is in some way connected with the events that took place when Set was dispossessed of his share of the kingship (56–8). The consecration of the king then begins. Milkmaids, slaughterers, and joiners are called in (59–65) ; food and wine are prepared (66–71) ; cornelian and faience ornaments are brought to the king (72–9) ; a procession encircles the two falcon standards (81–2) ; certain regalia are presented to him (83–8).

The next scene is that of the summoning of the Chiefs of Upper and Lower Egypt to attend the consecration of the king (89–90). Spices, resins and paints are brought in, and the keeper of the Great Feather meanwhile fastens on the crown (91–6). Half loaves are distributed among the Chiefs of Upper and Lower Egypt (97–100).

Events take another turn. A papyrus pectoral (Brustsatz), representing Osiris, is brought in and embraced by Horus, who thereby restores him to life (101–3). Bread and beer are brought, ' a flat cake of bread and a beer-jug ' (104–6) ; cloth is woven of two sorts (107–11).

Certain priests called The Seekers of the Spirit are sent to seek Osiris (111–13). They bring in his statue (114–16). They then make a ladder up which Osiris can climb to the sky (117–19). Two women are chosen to lament him (120–2).

The final scenes show the assembled Nome rulers being fed and anointed, while purifying elements are brought in for the dead king (132–9).

The scenes that are outlined so briefly are centred round the royal family, as is the universal rule. The chief actors are Geb, the father of Osiris; Thoth; Horus, the son of Osiris; Set, the brother of Osiris; Anubis; Isis, the wife of Osiris; Nephthys, the wife of Set, and sister of Osiris; the Children of Horus, sometimes called the Followers of Horus; and the Followers of Set. Osiris figures as an effigy.

One of the most tantalizing problems is that of defining the relationship between Geb and Osiris in the ritual.

It would seem possible to divide this ritual into three parts. The opening scenes, which centre round the outfitting of the royal ships, have constant references to Osiris. For example, while the d e d pillar is being raised, the following comment is made: ‘ It is Horus who has commanded his children to raise Set under Osiris ’ (48). Or, again, in the scene of the launching of the ships: ‘ It is Osiris set on the back of Set, the vanquished adversary ’ (21).

This association with Osiris appears to be severed after the embarkation of the royal party. The sham fight is associated with Horus and Set, and no mention is made of Osiris. The preparation of food for the consecration, the presentation of the ornaments and regalia to the king; the procession round the standards; the anointing of the king; the summoning of the Chiefs of Upper and Lower Egypt, and the presentation to them of loaves of bread in like manner ignore Osiris. On the other hand, frequent mention is made of Geb, grandfather of Horus. He is only named once in the earlier section of the papyrus, but he figures seven times in the ‘ consecration ’ scenes.

The final portion of the ritual, from the scene of introduction of the papyrus pectoral of Osiris onwards, is full of references to Osiris. Mention of Geb is made during the introduction of the papyrus pectoral; and in the following scene, in which bread and beer are brought in (101, 102, 103, 105, 106); but he does not appear to be mentioned after the seekers of the spirit appear on the scene.

Geb also is associated with the political events, in which Set is dispossessed, in the Memphis text. He does not seem to appear in connexion with the creative activities of Ptah, nor with the scenes of the drowning and burial of Osiris.

These conclusions lead to some interesting problems concerning the relationship between Geb, Osiris, Horus and Set. Both Geb and Osiris play an important part in the consecration of Horus. Geb's rôle is essentially mundane.

The part of Osiris is different. He is embraced by Horus, in the form of a pectoral (101–3). This is similar to the scene in the Memphis text, in which Horus appears as king ' in the arms of his father Osiris ' (164).

This duality in the consecration ceremony requires for its explanation an intensive examination of Egyptian texts. It will therefore have to be left on one side for the present.

The texts now being discussed, particularly the Ramesseum papyrus, have other general characteristics that are well worth consideration, though it must be brief. We find, for instance, that certain of the actors are silent. Osiris does not speak. This may sound a curious statement to make about a dead man. It must be remembered, however, that Osiris was supposedly brought to life again by his family, when he acquired once again all his faculties. He certainly is supposed to be able to hear. A text says : ' it is Horus who speaks to Osiris when he has found him whom he sought, and says that he will cling to him ' (107), and again Horus says words to Osiris : ' my father shall nestle to me ' (110). If Osiris could hear, surely he could be supposed to speak.

Set and his ' Followers ' are also silent actors. The only occasion on which we might have learned something of their point of view is in the final episode of the final scene of the Ramesseum papyrus which says ' the followers of Set speak to . . .' (139). What were they about to say ?

Geb, Horus and Thoth, together with the Followers of Horus, on the other hand, speak freely to one another, as well as to Osiris, Set and the Followers of Set.

The drama enacted in these texts therefore presents only one side of the story. It is evident that the Horus faction, so to speak, were dominant. Constant reference is made to this fact. The drama may be considered, from one point of view, as a series of events in the Horus-Set feud.

A yet more interesting feature is the frequent identification or association of Set and his Followers with sacrifices and offerings. Some examples will make this clear.

The comment on the bringing of certain jars on to the royal ship is as follows : Thoth says words to Set. ' Thou canst not stay long under him who is greater than thou (Osiris) ' (6). Set also supports the d e d pillar. One of the texts says, ' It is Horus who has commanded his Children to raise Set under Osiris ' (48). Set is said to ' stand smitten in fetters ' (52). Scene 13 deals with the offering of the heads of a kid and a goose before the d e d pillar. The last section of this scene runs : ' Geb says words to Thoth. Give him his head twice/the head of Set/offering of the goat head and the goose head/the gold-house/.'

Set was therefore sacrificed in the forms of a goat and a goose.

He suffers in yet other ways. For instance, part of the regalia consists of two high feathers and two sceptres. The texts read : ' It is Horus who incorporates into himself the testicles of Set that he may gain power of procreation thereby . . . thy power of procreation/the testicles of Set/gaining of strength/the way of the gods ' (83, 85).

Set's thighs are torn out by Horus and Thoth, and presented to Osiris (126–9). After this is done Horus says to Set, ' Depart from thence, be no more found ' (129), an extremely interesting and significant remark ! [1]

Many of the incidents of these rituals are life-giving. The regalia ; the ingredients used during the coronation ceremonies for the anointing of the king and his nobles ; the food offered to Osiris, Horus, and the nobles (18, 66, 69) ; all these have for their aim the acquisition of life in some form or other.

The dead king Osiris is identified with barley. In a scene called ' The Threshing of the Barley ' the following texts occur : ' It came to pass that the barley was laid on the threshing-floor. It came to pass that male cattle were brought in to tread it down. . . . Horus said to the followers of Set. Do not smite my father/smiting of Osiris. Dismemberment of the god. . . . Horus says words to Osiris. I have smitten for thee them that smote thee./ Followers of Set/Bulls ' (29–33).

The various sacrificial episodes, the killing of bulls, goats, and geese, are therefore closely connected with the drama of Osiris. He has been killed by Set, who consequently must suffer in order to restore his life.

Horus also restores Osiris. This is seen in the episode of the papyrus pectoral. ' It is Horus who embraces his father and makes entreaty to Geb. . . . I have twice embraced my father who is weary . . . he has become wholly restored again ' (101–3).

These texts show that the chief aim of the offerings of all kinds is to convey life, to both the quick and the dead.

We have already found that the great aim of ritual in America and in India was the securance of life. The Pawnee priests insisted with emphatic reiteration that the aim of every incident in the Hako ceremony was the securance of the breath of life from Tirawa, the source of all life. The Brahmana rituals are also concerned with the getting of life. They speak of breath

[1] Is Set the original scapegoat ?

as the highest thing in the universe. Egyptian ritual, we see, is concerned with the getting of life in all its aspects. Any and every ceremonial act had for its object the conferring of life, in the widest sense of that term. The royal insignia and regalia were magical, and were intended to protect the king from danger and to confer benefits upon him. For example, the two high feathers placed upon the king during his consecration were supposed to increase his powers of procreation. Gods are usually depicted carrying the ankh sign, with which they confer life. Every element of temple decoration was magical.[1]

The climax of these life-giving activities was, of course, the resurrection of Osiris. This was effected by the use of certain Givers of Life. It was, as it were, a mechanical process. It does not seem to have arisen from some preconceived theory of a soul that left the body at death and led a conscious existence in a hereafter. The sole and sufficient requisite was the exact performance of a ritual.

The body was embalmed and thus made physically immortal. Sometimes a portrait statue or portrait head of the deceased was made. When the body had been embalmed, or the statue carved, it was then ready to be brought to life.[2]

The aim of the Egyptians was to bring this mummified body or portrait statue, to life. The dead man was thus supposed to be alive once again, and to be able to enjoy the pleasures of the flesh to which he had been accustomed. A whole series of rituals were performed for this purpose. The body (i.e., mummy or statue) was placed upright on a heap of sand. It was then lustrated with water, anointed with oil, painted with pigments, and fumigated with incense. Then came the supreme series of actions, comprising the ritual opening of the mouth. The mouth, nostrils, eyes and ears were touched in turn by a series of life-giving objects. The dead man thus became alive. He was now Osiris. He could bring on the Nile flood by virtue of the powers that had now come into his possession. He was awakened from the sleep of death. At the same time he was dependent upon his relatives for food. He had not immortality as we define it. He was merely a man made alive once more, and as such he needed food. Consequently an important feature of his resurrection was the provision of vast quantities of food for his use.

This ceremonial procedure illuminates another dark place in Indian ritual. It will be remembered that in the story of the

---

[1] Maspero iii. 100.
[2] I group the mummy and the portrait statue together because there was no essential difference in the treatment of the two.

18

creation, as recorded in the Fire Altar ritual, Prajapati was not the first being in the universe. The text says that he was created by the Rishis out of the seven ' vital airs '.

The Rishis were the great priests of old who were responsible for the compilation of the Brahmanic rituals. It might seem at first sight, and indeed I presumed so for some years, that this account of the creation of Prajapati from the ' vital airs ' was an embellishment of later generations, added for some obscure purpose. I thus fell short of my canon of taking tradition seriously. For, having identified Prajapati with Osiris, by virtue of the numerous parallels between them, it is possible to suggest a meaning for this incident. It is obvious that Osiris, in the form by which we know him, was, as it were, created by priests out of the seven ' vital airs '. The central episode of the ritual of mummification was the series of incidents termed the ' Opening of the Mouth '. The seven ' vital airs ' in India were associated with the mouth, nostrils, eyes and ears, precisely those openings that were touched in the Egyptian animation ceremony. This additional parallelism intensifies the similarity between Prajapati and Osiris. It is of interest, moreover, in that it shows that life had to be put by human agency into these two great creators, before they could perform their life-giving activities.

The Children of Horus, sometimes referred to as the Followers of Horus, and the Followers of Set, are constant, if less important, actors in the ritual. The contrast in the titles of the two groups is interesting. Perhaps the Followers of Set were also the Children of Set. The two groups act both in concert and in opposition. For example, in one place the Chiefs of Upper and Lower Egypt are personated by the Horus Children and the Followers of Set. ' It came to pass that it was said " Come hither " to the Chiefs of Upper and Lower Egypt. . . . Geb says words to the Horus Children and the Followers of Set. " Attend on Horus. Thou (Horus) art the Lord of thy people " ' (89, 90).

These texts refer to the summoning of the minor rulers to the consecration of the king. The incident recalls the grouping in the Pawnee Creation ceremony. The Egyptian account has the added interest that the actors are all related.

This grouping was a constant feature of Egyptian State ritual. In the words of Naville, ' . . . It was a usual custom with Egyptian kings. For all the important ceremonies, especially those which were connected with a great event, or with the issuing of a solemn decree, they would call together the priests from different parts of the country, and also some civil officials.' [1]

[1] Naville iii. 21.

The Followers of Set also try to impede the Children of Horus. In an interesting incident in the coronation ceremony the Horus children, called here the Seekers of the Spirit, make a ladder for the dead king to go to the sky. The text then reads, ' Horus says words to Nut, " raise thy children to heaven, while thy hind-quarters are turned to the goats that surround (him) ". The raising to heaven of the Children of Nut in spite of the Followers of Set ' (117–19).[1]

The Followers of Horus and the Followers of Set, with their ritual relationships, correspond to the gods and Asuras in India. Both are created by Prajapati. The Indian king has to carry on the ceremonial, in spite of the attempts of the Asuras to frustrate him.

In Egypt the relationship between the two groups becomes clearer. The actors in the Egyptian drama bear more resemblance to living flesh and blood than do the lay figures of Indian cere-monial. We read of Set bringing actions against Osiris before the councils of the gods, and acting in a perfectly normal human manner, without any affectation of divinity.[2]

The king in India did not identify himself either with the Asuras or with the All-gods, the gods of the Four Quarters. During his consecration ceremony the king was identified with the group of solar gods called the Adityas. He merely placed the All-gods in their stations. The Asuras, as we have seen, tried to prevent the ceremonial from being carried out. The reason for these dis-tinctions is now clear. The four gods of the Quarters are the four sons of Horus, who are known to us by name. The followers of Set are the counterparts of the Asuras. There is therefore good reason for the distinction.

So far as I am aware, the Children of Horus usually act under the instructions of their father, and occasionally of Geb, their grandfather, as well as of Thoth. They do not appear to initiate incidents.

It will be remembered that the four posts of the Pawnee cere-monial lodge were brought in by four groups of people associated with the four quarters. The erection of these posts was accom-panied by a ceremonial fight. Four priests represented the gods of the four quarters in the rituals. These four groups, with their corresponding gods, or priests, have their counterparts in Egypt in the four Children of Horus, Hapi, Amset, Duamutef, Qebsennuf.

---

[1] The goats mentioned in this text are evidently the followers of Set (see pp. 259–60).

[2] See, for example, the Chester Beatty papyrus, edited by Alan H. Gardiner (p. 13 e.s.).

They are ' the four gods who stand by the pillar-sceptres of Heaven '.[1] We are told by Maspero that the Followers of Horus, or Children of Horus, founded most of the famous sanctuaries of Egypt, such as Denderah, Abydos, and Edfu.[2] They are identified with the four cardinal points, and with the four pillars which support the sky. It is interesting to note that at Denderah there is a zodiacal circle with two Horuses and a goddess at each quarter holding up the sky. It is still more interesting to note that these four sons of Horus stand at the four angles of the burial chamber of Osiris as the guardians of the corners of the world.[3] This configuration of Osiris at the centre surrounded by the four quarters recalls vividly the arrangements of Mexico City, where the mummified body of the dead ruler was situated in the midst of his people surrounded by the four quarters.

Egyptian ceremonial presents the same arrangement for the living king. This is found, for example, in the Sed Festival. In one of the most important episodes the king sits on a throne, placed on an open platform, approached by four stairways, leading from the four cardinal points. He has to turn in succession to face the south, north, west and east. Each time two divinities stand near him, and raise their hands above his head, ' as if they were giving him their blessing '. When he faces south three priests go up to the stairs and bring him emblems. Another text says, ' Horus rises and rests on his Southern throne, then happens the joining of the sky to the earth, four times.' [4]

Let us glance for a moment at the handiwork of the Children of Horus, the Egyptian temple. In the words of Maspero, ' The temple was built in the likeness of the world, as the world was known to the Egyptians. The earth, as they believed, was a flat and shallow plane, longer than its width. The sky, according to some, extended overhead like an immense iron ceiling, and according to others, like a huge shallow vault. As it could not remain suspended in space without some support, they imagined it to be held in place by four immense props or pillars. The floor of the temple naturally represented the earth. The columns, and if needful the four corners of the chambers, stood for the pillars. The roof, vaulted at Abydos, flat elsewhere, corresponded exactly with the Egyptian idea of the sky. Each of these parts was, therefore, decorated in consonance with its meaning. Those next to the ground were clothed with vegetation. The bases of the columns were surrounded by leaves, and the lower parts of the walls were adorned with long stems of lotus or papyrus, in

[1] Budge ii. CI.
[2] Maspero ii. 64.
[3] Lethaby i. 61 ; Naville ii. Pl. I, line 33.
[4] Naville iii. 13.

the midst of which animals were occasionally depicted. Bouquets
of water-plants emerging from the water, enlivened the bottom
of the wall-space in certain chambers. Elsewhere, we find full-
blown flowers interspersed with buds, or tied together with cords ;
or those emblematic plants which symbolize the union of Upper
and Lower Egypt under the rule of a single Pharaoh ; or birds
with human heads and arms, perched in an attitude of adoration
on the sign which represents a solemn festival ; or kneeling
prisoners tied to the stake in couples, each couple consisting of
an Asiatic and a negro. Male and female Niles, laden with flowers
and fruits, either kneel, or advance in majestic procession, along
the ground level. These are the nomes, lakes, and districts of
Egypt, bringing offerings of their products to the god. . . . The
ceilings were painted blue, and sprinkled with five-pointed stars
painted yellow, occasionally interspersed with the cartouches of
the royal founder. . . . The sun, travelling from east to west,
divided the universe into two worlds, the world of the north and
the world of the south. The temple, like the universe, was double,
and an imaginary line passing through the axis of the sanctuary
divided it into two temples—the temple of the south on the right
hand, and the temple of the north on the left. The gods and their
various manifestations were divided between these two temples,
according as they belonged to the northern or southern hemisphere.
This fiction of duality was carried yet further. Each chamber
was divided, in imitation of the temple, into two halves, the right
half belonging to the south, and the left half to the north. The
royal homage, to be complete, must be rendered in the temples
of the south and of the north, and to the gods of the south and
of the north. . . . Each sculptured tableau must, therefore, be
repeated at least twice in each temple—on a right wall and on a
left wall. Amen, on the right, receives the corn, the wine, the
liquids of the south ; while on the left he receives the corn, the
wine, and the liquids of the north.' [1]

The temple in Egypt thus faithfully reflected the universe, as
the Egyptians conceived of it, and the political circumstances of
the country under dynastic rule. This structure embodied in
itself, therefore, many lines of thought. Mention may be made
of one important characteristic, the duality of the temple, its
division into north and south portions. This was not, as Maspero
states, the result of the solar symbolism, but owed its origin to
historical circumstances. The union of the two kingdoms into
one was never forgotten in Egypt. Upper and Lower Egypt
always retained their distinctive personalities. The temple,

[1] Maspero iii. 90 e.s.

therefore, reflected this duality. It had its entrance to the east, towards the rising sun. This feature dates from the Third Dynasty, when the tombs were all placed on the west bank of the Nile, with their chapels on the east side. This east-west orientation was added to the duality of the country. In this east-west building, the duality of the state was expressed by the provision of a central aisle, that divided it into north and south halves. This feature of church architecture has survived into modern times, for our churches face east and west, and are divided into north and south by the aisle. But in our case the orientation and the division have lost their original meanings, and simply linger on as survivals.

The sanctuary of certain Egyptian temples was called ' the sky '. The king alone had right of entry through the folding doors that led to this holy of holies, where he met his father face to face. Likewise, in the Sed Festival, the king seats himself on a platform. He is then said to be in the sky-world.

The Egyptians therefore constructed artificial ' sky-worlds ', approached by stairways. It is important to discover how early this practice began. Certain inscriptions connected with the kings of that dim period when Egypt was emerging into history, depict the king seated on a throne at the head of a stairway.[1] We can only infer the meaning of these pictures ; but it would appear that the idea of a ' sky-world ' was already taking shape.

The ' sky-world ' of the Sed Festival, which Festival appears to have been in existence certainly as early as the beginning of the First Dynasty, has an important bearing on the general problem of ' sky-worlds '.

This ' sky-world ' is a square platform approached by a stairway from each quarter.[2] This ceremonial incident seems to solve a problem that has baffled some of us for many years. It is customary to class the pyramids of Egypt with those of Babylonia and America and of other countries. It has been pointed out, however, more than once, that there is a fundamental difference between Egyptian pyramids and the others. The Egyptian pyramid is essentially a tomb. The body of the king was placed inside it, while his temple was built east of the pyramid as a separate building. The other so-called pyramids, e.g., of Babylonia, were not sepulchral. Their essential feature was the temple on their flat summit. This temple was approached by one or more staircases, which were totally lacking in the Egyptian pyramid. We may take for example the pyramid in Mexico City,

[1] Petrie ii. I. 21 ; Pl. XI, 5, 14 ; XIV, 12 ; XV, 16.
[2] Naville iii. 13, Pl. II.

on top of which was a temple containing the mummified body of Huitzilopochtli. Like Osiris he is surrounded by the four quarters. Like the king of Egypt in his Sed festival, he is in the sky, also surrounded by the four quarters. Therefore it would appear that the platform in the Egyptian Sed festival corresponds exactly to the so-called truncated pyramid of Babylonia and America.

The similarity between Egyptian and other ' sky-worlds ' may be even closer. De Buck mentions a stone discovered near Heliopolis that bears what is assumed to be a drawing of a temple. This temple was built on a rectangular substructure, and was approached by a double stairway.[1]

The study of myth and ritual carried on in the past few chapters has vindicated the belief of the Pawnee in the truth of their origin stories. What appeared to be the products of imagination, far removed from reality, have been shown to be part of concrete living experience. The incident of the creation of land, drawn up from the bottom of the primordial ocean by beings in a sky-world, acting under the commands of a supreme ruler, is nothing more or less than a garbled account of royal ceremonials that find their most realistic expression in Egypt. It is true that it has not been possible entirely to close the gap between tradition and reality, and mention will be made of this point in a later chapter. But we have got near enough to reality for present purposes. For instance, the great sanctuary of Memphis was built on a mound supposed to have been drawn up by Ptah, the mummy god of that city, from the depths of the flood. Similarly with other great sanctuaries, some of which, at least, had a sky-world within them. In the Sed Festival the king ascends a platform, and is then seated both in the sky and on earth. That is to say the primordial ocean is real enough in Egypt ; the ' sky-world ' is real enough ; the mummy of the dead king is real enough. What cannot be witnessed is the act of creation of the primordial ocean by Osiris, either before or after his death. It is of course obvious that Osiris did not bring on the Nile flood, either before or after his death ; but there evidently must have been some foundation for the belief that he did.

It will be remembered that the Pawnee were taken as a type of society more or less at random, and that it was argued that their belief in the truth of their origin stories led to certain consequences. Among these consequences was the conclusion that gods were simply men who had performed certain rituals. The fusing of the human and the divine is fundamental in Egyptian

[1] De Buck 34.

religion. The word 'god' in the Egyptian language means a
mummy : the king himself actually goes so far as to carry on the
cult of himself as a god.   Moreover, as we have also seen, the
ritual of Egyptian temples centred round the royal family, and
not merely the royal family in general, but one particular family,
who, at some time in the past, underwent experiences that have
reverberated throughout the ages.

The rituals of India serve to make clear some of the dark places
in the ritual of the Pawnee. The ritual of Egypt, in its turn,
carries us still farther back into the past.   Egyptian ritual was
carried on in temples that, like the Pawnee ceremonial building,
represented the universe, so to speak.   Both had their axes running
from west to east ; both had roofs to represent the sky.   The
Egyptian temple was built on a mound that was claimed to be
the earth that first emerged, or was fashioned, from out of the
primordial ocean.[1]   I am not aware that the Pawnee made a
similar claim, though I feel certain that they did at one time.
The primordial ocean was represented in Pawnee ritual by a bowl
of water ; in Egypt it was the Nile flood ; it was also symbolized
by the temple pool.

The Egyptians constructed their sky-worlds in various ways,
but there does not appear to be any clear evidence as to how they
came by the idea.   The earliest ceremonial pictures known to
us show the king seated on a throne at the top of a stairway.
The sky-world presumably came into being at a very early date.

The great creator in Indian ritual, as we have seen, had a son
and a daughter, but no wife. He was the 'father' of the consecrated king, who, it will be remembered, was also a 'son of the
sun ', a member of a royal line that practised incestuous marriages.
Prajapati certainly had intercourse with his daughter, whom he
had created.

The situation is much clearer in Egypt. The great creator,
Osiris, appears to us in a much more concrete setting. He has
brothers and sisters, a son, grandchildren and possibly nephews.
He married his sister Isis, while his brother Set married their sister
Nephthys.   It is not known why this form of marriage took place.

Prajapati created the All-gods, the gods of the four quarters.
The same quartet appear in Egypt as the grandchildren of Osiris.
The Followers of Set probably were Set's sons.   As we have seen,
they correspond to the Asuras in India. The Followers of Set
carry on the feud between Horus and Set ; they have no quarrel
of their own.

[1] The Imperial cult in China was carried out on a mound at the Imperial
capital.   Wieger 12.

The Children of Horus and the Followers of Set sometimes acted together, as well as in opposition. The same happens in India between the gods and the Asuras. Indeed, some of the gods, Varuna for example, are called Asuras.

In India, so far as I am aware, the Asuras are simply the ritual enemies of the gods, with no apparent reason for this enmity. In Egypt, on the contrary, it is possible to discern some reason for the feud. The behaviour of Geb, in depriving Set of his kingdom, for purely sentimental reasons, is, to say the least, unwarrantable.

The treatment of Set in the rituals suggests that he murdered Osiris. For instance, an episode in the Ramesseum Papyrus speaks of male cattle treading down barley that was laid on the threshing-floor. These animals are the Followers of Set, and are killed in remembrance of the dismemberment of Osiris (29–33).

I mention this episode partly to point out that Osiris is not the personification of barley in the first instance, any more than Set is the personification of the cattle, goats, and geese that are killed in his stead. Barley merely symbolizes certain aspects of Osiris. The contrary assumption makes nonsense of the whole of Egyptian ritual.

The problems raised by the death and resurrection of Osiris are as yet insoluble. We may conjecture that Set killed him for revenge, but that at once involves the difficulty that it was Horus, and not Osiris, who deprived him of his kingdom.

It is likewise difficult to suggest how the royal family conceived the idea of embalming, and then reanimating, the dead, for the technical difficulties to be faced were tremendous.

Another difficulty is that of the consecration ceremony. What has it to do with the dead king ? It will be remembered that in the Ramesseum Papyrus the first part of the actual consecration, the bringing of food and wine ; the presentation of regalia and insignia ; the anointing of the king ; the assembly of gods of Upper and Lower Egypt, makes no mention of Osiris, but refers to Geb, the father of Osiris. The second part of the consecration refers almost entirely to Osiris. Geb is only mentioned in the texts referring to the introduction of the papyrus pectoral of Osiris (101–6).

The possession of Osiris seems to be of fundamental importance in the consecration ceremonies of Egyptian temples, just as the ' bundle ' dominated the ritual of North America. Twice in the Memphis text are we told that Osiris was buried in the newly founded capital of Memphis, which became the granary of Egypt and the source of all life.

Und so geriet Osiris in die Erde in der ' Königsburg ' auf der Nordseite dieses Landes, zu dem er gelangt war. Sein Sohn Horus erschien als König von Oberägypten und erschien als König von Unterägypten in den Armen seines Vaters Osiris inmitten der Götter, die vor ihm waren und (der Götter) die hinter ihm waren.[1]

In this instance the body of Osiris was taken out of the water by his family. In the Ramesseum Papyrus Osiris is said to have been dismembered. He is introduced into the ceremony as a papyrus pectoral, and is embraced by Horus his son.

The body of Osiris therefore was buried in the centre of the land, at the point of junction of Upper and Lower Egypt. Horus becomes the ruler of this dual kingdom by a ceremony in which he embraces the statue of his dead father. During this ceremony he is accompanied by the gods, or rulers, whichever you please, of Upper and Lower Egypt.

[1] And thus Osiris passed into the earth in the ' King's Castle ' on the north side of this land to which he had arrived. His son Horus appeared as king of Upper Egypt and appeared as King of Lower Egypt in the arms of his father Osiris in the midst of the gods who were before him and of the gods who were behind him.

CHAPTER XXII

THE ORIGINS OF IDEAS [1]

THE discussion of the past few chapters has led to the conclusion that many social institutions are what might be termed ' life-giving '. Certain definite results are supposed to accrue from carrying out certain stereotyped acts. The belief in the efficacy of these results is based upon the traditional nature of the necessary acts. The theory is presented in a concrete form ; the dramatic element is predominant.

There is no doubt that the mind of man, in elaborating these life-giving situations, and handing them on from generation to generation, has acted in a selective manner ; for it is obvious to any one that the ideas embodied in the rituals that have been examined are but a tithe of those that have been accessible to the mind of man throughout the ages. Obvious facts, for example, the influence of the sun on life, have been ignored by countless peoples throughout the ages.[2] Volcanic eruptions, floods, earthquakes, famines and other disasters, have been the experience of men in the past, but have been forgotten.

It has already been pointed out that the various incidents in these life-giving situations are of the most diverse character. Human beings, animals, plants, material objects, colours, actions, formulas and so forth, have been utilized. It is now necessary to inquire how these diverse elements have been selected out and retained in the memory of man for thousands of years.

It must be realized that the provenance of these elements of life-giving situations is not always obvious. The four quarters form a case in point. It is not clear at first sight why the Chinese Emperor in the Chou Dynasty should term his palace the Centre of the Earth, and surround it by the four quarters. The practice is not universal among rulers.[3] The inference, therefore, is that the process of selection has been a special one. If I ask my old Pondo friend Mtandama about the cardinal points, I find he has

[1] See Perry vi. Chaps. XXVII, XXVIII.
[2] See, for example, Chapters XI and XXI of ' The Megalithic Culture of Indonesia '.
[3] It is very widespread. Cf. Wensinck.

not gone far in thought.   If I point to the south, he says that it is the direction of the mouth of the river, the Umgazi, on the bank of which he lives ; if I point north, that is upstream ; if I point east or west, that is sunrise or sunset.   He has an accurate idea of direction, but it has never occurred to him to devise a framework to enable him to convey his ideas to other people in an abstract manner.   His ideas of direction are linked to natural phenomena that come within his own experience as matters of interest.   His upstream and downstream happen to be north and south ; but were he living on the banks of the Orange River they would be otherwise, but they would still be used. It is true that he uses sunrise and sunset as directions ; but these directions vary from day to day, and consequently would not readily give rise to a rigid framework.   Directions are indicated by pointing.   The time of day is likewise indicated by reference to the position of the sun.

This example shows, therefore, that the concept of the cardinal points is specific, and not general.   That is to say, it is not immediately derivable from personal experience.   It must have arisen in certain definite circumstances.

Human thought has developed along two different lines.   Man has acquired knowledge of facts ; he has also formulated theories. I will begin with the first category.

The consideration of the behaviour of the food-gatherers suggests that their interests are centred mainly on food and family life. Man's internal clock would tell him that it was time to feed, and would stimulate him to activity.   The industry of the Old Stone Age shows that primitive men were intent upon biological ends. They made implements in connexion with the preparation of food. They did not make many stone weapons, even for hunting ; they certainly do not seem to have made weapons for fighting. The art of Aurignacian man, in which he depicted animals that he hunted for food, was obviously utilitarian.   He was also influenced by the fact of death, for his actions betray it.

The evidence at our disposal suggests strongly that the great step towards the development of civilization took place in connexion with food.   It is impossible to be certain on this point, but the evidence appears to point that way.   In any case, it is possible to study the acquisition of knowledge under the stimulus of this urge.

The interest that food-gatherers take in the habits of their sources of food is revealed in their knowledge of animals and plants. But this knowledge is not necessarily dynamic, so to speak.   It does not inevitably lead on to the actual production of food.   The

Negritos of the Congo basin, the Semang of Malaya, the Punan of Borneo simply possess a fund of knowledge concerning their food supply. They have not been able to elaborate the idea of domesticating that food supply, although it would be to their interest to do so.

It would seem from this fact that the need for food is not necessarily productive of constructive thought concerning the food supply. There is some other factor in the situation. Somehow or other there must be the exercise of originality; a new idea must come into being.

Agriculture implies the recognition of certain natural phenomena of causation. For instance, it would involve presumably a recognition of the part played by the seed in the production of the plant.

This knowledge does not appear to have been acquired in a wholesale manner. It is generally agreed that agriculture began in one, or, at most, a few centres, and was diffused throughout the world. Complete agreement on this point has not yet been reached; but that does not matter so far as we are concerned at present. The present task is to search for the origin of new ideas, new knowledge or inventions. One country where this study can be carried on in detail is Egypt. I shall study the situation in Egypt without prejudice as to the claims of other countries to their share of originality.

Egyptian agriculture has for ages been based on irrigation. The country has no rainfall to speak of; so all agriculture depends on the Nile. There seems to me no doubt that the earliest Egyptians learned food-production in the Nile Valley, though the exact nature of the first step is still uncertain.[1]

We have already seen that the Nile flood was the Primordial Ocean, the great source of life. It is but fitting that this idea, derived directly from the objective world, as the result of the interest men take in their food supply, should be, as would seem, one of the supreme ideas in the mythologies of the world. It is likewise significant that Thales of Miletus, the founder of Greek philosophy and science, who knew Egypt well, should have chosen moisture as the foundation of his system of philosophy.[2]

The Nile flood, once it had become an object of interest, directed the attention of the early Egyptians to other matters. It caused them to measure time. The flooding of the Nile occurs every year practically at the same date. The Egyptians, once they had adopted agriculture, would be directly interested in the determination of the date of the next inundation. Their agricultural

[1] See Perry viii. 28 e.s.   [2] Lewes 4–6.

operations would be facilitated if they could measure the period
between the successive floodings of the Nile.

They ultimately measured this period. They found, moreover,
that this period was practically constant. They had therefore
made a discovery of fundamental importance to civilization.
They had measured the year.[1] The Egyptian word for ' month '
means ' moon '. This suggests that the year was first measured
by means of the phases of the moon. The Egyptians, however,
devised a far more accurate mode of measuring time, namely, the
solar calendar. This calendar was based originally on the movements of the star Sirius.[2] In this way the Egyptians stand
supreme among the nations. They were the first and only people
to invent the solar calendar.

The Nile flood was responsible for the discovery of the properties
of geometrical figures. The Egyptians were faced, year by year,
with the need for restoring the boundaries of their fields, which
had become obliterated by the flood waters. This led to an
empirical study of properties of figures. This study remained
empirical until it was taken up by the Greeks of Miletus, Thales
and others, who were the founders of Greek Mathematics.

The concept of the cardinal points was built up in Egypt.
Sethe has shown that the Egyptian words for north and south
originally meant ' downstream ' and ' upstream '.[3] The directions
' east ' and ' west ' presumably became added when interest was
directed towards the sun and his daily path.

We thus see that hunger directed the attention of the early
Egyptians towards certain natural phenomena. This interest
resulted in new ideas and new activities. These new ideas arose
as qualities and attributes of those ideas already formulated. As
we have just seen, the concept of the year arose in the minds of
the Egyptians as a statement of the nature of the Nile flood cycle.
This concept was then applied to the periodic movements of
the sun, which had also been observed. This shows that qualities sometimes detach themselves from their original sources.
They may then become independent ideas, or they may form
new attachments.

The process at work may be likened to the construction of a
mental scaffolding. As the structure of ideas grows from its
foundation, the attention of the mind is directed towards new
phenomena that had not previously been objects of interest. In
this way the Egyptians measured the year and laid the foundations

[1] The Egyptian year was divided into the three periods of inundation ;
winter, or ' emergence ' ; and summer, or ' deficiency '. This reveals its
origin. Gardiner vi. 203.

[2] Meyer 98–9. See also 159 e.s.   [3] Sethe i.

of geometry, and possibly also of astronomy. They were not destined to develop the study of geometry as did the Greeks. For some reason or other they never passed the purely empirical stage. Their study of geometry was not abstract. At the same time it must not be forgotten that the Greeks never used the solar calendar. They continued to use the lunar calendar which the Egyptians had discarded at least twenty-five centuries before. Lack of intelligence was obviously not the cause of the failure of the Egyptians to develop the abstract study of geometry. For some reason or other they had failed to detach their study of geometry from its concrete basis.

The Egyptians were certainly concrete-minded. This is borne out by Dr. Alan Gardiner : ' Most scholars would agree with the verdict that the Egyptians show no real love of truth, no desire to probe into the inner nature of things. Their minds are otherwise orientated : a highly gifted people, exhibiting talent in almost every direction, their bent was towards material prosperity and artistic enjoyment ; contemplation and thought for their own sakes—necessities to the peoples of Greece and India—were alien to the temperament of the Egyptians.' [1]

The body of knowledge accumulated by the ancient Egyptians as the result of their interest in the Nile flood was what might be termed empirical. It was purely objective. The Nile flood completed its yearly cycle with due punctuality. That could be verified. The movements of Sirius likewise were capable of exact study. Such ideas were the exact descriptions of facts.

There seems to be little doubt that the idea of the State as an agglomeration of a number of distinct family groups, incorporating a social hierarchy and a unified administration, was taught the Egyptians by the Nile. We have found that the food-gatherers had gone on for uncounted generations with their independent family groups, and that they show no tendency towards more complicated forms of social grouping. Each family group contends with its own food problem, and has its own hunting territory. Nothing has occurred to cause them to domesticate their food supply.

It was far otherwise with the pre-dynastic Egyptians. Once they had begun the cultivation of food they came under the domination of a unifying economic control.

This control, so far as is known, was originally in the hands of a family associated with the name of Horus. This state of affairs goes back into the days before the unification of the country under one throne. Egypt was dominated by this royal group

[1] Gardiner iii. 857.

during the early dynasties with a completeness that cannot be rivalled in any other place or period. As we have seen, however, this rigid control began to break down, certainly at the beginning of the Fifth Dynasty, when the nomarchs became independent and made their offices hereditary (see p. 76).

The early Egyptian kings were interested in the formulation of new ideas, because they were thereby enabled to attain a greater degree of control over the external world. In this they were merely acting as living organisms always do. By being able to predict the date of the oncoming Nile flood they would be able to take thought for the morrow, and to provide for this event. The acquisition of knowledge concerning the dimensions of fields was also useful. But they had another attitude towards these natural events. They sought to control them in a direct manner.

The early kingship was not merely concerned with exploiting the Nile flood, but assumed a directly causative attitude towards it. Osiris was supposed, as we have seen, to bring on the inundation every year.

How are we to fill up this gap between statement and reality ? The Pyramid Texts recorded in Chapter XXI (see p. 250) are open to a matter-of-fact interpretation. For example: ' It is Unis who inundates the land.' And again, ' The lakes fill, the canals are inundated, by the purifications that come forth from Osiris.' [1]

If we go back in thought to the early days of irrigation, it must be obvious that the central authority was able, by means of basin irrigation, to extend the area of the flood so as to bring new land under cultivation. The central authority would thus, in a sense, be causing the inundation. The quotations from the Pyramid Texts might possibly refer to this controlling activity. The act of predicting the date of the Nile flood, and of controlling it when it came, might conceivably have been interpreted as a creation of the flood itself.

A text of the time of Rameses II quoted by Erman is of interest. . . . ' Thy nature, Osiris, is more secret. Thou art the moon which is in heaven. Thou rejuvenatest thyself at thy desire, thou becomest young at thy wish. Thou appearest in order to dispel darkness, anointed and clothed, for the gods and magic come into existence to illuminate thy majesty and to bring thy enemies to the shambles . . . and men reckon that they may know the month, and work addition that they may know thy time.

[1] P.T. 388, 848.

' Verily thou art the Nile . . . men and gods live by the moisture which comes from thee.' [1]

The various statements made in this text show the many-sided attributes of Osiris. He is a great magician ; the gods are dependent on him ; he is connected with the observations and calculations associated with the annual inundation, which is identified with him.

This text, therefore, is a combination of rational and irrational ideas. It seems probable that the scientific and rational elements connected with the annual inundation of the Nile preceded the non-rational creative elements.

These two elements are associated most obtrusively with Osiris. The living king may possess the power of causing the inundation, but the texts appear usually to identify the inundation with Osiris. That is to say, the inference is that the idea of causing the inundation finds its fullest expression in connexion with mummification.

The essential problem with which we are faced is that of under-standing in what circumstances it came to be believed that a human being, living or dead, could perform superhuman feats. We have seen that men readily accept such claims at second-hand. The difficulty is that of understanding how such claims were originally formulated.

The royal family of Egypt in those early days may be assumed to have possessed all the existing knowledge concerning the irrigation system, as well as the knowledge of the ritual centring round the king, living or dead. The act of mummification of Osiris was the result of certain events that happened within the narrow circle of the royal family of Egypt. For some reason or other, they found it both necessary and practicable to embalm the body of Osiris, and produce in it a semblance of life. The motives that actuated them are as yet unformulated ; but we can be certain that somebody was to be persuaded of the resurrection of the dead. An important problem is to decide whether those responsible for the embalming and animation of the dead king really believed that they had achieved their supposed end. In other words, when they set out to renew the life of the dead king, did they believe it possible ; or did they act with intent to deceive ?

The situation is difficult and complicated. How do men take the mental leap over the gap between appearance and reality ? How are they to believe in events which never happened ?

The Egyptians at an early age, certainly as early as the beginning of the Third Dynasty, began to make portrait statues of their

[1] Erman ii. 80.

kings. Portrait statues were substituted for the actual mummy itself in the ritual of the dead. They are masterpieces of sculpture, and were made to appear as lifelike as possible. ' They were specifically funerary in character, and had an important practical function to perform. The corpse was doomed to perish, in spite of whatever precautions might be taken by the embalmer to stave off decay and corruption. None the less, it was necessary that the body should remain intact, and it was consequently hidden away in its sarcophagus at the bottom of a deep burial shaft, far from the reach of men. But immortality demanded assiduous attention, tending and care ; if the deceased was thus inaccessible, how was he to receive his daily meal of oxen and geese, beer and bread ? For this purpose a substitute had to be provided, and it was provided in the shape of a statue carved as true to life as the craftsman's art could make it—a realistic, and, to the Egyptians, even a real embodiment of the dead man's personality. It has not been emphasized sufficiently that every Egyptian statue was deliberately brought to life by magical passes and spells, before it was walled up in the recesses of the *serdab*. The sculptor in Ancient Egypt was called " the vivifier " and the word for " to carve " was the same as that for " to create ", " to give birth " ; it is perhaps not fantastic to think that, in the beginning, these expressions were literally understood. At all events, such funerary statues were mimetically vivified by the ritual of " Open the Mouth ", performed first, perhaps, at the sculptor's workshop (the " house-of-gold "), and again at the final interment. It was probably on this last occasion, and possibly then alone, that the statue was displayed to the admiring gaze of relatives, friends, and servants, afterwards to be walled up in a tiny outbuilding of the tomb, absolutely closed but for a chink before which the priestly officiant stood to make the daily funeral offering. Thus the living could remain in touch with the dead.' [1]

This is another example of the unfolding of one situation out of another. The Egyptian royal family found themselves in a situation which could be resolved by the mummification and resurrection of a dead king. This step led to others. As we have just seen, they began to make portrait statues of the dead, as the outcome of certain impelling reasons arising out of the specific circumstances in which they found themselves. The statue of the dead king was, like his mummy, the expression of a specific situation. Even the ornamentation of the statue was an integral part of the composition. Dr. Gardiner says : ' As an eminent critic has pointed out to me, the colours here are an essential

[1] Gardiner v. 2.

part of the artists' scheme, not a superfluous element, as in Greek sculpture they often seem to be.' [1]

These remarks suggest strongly that the minds of the sculptors themselves were imbued with the idea of the possibility of creating life. These portrait statues were made in the temple workshops, but it does not follow that the sculptors were very high in the priestly hierarchy. They may simply have been acting under the orders of those in authority. At the same time it must be realized that these portrait statues were quickly walled up in the confines of the serdab, never to be seen by mortal eye again. Also, as Dr. Gardiner remarks, the relatives probably only saw the likeness of the deceased but once.

This last fact suggests the desire to deceive. If we study any Egyptian ritual, whether temple or funerary, it is evident that the opposition between Set and his followers, on the one hand, and Osiris (or Horus and his followers), on the other, was fundamental. Evidently the aim of the ' Osiris ' party, so to speak, was to embalm and reanimate the body of Osiris in secret. The Set faction must be kept at bay at all costs. Both the story, as given by Plutarch, and the rituals themselves, make this point clear.[2]

It must not be forgotten, on the other hand, that Set and his followers sometimes assist in the rites. But on the whole Set and his followers are distinctly hostile. They are not to see the dead body, nor be allowed to handle it.

These considerations suggest the possibility of trickery on the part of the Egyptian royal family. They certainly deluded others, it may be they were not deluded themselves. Whatever be the truth of the matter, however, there is no doubt that mummification, and its attendant ritual, was the outcome of certain specific circumstances in which a group of people found themselves. They took action to deal with these circumstances, to solve the problems presented to them. In order to do so they had a fund of experience at their disposal. They were already well versed in the use of Givers of Life of various kinds. They added something new, that gave the situation its specific character. Henceforth the dead were enabled to live again, more or less, as they had lived on earth ; they no longer were condemned to the eternal slumber of their ancestors ; life abundant was in their grasp.

It is interesting to note how concrete was the reasoning of the Egyptians. They never attained to the idea of ' immortality ' as an abstract concept. They did not conceive of an immortal soul in the possession of every mortal being. On the contrary,

[1] *Ibid.*, 1. [2] Plutarch, De Iside et Osiride. Ubique.

Osiris was the first man with whom such ideas were associated. All they assert in their texts is that Osiris was the first man to escape death, to awaken to the life beyond the grave. Osiris was ' the immortal man '. Immortality was, as it were, attached to him in his guise of a reanimated mummy. The idea had not yet abstracted itself from its concrete basis. Thus every man who desired conscious life after death had to identify himself with Osiris in the closest possible manner. In fact, as is evident from the Pyramid Texts, he became Osiris and completely lost his individuality. So just as a Horus king became Osiris, so every living king is Horus during life and Osiris after death. The rituals and texts are not concerned with individual kings. Their aim is to derive life from its great sources.

Their concreteness often led the ancient Egyptians into serious contradictions. For example, there is no doubt that, throughout the ages, mankind has regarded the dead as being essentially associated with the grave. It is but natural that the final dwelling of the body should be especially associated, not merely with the mortal remains, but with the personality of the dead. Thus in Egypt the tomb was the mummy's eternal dwelling.[1] There the dead man lived, often emerging into the world to enjoy its pleasures. This he is enabled to do by virtue of the fact that he has been reanimated. But the dead man who had been embalmed had become identified with Osiris, who had been hidden away in the isles of the Delta, out of the reach of Set. Therefore the dead man was supposed to be in the isles of the Delta. Osiris was also in the sky-world, by virtue of his associations with Re ; so the dead man was there too. In these, and in other ways, the Egyptian texts reveal an uncritical accumulation of contradictory ideas, all of which are the outcome of the concrete-mindedness of the priests. In dealing with one situation they found themselves faced with others. These they dealt with in their usual matter-of-fact manner, regardless of the contradictions involved.

The formulation of the doctrine of theogamy is a beautiful example of the capacity of a concrete-minded people to deal with an awkward situation. So far as the facts tell us, the Heliopolitan priesthood found themselves in a situation based partly on mummification episodes, which led to the formulation of the doctrine of gods, and partly on the association of the kingship with the sun, that was based upon their scientific activities. They apparently argued that they could advance their interests by equating the sun to the dead king. To do so the sun had to become the father

[1] Gardiner i. 118 e.s.

of mortal men. That was obviously impossible of achievement in the ordinary manner, although the texts associated with Hatshepsut of the Eighteenth Dynasty depict him visiting the queen in her apartment, in the guise of the king. A child had to be produced, and as the trick of the warming-pan was evidently not known in those days, recourse was made to heroic measures. The aid of Khnum, the potter-god, was enlisted. He proceeded to make two models of children, Hatshepsut and her Ka or double, on his potter's wheel. These were animated with the breath of life, and thus Hatshepsut was born.[1]

These texts date from the fifteenth century B.C. but the doctrine of theogamy was formulated early in the third millennium.[2] In either of these cases the idea of the animation of statues and images would have been in existence. The priests of Heliopolis were therefore able to present a solution of the problem they had set themselves, though their logic was somewhat at fault, for it is hard to see how the sun-god could be claimed as the father of a child made on a potter's wheel !

It seems incredible, to me at least, that the priests of Heliopolis could have taken this play-acting seriously. Men who were realist enough to conduct the elaborate astronomical observations associated with the solar calendar, surely must have acted with intent to deceive. The doctrine surely was an elaborate piece of stagecraft, devised to meet a specific situation.

The activities of the Heliopolitan priests were not confined to the intellectual feats already mentioned. They were the first theologians, in the strict sense of the term. The contrast between Osiris and Re, the two great divine figures of Egypt, is remarkable. The associations of Osiris are concrete. He plays his ritual part in the bosom of his family. He may be compared to the Nile ; he may be figured as a ' barley bed ', to emphasize his association with corn ; he may be a creator ; but, above all, he is a homely figure, a real man.

Re, on the contrary, is not so human. He does not live in the midst of his family. He is more or less of an abstraction. Associated with him are such stories as the Destruction of Mankind, the Saga of the Winged Disc, the Stealing of Re's Name by Isis, that are less concrete than those of the Osirian cycle.[3]

---

[1] Naville i. II. 13–18. Pl. XLVI–LIV.

[2] Westcar papyrus. See Erman ii. 36. See also footnote 2.

[3] Elliot Smith devotes a chapter in his ' Evolution of the Dragon ' to Dragons and Rain Gods. He discusses these stories in detail, with full bibliographical details (see especially pp. 109–10). These stories are apparently late, and have been detached from their original ritual context.

The concreteness of Egyptian thought shows itself clearly in the association between Osiris and Re.   The identification of the dead king with the sun obviously necessitated the sky-world in which the sun lived, to which also the dead king could ascend. Thus we find that the land of the dead in the sky was identical with that on earth.[1]   The heavenly world had its Isles of the Blest, modelled on those of the Delta.   This, of course, causes confusion in thought, but that did not trouble the Egyptian priests.

The problem of access to this new world was solved in a direct manner by the priests.   The Ramesseum papyrus, for instance, has a scene in which Horus and his followers raise a ladder to enable the dead king to reach the sky.   Models of ladders were often put in graves, to enable the dead to climb up into their new home.   That is to say, the Egyptians, faced with a new situation that they wished to control, solved it in a direct manner. The dead king must be got to the sky ; what better means than a ladder ?   They had many other devices for attaining the same end—couches, canopies, thrones approached by staircases, and so on ; but the ladder surpasses them all in its directness, literally and metaphorically.

These examples suggest that the rituals of Egypt were the result of the formulation of theoretical propositions.   These propositions are concerned, broadly speaking, with the getting of life.   They are built up on preceding propositions.   But they are often something more than restatements of theory, or re-enactments of preceding events.   We have seen, from a brief survey of the rituals of the world, how important a part was played by the priesthood of early Egypt.   The rituals centring around mummification form the substance for religious and magical practices throughout the whole world.   The contemplation of these achievements must not, however, blind our eyes to the fact that these Egyptian priests had their forerunners certainly as far back as Aurignacian times (see p. 59).   It is interesting to note that circumcision, so prominent in ritual in many places, was practised by the pre-dynastic Egyptians, at a period that long precedes the invention of mummification.

One of the most interesting processes of the formulation of ideas is that of ' budding-off '.   We have already watched this process at work in connexion with the flood-cycle of the Nile.

The same process is at work in the domain of gods.   It is well

---

[1] It must not be forgotten, however, that the earliest pictures of ceremonial show the king seated on a throne placed at the top of a stairway.   See, for instance, the mace-head of Narmer figured in Quibell's Hieraconpolis, Part I, Pl. 26B.

known that particular qualities or attributes of deities can detach
themselves and assume a seemingly independent form.

Instances of this process have already been cited, in the chapter
on The Getting of Food. It was seen that the concept of the
Great Mother received all manner of elaborations associated with
the agricultural and pastoral activities of early men.

The Aditya gods of India, so closely associated with the kingship (see p. 235), are a good example. They are simply attributes
of the kingship. Indra stands for the king militant; Varuna is
the king as lawgiver; and so on.

These gods are in no way the products of naïve speculation.
They are the consequences of the interplay of several groups of
ideas. They are solar; they are named after their mother
Aditi; they attained immortality by getting to the sky-world;
and so on.

Egypt presents the problem of accounting for the diversity of
the gods of the different sanctuaries : Ptah of Memphis ; Min
of Coptos ; Amon of Thebes ; Re of Heliopolis. This diversity
accompanies the unity underlying the temple ritual of the whole
country. How, we may ask, has this unity in diversity arisen ?

It is only possible, in this place, to offer suggestions. Ptah of
Memphis is a useful example. He is associated with numerous
creative activities. He is identified with Nun, and with the two
lands of Egypt. He produced the primordial mound. He
established Memphis, and built a temple there. He created the
gods, and established their shrines. He produced men. His
temple contained workshops where statues were made. He was
said to have made the first statues of the kings and gods. He
was also said to form children as Khnum did. In short, he performed all manner of creative actions. He stands pre-eminent
in Egypt in this respect.

It would appear, at first sight, that Ptah was the personification
of creative activity, manifesting itself in various ways, from the
original creation of the land to the formation of children.

It must be remembered, however, that such an assumption is
dangerous. It is true, of course, that certain of his attributes
may have been the consequence of the application of the idea
of creative activity to certain situations.

One characteristic of Ptah must make us pause before invoking
an abstract idea of creation to account for him. Ptah is repre-
sented as a mummy. He therefore is, in that sense, a form of
Osiris that has become partially detached from its original context.
Ptah as creator must find his explanation in Osiris as creator.
This does not mean to say that the creative powers of Osiris

have been explained. All that is inferred is that these powers, accepted in the case of Osiris, have been reshuffled and have taken a new shape in the person of Ptah. Thus do abstractions arise.

Japan provides an instance of the derivation of the abstract from the concrete. It will be remembered that Erman expressed surprise at the absence of characteristic 'religious' sentiments in Egyptian ceremonial : ' would that there had been some trace of feeling for the sacredness of the place, the majesty of the god ' (see p. 253). There was, indeed, no essential distinction in Egypt between gods and kings.

The ruling family in early Japan likewise was very close to the gods. The house of the king was the shrine of the Kami, the gods. We are told that the articles and utensils for the latter were little distinguished from the former.[1]

A change took place in the course of time. ' When the first Emperor installed the sacred insignia in the palace where he himself dwelt, the instinct of filial piety and the principle of ancestor-worship were scarcely distinguishable. But as time passed and as the age of the Kami [gods] became more remote, a feeling of awe began to pervade the rites more strongly than a sense of family affection, and the idea of residing and worshipping in the same place assumed a character of sacrilege.' [2]

It is now possible to turn to the problem of the great dependence of peoples of all times and countries upon tradition for the sanction of their rituals. Among the great majority of peoples there appears to be an almost complete lack of conscious initiative in ritual. Even in Egypt no fundamental advance was made after the formulation of the propositions of the Pyramid Texts. All is concerned with the royal family, particularly with the destiny of the king after death. Later developments in Egyptian theology consist of an elaboration of ideas already in circulation. The coffin texts of the Middle Kingdom, and the Book of the Dead of the New Kingdom, have the same fundamental basis. Even the solar theology associated with Akhenaten of the Eighteenth Dynasty was but a modification of the solar theology of Heliopolis. But even with this apparent paucity of invention in later times, Egyptian religious thought seems to have dominated that of other peoples throughout the ages.

If we think for a moment of the significance of Osiris, the situation becomes clear. Osiris stands for the triumph of life over death. He incorporates the fundamental idea of godhead. It does not appear possible, as yet, to formulate exactly the process

[1] Brinkley 63. [2] Ibid., 79.

by which the resurrection of Osiris was achieved. We have yet
to learn the details of the events that led up to this stupendous
climax. For stupendous it was, whether the deception was witting
or unwitting. Therefore those who believe, as so many have
believed, in the reality of the resurrection of Osiris, and of all
who follow after him through the shadow of death into the life
beyond, base their belief on a partial knowledge of an original
situation. They know of certain events that happened ; they
know of certain ceremonial procedures. But they do not know
the ultimate reason for these ritual proceedings.

So far as this situation is concerned, the process is irreversible.
The concepts of the breath of life, of godhead, of royalty, of the
resurrection of the dead, have come down from the past, as the
end products of a process, the original nature of which is obscure.
The idea is accepted because of its vehicle, which acts as a concrete
setting for it. Once the setting is seriously damaged, the idea
becomes detached, so to speak, and can no longer be the basis
of supposedly effective action.

The behaviour of the Pawnee, the Toradja, and, say, the
Babylonians, is typical. All these peoples know of immortality,
but are unable to acquire it because the necessary mechanisms
have been lost. Knowing nothing about it, except that certain
people could acquire it, they could only regain it by fresh contact
with people corresponding, say, to the Children of the Sun. They
would be entirely unable to recapitulate the events that led up
to the resurrection of Osiris. This is what would be expected.
We of Western Europe, with all our resources of knowledge, cannot
reconstruct this series of events, so why should people of the lower
culture be able to perform this feat ? It is like trying to define
royalty on any other basis than birth and consecration. Royalty
throughout the ages can be witnessed in being or in disappearance.
Usurpers may arise, but they soon fasten on to the traditional
form. At any stage in history royalty signifies royal birth and
consecration. We are continually forced back into the past for
the origin of the concept. As a rule royalty can only be replaced
by royalty ; it is not designed afresh.[1]

The same may be said of many other social institutions. They
all derive their sanction from the past. Originally they had a
precise and definite meaning to society. They persist because of
their associations.

The State itself is a case in point. It is impossible to give
a satisfactory definition of what we mean by the words Britain,
France or Germany. Yet it is commonly assumed that each

[1] See Perry viii. Chaps. VII–IX.

represents a concrete unity. Britain stands for a multitude of things; the word actually is a mere abstraction. It includes people of different races, languages, with varying traditions and outlook. Its unity is often expressed by the kingship, itself an abstraction.

This concept of the unifying state had some meaning in Ancient Egypt. It must inevitably have been forced upon the Egyptian people by the economic factor of the Nile flood, that caused men to think of their food supply in terms of one predominating factor. Indeed, as we have seen, the Nile flood was the fundamental fact in many aspects of the lives of the ancient Egyptians.

The consequences of the transplantation of the idea of the unifying dominant state from such a country to, say, Rome, or Persia, or anywhere else, would therefore be obvious. Deprived of its concrete basis in economic fact, it would become a mere abstraction, serving theoretical ends, or the purposes of some group of men, and diverting men's minds from reality. We are to-day suffering keenly from this confusion of thought. A concept that was vital to an isolated country like Egypt, where men were forced to take concerted action for their own welfare, cannot be of the same use to Britain. The inhabitants of these islands are economically bound up with all parts of the world, and any attempt to isolate themselves is bound to be harmful. The conclusion to which this reasoning would seem to point is that all social institutions are ultimately derived directly from concrete situations in human society. That is not to say that every institution has a single source. On the contrary, many of them are extremely complicated, being built up out of strands of varied origin. At the same time every strand must ultimately reach back to an idea directly derived from experience.

If we wish to control these social institutions, we must follow them back to their sources in social experience. This is easy in some cases. The world of science is built up on concrete experience. The theoretical constructions of the scientist can only survive if they satisfy the test of application to concrete facts.

We master the world around us by means of our understanding. The more we know of it, the better can we control it. The need for control is obvious in the social world. Enough has been said in the preceding chapters to show that the great majority of mankind are unaware of the extent to which their lives are based on illusion, on faith in a reality where no reality exists. There never was a creation out of the primordial flood; the king does not control the welfare of his kingdom (except, perhaps, in a very abstract sense); the king's consecration ceremony is a farrago of meaningless nonsense ; there is no sky-world ; the ritual of mummification does not bring the dead back to life : yet all these ideas and practices have dominated the minds of millions of people for thousands of years. The vast majority of these people have believed more or less implicitly in the inherent value of the social institutions that have so moulded their lives. Divorced from reality, they have vainly imagined themselves in close contact with it.

After all, what is there of value at the back of all this welter of belief and practice ? Simply, it seems something very akin to a food-gathering society. In confining our attention to Egypt alone, and ignoring all questions of diffusion, we have the invention of agriculture by means of irrigation with its subsequent consequences, such as the invention of the calendar and the nilometer. This has grown out of man's interest in food, a wholesome, dynamic urge, that found specific expression in Egypt at least. In this way the foundations of civilization were laid in Egypt, if not in the rest of the world. For this process of development was in direct contact with reality. Along this path men's minds have travelled to build up our modern civilization.

Associated with this concrete, objective reasoning has been the grouping of the family. At the very dawn of Egyptian history we see one family dominating the country, possessing all power and knowledge. As in the case of the food-gatherers, this family lived mainly for itself, and showed no desire to amalgamate with the rest of the community. On the contrary, its actions show an intense desire to maintain its position of privilege. The earliest ruling group we can watch evidently considered its own existence to be an end in itself. To be of royal birth was in itself to be something different from the ordinary man and woman. This has been the attitude of ruling groups throughout the world.

I have already called attention to this exclusiveness of ruling groups. It is only necessary to think of pre-war Europe to realize that the ruling families of Germany and England, not to mention Denmark, Greece, and other countries, constituted a closely inter-related group. The members of this group were nearer to one another than to the subjects over whom they reigned. Royalty is something specific throughout the world. It is not derived from the community itself ; it has been imposed upon the community.

As has already been stated, the institution of ruling groups evidently grew directly out of the economic situation in early Egypt. Based originally on knowledge, it therefore had a firm

foundation ; but, beyond any doubt, the restriction of this knowledge to a narrow class must have been harmful, for that is the
lesson of history.   This early ruling group, moreover, led mankind
sadly astray when they tried to bring their father to life again.
For more than three thousand years the consequences of this
unreal act dominated Egypt, and, in the opinion of some of us,
the rest of the world also.   Based on illusion, the doctrine of the
resurrection of the body by human agency has obsessed mankind
for ages.   It has blinded men's eyes to reality.

The value of this development in human thought and action
is doubtful.   It hardly seems possible that a mass of hazy
reasoning, based on illusion, or self-deception, could have benefited
mankind.   It is true, of course, that chemistry grew out of
alchemy, and that alchemy was based upon the search for immortality, upon a whole complex of beliefs and practices concerned
with the getting of life.   Secondary consequences of this kind
have resulted from this chase after mirages.   But the search for
immortality was simply a selfish aim, based directly on man's
instinct of self-preservation, and not contributing to wholesome
social ends.

A strong case could be made out to show that the working of
family sentiments in human society has not always been beneficial.
The family stands for continuity.   Its social functions are partly
biological, partly cultural.   Much might be said for and against
its utility in the realm of culture.   In preserving certain aspects
of culture it has given them a definite twist, and thus obscured
reality, and impeded further development.

Every food-producing society possesses rituals associated with
illness.   Much of this ritual is concerned with individuals rather
than with groups.   I gained the impression that were it not for
the fact of illness the Pondo would hardly possess any magic.
They still possess several classes of medical practitioners—some
of whom I met, and others whom I did not succeed in meeting.
Such experts are but the survivors of a more highly complicated
hierarchy.   My Pondo friends told me that the rain doctors,
formerly so powerful, have died out.   Funerary ritual has gone ;
so has much of the marriage ceremonial.   The Chiefs no longer
hold the celebrations of the first fruits.   Circumcision has been
abandoned.   There remains but little.   The girls are initiated ;
beer-drinks are held.   Little else remains of group ceremonial.

This power of survival suggests that man's earliest constructive
thought may have been directed towards the treatment of illness.
We must not forget that the earliest members of our species as
yet known to us, Crô-magnon men, showed signs of a wide develop-

ment of magical thought (see p. 59). They were interested in the problems connected with their food supply, with death, and ill-health. That is to say, food-gathering man had already begun to cope with his surroundings in a way that is characteristic of the human race.

This development of early thought is well marked in Western Europe. There is little doubt, moreover, that the pre-dynastic Egyptians possessed a collection of magical beliefs and practices. These were utilized by those who built up the great rituals associated with the kingship. Such magical ideas may have existed through the ages in Egypt, quite independently of the State rituals. The same may be said of India and other countries.

Does it follow that all food-gatherers have developed some system of ideas round the experiences of death and illness ? This raises an extremely difficult problem, already discussed in Chapter VI. For instance, it does not seem possible to point to anything original about Australian magic. Its uniformity ; its associations with such things as quartz, pearl-shell, and, more especially, with the great beings of the sky-world, to whom all culture is ascribed ; the mode of initiation of the medicine men ; all these facts tend to exclude the possibility of an independent development of magical practices on the part of the Australian natives.

I do not propose to discuss this matter, for it would take us too far afield. I mention it simply to show that other problems concerning the original development of thought lie behind those already considered.

The getting of food, family life, illness and death are the things that matter to mankind. They provide the situations out of which most, if not all, of our social institutions have developed. These situations are enduring. Man must eat ; he procreates ; he falls ill ; and dies. That is the summation of his life. His food supply is within his control ; and in procuring it he does not depart far from reality. The action of his family sentiments, on the other hand, is for the preserving of the family group above all others. This often causes a departure from reality. Human behaviour is a mixture of rational and irrational.

CHAPTER XXIII

THE ACHIEVEMENT OF EXCELLENCE

THE Pondo living along the south coast of Cape Colony still make pottery. The importation of manufactured pots and pans has not quite killed the native craft.

The Pondo make pots by the coil method. Lumps of clay are prepared in the form and size of sticks of plasticine. A base of clay having been made, the pot is built up by coiling these sticks of clay round and round. It is smoothed over inside and out. It is then burned in a fire.

I commissioned my friend Nozinkilwani to make me some pots, so that I might study the methods adopted. The result was a pot of very poor quality.

This failure of the Pondo potter to make an article of beauty is well worth considering. The craft of the potter, in Africa, reaches back, to our certain knowledge, beyond 3300 B.C. Nozinkilwani, therefore, was one of a line of potters reaching back more than fifty centuries. Her craftsmanship is at the end of a process, not at the beginning. She turns out a pot of no artistic merit whatever.

When we go back to the other end of the line of potters, say to early Egypt, a surprise awaits us ; for these early people made pottery of extreme beauty, and displayed a superb craftsmanship. Sir Flinders Petrie, speaking of the early pre-dynastic period in Egypt, says : ' Pottery was the favourite product of these people. The care lavished on the perfection of shape and outline, the polish of the surface, the thinness of the body, the great variety of form, all show a love of artistic treatment. The whole of it was built up by hand without any wheel or circular motion, yet it is rarely that a lack of symmetry or any irregularity is obvious.' [1]

Professor Peet also comments on this achievement. He says : ' And it is here that in Egypt a paradox meets us, for, at the moment when he entered Egypt, the primitive potter was producing vases so admirable from the technical and artistic point of view that his successors never surpassed and seldom equalled them. He had learned to clean his clay by mixing it with water

[1] Petrie iv. 47.

290

and removing the coarser particles which settled first at the bottom ; knowing that a pure clay is apt to crack in the firing, he introduced into his paste a proportion of small grains of quartz or limestone ; despite his ignorance of the potter's wheel, he moulded his shapes so perfectly that its absence is never felt ; and, last but not least, he belonged to one of those rare and happy periods when the craftsman seems incapable of an error of taste, and in consequence almost every form that leaves his hands is a thing of beauty.'

. . . ' But the Egyptian pre-dynastic potter possessed a piece of knowledge more extraordinary than any yet described. Not only had he discovered that sand when combined with potash or soda and a metallic oxide will vitrify at a certain temperature ; but he had realized the possibilities of this glaze for decorative purposes ; he had learned to colour it blue with a salt of copper, to make it adhere to the substance on which it was to be laid, and to produce a fire of sufficient temperature to fuse it.' [1]

The pre-dynastic Egyptians made stone vases all through their period. The earliest were made out of calcite, aragonite, and other ' alabaster ' rocks, but after a time they were made of a great variety of hard rocks, such as basalt, diorite, syenite, and so forth. ' Here again, as in the case of pottery, he arrived at astonishing accuracy and beauty of form, and his achievements in the harder stones were never surpassed in later days . . . the hardness of stone had no terrors for the pre-dynastic craftsman.' [2] In the words of another authority, these vases ' reached perfection in the middle and later pre-dynastic periods ; they were already debased in proto-dynastic times, and disappear at the end of the Old Kingdom '.[3]

It is common to ascribe such craftsmanship as the pre-dynastic Egyptians show in all aspects of their industries, to a long process of development. There appears at first sight to be much support for this interpretation. The study of organic evolution, with its evidence for the long development of the different varieties, species, genera and families of living creatures, usually arranged in a series of increasing complexity, has strongly influenced anthropologists. These base their reasoning upon two bodies of facts ; those derived from the study of prehistoric man, and those derived from the study of modern savages. The Old Stone Age reveals a steady process of development in the technique of the manufacture of stone implements. The beautiful products of the industry of the so-called Solutrean Age come at the end of a process of development reaching back for thousands of years.

[1] Peet 243.　　　[2] *Ibid.*, 243–4.　　　[3] Glanville 53.

Modern savages frequently display crudeness in their arts and crafts. As we have already seen, in the case of the food-gatherers, some of these savages are really primitive. At the same time it must not be assumed that all their culture is necessarily primitive. Still less can we assume that the culture of food-producers is always their own product. As we have seen already, the opposite is the case. Such peoples are not primitive in the sense that the food-gatherers are primitive ; they usually can be shown to be relatively recent arrivals in the area in which they are found . . . Their arts and crafts can often be shown to have been acquired by them from elsewhere. The Pondo, for example, only came into existence as a tribe within the last few centuries. They are a branch of the Bantu, themselves of recent origin.

All these facts, and many others that could be added to them, go to show that the crude craftsmanship exhibited by modern savages is the result of a long past history. It is in no way primitive, and until a sufficiently coherent body of facts can be brought forward to the contrary, this generalization will continue to hold the field.

When we turn to the other end of the scale, and inquire of the highest manifestations of the artist or craftsman, we are met with an arresting series of facts. They can be included under a generalization, namely, that any new development of an art or craft, involving the factor of skill alone, rapidly achieves its summit of perfection, and then degenerates more or less continuously.

Mention has already been made of the craft of the potter. The early pre-dynastic Egyptian potter was a superb craftsman. He may, or he may not, have profited by the experience of generations of forerunners ; [1] we are ignorant upon this point ; but we do know that he was not surpassed by his successors. He stands, in his skill, in strong contrast to the myriad communities that have profited by his example, and have failed to achieve equal results.

Innumerable examples could be quoted of this early excellence. For instance, here is Sir Flinders Petrie's comment on the jewellery discovered by him in a royal tomb of the First Dynasty. He says : ' Such is this extraordinary group of the oldest jewellery known, some two thousand years before that from Dahshur. Here, at the crystallizing point of Egyptian art, we see the unlimited variety and fertility of design. Excepting the plain gold balls, there is not a single bead in any bracelet which would be interchangeable with those in another bracelet. Each is of independent design, fresh and free from all convention or copying.

[1] For example, see Childe ii. 49 e.s.

And yet not any one of these would be in place among the jewellery
of the Twelfth Dynasty ; they all belong to the taste of their age,
—the purest handwork, the most ready designing, and not a
suspicion of merely mechanical polish and glitter. The technical
perfection of the soldering has never been excelled, as the joints
show no difference of colour, and no trace of excess.' [1]

Certain facts suggest that the generalization concerning the
early achievement of excellence is capable of extension in certain
directions. The formulation of new systems of ideas often proceeds with amazing rapidity. The mind quickly grasps the reality
of the new situation, and often goes a long way towards exhausting
its potentialities.

The invention of writing, and particularly of the alphabet,
illustrates this process.

The Egyptians and Sumerians possessed a system of writing
from the beginning of historical times, that is to say, from about
3300 B.C. in Egypt. Both systems possessed signs representing
syllables. The Egyptians, however, possessed also an alphabet,
a single sign representing a single sound. The Sumerians, and
the Babylonians who followed them, never possessed an
alphabet, but continued to use syllable signs. Egypt remained
alone in the use of the alphabet for more than twenty centuries.
For the alphabet, spread abroad mainly by the Phoenicians
and Greeks, only came into general use after the tenth century B.C.

How long did it take the Egyptians to devise their alphabet ?
The comments of Professor Peet are worth quoting. He says
that ' in certain of the royal tombs of the First Dynasty we find
the system of hieroglyphic writing so highly developed that it
must already have been long in use, and had already acquired
a cursive or hieratic script, written in ink. A slate palette of
undoubted pre-dynastic date, found at el-Amrah, has in relief
two signs which might conceivably be hieroglyphs ; one of these
may be an early form of the cult object of Min, but the other is
no known hieroglyph, and no conclusion ought to be drawn from
the group. Of the early inscribed cylinder-seals none can be
definitely proved to be earlier than the rise of the First Dynasty,
the pre-dynastic examples showing only designs of animals or
birds, with in one case a star, and in another what appears to be
a building. Further, it is doubtful whether any of the slate
palettes which show undoubted hieroglyphs can be dated as
pre-dynastic. On the other hand, the crude combination of
elementary true writing with pictorial representation so admirably

[1] Petrie ii. II. 19.

20

illustrated by the great palette of Narmer warns us that if this document is a fair sample of the stage which writing had reached at this moment (beginning of the First Dynasty) or just earlier, and not an archaism, very little in the way of writing is to be expected from the period which preceded it. At the same time it is singular that nothing at all has up to the present made its appearance.' [1]

Professor Griffith also comments to the same effect. ' Egyptian writing developed rapidly during the Old Kingdom ; the beginning of the Fourth Dynasty was especially a period of rapid improvement, and it has long been recognized that the graffiti of Khufu were written with considerable freedom. It is, however, somewhat startling to find cursive writing in the time of the First Dynasty.'

. . . ' Another fact which it is interesting to observe is that, with one exception, all the essential features of the Egyptian system of writing appear well developed at this remote period. The rapid change from the inscriptions at the end of the Third Dynasty to those of the Fourth Dynasty would have prepared us to find some radical difference in the writing of the First Dynasty. But apparently no such difference exists in fact ; at present, indeed, we find no clear evidence of the employment of determinative signs in these primitive writings, but even as late as the Fifth Dynasty their use was very restricted in the monumental writing, though it was common in the cursive, and in the freely written texts of the Pyramids.' [2]

The Egyptians were accustomed to carve portrait statues of their kings from a remote period of their history. From the beginning they exhibited a perfect mastery over diorite and other intractable materials, and reached a pitch of perfection that they never surpassed. Competent authorities maintain that the sculpture of the Third and Fourth Dynasties has never been surpassed, even by the Greeks.

The wooden bas-reliefs of the noble Hesy, masterpieces of their kind, belong to this period. This last work is astonishing in its perfection. In the words of Maspero, ' Never has wood been cut with a more delicate chisel or a firmer hand.' [3]

The beginning of the Dynastic Period itself was marked by the sudden development of a living and powerful art. ' It had no traditions to spoil it or hold it back : it was full of observation as the only method for its work. It is always simple and dignified, and shows more truth and precision than any art of a later

[1] Peet 245–6.　　　　　　　　[2] Griffith ii. 34.
[3] Maspero iii. 211.

age.' Petrie tells us, moreover, that this stage was reached ' at
the very beginning of the history '.[1]

Petrie comments on the new development of art at the beginning
of The Pyramid Age. He points out that ' the greater part of
the really fine sculpture that we possess in Egypt comes from
this time. . . . For the expression of royal energy, dignity, and
equanimity the figures of Khufu and Khafra are unsurpassed.' [2]

I cannot resist the temptation to quote Petrie's description
of a minute carving in ivory of Khufu. The face of the king
is only a quarter of an inch high. ' Yet in this minute space one
of the most striking portraits has been given. The far-seeing
determination, the energy and will expressed in this compass,
would animate a life-size figure ; . . . quite apart from the
marvellous minuteness of the work, we must estimate this as one
of the finest character-sculptures that remain to us.' [3]

Architecture provides other instances. The Egyptians began
building with mud bricks just before the beginning of the dynastic
period. The kings of the first two dynasties built large tombs of
brick, and displayed considerable skill in this craft. For instance,
Petrie describes the tomb of Merneit. He states that, ' the central
chamber is very accurately built, with vertical sides parallel to
less than an inch. It is about 21 feet wide and about 30 feet
long.' [4]

The earliest people to build large stone structures were the
Egyptians. Early Susa used brick, and so did early Sumer.
The First Dynasty cemetery at Ur, as well as Eridu, had a
certain amount of stone construction. It was very crude, and
did not give rise to any development, for thereafter in Sumer stone
was not used for building. In Egypt, on the contrary, there
was a marvellous development of stone construction. The tomb
of Den, a king of the First Dynasty, had a granite floor in one of
the chambers. The tomb of Khasekhmui, the first king of the
Third Dynasty, had a chamber made of limestone blocks.

The great development of stone construction in Egypt took
place at the beginning of the Third Dynasty, round about 3000
B.C. Zoser, an early king of the Third Dynasty, built the first
known pyramid. It was shaped like a gigantic staircase, facing
four-square to the cardinal points. On the eastern side of this
pyramid he built a temple, the first built in stone that is known
to us.

The perfection of skill and craftsmanship displayed in this

---

[1] Petrie iii. 14–15.   Also 32, 33.   See Howard Carter II. 1–11 for an interesting discussion of Egyptian art.
[2] Petrie iii. 16–17, 36.   [3] *Ibid.*, 135.   [4] *Ibid.*, ii. 10.

remarkable monument moved Mr. Firth to the following utter-
ance : ' The stone cutting and masonry of all these Third Dynasty
buildings is so perfect that the Manethonian tradition that Zoser
or his *Vezir* Imotep were the first builders in hewn stone cannot
be accepted. Behind these buildings there must be a long
tradition of stone masonry. This is corroborated by the entry
in the Palermo stone which records the building in stone of the
temple called *The goddess abides* in the Second Dynasty. But
these earlier buildings still await discovery or have perished.
The remarkable temples and chapels around the Step Pyramid
are perhaps the oldest constructions in stone remaining from the
ancient world.' [1]

It may be, of course, as Mr. Firth says, that the Egyptians had
had long experience in stone-building ; but it must be realized
that the evidence for this long training is not there. The temple
of the Step Pyramid stands forth as the work of a man whose
genius was known to the Greeks ; for Imhotep survived in Greek
tradition as Aesculapius.[2]

Egyptian stone-work reached its summit of perfection in the
Great Pyramid of Khufu, the largest and most perfect of all
pyramids. The survey of Petrie revealed an almost incredible
degree of accuracy in the lay-out of this vast heap of stone. ' The
highest pitch of accuracy on a large scale was reached under Khufu
in the Fourth Dynasty ; his pyramid had an error of less than
·6 of an inch on its side of 9,069 inches, or 1 in 15,000 ; and its
corners were square to 12 inches. A change of temperature during
a day would make larger errors than this in a measuring-rod.
The accuracy of levelling, and of finish of the stones, is on a par
with this ; joints over six feet long are straight to a hundredth
of an inch.' [3]   The pyramid of Khafra, his successor, had an error
three times as great, while that of Menkaura was worse.[4]

The casing blocks of the Pyramids of Khufu weighed sixteen
tons. They had vertical joints five feet high and seven feet long
that were filled with a film of plaster only a fiftieth of an inch
thick. ' How it was introduced into the joints of the pyramid
casing is a mystery.' [5]   ' The later ages, so far as we know, have
left nothing that can be compared with the accuracy of the early
dynasties.' [6]   Truly a wonderful age. Well might Lethaby say
that Khufu's pyramid is ' the greatest and most accurate structure
ever built '.[7]

Petrie's small book on ' The Arts and Crafts of Ancient Egypt '

[1] Firth iii. 159.   [2] See pp. 303 e.s.   [3] Petrie iii. 81.
[4] *Ibid.*, 81–2.   [5] *Ibid.*, 142 ; see also Petrie i. 169.   [6] *Ibid.*, 82.
[7] Lethaby ii. 40.

abounds in examples of this principle. He states, concerning the pre-dynastic period, that 'there is no sign of progress in art during this time'. The representation of human and animal figures, flint-working, and pottery-making all decline in achievement. [1]

The period of the First Dynasty witnessed, as we have seen, the sudden rise of 'a living and powerful art'.[2]

This was followed by the Pyramid Age, some of the achievements of which have already been mentioned.

The study of sculpture reveals the same process at work. The earliest portrait statues were the best. The figures of the Fifth and Sixth Dynasties are hardly of the same standard.[3]

The statuary of the Twelfth Dynasty was good, but on a lower level. That of later times was purely conventional, 'and it is seldom that any one feature even approaches the truth of the early art'.[4]

The following quotation from Professor Lethaby's little book on Architecture shows that the early excellence of the Egyptian craftsmanship was the result of intelligence: 'Minutely careful measurements have demonstrated that the Egyptians worked according to schemes of proportion, as part of these ideas for perfect building . . . these results, worked out by actual measurement, coincide exactly with what is reported to us of Greek ideas of proportion—ideas based on the feeling that an object to be perfect must have all its dimensions related according to some scheme of simple measurement which avoids fractional parts. The builders, it is clear, had before them some idea of perfection, and endeavoured to realize a type which should rise above the accidental.' [5]

The lowest levels investigated at Susa by the French Expedition to Persia, led by de Morgan, are of interest; for the earliest inhabited site contained painted pottery superior to that made by later inhabitants of the same city.[6]

Painted pottery, of obvious affinities with that of Susa, but of inferior artistic merit, has been discovered in the earliest food-producing settlements of a vast portion of Asia, extending as far as Eastern China.[7]

There is no common agreement as to the history of this early painted pottery of Susa. There is no evidence that its makers elaborated their culture on the spot. It seems to be admitted

[1] Ibid., 13.   [2] Ibid., 14.   [3] Petrie, op. cit., 34.
[4] Ibid., 36.   [5] Lethaby ii. 63.
[6] de Morgan, I, VII, VIII, XII, XIII.
[7] V. Gordon Childe : Pumpelly : Andersson.

that they came from elsewhere. It cannot therefore be stated
that their pottery was a new development ; but everything goes
to show that the standard of achievement soon fell, and never
again reached its original high level.

The early civilizations of Sumer, as shown by recent excavations, had already achieved excellence in the arts and crafts
when it first appears on the scene. The earliest jewellery was
never surpassed. The following quotation from Professor
Langdon will show how this early excellence compared with what
came after : ' The surprising feature of it all is that the art of
the period 3500–3200 B.C. surpasses all that came after it. Field
Museum now has painted pottery of 3500 B.C. never again produced
before the Greek period, and statuettes of remarkable beauty of
3300 to 2900 B.C. entirely superior to anything subsequently
produced in Western Asia before the Greek schools of sculpture.
It is difficult to understand how human endeavour fails to maintain its noble achievements. Least of all had one expected to
find men endowed with such genius at the dawn of history . . .
But our records prove it, and the Museum possesses full evidence
of this tragedy of human history.' [1]

Similarly, at Ur, the later jewellery did not equal the earlier.
Instead of solid gold beads, there are beads of copper plated with
gold. The technique of the earliest finds is described as ' that
of practised master hands '.[2] Having achieved this summit of
excellence, Sumerian craft remained stagnant for a thousand
years.

In another place we read of early Sumerian potters, that ' they
had not learned the use of a potter's wheel, but turning the clay
by hand they had the skill to fashion vessels of really artistic
shapes, admirably regular and sometimes so delicate that they
can only be called " egg-shell " ware, and to decorate them with
designs painted in black and red which, though composed of
single elements, are masterpieces of ornament. None of the later
pottery of Mesopotamia can be compared for excellence with these
earliest vases. . . .' [3]

Mention has already been made of the excellence and accuracy
of Egyptian architecture. Petrie shows the extreme care taken
by the builders of the earlier royal tombs of Egypt. These are
among the earliest brick buildings known to us. It is therefore
interesting to compare these buildings with those of other countries.
An illuminating instance is given in the report on the excavations

---

[1] Langdon iii. The dates are Professor Langdon's own. They are much
higher than those usually accepted.

[2] Hall 447.   [3] Hammerton 513–14.

at Mohenjo-daro in Sind, published by Sir John Marshall. He says : ' It is evident that the bricklayer's art deteriorated remarkably in the Late Period, but for what reason it is difficult to say with certainty.

' The majority of the rooms and buildings at Mohenjo-daro are out of truth in the Late Period, and this feature is noticeable in even the largest buildings. This is at variance with the accuracy of the more important ancient buildings of Sumer, where attempts were made to obtain a proper degree of squareness.' [1]

Inferiority in technique by imitators appears to occur either in the place of origin or as the result of transmission to some new home. Wherever inquiry be made the answer seems to be the same. For example, I open Messrs. Wace and Thompson's work on ' Prehistoric Thessaly ', and look up their remarks on pottery. Speaking of a variety with red decorations on a white background, the authors say that ' at a very early date also, almost at its first appearance, it reaches its highest development, both in decoration and technique.   As time goes on, however, it decreases in quality and quantity alike ; the designs become cruder and the vases coarser and clumsier in shape.'

They say in another place, ' thus almost from the very beginning, we have to deal with a degeneration ; for in the earliest strata the pottery is better in technique and painted wares are more plentiful.' [2]

My Pondo friend, Nozinkilwani, therefore has her counterparts in ancient Greece. There are multitudes of others.

Another interesting example of the early achievement of artistic triumph is provided by the Aurignacian and Magdalenian peoples of the Upper Palaeolithic Age in western Europe. These men, the first known of our species, rapidly achieved a complete mastery over line. There are very few signs of crude beginnings. This is all the more surprising, in view of the fact that this work was, so far as I know, always carried out in the dark recesses of caves, sometimes many hundred yards away from the opening. The contrast between this art and that, say, of the Australian natives, is remarkable. For the work of these latter is crude in the extreme ; in fact there is nothing throughout the whole range of savagery that surpasses the art of the cave men. Indeed, there is little of any age that can be compared with it.

The achievements of Classical Greece and its precursors serve further to illustrate the general principle of the early achievement of excellence. This is shown not only in the arts and crafts, but

[1] Marshall 262.   [2] Wace and Thompson 240.

also in the foundation of systems of ideas such as philosophy and mathematics.

The Greeks were eminent in so many branches of learning and inquiry that it is difficult to know which topic to choose first. A beginning may be made with philosophy. We cannot do better than to remember the opening passages of Lewes's ' History of Philosophy '. His opening sentence says : ' It is the distinguishing peculiarity of the Greeks, that they were the only people of the Ancient World who were prompted to assume a scientific attitude in explaining the mysteries which surrounded them.' [1]

The early Greeks started from the beginning. ' Eastern philosophy, as far as we know it, seems to have been a traditional development ; but the early Greek had no real predecessor from whom to learn.' [2] Nevertheless, ' progress was so rapid that the brief period of three centuries saw the full development of all the chief phases of philosophy, and the origination of all its fundamental solutions '.[3]

Greek mathematics shows a similar rapidity of achievement. Sir Thomas Heath describes this phenomenon in his Greek Mathematics as follows : ' Of all the manifestations of the Greek genius none is more impressive and even awe-inspiring than that which is revealed by the history of Greek Mathematics. Not only are the range and the sum of what the Greek mathematicians actually accomplished wonderful in themselves : it is necessary to bear in mind that this mass of original work was done in an almost incredibly short space of time, and in spite of the comparative inadequacy (as it would seem to us) of the only methods at their disposal, namely, those of pure geometry, supplemented, where necessary, by the ordinary arithmetical operations.' [4]

The early Ionian Greeks of Asia Minor supply one of the best examples of the principle. Among them was Homer, the greatest epic poet the world has known. We are told that he comes at the end of a long period of development ' about which we have no direct information '. That is to say, the suggestion that there has been any prior period of development of epic poetry leading up to the Homeric climax rests upon no foundation of fact, but merely of inference. It is assumed that such great excellence must have been the result of a long period of experience on the part of the epic poets. Mention is made of ' the disappearance of pre-Homeric poetry about which the Greeks themselves knew nothing '.[5] The period between the Homeric poems and the beginnings of Greek drama is obscure. In the eighth and seventh

---

[1] Lewes 1. [2] Id., 2. [3] Id., 2.
[4] Heath 1. [5] Bury 471.

centuries the Cyclic poets imitated Homer. We are told, however, that they ' were uninspired and dull, and we shall hardly
be doing them an injustice if we surmise that any of them had
mastered the Homeric technique in construction or introduced
a new note of their own '.[1]

Hesiod, who flourished not later than the ninth century B.C.,
was, we are told, second only to Homer as an epic poet. He
broke new ground, ' abandoning the self-suppression of Homer,
he comes forward in his own person, names himself and his home
and mentions some biographical details '.[2] He therefore constitutes an early instance of that awakening of consciousness and
individuality which so characterizes the early Ionian writers both
poetic and prose. But Hesiod was not the equal of Homer.
' The second-class kind of poetry which Hesiod created, didactic
and expository, offers little room for artistic construction and
invention.' Neither of the two works which have come down to
us can be judged as a work of art, notwithstanding the merits
of particular passages.[3]

' If we survey the body of post-Homeric rhapsodic poetry that
we possess—Hesiod, the Hymns, and the fragments of the Cyclic
poets—and compare it with the " Iliad " and the " Odyssey ",
we see that many poets trained in Homeric tradition and with
Homer's work as a model reached a high standard of skill but
that none of them had learned his secret. None of them had
his greatness of spirit, none of them his power of telling a story ;
much less could any of them create immortal figures, like Nestor
and Odysseus and Penelope, and the witch Circe and, portrayed
by a few touches, Helen, so curiously attractive. Of such powers
of artistic creation we find indeed no trace in Greek poetry till
we come to the great Attic tragedians. None of the epic poets
achieved that easy loftiness which impressed and astonished later
Greek critics and of which they were fond of quoting as an example
the description (in Iliad, xiii. 14 seq.) of Poseidon driving over
the sea in his chariot. " The mountains trembled throughout all
their length, and their woods and their parks, and the towers of
the Trojans, and the ships of the Greeks, under the immortal
feet of Poseidon as he went. He drove over the waves, and rising
from their caves the sea-beasts played all around beneath him
and well they knew their lord ; and in joy the sea parted asunder
and his horses flew." ' [4]

Dr. Livingstone finds it hard to believe in the suddenness of
Homer's achievement. ' The primitive conditions that preserve

[1] *Ibid.*, 473.   [2] *Ibid.*, 474.   [3] *Ibid.*, 479.
[4] *Ibid.*, 480–1.

simplicity are apparently incompatible with technical perfection, which is a late-born child of literature and the creation of mature taste, long experiment, and patient work. But in Greek, and perhaps only in Greek, *naïveté* and art go hand in hand. There is something almost uncanny in Homer's union of the two ; it is a paradox that the character of Achilles, the death of Hector, the primitive cunning of Odysseus, should be portrayed in such a metre and such a vocabulary ; it seems unnatural that a so highly wrought and refined medium should be used to depict the life and ideas of a society which is nearer to savagery than civilization. But unnatural or not, so it is.' [1]

Another great master of poetry was Archilochus of Paros. I quote from ' The Cambridge Ancient History ' : ' During the age of the post-Homeric rhapsodies there appear in Ionia, alongside of the hexameter, poetical forms, the iambic, and the elegiac, but they have reached such an advanced stage of perfection when we first meet them early in the seventh century, that they must have been in use long before.' [2] Mention is made of traces of iambic poetry in the eighth century B.C. ; but early in the seventh century B.C. came the great master, Archilochus, who is sometimes compared with Homer. The author says : ' The influence which he exerted on the forms of subsequent poetry was immense. We may call him the father of iambic poetry, and perhaps of elegiac, in the same sense that Homer may be called the father of epic. This does not mean that he created either, though in Greek traditions he has been described as the inventor of both, but that he fashioned them into perfect instruments for poetical expression. His elegiacs are the earliest elegiacs we have. In his hands the technique of the iambic trimeter, which was to be the metre of the Attic dramatists, has reached perfection ; and the trochaic tetrameter was handled as skilfully by him as by any later poet. He appears to have made, though we must speak diffidently because our knowledge is so imperfect, signal contributions to what was one of the most remarkable feats of the intelligence of the Greeks, the construction of their wonderful system of poetical measures obedient to severe laws. His experiments in combining different rhythms the imitations of Horace have made familiar.' [3]

Archilochus handles the elegiac and iambic forms of poetry with such perfection in the early seventh century B.C., that classical scholars assume a long period of preparation. But for this assumption there is no evidence. Like Homer, to whom he has been compared, Archilochus appears suddenly, and at once

[1] Livingstone 259.   [2] Bury 482.   [3] Op. cit., 485.

we find complete certainty and assured mastery of the medium employed.

There is the same surprising element of suddenness in the way in which the three great tragic dramatists, Aeschylus, Sophocles, and Euripides, in one generation raise the Greek tragic drama to a height which has only been approached by one dramatist, our own Shakespeare.

The classical period of Greece, from 480 B.C. to 430 B.C., was one of astounding originality. It was therefore less than two centuries in date from the time of Thales of Miletus (624–548 B.C.), who marks the beginnings of Greek science and philosophy. In the course of the sixth and seventh centuries B.C. all the main streams of modern intellectual activities began their course. The culminating point of this process was the classical period, when, in the words of Neuburger, ' " the tree of mankind was in full flower ". It is the epoch which brought forth the statesmanship of Pericles, the philosophy of Socrates, the historical writings of Thucydides ; the era of Sophocles and Euripides, of Pheidias, Polycleitos and Praxiteles ; of Polygnotus, of Zeuxis and Parr-hasios. Never before nor since has so confined a space in so short a time contained such a wealth of intellect and nobility. The liveliest representation must fall short of a reality where the only bounds to creative energy were those of symmetry, beauty, and harmony, and where the rights of the individual were only restricted by the interests of the community.' [1]

Professor P. N. Ure summarizes the situation in an equally emphatic manner. He states that the Greek civilization of the Classical Period ' does not appear to have been the result of a long period of evolution. It was a rapid and almost sudden renaissance '.[2]

Hippocrates the physician (460–377 B.C.) was one of the greatest figures of this period. In the early days Greek medicine was at the mercy of philosophical systems. The facts were studied in association with theoretical constructions of a priori character. Pythagoras stands out among these early philosopher-scientists, who busied themselves, among other activities, with medicine.[3] He made certain contributions to medicine, particularly as regards hygiene. His school was dispersed about 500 B.C., and his follow-ers were scattered throughout the Greek world, with important results.

Various schools of medicine existed in early Greece, mostly in colonies actively influenced by Egypt or the Asiatic kingdoms. These places had schools of philosophy or temples of Asclepios

[1] Neuburger 126.   [2] Ure i. 4.   [3] Neuburger 105.

(originally Imhotep of the Third Dynasty in Egypt), where the Asclepiads started a rational school of medicine, free from the influence of the priests.

The Asclepiads were members of a guild, which had branches at Cnidos and Cos. They formed a closed corporation for a century before the time of Hippocrates. It is thought that they were originally a band of brothers, claiming descent from Asclepios.[1] If this be so, we have before us an interesting example of the interaction between the family grouping and a social institution.

Cnidos and Cos, the two great Asclepiad schools, diverged somewhat in the course of time. Both of them aimed at making of medicine something more than a crude empiricism. But each had certain theoretical preconceptions blinding them to the actual facts.

Out of the Coan school, however, there soon emerged a man who was destined to place medicine on a purely scientific basis, and to be the model for physicians of all time. This man was Hippocrates. He is known through the Hippocratic writings, which were put together in the third century B.C. by a commission of Alexandrian scholars. But through them all, it is said, shines the personality of one man.[2]

Hippocrates was the son of an Asclepiad. He was born in 460 or 459 B.C. in Cos. He was thus a member of a fraternity that incorporated more than any other the true scientific spirit of medicine. This school was freest from the speculative element that so obscured observation. It based its methods more than any other school upon observation and reflection. Hippocrates performed the great service of leading the school towards rational science. He looked at his profession from a high ethical stand-point, and made the good of the patient the supreme aim of the physician. He also paid proper attention to tradition. He writes in ' Ancient Medicine ' : ' I do not say that the old art of healing should be abandoned as of no account or as though its investigations were wrongly conducted ; on the contrary, I maintain that its way of thinking came so near to truth that one should take it more into consideration and wonder at the discoveries made in spite of so great a lack of knowledge.' He abandoned the speculative habit which assigned overmuch weight to preconceived schemes, as compared with the knowledge acquired in the past. He insisted throughout upon the practical aims of medicine. He made the empirical method the sole method of science ; not crude empiricism, but the observation of facts that

[1] Neuburger 98.   [2] *Ibid.*, 116, 117, 121.

were to be built up into generalizations. That is to say, he employed the method of induction. He first thoroughly instituted the system of paying attention to the patient in the first instance, of attending to the most salient phenomena first of all. Unessential details were to be excluded.[1] The following extract from Neuburger's ' History of Medicine ' describes the essential characteristics of Hippocrates, as compared with his predecessors.

' Between Cnidian and Hippocratic methods there is the same contrast as may be seen between the historians Herodotus and Thucydides. The former concerns himself more with stories than with history ; in his descriptive mosaic there is no complete representation of events, hence no real picture of battles, warlike operations and personalities such as occurs in Thucydides. This brings us to a new essential of Hippocratism which explains a whole series of its peculiarities, both in respect of methods of thought and therapeutics, viz. individualism.

' The spirit of the age assigned greater prominence to personality in drama, sculpture and painting ; looking gave way to seeing ; in place of the older art which only took account of two dimensions was developed a perception of three. As Socrates individualized abstraction, as Thucydides placed personality in the foreground, so does Hippocratic medicine find its starting-point from the physician as exponent of an art, and its goal, not in the micrography of symptoms, not in speculatively conceived schemes of disease, but in the sick individual.

' Hippocrates unites the idealistic tendency and the realistic, empiricism and widest generalization, in a form of individualism, which had nothing but the name in common with the individualistic caprice of the sophist physicians of his day.

' Each separate case of illness was to him a natural phenomenon, which was to be studied with all the available aids to observation ; personal and vicarious experience being brought to bear upon it with due regard to individual peculiarities and to its affinity with nature as a whole.' . . .

' Not so much sickness as the sick individual, rather cure than scientific pathology, prognosis more than diagnosis, these constitute the foci of his interests.' [2]

Greek sculpture had a brief but exalted career that has been summed up by Lethaby in his small work on ' Architecture '. He speaks of ' a couple of generations of intense training, then attainment by another generation, and the beginning of decay at once followed.' [3]

The earliest possible date for the beginnings of the Classical

[1] *Ibid.*, 125–32.   [2] *Ibid.*, 133–4.   [3] Lethaby ii. 83.

Greek Sculpture is about 600 B.C. The great period of Greek sculpture, 450–430 B.C. followed the Persian Wars, ' when Greek sculpture in its perfected form suddenly burst forth on the world '.[1]

The story of Greek painting is similar. Polygnotus first established painting as an independent art. He came to Athens from Thasos about 463 B.C. His painting was still probably still rather crude. Apollodorus, the first great master of chiaroscuro (light and shade), was born in the middle of the fifth century, and carried the art far beyond Polygnotus. The greatest Greek painter, however, was Apelles, who flourished between 350 and 300 B.C., about a century after Polygnotus. In the words of Poynter, ' The perfect art of painting perished with the generation of Apelles—not to be known again until, eighteen centuries later, came its new birth in mediaeval Italy.'

The same author, comparing the two phases, says that it was ' in all probability as perfect in its kind as the finest works of their sculpture which have been preserved to us ; in qualities of colour, light and shade, and expression in gesture and face, it could hardly have fallen short of the best work of the Italian Renaissance ; while in beauty of form and composition it may have been superior to anything that we know '.[2]

It may be mentioned, as another instance of the lack of originality of mankind, that the Greeks evidently were ignorant of perspective. They never seem to have realized that all parallel lines seen in perspective converge to one point on the horizon.

The Romans attracted many Greek artists after the fall of Corinth in 146 B.C. ; but painting was on a low level, and never attained the standard of the lesser Greek painters. This is true likewise of Roman poetry, drama, and the arts and crafts in general.

The next advance in painting took place in the Renaissance and subsequent periods.

Painting in Renaissance Italy was largely confined to a few northern centres, particularly Florence and Venice. The dawn arrived at about the beginning of the fourteenth century, when Giotto (1265–1336) was at work. The full blaze of glory burst forth with the middle of the fifteenth century, and lasted for about a century. This period included Botticelli (1447–1510), Leonardo da Vinci (1452–1519), Michelangelo (1475–1564), Raphael (1483–1520), Titian (1477–1576), and Veronese (1528–1588). Truly a marvellous constellation. Unfortunately it lacked the permanency of a stellar grouping. It had its little day, and was gone. The torch was handed on to the peoples of western Europe, to Germany, Flanders, Holland, France, Spain, and finally England.

In each country so favoured the same cycle of early brilliance and subsequent decay is clearly to be observed.

The history of painting outside Italy reveals the usual rapid achievement of excellence and subsequent steady decline. The German schools of painting, for example, produced nothing of note for a century after Florence and Siena had emancipated themselves from Byzantine influence. The school of Bohemia, which lasted from 1348 to 1378, was under Byzantine influence. The school of Cologne, which lasted from 1358 to 1556, was the parent of the later schools of Germany and the Netherlands. Meister Wilhelm worked in Cologne from 1358 to 1372, and Meister Stephan about 1442, but they are shadowy and half-forgotten figures. The greatest figure of German painting was Albrecht Dürer, who was born at Nuremberg in 1471. With him the glory of German art died out. After the death of Dürer, Holbein, and Kranach, German painting fell into a sleep from which its awakening was long delayed. German painters became mere copyists of the Italians, and lost all originality.

The same rapid advance and decline was observable in Flemish art, which flourished at Bruges. The founders of this school were the Van Eycks. Hubrecht was born in 1366, and Jan about 1390. We are told that the school of Bruges began, grew and reached its highest point during the lives of these two men, and none of their scholars equalled them.

The earliest school of painting of the Netherlands was founded at Antwerp by Quentin Matsys (1466–1531). After his death this art rapidly degenerated, and the painters started imitating the Italians. This school of art was revived in 1600 by Paul Rubens, born 1577, and carried on by his pupil Anton van Dyck. None of the successors of these two men equalled them as painters.

The great period of Dutch art was in the sixteenth and seventeenth centuries. It contained all the greatest masters. Within the space of less than a century ' that school sprang into vigorous life, full-grown as it were without preparation, and died as quickly '. The founder of the school was Franz Hals, born 1584, followed by Rembrandt, born 1607. It is said that ' of the pupils of Rembrandt many attained to great excellence as portrait painters ; their works are frequently but the shadow of the great masters '. ' Art, which was born vigorous and full of life when Holland became free, died out after the Peace of Utrecht (1713) when a purely popular government was exchanged for that of hereditary Stadtholders, who quickly became kings.' [1]

Painting in England supplies similar instances. The great school of portrait painters of the eighteenth century is a case in point. It began with Hogarth (1697–1764). He was followed by Reynolds (1723–1792), Gainsborough (1727–1788), Romney (1734–1802), Hoppner (1758–1810), and Lawrence (1769–1830).

This series is, roughly speaking, one of descending magnitude. Its greatest period included Hogarth, Reynolds and Gainsborough. The claims of Romney to an equal greatness are not so strong. Hoppner has been said to be ' the least and . . . the last ' of this great line of artists.

The same story is true of English landscape painters. The father of the school was Richard Wilson (1713–1782). The next name is that of old Crome (1768–1821). He was the contemporary of Constable (1776–1837) and Turner (1775–1851). Thus English landscape painting witnessed its greatest brilliance during the lives of three men of practically the same age. Indeed, if we take Wilson as our starting-point, that man was 55 years of age when Crome was born, and 63 years of age when Constable was born. Since the days of these giants England has not produced their like.

Music reveals the same process at work. We may take for an example the Italian composer Palestrina (1524–1594). He wrote choral music, and achieved the highest summits of his art. In the words of Sir Hubert Parry, ' It is like Greek statuary or the painting of the greatest Italian masters, or the architecture of the finest English cathedrals ; its beauty is so genuine and real that the passage of time makes no difference to it. As long as religion and religious emotions last, Palestrina's music will be the purest and loftiest form in which it has been expressed.' [2]

He goes on to say, ' His music itself was, of course, from the moment of its triumph in 1565, recognized as a model for composers of church music to imitate : but, curiously enough, the perfection of his art was so great and wonderful that it took the heart out of composers who would have followed in his steps. It seemed impossible to compete with him, or to produce anything of the same kind which was worth hearing by the side of his work. . . . Palestrina's art of his own kind was complete with him ; and in order to do anything more in art it was necessary to begin on another road. It is much as if men had been climbing a big mountain for a long while. When Palestrina finished his work

[1] Poynter.   [2] Parry 17.

they were at the top, and could not go any higher that way ; and in order to get to the top of another high point they had to go back almost to the bottom again.' [1]

Many more illustrations might be taken from music. John Sebastian Bach was a phenomenal genius, none of whose followers approach him in mental stature. With him began and ended the development of the fugue.

Bach and Palestrina were the greatest exponents of Counterpoint. Palestrina was supreme in strict Counterpoint, which employs no discords ; and Bach was supreme in Free Counterpoint, which employs discords.

The development of the sonata and symphony was rapid. Emanuel Bach (1714–1788), the second surviving son of John Sebastian Bach (1685–1750), has been called the Father of the Sonata. Haydn (1732–1809) was practically his pupil. Mozart (1756–1791) and Beethoven (1770–1827) were contemporaries of Haydn. One of the greatest developments in music therefore was the work of a group of men who were contemporaries.

It is not necessary to seek far for instances. The year 1597 marked the birth of opera at Florence, so we are told by Mr. Ernst Schoen in the ' Radio Times ' for July 13, 1934. Eleven years later Claudio Monte Verdi wrote the opera ' Ariadne ', ' of which nothing remains but the famous Lament that will ever remain the prototype of musical and dramatic expression of human suffering '. [2] . . .

It is surprising in what curious and unexpected quarters the principle of early excellence appears to hold good. For example, I happened one day to take down from the bookshelves of a friend a work totally unfamiliar to me, dealing with a subject about which I had read nothing. It was by W. H. Woodward, and dealt with the life of an Italian named Vittorino da Feltre, who was born in 1378, and thus was a young man when Manuel Chrysoloras came from Byzantium to lecture in Florence in the year 1397. The visit of this remarkable man, who brought back with him the lost treasures of Greek learning, marks the turning-point of the Renaissance. Access to Greek authors, who for a thousand years had been practically unknown to Western Europe, became possible ; a revival of learning set in in earnest.

Vittorino da Feltre was a schoolmaster who played a prominent part in the founding of what is called ' classical education '. We are told that he established and perfected the first great school of the Renaissance during the years 1423 to 1444, a school whose

---

[1] *Ibid.*, 20–1.   [2] Loc. cit., 85.

21

spirit, curriculum, and method, justify us in regarding it as a standard of greatest importance : indeed it was the first typical school of the humanities.[1]

Humanistic education apparently achieved its summit of perfection within the lifetime of this man. The author comments on ' the little band of students and schoolmasters who within the space of hardly more than one generation, could establish a concept of education wholly new to the modern world, and could devise from its material, a large part of it wholly unfamiliar, a working method which has for five centuries remained, with but slight modification, adequate to the highest needs of intellectual culture '.

Even this new flowering soon began to wilt. Speaking of the period following the year 1407, the author says : ' We may claim for the Latinity of this particular stage of the revival a spontaneity and Italian colour which we look for in vain when the middle of the century has been turned.' [2]

Examples of the principle may be found in all manner of arts and crafts. It might be thought, for instance, that the novel, so popular in our country, would have been produced spontaneously in all times and places. Yet the novel is a product of the last few centuries, and its early fashioners were no mean craftsmen. We are told, for example, that Fielding's ' Tom Jones ' is one of the earliest and one of the finest novels ever written. For example, Professor Saintsbury says, in his work on ' The English Novel ', ' " Tom Jones "—by practically universal consent one of the capital books of English literature.' [3]

This achievement is noteworthy in view of the stupendous output of novels that characterizes our own time.

The principle of early excellence seemingly holds in the domain of bookbinding. This is shown by the following quotation from the diary of Sir James Lacaita. He mentions a visit to Signor Libri. ' He showed me some very fine specimens of ancient bindings, of which he has a very large collection. He maintains that the finest bindings were the Italian bindings of the fifteenth and beginning of the sixteenth centuries ; next come French bindings, as Grolière and others ; next English and German. That they continued more or less fine throughout the sixteenth and got spoiled in the seventeenth and totally deteriorated in the eighteenth century.' [4]

It is hardly necessary to cite the example of Shakespeare. He stands supreme as a poet and dramatist. His forerunners

[1] Woodward 26–7.   [2] *Ibid.*, 11.   [3] Saintsbury 106.
[4] Lacaita 99.

were few and his successors many, but none of them approached
him in any branch of his art.

These examples cover a wide range. They include all manner
of creative activities. Pottery-making, the fabrication of stone
vases, stone-carving, wood-carving, painting, music, stone construction, poetry, prose, medicine, mathematics, philosophy,
education, can be called to witness. It is indeed interesting to
find such diverse activities apparently subject to the same general
principle.

These activities seem to fall into two groups : those involving
manipulative skill, and those concerned more especially with
ideas, and not involving manual dexterity. In spite of this
diversity, the two appear to be the expression of an underlying
unity. Both are products of the human mind, both are creative.
In the one case the mind gives itself concrete expression by
manipulative acts ; in the other the mind's creative power is
expressed verbally. Both activities spring from specific concrete
situations. For some reason or other, the first potter found himself in a situation that he resolved by making a pot ; the sculpture
of the Old Kingdom in Egypt was, in like manner, the expression
of a situation. Both were the outcome of a spiritual experience
of mankind, and therefore are comparable to such works as the
Epics of Homer. The imitator, in each case, is in a position of
like relationship to the innovator. Degradation series occur in
all creative activities of mankind.

These few examples, taken more or less at random, all seem to
support the general principle laid down at the beginning of this
chapter. We see in the course of history new developments in
arts and crafts coming to a sudden fruition, then fading away,
sometimes slowly, sometimes rapidly. In some instances we
know for certain that the new development was based upon the
genius of one man, or of a small group of men who led the human
mind in a new direction. Aeschylus, Sophocles and Euripides
founded Greek tragedy within a generation, and the greatest of
these was the first. On the other hand, we do not know the background of Homer, but, for all we know, he was, like Aeschylus
and Archilochus, a real innovator. Certainly none of his successors
equalled him. In fact, we may say in general that, although we
are not certain that men like Homer were the innovators of their
craft, we almost invariably find that their successors and imitators
are their inferiors.

It will have been noticed that several of the authorities quoted
in this chapter express surprise concerning the excellence of early

originators, whether in architecture, jewellery, poetry or some other branch of human activity. They seem convinced that such brilliance of achievement must be the outcome of a long experience.[1] Our knowledge of the circumstances accompanying each outburst varies considerably, but it can at least be said that the earliest known examples of new developments in an art or craft are usually superior to those that follow. Therefore the principle stands until some new facts should overturn it.

Certain authorities have, as it were, ' sensed ' the existence of the general principle just outlined. First, Sir Flinders Petrie. Speaking of a revival of art at the end of the Eleventh Dynasty, he says : ' Like all great developments of art it arose with extraordinary rapidity, and within a generation or two the new movement was fully grown.' [2]

The late Dr. Hall of the British Museum, speaking in 1928 of the artistic achievements of the early Sumerians, comments thus : ' One wonders how long a period of development preceded that artistic motive. Still it must be remembered that development in such matters was often swift.' [3]

Another instance is that of Mr. Woodward, in his work on Vittorino da Feltre, the great Italian schoolmaster. He says : ' In any art genius, as we know, often makes swift intuition towards a right method.' [4]

There may be exceptions to this general principle ; but I have as yet failed to detect any, in spite of conversations with experts in various branches of learning. One difficulty to be faced in studying this principle, is that of distinguishing between skill and knowledge. It is obvious that modern microscopes are better than their predecessors. It does not follow that the man who looks down the modern microscope is necessarily superior to his forerunners. Indeed, many of the greatest scientific discoveries have been made with the crudest of apparatus. We know that many great discoverers have had a far surer grasp of general principles than their followers. Their discoveries give a great

---

[1] Professor Hocart supplies an interesting example in his latest work, ' The Progress of Man '. He is speaking of inventions. He says that an invention usually does not become known to us ' till some considerable time, it may be millenia, after its first beginnings '. He then goes on to say, ' Yet when we find the first evidences of domestication all clustering on our time chart close to a certain period, the Neolithic, it becomes evident that domestication came in about then with a rush, not as a long series of accidents.' *

[2] Petrie iii. 17.   [3] Hall 447.   [4] Woodward 63.

---

* Op. cit., 110.

stimulus to research, but the disciples have not the insight of the master. The result is that knowledge is heaped up more or less mechanically, and the significance of this new knowledge is often lost sight of, until a new genius arises to make clear the path once again.

Hippocrates may be taken as a typical example of genius. His superiority lay in the fact that, as Neuburger remarks, he had realized that ' natural powers are the healers of disease ' (see p. 304). In other words he had recognized the reality that lay behind appearance. He was, in fact, able to sweep aside the mass of illogical reasoning that had accumulated around the treatment of disease, and to realize that the most that medicine can do is to help the patient to help himself.

The like may be said of Homer, of Aeschylus, of Shakespeare. Their claims to greatness do not rest on their capacity for invention, but on their power to depict reality, on their fidelity to truth.

The contrast between knowledge and insight is brought forcibly into prominence, when it is remembered that generations of art students have studied the works of the great masters, and yet have failed to achieve even a fraction of their power. They know more about painting than Vandyck, but they are not producing Vandycks. Think again of the dramatic critics, the musical critics, the countless professors of literature. These students are perpetually engaged in dissecting the creatures produced by the mind of genius, but they are unable to infuse new life into their dissections.[1] Knowledge and vision are not the same thing.

We might perhaps distinguish between insight and knowledge in the following way. Insight is the power to detect the reality that lies behind knowledge. Galen probably knew more about medicine than Hippocrates, but Hippocrates, on the other hand, with his greater insight, recognized the essentials among the mass of facts presented to him. The same is certainly true of all great artists, writers, poets, musicians. The genius of Mozart and of Bach lies in their power of saying what they want to say with the least possible expenditure of material. The genius of the portrait painter lies, not so much in detail, as in his power of depicting character.

The mere accumulation of knowledge for its own sake is often of doubtful use. Knowledge should lead us ultimately to reality, to the formulation of general principles that should guide human conduct, and must therefore be combined with insight ; and as

[1] M. Alderton Pink in his ' If the Blind Lead ' (1933) has some interesting remarks concerning modern scholarship. See especially pp. 108 e.s.

the element of insight increases, so does knowledge become more scientific.

It is possible to approach the study of originality from many directions. Race, climate, economic and political conditions, religion, the analogy of the life-cycle of the living organism, these and many other factors have been invoked to explain the outstanding contributions of Renaissance Italy or Classical Greece to civilization.

These are two of the great productive periods of human history. Others lie behind them, of which something will shortly be said. The periods of the Renaissance and of Classical Greece are alike in this particular ; they are characterized by a sudden outburst of originality in all directions. Sculpture, painting, poetry, the drama, science, mathematics, medicine, these and other branches of human thought develop with amazing rapidity and brilliance for a brief space. The whole of society is affected.

The two phenomena, the Renaissance and Classical Greece, are connected with each other. The stream of originality which flowed from Ancient Athens began to dry up at the beginning of the fourth century B.C. The transference to Alexandria of the great bulk of Athenian learning continued the process. The domination of Alexandria by Rome carried it a stage further, and the downfall of the Roman Empire completed it. Henceforward, with the exception of Byzantium, Greek learning was almost forgotten in Europe until the dawn of the Renaissance in Italy. For a thousand years the originality displayed by European nations is hardly worth the mention. Scholarship descended to puerile depths.

It is true that the spread of Islam had enabled western Europe, from the thirteenth century onwards, to acquire a small measure of Greek learning from translations through Syriac, Arabic and other sources ; but all this was as nothing compared with the ultimate effects of the invitation extended to Manuel Chrysoloras, a Greek scholar from Byzantium, in the year 1397, to lecture in Florence. From this time onwards access was had once more to the learning of the Greeks ; originality made its sudden appearance, and the modern world of thought was born.

This would suggest the simple conclusion that originality is derived from originality. The Greeks of Athens saw clearly, and only those who knew their thoughts were able also to see clearly. The mass of traditional lore that formed the mental pabulum of the Middle Ages could only produce such products of mental indigestion as the scholastic philosophy. But when the eyes of men were once more opened to reality, they were able to proceed with the extension of the mental scaffolding that the Greeks had erected so skilfully a thousand years before.   To alter the metaphor, the streams of thought that were dried up during the Middle Ages were filled once again, and enabled to flow on down through the ages.

What was the source of the originality of the Greeks ?   In the minds of some of us there seems to be little doubt about the answer.   One starting-point of Greek originality was in Miletus, one of the early Ionian colonies on the coast of Asia Minor.   The Milesians were active merchants whose ships sailed in every part of the Levant.   In the seventh and sixth centuries B.C., they had trading stations in Egypt.   The earliest was known as the Milesians' Fort.   This gave rise to Daphnae and Naucratis, at the east and west mouths of the Nile.   At this time the Egyptians were indulging in what might be termed a revival of learning. They were striving to reproduce the glories of the Old Kingdom of twenty-five centuries ago and more, one of the periods of greatest originality in the history of the world.   As we have seen, the alphabet, stone-building, various forms of art, all these reached their highest perfection in that period.   The Milesians would have had the chance of acquiring knowledge of some of these products of Egyptian originality.[1]

Thales, in a way, was to Miletus what Manuel Chrysoloras was to Florence.   He transplanted the old learning to a new soil, where it could flourish and perpetuate itself.

I do not propose to labour this point.   It is controversial and complicated.   I urge, however, that the scheme so briefly outlined in the last few paragraphs is in harmony with what has gone before.   It serves to round off the argument.   It enables us to suggest why, at certain periods in the history of mankind, men saw clearly and were able to add to the store of knowledge already accumulated.   Apparently those who saw clearly at any stage, such as the Renaissance or in Classical Athens, or in the Old Kingdom of Egypt, did not do so on their own initiative.   They did so because they had access to the original thought of an earlier group of innovators.   We of western Europe, for instance, get our inspiration from the Renaissance or from Classical Greece, the men of the Renaissance got theirs from Classical Greece, and so on.   The process is one of continuous development, of the extension of a mental scaffolding out into the unknown, or the growth of a tree ; it is a continuous process going down through the ages.

[1] See Bury 518 e.s. for a further account of the indebtedness of Miletus to Egypt, e.g. Hecateus.

We have already seen that, as a rule, only the originators of a new form of activity have a firm grasp of reality. The vision of their followers and imitators is obscured. This obviously is because the personality of the innovator interposes itself in between the mental eye of the disciple and the reality. We have already seen also that certain innovators made false interpretations of reality. The most important of these false interpretations were built up into the fabric of the theory of the State elaborated by the Egyptians at the dawn of history. The Egyptians achieved intellectual triumphs that make them unsurpassed among mankind. They were, at the same time, building up a theory of the kingship, the completeness of which has never been surpassed. The Egyptian kingship has its roots in the economic, political, and religious structure of the State to a degree unapproached in the history of man. This institution, partly logical and partly illogical, dominated the country for thousands of years so completely that any fundamental divergence from the traditional pattern of thought became difficult.

The Milesians, on the other hand, were apparently not dominated by a corresponding theory of the State. In the words of Lewes, progress was rapid 'owing to speculative activity being entirely untrammelled by Theology, Tradition, or Political Institutions, and left to run its own free course'. [1]

It is interesting to note, moreover, that the early Ionian thinker was 'generally concerned either with the whole universe or with his own individual soul'.[2] Self-knowledge was the aim of Archilochus, Alcaeus, and Sappho. 'They led the way in the line of great writers who have held self-knowledge as a passionate faith and preached the doctrine in the only practicable way by publishing confessions of their own.'[3] These early thinkers of the seventh and sixth centuries B.C. were above all interested in themselves and the people and happenings of their own age.[4] Their attitude was in marked contrast to the traditional outlook with which we have been so concerned. They had penetrated the mist of illusion and discovered the human reality behind it. In the words of Ure, 'It is among the Greeks of the seventh and sixth centuries B.C. that we first find men who intellectually and politically share our outlook in a way that is becoming more and more striking the more the world emancipates itself from the mediaevalism that it is in the process of casting off.' He goes on to say that this development was not the result of a long period of evolution. 'It was a rapid and almost sudden renaissance.' [5]

[1] Lewes 2. See also C.A.H., IV. 538.   [2] Ure iii. 121.
[3] *Ibid.*, i. 98.   [4] *Ibid.*, 94.   [5] *Ibid.*, 4.

That is to say, their minds were not built up on a set, formalized framework of thought. They inherited, it would seem, the trading activities of the old Aegean civilization. Their calling would tend to induce in them a matter-of-fact prosaic frame of mind. They would learn, for instance, from the Egyptians certain facts about the properties of figures. These facts would not have the same meaning to them as to the Egyptians. They would not necessarily be interested in the dimensions of fields in the same way as the Egyptians. Thales may well have heard from Egyptian priests about the Primordial Ocean. That fact, detached, in his mind, from its original context, simply became a philosophical abstraction.

It is significant that Hippocratic medicine was developed in a school of thought that was apparently free from priestly domination.

This fertile movement of thought slowed down when it came in contact with the State theory, as the result of the conquest of Greece by Philip of Macedon and his son, Alexander the Great. The domination of Alexandria by Imperial Rome, as we have seen, continued the process. From then until the Renaissance originality was almost completely blotted out.

The Renaissance was begun in a manner that recalls the dawn of Greek originality. The great reservoir of Greek learning in the Middle Ages was Byzantium. From the days of its founder, Constantine, until its final eclipse in the fifteenth century, Byzantium was dominated by the state theory. Greek learning became almost completely sterile, like insects imbedded in amber, in that formalized atmosphere. There were new revivals of learning from time to time ; these were due to renewed interest in Greek learning.

The Italian Republics, such as Florence of the fourteenth century, could, on the other hand, be compared with Miletus. They were City States with no definite ruling group, and very little religion. Whatever Chrysoloras told them in his lectures, they certainly would not be interested in the constitution of Byzantium. Their attention would be directed towards the concrete aspects of his learning.

Professor Ure has called attention, particularly in his work with the significant title ' The Greek Renaissance ', to the similarity between these two periods. The Greek Renaissance begins about the time when coinage was first introduced, probably in Lydia. This was the age of the tyrants, who founded their power on commerce, and not on the claim to divine birth.[1]   Professor

[1] P. N. Ure ii. 1–2.

Ure considers that the development of this new social system began in Egypt, particularly under Psammetichus I.[1]

He compares this Greek Renaissance with the Italian Renaissance. ' The commercial tyrant is not a phenomenon peculiar to this early period of Mediterranean history. He reappears some 2,000 years later in Italy. Of these commercial despots of the early days of our own renaissance the most notable are the Medici of Florence.' [2]

It is significant that banking began in Florence, which constitutes an interesting parallel to the invention of coinage during the earlier renaissance.

The receptiveness of the Florentines and others of northern Italy is illuminated by their historical background.

For it would seem that the revival of learning in Europe, which came about in the twelfth and succeeding centuries, was the work of independent laymen, rather than of members of the schools that had sprung up under the patronage of the Church.[3]   This revival took place principally in northern Italy, not in France or northern Europe.   As is said by the same eminent authority :

' In truth, the differences between the two educational systems, if such they can be called, are all explained by the one great contrast which is presented by the social and political conditions of the two regions.   In northern France all intellectual life was confined to the cloister or to schools which were merely dependencies of the cloister, because the governing class itself was composed of but two great orders : the military and the clerical— in the latter of which alone was there any demand for learning. In Italy, in place of a régime of pure feudalism tempered only by ecclesiastical influence, there had survived all through the darkest ages at least the memory of the old Roman municipal system, and with it at least the germ and the possibility of a free and vigorous municipal life.   Hence, in Italy it was in the political sphere that the new eleventh-century activity first manifested itself ; while the consequent or concomitant revival of culture took a correspondingly secular turn.' [4]

The same author goes on to say in another place, the intellectual Renaissance of the twelfth centary found the Italian cities just entering upon a struggle for independence.   The intellectual Renaissance of this period was only another side of the political renaissance.   ' As the Lombard cities awoke to a consciousness of their recovered liberty, their energies were absorbed by a political life as engrossing, as interesting and dignified, as it had been in

[1] P. N. Ure ii. 292–3.   [2] *Ibid.*, i. 158, 159.   [3] Rashdall I. 92.
[4] *Ibid.*, 95.

the cities of ancient Hellas.' So close, indeed, was the parallel between the two cases that, ' The conception of citizenship prevalent in the Italian Republics was much nearer to the old Greek conception than that which prevails in modern States. Citizenship, which is with us little more than an accident of domicile, was in ancient Athens or mediaeval Bologna an hereditary possession of priceless value.' [1]

Thus released, the people of the Italian republics of the north bounded ahead, and produced the triumphs of the Renaissance, that in its turn gave rise to our modern period of originality in thought. The combination of two things, contact with original Greek thought, and freedom from theoretical preoccupations, based on Church and State, were the main contributing causes of the Renaissance.

The parallel between Miletus and Florence is therefore close. Both were independent City States, the survivors of the break-up of civilization. They were Merchant States, and therefore full of knowledge of different countries. They were not dominated by rigid state theory, nor at the mercy of a hierarchy of priests.

Two main conditions therefore appear necessary for originality in thought—freedom from the domination of a state theory, and contact with originality. Omne vivum ex vivo is as true of thought as of life in general.

These conclusions seem to supply a consistent explanation of the facts. We have to account for the sudden appearance of skill in small communities such as Athens and Florence. The explanation for these facts appears to lie in the workings of Man's most important organ—his brain.

The astounding wealth and fertility of invention among these small communities suggests that genius is not so much individual as social. The manner by which thought is acquired by any community tends to mould that community into shapes almost unknown to itself. The more we realize this fact, the more we can control our destinies. We have but to remove the obstacles to clear thought, and clear thinking would be the possession of us all. The human mind, free from its clogging poisons, will rise to artistic triumphs in all directions.

We may go further. The standard of behaviour determined by the study of food-gathering peoples, was simple and harmonious. Divergence therefrom, it was urged, was the result of the action of social institutions. All social institutions, we have seen, rest on a basis of theory or fact, or a combination of both. Some of these institutions have produced much destruction

[1] *Ibid.*, 98, 152.

and unhappiness. It may be that this is the price we pay for civilization. On the other hand, it is possible that undesirable traits of human behaviour in civilized communities result from an erroneous interpretation of reality. In that case it will be possible ultimately to remove these defects. The nearer we approach to the appreciation of reality, the more harmonious will our behaviour become. Human thought, it would seem, is the most powerful instrument for good or evil that we possess. Race, climate, factors such as these are negligible in comparison with it. Science has given us control of nature ; we must learn to control ourselves.

CHAPTER XXIV

MAN AND SOCIETY

MODERN peoples of western Europe contrast generally with the rest of the world, past and present, in their greater freedom of thought and action. We play games of various kinds; we dance; we go to the theatre; we have a multitude of social activities that appear to us to be entirely spontaneous.

We usually go to the theatre for amusement. The performances we witness there are generally written to please, rather than to edify or instruct. Theatrical performances in our country rarely have any ceremonial characteristics. When we consider other countries, we often find the theatre fulfilling much more definite functions. For instance, we may take the following quotation from an authority on the theatre of India :

'According to Hindu authorities, the occasions suitable for dramatic representations are the lunar holidays, a royal coronation, assemblies of people at fairs and religious festivals, marriages, the meeting of friends, taking first possession of a house or a town, and the birth of a son. The most ordinary occasion, however, of a performance was, as will be seen, the season peculiarly sacred to some divinity. All the modern compositions, however, are of a mythological and sectarial character, and are intended to celebrate the power of Krishna, or of Siva.'[1]

It is not easy for us to realize the formalism of the lives of other peoples. We are perhaps not even aware to the extent to which our own lives are formalized. It comes as a surprise to learn that some peoples confine their theatrical representations to ceremonial occasions. Such peoples obviously enjoy going to the theatre; therefore, we may ask, why don't they have theatrical performances purely for pleasure ?

We play our games at any convenient season. We are not like the people of Bali, in the East Indian Archipelago, who, so Sir Grafton Elliot Smith tells me, spend their afternoons in the temple courts, and there play their games, and hold their cock-fights.

We smoke tobacco for pleasure. There is no ceremonial con-

---
[1] Wilson i. XIV–XVI.

nected with it ; although our grandfathers wore ' smoking-caps ' and ' smoking-jackets ', and retired to ' smoking-rooms ' and told ' smoking-room ' stories. The North American tribes formerly only smoked tobacco on ceremonial occasions.

Wrestling matches are not ceremonial in this country ; at least, not so far as I am aware. But it is different in Japan, as may be seen by the following quotation :

' Wrestling, or *sumo*, goes back to hoary antiquity, and is taught with the sanctity of remote religious associations. So that to-day, when a temple is in need of funds, it turns not to the chicanery of a bazaar, but to the large-hearted innocence of a wrestling match. Such matches are almost always held in the grounds of a temple, in any case. The umpires wear a sumptuous ceremonial dress belonging to the Kamakura era of seven or eight hundred years ago—whilst the champion wrestler of the company, called the *yokozuna*, appears in full ceremony, wearing a belt of twisted rope and paper streamers, the Shinto symbol of divinity.

' To describe the humours and excitement of a wrestling match would need as much space as a wrestler's paunch occupies. Suffice it to say that, in the centre of a large tent, is set up a small plat-form built on 16 bales of rice, in the midst of which a 12 ft. circle is marked out with straw ropes. Yes—the wrestling ring is straightforwardly a ring and not a roped-in square. Victory is achieved by depositing any part of your opponent outside this ring.

' The contest consists of a long series of bouts between pairs of wrestlers belonging to parties drawn from the east and west of Japan. Forty-eight specified kinds of falls are allowed. But often the bout is finished off with the use of about one and a half. Yet, when a well-matched pair meet, the bout may last a tense five or ten minutes.

' It is impressive to watch a group of these almost naked bronze giants, their long black hair drawn up into a quaint chignon, seated, with the effect of a range of primitive monoliths, round the ring waiting their turn—whilst within the ring itself is being strenuously decided which of the two Titans is to be left in vic-torious possession. The thousand and more spectators squatting round look Lilliputian indeed by contrast, and even an average-sized Englishman feels small not only in body, but also in the knowledge which had never prepared him for the sight of such earth-shaking giants as these.' [1]

Accounts such as these read strangely to us, accustomed, as we are, to playing games as part of our ordinary everyday life. It

[1] Pickering.

seems the most natural thing in the world for those intending
to play a game to divide up into two parties, each with its territory
to defend. We take great pleasure in such games, which appears
at first sight to be a sufficient cause for their existence. But,
seeing that our modern civilization owes its foundation ultimately
to the Ancient East, such an explanation cannot be accepted
without further inquiry. A game of football, for example, is not
quite so simple as would appear. Where and how and why
should men begin to divide themselves up into two parties, wearing
garments or badges of different colours, struggling for the possession of a ball which they endeavour to kick through or over a goal
in the opponents' territory ? If we are to follow the working
hypothesis, this kind of game was the outcome of a concrete
situation in society. It must originally have had some definite
social meaning, and cannot have been simply the outcome of
some generalized tendency to play games.

In order to solve this problem it will be necessary to recapitulate
some of the discussions of earlier chapters.

The studies carried on in the previous chapters suggest that
early thought and action were expressions of social situations.
The arts of engraving, painting, and sculpture provide striking
instances of this generalization. We have already seen that the
cave art of the Aurignacian people was concerned, for the greater
part at least, with their food supply.

We have seen also that the carving of portrait statues in Ancient
Egypt was the direct outcome of certain social circumstances,
and not the expression of an artistic impulse. Dr. Alan H.
Gardiner remarks, in his article dealing with these statues, ' To
ourselves, accustomed to regard Art as a thing in and for itself,
it may seem incredible that such skill, such manifest creative
feeling, were expended for a mainly utilitarian purpose. But
history points unmistakably in that direction : Art is but the
by-product of men's practical ends, nay more, of men's early
superstitions.' [1]

We may take another example. The title ' Son of the Sun ',
adopted by the kings of Egypt, was dependent on the existence
of a royal family ; on the concept of a god as the father of a king ;
which concept was based upon the invention of mummification ;
which practice ultimately grew up out of certain circumstances
attending the kingship of the time. This kingship was based
upon the economic needs of Egypt. These economic needs were
largely the outcome of the periodicity of the Nile Flood, and its
function as the great source of life of the country. Only by the

[1] Gardiner v.

erection of a scaffolding of thought, based originally on concrete phenomena, and built up partly with the aid of the power of the human mind of accepting the appearance of reality for reality itself, could the sun become an object of interest, and acquire a significance that it had not previously possessed.

Not only does the thought arise out of the social situation, but in return it moulds it directly and indirectly. The royal family, for instance, once in existence, went far beyond its original function. Its privileges were based upon the hereditary principle, and thus family considerations have played a great part in shaping its characteristics.

Its self-esteem was awakened, and every effort made to emphasize its position. Its power was used for its own self-glorification. It was not satisfied until it had raised itself to the highest pinnacle of human majesty. The Pharaoh of the late Fifth Dynasty who called himself the ' Son of the Sun ' stands out on the summit of human magnificence.

This process of development of a special group has had some remarkable effects upon human behaviour. It has preserved and transmitted down to our days the memory and consequences of certain events which happened within this small family group at the beginning of history.

It is well known, as has already been stressed in previous chapters, that the ritual of Egyptian temples and tombs was based mainly on the drama of the death and resurrection of Osiris. The consecration of the Egyptian king included dramatic performances of events that happened, or are supposed to have happened, in that connexion. The re-enactment of these events was essential to make the king into a god, either during his life, when he sat on the throne, or after death, when he became united with his ancestor. In the beginning these rituals were reserved for the royal family ; but in course of time the privilege was extended to the nobles, and ultimately, after about three thousand years, to the whole of the community.

These rituals were extremely complicated. The central element was the dramatic performance based on the passion of Osiris. In addition there were many activities such as processions, dancing, singing, instrumental music, acrobatics, juggling, wrestling and so forth.[1]

It is possible to urge that many of our social activities, such as certain kinds of games, the drama, architecture, dancing, have largely received their scope and form from this primordial source.

[1] Pictures of these performances are to be found in the rock-cut tombs at Beni Hasan. See Griffith i.

We may take as an example the ball games and other two-sided struggles that have just been mentioned. Rituals the world over, particularly the more elaborate, such as those of the Indian Brahmanas, include demons who try to prevent the proper performance of the ceremonial. In Egypt the leader of these hostile beings is Set, the brother of Osiris, who plays in the ritual almost as important a part as Horus, the living king. In the Pyramid Texts of the Old Kingdom, the Coffin Texts of the Middle Kingdom, and the Book of the Dead of the New Kingdom, as well as in countless temple inscriptions, victory over Set is a prominent feature of the ritual.

A few quotations from the Egyptian ' Book of the Dead ' will illustrate the importance of this theme.

' Oh Thoth, who makest Osiris triumphant over his adversaries, let (the dead king) be made triumphant over his adversaries. . . .'

. . . ' Horus son of Isis and son of Horus repeateth an infinite number of festivals, and all his adversaries fall down, are overthrown and slaughtered.'

' Thoth abideth at the prow of thy bark that he may destroy all thine adversaries.'

' I come forth victoriously against the adversaries.' [1]

It can hardly be claimed that there is anything essential in this part of the ritual. Yet the episode has played a part of enormous importance in the world's history. We do not know the exact details of the quarrel. All that we know goes to suggest that Set may have been unjustly dealt with by his family. We only hear the point of view of the successful branch of the royal family. Royal chroniclers have made Set the embodiment of evil. They forget that the early texts show him to have been a colleague of Horus in many incidents.

This primordial quarrel between two members of the early Egyptian royal family appears to have had remarkable consequences on human behaviour. It has generalized itself into an attitude between states, as well as between divisions of states. Throughout the world each state ruled over by a king who has a consecration ceremony has its official enemies, whom it is the duty of the king to conquer. A definite attitude is therefore aroused, and the way made open for regular warfare.

This warlike attitude of mind has been greatly reinforced in many parts of the world, as we have seen, by the spread of the dual organization, with its organized hostility.

This struggle between two parts of the country appears to have had another consequence. In all probability it is responsible

[1] Renouf, Chaps. XVIII, XIX, XV, X, 53, 60, 24, 20.

22

for our modern games, such as football, cricket, hockey, lacrosse, and others in which two parties contend against each other on a ground divided into two parts.

I do not mean to suggest that there would be no two-sided games if it were not for this primordial struggle in Egypt. Play is instinctive, in the sense that every normal child exhibits that activity. The young of certain animals, particularly the higher mammals, also play. But when we say that the play of children is instinctive, are we always certain what we mean ? The play of children is largely imitative. It is a means whereby the child learns to take its place in society. A child likes nothing better than to do what its mother does. A small girl puts her dolly to bed with the appropriate gestures and phrases. She cleans up the hearth, if she is allowed. She sweeps the carpet. In everything the young child imitates its elders and companions, and does not display any sign of elaborating games for itself. In fact, it can be said of children's games in general that they are traditional. Many of them, as is known from the study of folklore, are imitations of ceremonials carried on by their elders.[1] *London Bridge is Falling Down*, for instance, probably harks back to the practice of offering up human sacrifices when a new construction is being made. Courting games, again, are imitations of marriage ceremonies. Funeral games imitate funeral ceremonies. Children do nothing original, they simply imitate their elders, and make games even of the serious affairs of life.

This characteristic of children's games affords another instance of the working of the human mind. The interest of the young is fixed on concrete situations. The child draws its material from the life surrounding it ; it apparently has no other source.

Therefore when children play ball games, such as football, hockey, cricket, they are imitating their elders. They can give us no help when we inquire into the beginning of ball games, or struggles between two sides, such as tug-of-war. Nor can their elders help us much, for they too are playing a traditional form of game.

The inquiry into the reason why men began to play two-sided games in England is illuminating. Shrove-Tuesday is an interesting day throughout Britain. In Dorking, for instance, the quaint old-world town in Surrey, a game of football was formerly played up and down the street of the town. The two sides were drawn from the inhabitants living east and west of the church, and were distinguished by the wearing of red and white colours.

[1] See, for example, Haddon i. 219 e.s.

The game went on for hours, and usually was nothing more than a tussle.

The people of Ludlow in Shropshire had a tug-of-war on the same day. The two sides were drawn from Corve Street and Teme Street, and many people took part in the game. We read accounts such as the following :

' At Derby there was a football contest between the parishes of All Saints' and St. Peter's. The ball was thrown into the market-place from the Town Hall. The moment it was thrown the " war-cries " of the rival parishes began, and the contest, nominally that of a football match, was in reality a fight between two sections of the town, and the victors were announced by the joyful ringing of their parish bells.' [1]

Another example comes from Hawick. ' The game is called Hawick Handba'. It is a very old custom in Hawick. The west-enders play the east-enders. The ball is given by owners of public-houses and mills. The ball is covered with threepenny pieces, and the first man to get the ball takes off the money and the ribbons. The ball is thrown over the Slitrig or Teviot ; if it goes into the water, they have to go in after it. This goes on all afternoon. The one who wins gets treated to beer or something like that. In some places the brides of the year provide the ball.' [2]

My final example is taken from Ashbourne in Derbyshire. This is an account taken from the ' Daily Herald ' (Feb. 2nd, 1929) :

' At Ashbourne, in Derbyshire, on Shrove Tuesday, brawny toilers from the town and villages around gather in their hundreds, and a ding-dong battle for the " ba' ", tossed up in the Shaw Croft, ensues.

' The players care little for hard knocks. If you are merely a spectator " Tha' moan't get in t' way "—to be caught in the " hug " when the game is in full swing is apt to be a somewhat rough experience. Duckings are common, and when the " ba' " is thrown into Henmore Brook there is a lot of fun.

' The players usually take sides according to the place of their birth, and are known as the " Up'ards " and the " Down'ards ". The game begins with a wild scramble for the big ball, which is stuffed with cork and painted in gay colours. The " Down'ards " endeavour to force the play into the bed of the shallow river whilst their opponents attempt to drive the ball into the open country. The goals are the water-wheels at Sturston and Clifton Mills, some three miles apart.

[1] Gomme I. 135.   [2] I owe this to my friend, Mr. J. Lewis.

' The lads thoroughly enjoy the rough-and-tumble.   Even to
be thrown full-length into the ice-cold water fails to damp their
ardour.   Shrovetide foot-ba' is in the very blood of these Ashbourne men, and honoured are the scars—and the sticking plaster
—that they carry with them after the event.

' The side which gets the ball to the goal is the winning side.
But sometimes play goes on for hours without either side scoring.
The game is characterized by bulldog tenacity, the worthy foemen
battering each other for all they are worth, ever ready to give,
or take, a knock or a dowsing.'

These games are definitely ceremonial, though their original
significance has usually disappeared.   Mr. J. M. Wheeler cites,
in his work on ' Paganism in Christian Festivals ', evidence that
suggests a religious background for these struggles.

He refers to Chambers' ' Book of Days ', where it tells how
formerly Bishops and Deans took a ball into the church at Easter.
They danced at the beginning of the antiphon, meanwhile throwing
the ball to the choristers.[1]

This curious Easter ritual took place formerly in other countries.
We learn, for instance, that the Easter Pelota of Auxerre, which
lasted until 1538, took place in the nave before vespers. . . .
' The dean and canons danced and tossed the ball, singing the
Victimae paschali.' [2]

It is remarkable to read of ball games in Christian churches.
This practice opens up a fascinating field of research.   One of the
most interesting, but obscure, instances comes from Egypt.   The
great temple constructed by Queen Hatshepsut of the Eighteenth
Dynasty at Deir el Bahri contains a picture of the king playing
ball.   The text reads, ' to strike the ball to (in honour of) Hathor
the protectress of Thebes '.

Naville remarks that it would appear from the text accompanying a similar representation in the temple at Denderah, that the
throwing of balls was a kind of emblem of victory : ' the enemies
are struck before them '.   He also cites the incident depicted
on the wall of the temple at Edfu, in which the king strikes a ball
in honour of his mother.[3]

Such ball games, evidently, as we see, originally ceremonial,
gradually became divorced from their connexion with the Church.
Men found pleasure in such contests.   They were enabled to

---

[1] Wheeler 23 e.s.

[2] Chambers I. 128, n. 4.   See Professor E. O. James, 277 e.s.

[3] Naville i. 4.   The Deir el Bahri temple also depicts Anubis rolling a
large disc.   Naville remarks that this scene is found in all birth temples.
Op. cit., II. 18.

exercise their skill, and satisfy their self-esteem when they beat the opposing team.

Spectators also took an intense pleasure in watching such contests. They were a form of relaxation. They also afforded the pleasure which comes from watching skilled movements. This has given the cult of such games a wide vogue. Starting in a few countries, such as England and France, they are gradually extending over the whole world. In short, what was once purely ceremonial, has now become, in western Europe, secular, except for a few traditional survivals, such as have been described.

This secularization of activities once ceremonial, serves to distinguish modern civilization from the rest of the world. There is a widespread occurrence throughout the world, among peoples with the dual organization, of ball games, in which one half of the group plays against the other half.

Lacrosse, for example, was learned by the European population of Canada from the Indians. 'The Handbook of American Indians' has an article on the subject that I venture to quote as a whole. It is entitled Ball Play, and runs as follows: 'The common designation of a man's game, formerly the favourite athletic game of all the eastern tribes from Hudson Bay to the Gulf. It was found also in California and perhaps elsewhere on the Pacific coast, but was generally superseded in the west by some form of shinny. It was played with a small ball of deer skin stuffed with hair or moss, or a spherical block of wood, and with one or two netted rackets, somewhat resembling tennis rackets. Two goals were set up at a distance of several hundred yards from each other, and the object of each party was to drive the ball under the goal of the opposing party by means of the racket without touching it with the hand. After picking up the ball with the racket, however, the player might run with it in his hand until he could throw it again. In the north the ball was manipulated with a single racket, but in the south the player used a pair, catching the ball between them. Two settlements or two tribes generally played against each other, the players numbering from 8 to 10 up to hundreds on a side, and high stakes were wagered on the result. Preceding and accompanying the game there was much ceremonial of dancing, fasting, bleeding, anointing, and prayer under the direction of the medicine-men. The allied tribes used this game as a stratagem to obtain entrance to Fort Mackinaw in 1764. Numerous places bearing the name of Ball Play give evidence of its old popularity among the former tribes of the Gulf states, who have carried it with them to their present homes in Indian Ter., where it is still kept up with the old cere-

monial and enthusiasm.   Shorn of its ceremonial accompaniments
it has been adopted by the Canadians as their national game under
the name of *la crosse*, and by the Louisiana French creoles as
raquette.   The Indians of many tribes played other games of ball,
noteworthy among which is the kicked ball of the Tarahumare,
which, it is said, gave the name to the tribe.' [1]

I cannot resist the temptation to make further quotations from
this work.   For example, the article on Games says that, ' In
general, in all Indian games, . . . the conceptions of the four
world quarters [constitute], the fundamental idea . . . back of
each game is found a ceremony in which the game was a significant
part.   The ceremony has commonly disappeared ; the game
survives as an amusement, but often with traditions and observances which serve to connect it with its original purpose.   The
ceremonies appear to have been to cure sickness, to cause fertiliz-
ation and reproduction of plants and animals, and, in the arid
region, to produce rain.   Gaming implements are among the most
significant objects that are placed upon many Hopi altars, and
constantly reappear as parts of the masks, head-dresses, and
other ceremonial adornments of the Indians generally.'

As an example we may take the hidden ball game.   This consists of four wooden tubes or cups.   These represent the four
world quarters.   A ball or stick is hidden under one of these
tubes and the game is to guess where it is.[2]

These quotations illustrate the ceremonial nature of the games
of the North American Indians.   They are still partly ritual in
their ceremonial contact, and there is little doubt that the more
important games were derived from the tribal ritual.   That is
to say, they come from the same source as the rest of savage ceremonial, viz. the ritual of the royal family.

The civilization of the native tribes of the United States came
from the direction of Mexico and Central America.   The earliest
of these parent civilizations was that of the Maya of Guatemala,
Honduras and Yucatan.   One of the later Maya settlements of
Yucatan, Chicuen-Itza, now in ruins, possessed a special building
used for ball games.   This building, like so many other ceremonial
buildings, was on the top of a stone platform, in the form of a
truncated pyramid.   It was rectangular in shape, with its longest
side running north and south.   It was divided into two parts,
after the fashion of the modern tennis court.

The players in these games must have been exalted in more
senses than one.

[1] ' Handbook of American Indians.'   Art. ' Ball Play ', p. 127.
[2] *Ibid.*   Art. ' Games ', 484, 5.

The pre-Columbian inhabitants of the West Indies were greatly given to ball games. The archaeological literature abounds in evidence of this activity. Mention is made of ball courts in Cuba, Porto Rico, and Santo Domingo. These consisted usually of two parallel earth walls. In one example the walls were eighty metres long, one metre high, four to seven metres broad, and sixty metres apart. [1]

It may sound incredible that a multitude of human societies, ranging through a period of more than 5,000 years, and extending from one end of the world to the other, should derive games, ceremonial or secular, as well as their animosities, from one incident in the history of a single royal family at the dawn of history. Yet there does not appear to be any other hypothesis to account for the facts. The hostility between Upper and Lower Egypt has been caught up in the stream of ritual that has flowed down through the ages from its original source in Egypt. By this means millions of mankind have become parties to a quarrel that is none of their seeking. There is no inherent reason why societies with a dual organization should carry on a traditional feud, or play ceremonial ball games. They do so seemingly because of a series of historical accidents.

The Pondo provide negative evidence on this point. They are singularly devoid of amusements. Pondo boys between the ages of six and sixteen occupy their days herding cattle. There is usually a band of them, spending the day together, while the cattle graze around them. We never observed any of them playing any kind of game. The most that any of them did was to make small clay models of cattle ; but even that is rare nowadays. They seem to spend the whole day loafing about, cooking meals, and so on.

The Pondo have one ceremonial practice that might have developed into a game. Their ceremonial occasions centre round the killing of cattle. The victim is driven, usually down a hillside, into the cattle kraal that forms part of each Pondo settlement. A band of young men, armed with sticks, try to prevent the cattle from entering the kraal. Another group, also armed with sticks, likewise try to force an entrance for the cattle. This fencing goes on for some minutes, and while it is on there is much excitement. It is the supreme moment of the day.

Certain young Pondo men were pointed out to me as famous fighters with these sticks ; but I was always told that they only fight on ceremonial occasions. It evidently had not occurred to the Pondo to turn the fencing into a pastime. They simply

[1] Hatt.

accepted it as part of the ritual.   It does not seem to occur to
them to fence for fun.

This is a good instance of the passivity of the human mind.
The Pondo accept the fencing, seemingly without qualification.
It is part of the procedure of getting the cattle down into the
kraal. ' It's a custom,' they invariably reply, when you ask why
they do it.   I have no doubt whatever that this ceremonial
contest comes from the same source as the others.   It has been
practised in Africa for 5,000 years, and would be practised for
5,000 more if it were not for the disruptive tendencies of
civilization.

The same might be said of dancing.   Some time ago I asked
a friend of mine, who had studied native culture in the New
Hebrides, whether the natives in any islands he knew ever danced
for fun.   They have an enormous number of dances, most of
which I knew to be ceremonial.   His answer was illuminating.
' Well, Perry, that sounds as if you were talking nonsense.'   I
then inquired of another friend, who had spent many years in the
Solomon Islands.   His reply was similar.   ' Certainly not; if
so, the ghosts of the dead would punish them.'

I do not wish to infer that savages never dance purely for
amusement.   The Pondo do ; but in general their dancing is
part of a ritual, and usually occurs on ceremonial occasions.   The
songs sung while dancing are also traditional.   Some of them are
now entirely meaningless.

I am the more loath to insist on the ceremonial nature of all
early dancing, because I have an uneasy feeling that the Egyptians
of the Pyramid Age had secular as well as sacred dancing.   The
funerary monuments of the Pyramid Age depict ballets of dancing
girls, clad in the orthodox classical style.   This suggests that the
great ones of this time kept troupes of dancing girls for their
amusement.   It must not be forgotten, however, that these
dancing girls may really have been dancing a ballet that had
some definite meaning.   We are told by Dr. Alan Gardiner that
Egyptian dancing girls almost invariably represented Hathor.
Their dancing ' displays the goddess in the act of conferring her
favours upon the lord of the feast '.[1]

Hathor was especially associated with dancing.   The sistrum,
or rattle, was in the shape of a Hathor head.   Dr. A. M. Blackman
tells me that Qenna, near Denderah, itself famous for the temple
of Hathor, is still one of the headquarters of the dancing girls.
Miss Blackman tells me that she has seen girls dancing on the
birthday of the Prophet.   The dance simulated the birth of

[1] Gardiner i. 95.

Mohammed. This dance, the *danse à ventre*, is always danced at the weddings of villagers. Dr. Blackman infers from this that the *danse à ventre* originally simulated the birth of the sun-god.

Dr. Alan Gardiner has clearly shown that the scenes in Egyptian tombs so often represent incidents of daily life. The dead man was awakened from his sleep, and brought to life, either as a mummy or a portrait statue, so that he might enjoy life as he had before he died. This evidence may, of course, be interpreted in two ways. Either dancing started as a secular amusement, and became incorporated in tomb and temple ritual ; or it was originally concerned with the dead or gods, and became secularized.

There is no doubt, on the whole, that dancing throughout the world was originally ritual ; dancers were actors in a sacred drama. Secular and ball-room dancing are of recent origin in western Europe. Our modern ball-room dancing, for instance, has developed from the country dance, which, in its turn, was a modification of dances such as the Maypole dance, associated with certain times of the year.

That is to say, a form of amusement, that would appear to be more or less spontaneous, owes its modern form, at least, to the fact that it was originally ritual and dramatic. The movements involved in ritual dancing were originally mimetic. The arrangement, in the Morris dance, of two opposing parties, has characteristics highly suggestive of the ceremonial fights, in Egyptian ritual, between the Followers of Horus and the Followers of Set. It is noteworthy that Egyptian dancers wore shoulder straps similar to the baldrick of Morris dancers. Processional dances hark back to the same period. Other modern survivals in England of ceremonial dances, such as the sword dance, have characteristics betraying their affinity with the world-wide group of rituals that we have been studying.[1]

It is interesting to note that Morris dances, Maypole dances, and other seasonal dances, are called Folk Dances. This would appear to infer that they are in some way or other a development welling-up from the ' folk mind ', if such an expression may be used. Yet all these folk dances betray their origin in royal ritual. The Basque dances form a case in point. Their Mascardes, which they dance at Carnival time, include a Lord and Lady, in addition to the Hobby-horse, the Man-woman, and other stock characters. They have, likewise, a Royal dance.

Do we not hear of the King and Queen of the May ? Are not King and Queen important actors in modern carnivals ? It is

[1] A delightful account of the story of the dance is given in Miss Evelyn Sharp's ' Here we go round ' (Gerald Howe).

difficult, if not impossible, to abstract the royal element, particularly in the archaic forms of these ceremonials. The Basque dances are also connected with churches. The sword-dance is sometimes danced in churches. When, therefore, the word ' folk dance ' is used it should be realized that the term has a limited meaning. The term ' folk ' applies to their modern association ; even in their existing form in England they are still ritual dances. The further back we go in history the less obtrusive becomes their ' folk ' element.

The story of the theatre is similar to that of contests. European drama originated from ritual performances of a religious nature. It came down to us partly by way of the Christian Church, partly through secular channels. The origin was religious in all cases.

The mediaeval Church had many dramatic religious ceremonies. They were held originally, like the ball games, in the church itself. Then came a time when the drama was performed in the graveyard and the neighbouring market-place, and thus lost part of its religious significance.

The secularization, as it may be termed, of the sacred drama, went still further. The original drama acted in the church contained secular and comic elements. These became emphasized. The plays became more human and less ecclesiastical. They began, moreover, to be acted in the vernacular, instead of, as before, in Latin. Thus we began in this country to act plays for the sheer joy of witnessing the representation of human experiences that interest us. But the drama long retained traces of its origin.

The beginnings of the drama lie still further back. Tragedy and comedy in Europe have been traced to Greece of the sixth and following centuries before Christ. The generally accepted theory is that comedy and tragedy both originated, particularly in Athens, as performances imitating those held on certain occasions in connexion with the religious rites that centred round Dionysus. The drama became secularized. Aeschylus, Sophocles and Euripides laid the foundations of tragedy, basing their plots on the religious drama that was already being performed. Aristophanes and others wrote comedies that likewise were based upon the dramas of the cults of Dionysus. Their works found a ready response, because they presented human beings in characteristic situations, and thus satisfied the feelings of their audiences.

The original dramatic performances out of which comedy and tragedy developed were performed in connexion with what are known as the Mystery Religions. These consisted of rites and beliefs connected with certain personages, Dionysus, Attis, Mithra, Serapis, whose cults moved about the Mediterranean during the few centuries before and after Christ. The religious associations connected with these personages were joined by men because they believed that they thereby gained the privilege of immortality, and of a glorious hereafter.

Each Mystery had an elaborate ritual, based on the common general plan. The central feature was the dramatic performance of the death and resurrection of the person in whose memory the Mystery was founded. The novice witnessed this drama, and, in some cases, seems to have participated in it. He was subjected to a ritual death and rebirth, based on this drama, and henceforth was one of the elect.

To mortal man the appeal of immortality is tremendous. He therefore takes an intense interest in any promise that assures him of this benefit. The dramatic performance that took place in each Mystery played a part of fundamental importance in the ritual. It was the concrete symbol of the reality of the events upon which the hope of immortality was based. It kept the aspirant after immortality in the closest possible contact with the original series of events in the lives of Attis, Mithra or Osiris, which were fraught with such tremendous significance for him.

The origin of the drama can be well understood when it is realized that it was intended to play so important a part in the lives of mankind. The drama, as we know, was, however, destined to go further than that. It awakened in the minds of men a pleasure in such performances. The appetite for the theatre was whetted. So when the opportunity arose the transition took place to the secular drama, to tragedy and comedy, and, ultimately, to all branches of the modern theatre.

Comedy and tragedy came out of the sacred drama. Whence, in its turn, came the sacred drama ? The answer is not difficult. It can be detected from the most cursory inspection of comedy and of tragedy. The whole setting of the drama of the Mysteries was that of royal families. Dionysus, for instance, in his latest form, was the son of Zeus and of Semele, daughter of Cadmus, founder of Thebes in Boeotia in Greece ; Adonis was a son of the king of Byblos in Phoenicia, or of Paphos in Cyprus ; Mithra was closely connected with the kings of Persia ; Osiris was the king of Egypt, and Isis was his sister and queen-wife. The Mysteries, therefore, although they were patronized by all ranks of society in Greece and Rome, were based on a series of events that happened in the royal families of the countries that bordered on Greece. A process of generalization has, therefore, taken place. Events which happened in royal families have come to awaken a new and universal interest among mankind, and have ultimately

given rise to performances that are entirely secular and democratic.

The study of the beginnings of the Mysteries reveals this process
still further. The earliest known Mystery was evidently that
of Osiris in Egypt. The others were, in all probability, derived
from it. At least they appear to have sprung up in Greece and
Rome at least three thousand years later than in Egypt. One
of them, the Isis Mysteries of Rome, was certainly brought from
Egypt.

As we have already seen, the Mysteries of Egypt were connected
with the royal family and their mummified and resurrected
ancestor. Evidently the appeal of the ritual was so great that
after many centuries it permeated the community. But it never
lost its royal character. Even when the dramatic performance
had become entirely secularized, it still contained traces of its
original nature, in that so many of the characters in tragedy were
of royal rank.

The study of dramatic performances thus introduces us to
a generalization so wide in its scope as to appear almost incredible.
It may be fairly stated that our modern dramatic performances
owe their origin, partly at least, to the ritual associated with the
funeral ceremonies of one man. By a gradual process of generalization, more and more people have come to take an interest in
this form of activity, until now it forms a large part of our modern
social life. It is curious to think that there are definite links
between ancient Egypt and Hollywood, but the connexion is
there, and cannot be denied.

It must not be thought from this that the dramatic art does
not rest on some deep-seated tendency. It is certain that the
tendency to dramatize is innate. It plays a large part in the
lives of mankind all the world over. But it would seem that the
early dramatic tendency was only called into activity by certain
events. Men only performed dramas for some definite purpose,
usually to obtain some supposed benefit.

The earliest example known to me of dramatic activity is the
animal disguise adopted by hunters, in order to decoy or otherwise
deceive the animal that is being hunted. This practice may indeed
go back as far as Aurignacian times in western Europe. A widespread series of rock carvings in North Africa depicts hunters
wearing animal disguises. This same device was practised by
the Bushmen of South Africa.

The aim of the hunters is obvious. Their interest is in the
acquisition of food, and the disguise is a ready means of acquiring
this food. In this these ancient hunters are on a level with the

performers of ceremonial all the world over. Ritual is universally dramatic, and is designed to gain something. The idea of an artistic appreciation, of the correct portrayal of situations, did not enter the minds of the Egyptians. They were too intent upon the inner meaning of the ceremonial. The transition to the dramatic art only came when the dramas became secularized, as it were, when they were detached from their original setting. Then arose the interest in the play for its own sake.

The generalization that ritual usually begins in royal families can be sustained with a vast mass of facts drawn from every people of whom we have records.[1] In the original communities of early Egypt the commoners could have taken very little part in the ceremonial life of the country. They had to get on with their hereditary tasks. The king and his nobles were there to carry on the ceremonial, to manage the religious part of the state. There were no Saturday afternoon football or cricket matches, no Saturday evening pictures, no special editions of the evening papers with the latest winners. All that had to develop, through the Greek games, the chariot races of the hippodrome of Rome and Byzantium, the ritual contests of the Churches, and by a multitude of other channels. Ritual was the concern of the rulers in the beginning. All that follows is an imitation of the royal initiators. This reminds me of a remark made by my old Pondo friend Mtandama. We were talking one morning about the cessation among the tribe of the circumcision of young men. He was saying that the paramount chief of the Pondo decided some years ago not to have this rite performed on behalf of his son. Consequently no Pondo boys have been circumcised for many years. Mtandama explained that if the Chief were to give the word, the custom would revive. He then electrified us by remarking, ' All customs come from the Chiefs ', which seems to be a fair approximation to the truth.

The gradual break-up of old ritual, and the consequent detachment of certain elements which begin to lead an independent existence, has made our lives vastly richer in content than were those of our remote ancestors. Games, dancing, art, architecture, are only some of a multitude of instances of this process. So-called ' folk tales ' also illustrate the process. The late G. A. Dorsey tells us that ritual stories are usually the prized possession of the owners of the ' bundles ' to which they refer. These stories, we have seen, are among the most cherished possessions of the Pawnee.

Dorsey tells us that these stories tend to become common

[1] See Hocart's ' Kingship ' for a wealth of illustration of this thesis.

property. ' Naturally, these myths of the origin of bundles and dances do not always remain the exclusive property of the priesthood ; they find their way among the ordinary people, where, when told, they lose much of their original meaning. Thus, by a gradual process of deterioration, they come to be regarded as of no special religious significance.' [1]

It is well known that many people throughout the world tell stories of the ' Brer Rabbit ' type. These stories recount battles of wits between opponents. In the versions carried by the negroes to the United States, Brer Rabbit is the hero. In Borneo, the hero is Pelandok, a small deer about as big as a rabbit. G. A. Dorsey tells us that the Pawnee invent these stories, and tell them for fun.

I was inclined until quite recently to assume that this explanation was enough to account for them, but some remarks let fall by Professor Hocart in the course of lectures delivered at University College, London, suggested to me quite another explanation. It would appear that many peoples throughout the world who possess the dual organization (that complicated but fertile and fascinating group of social institutions) have customs that suggest an origin for these stories. It will be remembered that in such communities the people are arranged in two inter-marrying groups, which at the same time are hostile. That is to say, a man's relatives in-law belong to the opposite group to himself. They are accustomed to play tricks on each other, and constantly endeavour to get the better of one another. I do not propose to discuss this question here, but I cannot refrain from commenting on the fact that a similar condition of affairs existed among the earliest known dual organization, that of Egypt. Stories such as that published by Dr. Alan Gardiner, in the Chester Beatty Papyrus, contain incidents in which Horus and Set, in their fights, changed into animal shapes in order to circumvent each other.[2] The practical joking and buffooneries of Fijian and North American tribes may therefore be derived from this primordial struggle, and, in their turn, have given rise to the vast series of Brer Rabbit stories throughout the world.

The Chester Beatty Papyrus, recently edited by Dr. Alan Gardiner, illustrates the same principle. It contains a popular story about Horus and Set. But we are assured by the editor that it is simply a re-hash of various ' mythical ' incidents, and contains no original elements. As he says, ' The probability is that the Ramesside author has invented nothing.'

Dr. Gardiner contrasts this composite story with ' the simple,

[1] Dorsey i. XXII.   [2] Gardiner iv. 19, 23.

comparatively spontaneous myths of a postulated naïve tribal
age ' ; [1] an age which, we have reason to believe, never existed.
Myth-making man is a myth.[2]

The widespread popularity of the professional story-teller in
the East would lead many to conclude that the telling of stories
would be found developing spontaneously in any human society ;
but such evidently is not the case.   The following remarks of
Monsieur Saintyves, in his work ' Les Saints Successeurs des
Dieux ', are of interest.   He says :

' Que nombre de contes soient nés contes, et nombre de fables
soient venues au monde fables, c'est possible, mais on peut être
assuré que fables, contes et mythes sont faits à l'ordinaire d'une
étoffe commune et que la plupart remontent à une époque mytho-
logique, ou mieux à un état d'esprit analogue à celui des sauvages
modernes.   Ceux qui créèrent des mythes forgèrent des contes
et réciproquement.   Mythes, contes et fables sont des façons
enfantines de répondre aux questions que l'esprit se pose sur la
nature et sur la destinée.   Les fables comme les mythes relatifs
aux règles de conduite justifient d'une semblable façon la morale
et le devoir.   Si l'on a pu les accuser de propager une morale peu
élevée, fort intéressée et parfois même plus qu'egoïste, c'est
qu'elles se ressentent de leur origine primitive, de leur parenté
avec les vieux interdits totémiques.   Les contes comme les mythes
relatifs à l'univers, à sa constitution, à son origine et à sa fin sont
une sorte de physique de la nature, balbutiante, naïve et poétique.

' On peut présumer qu'à leur naissance, fables, contes et mythes
furent également localisés et se rapportèrent aux choses et aux
gens d'un pays déterminé.   Tous étaient attachés à la source, ou
à la montagne, liés à quelque totem ou à quelque ancêtre dont on
redisait, aux veillées, les exploits.

' Ce n'est que beaucoup plus tard, en voyageant de famille
à famille, de tribu à tribu, de nation à nation qu'ils perdirent leur
couleur locale primitive.   Pour s'universaliser, la fable, le conte
et le mythe ont dû perdre leur caractère de traditions familiales,
tribales ou ethniques ; mais, en revanche, ils y ont gagné des ailes.

' Lorsqu'une légende sainte se déplaçait avec les reliques qu'elle
accompagnait, surtout lorsqu'il s'agissait de déraciner un vieux
culte païen, on se préoccupait d'abord de lui rendre une couleur
locale pour l'adapter au paysage nouveau, au lieu déjà saint, où
l'on allait l'installer.   On n'y parvenait guère si l'on ne s'efforçait
de faire oublier les anciennes fêtes du culte antérieur.' [3]

Saintyves discusses the origins of popular stories.   He says that
at the present moment we may consider India, Egypt, and Asia

[1] Op. cit., 9, 11.   [2] See Hocart i.   [3] Saintyves 262-3.

Minor as the three great centres of diffusion.[1]   India was formerly much favoured as an originator.[2]   Miletus finds a strong supporter in Monsieur Monceaux.[3]   But Saintyves himself agrees with Salomon Reinach and Maspero in regarding Egypt as the home of the popular story.   He says :   ' The Egyptian theory of which Monsieur Salomon Reinach is, I believe, the father,[4] seems to me to have a very brilliant future.' [5]

He also quotes Maspero.   ' We must consider Egypt, if not as one of the countries where popular stories originated, at least as one of those where they were first naturalized, and where they have assumed a truly literary form.   I am convinced that those most competent to judge will agree with this conclusion.' [6]

The remarks of Saintyves concerning the popular story are surprising.   It is hardly credible that mankind throughout the ages has not been able spontaneously to develop even the small amount of imagination involved in inventing a story.   But when we learn that Aesop is said probably to have owed his tales to oriental sources, it is surely not surprising that less exalted peoples than the Greeks show an almost complete lack of originality in this direction.[7]

This lack of originality is a striking illustration of the concrete working of the human mind.   It would appear that what is called ' imagination ' is almost entirely absent from the human mind.   The savage appears to be like us.   He spends much of his time gossiping and in general conversation.   Like us, again, he often knows some traditional stories, but usually does not trouble to invent any for himself.   This is not to be wondered at when the simplicity of his daily life is borne in mind.   The average savage is usually almost entirely ignorant of his tribal religion.   There is no reason to believe that he has taken any part in fashioning his tribal beliefs, therefore why should he invent stories ?   He is quite content to do nothing.

The consideration of the intellectual output of the Dark Ages in Europe reveals a woeful lack of initiative.   For about a thousand years the combined intellects of Europe produced practically no literature.   It needed the vitalizing breath of Greek inspiration to rekindle the embers.   The literary products of the Middle Ages are for the most part concerned with stereotyped themes.   As an example we may take Miss Jessie Weston's work, ' From Ritual to Romance ', in which she deals with the Arthurian legend.   She shows that this legend, dealing, as it does, with

[1] Saintyves 261 n. 1.   [2] *Ibid.*, 204 e.s.   [3] *Ibid.*, 261 n. 1.
[4] Reinach ii. I. 409.   [5] Saintyves 208.
[6] Saintyves 209, n. 1 : Maspero i. LXXII.   [7] C.A.H. IV. 520–1.

the search for the Holy Grail, was based originally upon a ritual. This ritual, although Miss Weston herself does not state it, bears every trace of being a variant of the original ritual concerned with the death and resurrection of Osiris. The compilers of the different versions of the Arthurian romance were therefore using the common source of inspiration of so many social activities of modern men.

The development of modern literature in Europe is displaying once again the fundamental tendency of the human mind. The romantic stories, such as those of the Arthurian cycle, have floated so far away from their original moorings that their interest is now mainly antiquarian. They correspond very little to reality, as we conceive it in our days. Stories of knights seeking adventure, even though the knight be the immortal Don Quixote, are no longer universally enjoyed. The tendency is to depict social reality.

This process is also discernible in the theatre. The day of the melodrama, with its stock characters, and stereotyped plot, has almost ended. Plays and literature aim at concrete represent-ation of social situations. They succeed or fail according as they are or are not faithful to reality as we conceive it. The general aim is to give a ' slice of life ', the ' happy ending ' is no longer imperative.

We have already seen that art was originally based on utility, real or imagined. The cave-men of western Europe, like the Egyptians of the Old Kingdom, painted, drew, or carved for use in the first place. Every item of ornamentation in an Egyptian tomb or temple forms part of a great ' life-giving ' scheme. The lotus, for instance, was a symbol of life to the Egyptians. Horus is often depicted rising from a lotus that is floating on the pri-mordial flood.

The Greeks acquired the lotus *motif* from Egypt ; but ignored the symbolism attached to it. It had a purely artistic meaning for them.[1]

The well-known Greek ' key ' pattern was likewise borrowed from Egypt. It was a development of the Egyptian sign for a house. This sign represented the ground-plan of a ' but-and-ben ' house ⌐⌐.

The history of human behaviour, as we have seen, provides many surprises. Activities that appear to us natural and in-evitable, that appear to require no special stimulus, are found to be specific in nature.

[1] Ward 262.

23

Instances of this kind have already been given. Saintyves provides us with yet another. He speaks of professional wailers for the dead, such as are met with in certain countries. He remarks that they existed in Egypt, and that Greece and Rome presumably borrowed the custom from that country.[1] These professional mourners doubtless represent Isis and Nephthys, wife and sister of Osiris, mourning for their dead lord.

Saintyves tells us likewise that the Egyptian custom of holding funeral feasts has given rise to modern hymns and funeral orations, and has blossomed into the masterpieces of a Prudence or a Bossuet. These were at first merely a kind of incantation intended to avert magical influences from the deceased during his journey to the land of the dead. The Egyptians feared being devoured by Set, Nephthys or some other deity before they arrived at their future home.[2]

Another interesting instance of the spread of a practice, though of a somewhat different nature, is supplied by Dr. E. J. Dingwall. He has studied the practice of artificial cranial deformation throughout the world. In many parts of the world people of noble or royal rank deform the heads of their children, which is regarded as a sign of rank It is, or was, practised more especially in certain centres, such as pre-Columbian Peru. Adjoining peoples possessed the practice, but the deformation was slighter. In like manner peoples more remote, made still slighter efforts, often merely stroking the heads of their babies.

This process of ' fading out ' has been described by Dr. Dingwall in Asia, Africa, Oceania, and America. It strongly suggests the implantation of the practice in certain centres, and a subsequent spread into neighbouring areas, with the inevitable degradation.

The evidence all goes to suggest that the practice arose in the countries of western Asia, whose rulers imitated in an artificial manner the shape of the head of Akhenaten, of the Eighteenth Dynasty in Egypt. Akhenaten's head was deformed as the result of illness. His family and the members of the court are depicted with the same form of head. It seems that they wore head-dresses for the purpose, and did not deform the heads of their children.

The actual deformation of the head evidently arose in neighbouring countries such as Cyprus or among the Hittites, and spread thence over the world.[3]

These facts show that, although man possesses certain deep-seated tendencies, they do not manifest themselves spontaneously. Something more is necessary. Some specific set of circumstances must be present, calling into being a form of activity that ulti-

[1] Saintyves 61. [2] Ibid., 64–5. [3] Dingwall 237, 238.

mately becomes so widespread throughout mankind as to seem spontaneous. Painting, dancing, the drama, games, all appear to us to be ' natural ', to spring immediately from innate tendencies. But the study of these activities shows that this conjecture is false. They came into play for some definite purpose. But, once initiated, they were eagerly seized upon by men, and practised for their own sakes.

LIST OF AUTHORITIES [1]

A . . .	' Anthropos ', Vienna.
AA . . .	' The American Anthropologist ', Washington, New York, Lancaster.
AAE . .	University of California Publications in ' American Archaeology and Ethnology ', Berkeley, California.
AJ . . .	' The Antiquaries' Journal '.
AKAW .	' Königliche-Preussische Akademie der Wissenschaften zu Berlin ', Abhandlungen.
ARBE . .	' Annual Report of the Bureau of Ethnology ', Washington, D.C.
ASAM . .	' Annals of the South African Museum ', Cape Town.
ASE . .	' Archaeological Survey of Egypt ', Cairo.
ASN . .	' Archaeological Survey of Nubia ', Cairo.
BBE . .	' Bulletin of the Bureau of Ethnology ', Washington, D.C.
BTLV . .	' Bijdragen tot de taal-land-en volkenkund van Neder, landsch-Indie ', 's Gravenhage.
CAH . .	' Cambridge Ancient History ', Cambridge.
ERE . .	The ' Hastings Encyclopaedia of Religion and Ethics '.
FL . . .	' Folk-Lore '.
HJ . . .	' The Hibbert Journal '.
JAI . .	' Journal of the Anthropological Institute '.
JAS. . .	' Journal of African Studies '.
JBORS .	' Journal of the Bihar and Orissa Research Society ', Patna.
JEA . .	' Journal of Egyptian Archaeology '.
JRAI . .	' Journal of the Royal Anthropological Institute '.
PBA . .	' Proceedings of the British Academy '.
PSBA . .	' Proceedings of the Society of Biblical Archaeology '.
RA . . .	' Revue Archéologique ', Paris.
SBE . .	' The Sacred Books of the East ', Oxford.
TES . .	' Transactions of the Ethnological Society of London '.
TNAG .	' Tijdschrift van het (Koninklijk) Nederlandsch Aardrijkskundig Genootschap ', Amsterdam, Leiden.
TRSSA .	' Transactions of the Royal Society of South Africa ', Cape Town.

---

[1] Place of Publication is London, except when otherwise stated.

VBG . . 'Verhandelingen van het Bataviaasch Genootschap van kunsten en wetenschappen', Batavia.
VMKAW . 'Verslagen en mededeelingen van het . . . (koninklijk) Akademie der wetenschappen', Amsterdam.
ZAS. . . 'Zeitschrift für Aegyptische Sprache', Leipzig.
ZFE . . 'Zeitschrift für Ethnologie', Berlin.

ACOSTA, JOSEPH DE : ' The Natural and Moral History of the Indies ', Trans. by C. R. Markham, 2 vols., 1880.
ANDERSSON, J. G. :
   (i) ' An Early Chinese Culture ', Bulletin of the Geological Survey of China, No. 5, 1923.
   (ii) ' The Cave-Deposit at Sha Kuo T'un in Feng-tien ', Palaentologia Sinica, Geological Survey of China, Pekin, 1923.
ASTON, W. G. : ' Shinto ', 1905.

BAILEY, J. : ' Wild Tribes of the Veddahs of Ceylon ', TES, II, 1863.
BANCROFT, H. : ' Native Races of the Pacific States ', 1875–6.
BANDELIER, AD. F. : ' On the Art of War and Mode of Warfare of the Ancient Mexicans ', Report of Peabody Museum, Vol. II, 1876–9.
BARBEAU, C. M. : ' Huron and Wyandot Mythology ', Ottawa, 1915.
BARTLETT, F. C. : ' Psychology and Primitive Culture ', 1923.
BARTLETT, H. H. : ' The Sacred Edifices of the Batak of Sumatra ', University of Michigan, Occasional Contributions from the Museum of Anthropology, No. 4. Ann Arbor, Michigan, 1934.
BASTIAN, A. : ' Indonesien ', Berlin, 1884–94.
' Beni Hasan '. By various authors. (Archaeological Survey of Egypt), 1893–1900. See GRIFFITH, NEWBERRY.
BERGH, VAN DEN, L. J. : ' On the Trail of the Pygmies ', 1922.
BEVERIDGE, P. : ' The Aborigines of Victoria and Riverina ', Melbourne, 1889.
BIOT, E. : ' Le Tcheou Li ', Paris, 1851.
BISCHOFS, J. : ' Die Niol-Niol, ein Eingeborenenstamm in Nordwest Australien ', A, 3, 1908.
BLACKMAN, A. M. : ' Sacramental Idea and Usage in Ancient Egypt ', PSBA, XL, 1918. See also HOOKE, ERMAN.
BOAS, F. : ' Central Eskimo ', ARBE, 6, 1884–5.
BONNEY, F. : ' On Some Customs of the Aborigines of the River Darling ', New South Wales, JRAI, 13, 1884.
BONWICK, J. : ' The Australian Native ', JAI, 16, 1887.
BORCHARDT, L. :
   (i) ' Nilmesser und Nilstandmarken ', AKAW, 1906.
   (ii) ' Das Grabdenkmal des Königs Sahure ', Leipsic, 1913.
BOVET, P. : ' The Fighting Instinct ', 1923.

BREASTED, J. H. :
(i) ' Ancient Records of Egypt ', 1907.
(ii) ' A History of Egypt ', New York, 2nd Edition, 1909.
(iii) ' The Development of Religion and Thought in Ancient Egypt ', 1912.
(iv) ' The Conquest of Civilization ', 1926.
BRIDE, T. F. : ' Letters from Victorian Pioneers : being a series of papers on the early occupation of the Colony, the Aborigines, etc.' Edited by Thomas F. Bride, Melbourne, 1899.
BRINKLEY, P. : ' A History of the Japanese People.'
BROWN, A. R. RADCLIFFE :
(i) ' Three Tribes of Western Australia ', JRAI, XLIII, 1913.
(ii) ' The Andaman Islanders ', Cambridge, 1922.
(iii) ' The Social Organization of Australian Tribes ', ' Oceania ' Monographs, No. 1, 1931.
BUCHANAN, F. H. : ' Journey through the Countries of Mysore, Canara, and Malabar ', 1807.
BUCK, A. DE : De Egyptische voorstellingen betreffende den oerheuvel. Leiden, 1922.
BUDGE, SIR E. A. WALLIS :
(i) ' The Mummy. Chapters on Egyptian funereal Archaeology', 1893, 2nd Edition, 1925.
(ii) ' The Papyrus of Ani ', 1895.
(iii) ' On the Hieratic Papyrus of Mesi-Amsu ', Archaeologia, 52.
BURNET, JOHN : ' Early Greek Philosophy ', 1892, 4th Edition, 1930.
BURY, J. B. : ' Greek Literature ', CAH IV, 1926.

CAPART, J. : ' Primitive Art in Egypt ', 1905.
CAREY, B. S., and TUCK, H. N. : ' The Chin Hills ', Rangoon, 1896.
CARTER, HOWARD T. : The Tomb of Tutankhamen ', 1923, etc.
CHAMBERS, E. K. : ' The Mediaeval Stage ', 2 vols., 1903.
' Chester Beatty Papyrus '. See GARDINER, A. H.
CHILDE, V. GORDON :
(i) ' The Most Ancient East ', 1928.
(ii) ' New Light on the Most Ancient East ', 1934.
CHRISTY, CUTHBERT : ' Big Game and Pygmies ', 1924.
COOPER, JOHN M. : ' Analytical and Critical Bibliography of the Tribes of Tierra del Fuego and adjacent Territory ', BBE, 63, 1917.
CUSHING, F. H. : ' Outlines of Zuni Creation Myths ', ARBE, 13, 1891-2.
' Customs of the World ' : Edit. by Walter Hutchinson, 1913.

DARMESTETER, J. : ' The Zend-Avesta ', Part I, The Vendîdâd, SBE, IV, 1880.
DAVIDSON : ' The Island of Formosa ', 1902.
DAVIES, N. DE G. : ' The Tomb of Amenemhet ', 1915. See also GARDINER, ALAN H.

DAWSON, JAMES : 'Australian Aborigines', Melbourne, Sydney, Adelaide, 1881.

DAWSON, R. : 'The Present State of Australia', 1831.

DAWSON, WARREN R. See Elliot Smith.

DINGWALL, E. J. : 'Artificial Cranial Deformation', 1931.

DORNAN, S. S. : 'Pygmies and Bushmen of the Kalahari', 1925.

DORSEY, G. A. :
    (i) 'Traditions of the Skidi Pawnee', Boston and New York, 1904.
    (ii) 'Traditions of the Wichita', 1904.
    (iii) 'The Arapaho Sun Dance', Field Columbian Museum, Pub. 75, Anthr. Ser., Vol. IV, 1903.

DU PRATZ, LE PAGE : 'Histoire de la Louisiane', 1758.

EGGELING, J. : 'Satapatha Brahmana', SBE, 5 vols.

ELKIN, A. P. : 'Studies in Australian Totemism', Oceania, III, 4.

ELLIOT SMITH, SIR G. :
    (i) 'The Migrations of Early Culture', Manchester, 1915.
    (ii) 'Primitive Man', Proc. Brit. Acad., VII, 1917.
    (iii) 'The Ancient Egyptians and the Origin of Civilization', 1911, 2nd Edition, 1923.
    (iv) And WARREN R. DAWSON : 'Egyptian Mummies', 1924.
    (v) 'Human History', 1930, 2nd Edition, 1934.
    (vi) 'The Evolution of the Dragon', Manchester, 1919.
    (vii) 'The Diffusion of Culture', 1933.

ELLIS, HAVELOCK : 'The Dance of Life', 1923.

ENRIQUEZ, MAJOR C. : 'Malaya, an Account of its People, Flora, and Fauna', 1927.

ERKELENS, B. : 'Geschiedenis van het rijk Gowa', Batavia, 1897.

ERMAN, A. :
    (i) 'Aegypten, Tübingen', 1922.
    (ii) 'The Literature of the Ancient Egyptians', 1927. Trans. by A. M. Blackman.
    (iii) 'A Handbook of Egyptian Religion', 1907.

EVANS, SIR ARTHUR : 'The Mycenaean Tree and Pillar Cult', 1901.

FIRTH, C. M. :
    (i) 'The Archaeological Survey of Nubia', Bull., 7, Cairo, 1911.
    (ii) 'The Archaeological Survey of Nubia', 1909–10, Cairo, 1915.
    (iii) 'Excavations of the Dept. of Antiquities at the Step Pyramid. Saqqara' (1924–5). Annales du Service des Antiquitès de l'Egypte, XXV.

FLETCHER, A. C. (MISS) :
    (i) 'The Hako, a Pawnee Ceremony', ARBE, 22, 1900–1.
    And LA FLÈSCHE, F. (ii) : 'The Omaha Tribe', ARBE, 27, 1911.

FORBES, C. J. F. : 'British Burma', 1878.

FORBES, H. O. :
    (i) 'On the Kubus of Sumatra', JRAI, 14, 1885.
    (ii) 'A Naturalist's Wanderings in the Eastern Archipelago', 1885.

LIST OF AUTHORITIES 349

FORDE, C. D. : ' Habitat, Economy and Society ', 1934.
FOX, C. E. :
  (i) ' Social Organization in San Cristoval, Solomon Islands ', JRAI, 49, 1919.
  (ii) ' The Threshold of the Pacific ', 1924.
FRIEDERICI, G. : ' Skalpieren und Ähnliche Kriegsgebräuche in America ', Brunswick, 1906.

GARCILASO DE LA VEGA. See VEGA.
GARDINER, ALAN H. :
  (i) ' The Tomb of Amenemhet ', 1915. See also DAVIES N. DE G.
  (ii) JEA, II, 1915. Review of Sir J. G. Frazer's ' Attis, Adonis and Osiris '.
  (iii) Article ' Philosophy (Egyptian) ', ERE.
  (iv) ' The Chester Beatty Papyrus, No. 1 ', Oxford, 1931.
  (v) ' A New Masterpiece of Egyptian Sculpture ', JEA, IV, i, 1917.
  (vi) ' Egyptian Grammar ', 1927.
GEIGER, W. : ' The Mahavamsa ', 1912.
GLANVILLE, S. R. K. : ' Egyptian Theriomorphic Vessels in the British Museum ', JEA, 12, 1926.
' Glass Palace Chronicles '. See TIN, PE MAUNG, and LUCE, G. H.
GODDARD, P. E. : ' Life and Culture of the Hupa ', AAE, 1, 1903–4.
GOMME, ALICE B. : ' Dictionary of British Folklore ', 1898.
GOMPERTZ, M. : ' Corn from Egypt ', 1927.
GOODWIN, A. J. H. :
  (i) And C. VAN RIET LOWE : ' The Stone Age Cultures of South Africa ', Annals of the South African Museum, Vol. 27.
  (ii) ' Some Developments in Technique during the Earlier Stone Age ', Trans. Roy. Soc. Sth. Afr., XXI, Cape Town, 1933.
GREY, G. : ' Journals of the Journeys of Discovery in North West and Western Australia during the years 1837–8–9 ', 1841.
GRIFFITH, F. LL. :
  (i) ' Beni Hasan '. Part III, 1896 (Archaeological Survey of Egypt).
  (ii) ' The Royal Tombs of the First Dynasty ', 1900. See also PETRIE.
  (iii) ' Two Hieroglyphic Papyri from Tanis ', 1889. See also PETRIE.
GRIFFITH, R. T. H. : ' The Hymns of the Atharva-Veda ', 1895.
GRINNELL, G. B. :
  (i) ' Pawnee Hero Stories ', 1893.
  (ii) ' The Cheyenne Indians ', New Haven, 1923.
  (iii) ' The Indians of To-day ', in P. S. Dellerburgh, ' The North American Indians of Yesterday ', 1931.
GROOT, J. J. M. DE : ' The Religious System of China ', 6 vols., Leyden, 1892–1910.
GRYZEN, H. J. : ' Mededeelingen omtrent Beloe of Midden-Timor ', VBG, 54, 1904.

HADDON, A. C. :
    (i) ' The Study of Man ', 1898.
    (ii) ' The Wanderings of Peoples ', Cambridge, 1911.
HALE, A. : ' On the Sakais ', JRAI, 15, 1886.
HALL, H. R. : ' Antiquaries' Journal ', 8, 1928.
HAMMERTON : ' Universal History of the World '.
' Handbook of American Indians ', BBE, 30, Washington, D.C., 1912.
HANDY, E. S. C. : ' The Native Culture in the Marquesas ', Bull. 9,
    Bernice P. Bishop Museum, Honolulu, 1923.
HARDY, R. S. : ' A Manual of Buddhism ', 1853.
HARRINGTON, M. R. : ' Sacred Bundles of the Sac and Fox Indians ',
    Univ. Penn. Mus. Pub., 1914.
HATT, G. : ' Notes on the Archaeology of San Domingo ', Saertryk
    af Geografisk Tidsskrift, 1932.
HAWKES, E. W. : ' The Labrador Eskimo ', Geol. Survey, Mem. 91,
    Ottawa, 1916.
HEATH, SIR T. : ' Greek Mathematics ', 1921.
HILL-TOUT, C. : ' British North America ', 1907.
HOCART, A. M. :
    (i) ' The Commonsense of Myth ', AA, 1916.
    (ii) ' Kingship ', Oxford, 1927.
    (iii) ' The Four Quarters ', Ceylon Journ. Science, I, 1927.
    (iv) ' The Progress of Man ', 1933.
HOOKE, S. H. : ' Myth and Ritual ', Oxford, 1933.
HOOPER, L. (MISS) : ' The Cahuilla Indians ', Univ. Cal., AAE, 16,
    1920.
HORNE, G., and AISTON, G. : ' Savage Life in Central Australia ',
    1924.
HOSE, C., and McDOUGALL, W. : ' The Pagan Tribes of Borneo ',
    1912.
HOWITT, A. W. : ' The Native Tribes of South-East Australia ', 1904.
HUETING, A. : ' De Tobeloreezen in hun denken en doen ', BTLV,
    77, 1921.
HUNTINGTON, E. :
    (i) ' The Pulse of Asia ', Boston, 1907.
    (ii) ' The Climatic Factor ', Washington, D.C., 1914.
HUTCHINSON, W. : ' Customs of the World ', 1913.
HUTTON, J. H. :
    (i) ' The Angami Nagas ', 1921.
    (ii) ' The Sema Nagas ', 1921.

INNES, C. A. : ' Madras District Gazetteer ', Madras, 1908.

JAMES, E. O. : ' Christian Myth and Ritual ', 1933.
JENKS, A. E. : ' The Bontoc Igorot ', Manila, 1905.
JUNKER, H. : ' Die Stundenwachen in den Osirismysterien nach den
    Inschriften von Dendera, Edfu, und Philae ', Denkschrift. K.A.,
    W., Wien. Phil. Hist. Klasse, 54, 1911.

KARSTEN, R. :
  (i) ' Blood revenge, War, and Victory Feasts among the Jibaro
      Indians of Eastern Ecuador ', BBE, 79, Washington, D.C.,
      1923.
  (ii) ' The Civilization of the South American Indians ', 1926.
KING, L. W. : ' The Seven Tablets of Creation ', 1902.
KRÄMER, F. : ' Die Samoa-Inseln ', Stuttgart, 1902.
KROEBER, A. L. :
  (i) ' Types of Indian Culture in California ', AAE, II, 1904–7.
  (ii) ' Elements of Culture in Native California ', AAE, 13, 1922.
KROEBER, H. R. : Pima Tales. AA, New Ser. 10, 1908.
KRUYT, A. C. :
  (i) ' Het Animisme in den Indischen Archipel.', 's Gravenhage,
      1906.
  And ADRIANI, N. (ii) : ' De Bare'e Sprekende Toradja's van
      Midden-Celebes ', 's Gravenhage, 1912.
KRUYT, J. : ' De Moriërs van Tinompo ', BTLV, 80, 1924.
KUBARY, J. : ' Ethnographische Beiträge zur Kenntniss der Karo-
      linischen, Inselgruppe und Nachbarschaft, Heft 1. Die Sociale
      Einrichtungen der Pelauer ', Berlin, 1885.

LACAITA, C. : ' An Italian Englishman ', 1933.
LANGDON, S. : ' Art and Archaeology ', 24, 1927.
LAYARD, J. W. : ' Degree-taking Rites in South-West Bay, Malekula ',
      JRAI, 58, 1928.
LEHMAN, H. C., and WITTY, P. A. : ' The Present Status of the Tend-
      ency to Collect and Hoard ', Psych. Review, New York, 34, 1927.
LE PAGE DU PRATZ. See DU PRATZ.
LETHABY, W. R. :
  (i) ' Architecture Mysticism and Myth ', 1892.
  (ii) ' Architecture ', Home Univ. Lib. Ser., 1912.
LEVIN, MARY : ' Mummification and Cremation in India ', Man, 1930.
LEWES, G. H. : ' History of Philosophy ', 1871.
LING ROTH, H. : ' The Natives of Sarawak and Brit. North Borneo ',
      1896.
LIVINGSTONE, R. W. : ' The Legacy of Greece '. Oxford, 1921.
LOISY, A. F. : ' Les Mystères païens et le mystère Chretien ', Paris,
      1914.
LOWIE, R. H. : ' Primitive Religion ', 1925.
LUCE, G. H. : See TIN.

MCCONNEL, URSULA : ' The Wik-Munkan and Allied Tribes of Cape
      York Peninsula, N.Q.' Oceania IV, Sydney, 1934.
MCDOUGALL, W. : ' Introduction to Social Psychology. See also
      HOSE, C.
MACE, A. C. : ' Early Dynastic Cemeteries of Naga ed Deir ', II,
      Univ. Cal. Pub. Egypt Arch., II., Pt. I, 1908.
MACKENZIE : ' History of the Fur Trade '.

MAHAVAMSA : See GEIGER, W. : TURNOUR, G. : UPHAM, E.
MALINOWSKI, B. :
(i) ‘ The Family Among the Australian Aborigines ’, 1913.
(ii) ‘ Argonauts of the Western Pacific ’, 1922.
(iii) ‘ Lunar and Seasonal Calendars in the Trobriands ’, JRAI,
57, 1927.
(iv) ‘ Myth in Primitive Psychology ’, 1926.
(v) ‘ Kinship ’, Man, 1930.
MAN, E. H. :
(i) ‘ On the Andaman Islands and their Inhabitants ’, JRAI,
1885.
(ii) ‘ The Andaman Islanders ’, 1883.
(iii) ‘ On the Aboriginal Inhabitants of the Andaman Islands ’,
JAI, 12, 1883.
MARKHAM, C. R. :
(i) See VEGA.
(ii) ‘ History of Peru ’, Chicago, 1892.
(iii) ‘ The Incas of Peru ’, 1910.
MARSHALL, SIR J. : ‘ Mohenjo-daro and the Indus Civilization ’,
1932.
MASPERO, G. :
(i) ‘ Les Contes Populaires de l’Egypte Ancienne ’, 1881, 2nd
Edition.
(ii) ‘ Études de Mythologie et Archaeologie égyptiennes ’, 1889.
(iii) ‘ Manual of Egyptian Archaeology ’, 1895.
MATHEW, J. : ‘ Eaglehawk and Crow ’, 1899.
MEYER, E. : ‘ Geschichte des Altertums ’, 1909.
MOORE, R. D. : ‘ Social Life of the Eskimo of St. Lawrence Island ’,
AA, 1923.
MORET, A. :
(i) ‘ Le Rituel du Culte Divin Journalier en Egypte ’, Ann. de
Mus. Guimet, Bibl. d’études, XIV, Paris, 1902.
(ii) ‘ Mystères Egyptiens ’, Ann. Mus. Guimet, Bibl. de Vulgarisa-
tions, Paris, 1912.
MORGAN, J. DE : ‘ Mémoires de la Délégation en Perse ’, Paris.
MORLEY, S. G. : ‘ The Inscriptions at Copan ’, Washington, 1920.
MÜLLER, S. : ‘ Reizen en onderzoekingen in den Indischen Archipel ’,
Amsterdam, 1857.
MÜLLER (WISMAR), W. : ‘ Yap, Ergebnisse der Südsee Expedition ’,
1908–10. Hamburgische Wissenschaftliche Stiftung, Hamburg,
1917–18.
MURIE, J. R. : ‘ Pawnee Indian Societies ’, Anthropological Papers
of the Amer. Mus. Nat. Hist., New York, 1912–16 (1914).
MURRAY, M. A. : ‘ Royal Marriages and Matrilineal Descent ’,
JRAI, 1915.
‘ Myth and Ritual ’, Edit. by S. H. Hooke, Oxford, 1933.

NANSEN, F. : ‘ Eskimo Life ’, 1893.

NAVILLE, E. :
    (i) ' Deir el Bahari ', 6 vols., 1895–1908.
    (ii) ' Textes relatifs au Mythe d'Horus, Geneva and Bâle ', 1870.
    (iii) ' The Festival Hall of Osorkon II in the Great Temple of
        Bubastis ', 1892.
NELSON, E. W. : ' The Eskimo about Behring Strait ', ARBE, 18,
    1896–7, 1899.
NEUBURGER, M. : ' History of Medicine ', Vol. I, Oxford, 1910.
NEWBERRY, P. E. : ' Beni Hasan ', 1893–1900 (' Archaeological
    Survey of Egypt ').

OLSON, R. L. : ' Clan and Moiety in Native America ', AAE, 1933.
OSSENBRUGGEN, VAN F. D. E. : ' De Oorsprong van het Javaansche
    Begrip Montja-pat ', VMKAW, Afd. Lett. Series V, Pt. III,
    Amsterdam, 1917.

PARKER, E. H. : ' A Thousand Years of the Tartars ', 1895.
PARRY, SIR H. H. : ' Studies of Great Composers ', 11th Edition.
PEET, T. E. : ' Egypt: The Pre-dynastic Period ', Chap. 6, CAH,
    Vol. I.
PE MAUNG TIN, and LUCE, G. H. : ' The Glass Palace Chronicles of
    the Kings of Burma ', Oxford, 1923.
PERINGUEY, L. : ' The Stone Ages of South Africa as represented in
    the Collection of the South African Museum ', Annals of the
    S.A. Museum, Vol. VIII, 1911, Cape Town.
PERRY, W. J. :
    (i) ' The Orientation of the Dead in Indonesia ', JRAI, 44, 1914.
    (ii) ' Myths of Origin and the Home of the Dead ', FL, 26, 1915.
    (iii) ' An Ethnological Study of Warfare ', Mem. Proc. Man-
        chester Lit. and Phil. Soc., 1917.
    (iv) ' The Peaceful Habits of Primitive Communities ', Hibbert
        Journal, 1917.
    (v) ' The Megalithic Culture of Indonesia ', Manchester, 1918.
    (vi) ' The Children of the Sun ', 1923, 2nd Edition, 1926.
    (vii) ' The Origin of Magic and Religion ', 1923.
    (viii) ' The Growth of Civilization ', 1924, 2nd Edition, 1926.
    (ix) ' Gods and Men ', 1927.
    (x) ' The Age of the Gods ', The Frazer Lecture delivered at
        Glasgow University 1924, Published in ' The Frazer
        Lectures ', 1932.
    (xi) ' Sumer and Egypt ', Man, 1929, 18.
PETRIE, SIR W. M. FLINDERS :
    (i) ' Pyramids and Temples of Gizeh ', 1883.
    And GRIFFITHS, F. LL. (ii) : ' The Royal Tombs of the First
        Dynasty ', 1900.
    (iii) ' Arts and Crafts of Ancient Egypt ', 1909.
    (iv) ' Two Hieroglyphic Papyri from Tanis ', 1889.   See also
        GRIFFITH.
PINK, A. : ' If the Blind Lead ', 1933.

PLEYTE, C. M. : ' De Geogr. Verb. v.h. Koppensnellen in den Ost. Arch.', TNAG, VIII, 1891.

PLUTARCH : ' De Iside et Osiride ', Camb., 1744, Trans. by Samuel Squire.

PORTMAN, M. V. :

(i) ' Notes on the Andamanese ', JRAI, 25, 1896.

(ii) ' A History of our Relations with the Andamanese ', Calcutta, 1899.

POWELL-COTTON, P. H. G. : ' Notes on a Journey through the Great Ituri Forest ', JAS, 7, 1907.

POYNTER, SIR E. : ' Painting, Classic ; Early Christian ; Italian and Teutonic ', 1882.

PRATT, G. : ' Some Folk-Songs and Myths from Samoa ', Journ. Roy. Soc., N.S.W., 25, 1891, Sydney.

PRATZ : See DU PRATZ.

PUMPELLY, R. : ' Explorations in Turkestan ', Washington, D.C., 1907.

QUATREFAGES, A. DE : ' Les Pygmies ', Paris, 1887.

QUIBELL, J. E. : ' Hieraconpolis ', Brit. Sch. Arch. in Egypt, 1900–2.

RADIN, PAUL :

(i) ' The Social Organization of the Winnebago Indians ', Geol. Surv. Canada, Dept of Mines, Museum Bull. 10, Ottawa, 1914.

(ii) ' The Winnebago Tribe ', ARBE, 37.

RAE, E. :

(i) ' On the Esquimaux ', TES, 1866.

(ii) ' Land of the North Wind ', 1875.

RAJAH, K. R. V. : ' Comparative Studies in Cochin History.'

RAPSON, E. J. : ' Ancient India ', 1914.

RASHDALL, HASTINGS : ' The Universities of Europe in the Middle Ages ', 2 vols., Oxford, 1895.

RATZEL, F. : ' History of Mankind ', 1897.

RAY, P. C. : ' The Mahabharata ', Calcutta, 1892.

REINACH, SALOMON :

(i) ' La representation du galop dans l'art ancien et modèrne ', RA, 3rd Ser., 37–9.

(ii) ' Cultes, Mythes et Religions ', Paris, 1913.

REISNER, G. A. :

(i) ' The Early Dynastic Cemeteries of Naga-Ed-Dêr ', Univ. California, 1908.

(ii) ' Archaeological Survey of Nubia ', 1907–8, Cairo, 1910.

(iii) ' Excavations at Kerma ', Harvard African Studies, Cambs., Mass., 1923.

(iv) ' Mycerinus. The Temples of the Third Pyramid at Giza ', Harvard, 1931.

REITZENSTEIN, R. (the elder) : ' Die hellenistischen Mysterien-religionen ', Leipzig and Berlin, 1910.

RENOUF, SIR P. LE PAGE : ' The Book of the Dead ', Edit. by E. Naville, Paris, 1907.

RICHARDS, AUDREY : ' Hunger and Work in a Savage Tribe ', 1932.

RIEDEL, J. G. F. : ' De sluik-en kroes-haarige rassen tusschen Selebes en Papua ', 's Gravenhage, 1886.

RIVERS, W. H. R. :
    (i) ' The Todas ', 1906.
    (ii) ' The Disappearance of Useful Arts ', Festsscrifts Tillägnad Edward Westermarck, Helsingfors, 1912.
    (iii) ' The History of Melanesian Society ', Cambs., 1914.
    (iv) ' Instinct and the Unconscious ', Cambs., 2nd Edition, 1922.
    (v) ' Social Organization ', 1924.
    (vi) ' Psychology and Ethnology ', 1926.

ROTH, H. LING : See LING ROTH.

SAINTSBURY, G. : ' The English Novel ', 1913.

SAINTYVES, P. : ' Les Saints Successeurs des Dieux ', Paris, 1907.

' Satapatha Brahmana ', see EGGELING.

SCHADENBERG, A. : ' Ueber die Negritos in den Philippinen ', ZFE, 12, 1880.

SCHAEFER, H. : ' Die Mysterien des Osiris in Abydos unter König Sesostris III ', Berlin, 1904.   See SETHE (iv) IV, 2, 1904.

SCHAPERA, I. : ' The Khoisan Peoples of South Africa ', 1930.

SCHEBESTA, P. :
    (i) ' Among the Forest Dwarfs of Malaya ', 1929.
    (ii) ' Among the Congo Pygmies ', 1933.

SCHMIDT, P. W. :
    (i) ' Die Stellung den Pygmäenvölker in der Entwicklungsges-chichte des Menschen ', Stuttgart, 1910.
    (ii) ' Der Ursprung der Gottesidee ', Münster i W, 1912 : L'Origine de l'idée de Dieu, A., vols. 3–5, 1908–10.

SCHOOLCRAFT, H. R. : ' Information resp. the Hist., Condition, etc., of the Indian Tribes of the United States ', Philadelphia, 1853–7.

SCHWARZ, J. A. T. : ' Tontemboansche Teksten ', Leiden, 1907.

SELIGMAN, C. G. :
    (i) ' The Melanesians of Brit. New Guinea ', Cambridge, 1910.
    and B. Z. SELIGMAN, (ii) : ' The Veddas ', Cambridge, 1911.
    (iii) See ' Customs of the World ', re Veddas.

SENART, E. : ' Les Castes dans l'Inde ', Paris, 1896.

SETHE, K. :
    (i) ' Die Namen von ober- und unter-Ägypten und die Beziehungen für Nord und Sud ', ZAS, 44, 1907.
    (ii) ' Dramatische Texte zu Altaegyptischen Mysterienspielen '. See SETHE (iv) 10, 1928.
    (iii) ' Die Aegyptischen Pyramiden Texte ', Leipzig, 1908, etc.
    (iv) ' Untersuchungen zur Urgeschichte und Altertumskunde Ägypten ', Leipzig.

SHARP, MISS E. : ' Here We Go Round ', 1928.

SKEAT, W. W., and BLAGDEN, H. O. : ' Pagan Races of the Malay Peninsula ', 1906.

SMITH, S. P. : ' Hawaiki : the Original Home of the Maori ', 1910.

SOLLAS, W. J. : ' Ancient Hunters and their modern Representatives ', 3rd Edition, 1924.

SPECK, F. G. : ' The Family Hunting Band as the basis of Algonquin Social Organization ', AA, 1915.

SPENCER, B. (SIR), and GILLEN, F. S. :
(i) ' The Northern Tribes of Central Australia ', 1904.
(ii) ' The Arunta ', 1924.

SPITTEL, R. L. : ' Wild Ceylon ', 1925.

STEVENSON, M. C. (MRS.) : ' The Zuni Indians ', ARBE, 23, 1901–2.

STOW, G. W. : ' The Native Races of South Africa ', 1905.

STUHLMANN : ' Die Zwergvolker von Africa, besonders über die des oberen Ituri ', ZFE, 25, 1893.

TEMPLE, SIR R. : See ' Customs of the World ', re Andaman Islanders.

THOMAS, E. S. : ' A Comparison of Drawings from Ancient Egypt, Libya, and the South Spanish Caves ', JRAI, LVI, 1926.

THURM, SIR E. IM : Pres. Add. Section H, Brit. Ass., 1914.

TIN, PE MAUNG : See PE MAUNG TIN.

TONGUE, M. HELEN : ' Bushman Paintings ', Oxford, 1909.

TORDAY, E. : ' Dualism in Western Bantu Religion ', JRAI, 58, 1928.

TORRES STRAITS : ' Report of the Cambridge Anthropological Expedition to Torres Straits ', vols. 5 and 6, 1904, 1908, Cambridge.

TROTTER, W. : ' Instincts of the Herd in Peace and War '.

TURNOUR, G. : ' Mahavamsa ', 1836.

UPHAM, E. : ' The Mahavansi, the Raja-Ratnacari, and the Raja-Vali ; forming the sacred and historical books of Ceylon ', 1833.

URE, P. N. :
(i) ' The Greek Renaissance ', 1921.
(ii) ' The Origin of Tyranny ', Cambridge, 1922.
(iii) ' The Outer Greek World in the Sixth Century ', CAH, IV, chap. IV.

VAN DEN BERGH : See BERGH.

VAN OSSENBRUGGEN : See OSSENBRUGGEN.

VANOVERBERGH : ' Negritos of Northern Luzon ', Anthropos, 20, 1925.

VEGA, GARCILASO DE LA : ' Royal Commentary of the Incas ', Trans. by C. R. Markham, 1869.

WACE, A. J. B., and THOMPSON, M. S. : ' Prehistoric Thessaly ', 1912.

WALTERS, H. B. : ' Greek Art ', 1904.

WARD : ' Historic Ornament ', 1897.

WENSINCK, A. J. : ' The Ideas of the Western Semites concerning the Navel of the Earth ', Kon. Akad. V. Wetensch, etc., Amsterdam. Afd. Lett. N.R., 17, 1916.

WEST, E. W. : Pahlavi Texts, Part I, SBE, vol. V, Oxford, 1880.

WESTGARTH, W. : ' Australia Felix ', Edinburgh, 1848.

WHEELER, J. M. : ' Paganism in Christian Festivals ', 1933.

WIEGER, L. : ' Histoire des Croyances religieuses et des Opinions philosophiques en Chine ', Hien-Hien, China, 1922.

WILKEN, G. A. : ' Verspreide Gescriften ', 's Gravenhage, 1912.

WILLIAMS, F. E. : ' The Natives of the Purari Delta ', Port Moresby, Papua, 1924.

WILSON, H. H. :
(i) ' Select Specimens of the Hindu Theatre ', 1826–7.
(ii) ' Rig Veda Sanhita ', 1850.
(iii) ' The Vishnu Purana ', 1840.

WOOD, W. : See ' Customs of the World ', re Arctic America.

WOODWARD, W. H. : ' Vittorino da Feltre ', Cambridge, 1897.

WORCESTER, DEAN C. : ' The Non-Christian Tribes of Northern Luzon ', Manila, 1906.

WORSNOP, T. : ' The Prehistoric Arts, Manufactures, Work, Weapons, etc., of the Aborigines of Australia ', Adelaide, 1897.

ZUCKERMAN, S. : ' The Social Life of Monkeys and Apes ', 1932.

ZWAAN, J. K. DE : ' Die Heilkunde der Niasser ', Den Haag, 1913.

24

INDEX

Printed in Great Britain by Butler & Tanner Ltd., Frome and London

METHUEN'S
GENERAL LITERATURE

A Selection of
METHUEN'S
PUBLICATIONS

This Catalogue contains only a selection of the more important books published by Messrs. Methuen. A complete catalogue of their publications may be obtained on application.

ABRAHAM (G. D.)
MODERN MOUNTAINEERING
Illustrated. 7s. 6d. net.

ARMSTRONG (Anthony) ('A. A.' of Punch)
WARRIORS AT EASE
WARRIORS STILL AT EASE
SELECTED WARRIORS
PERCIVAL AND I
PERCIVAL AT PLAY
APPLE AND PERCIVAL
ME AND FRANCES
HOW TO DO IT
BRITISHER ON BROADWAY
WHILE YOU WAIT
　　　　Each 3s. 6d. net.
LIVESTOCK IN BARRACKS
Illustrated by E. H. SHEPARD.
　　　　3s. 6d. net.
EASY WARRIORS
Illustrated by G. L. STAMPA.
　　　　5s. net.
YESTERDAILIES. Illustrated.
　　　　3s. 6d. net.

BALFOUR (Sir Graham)
THE LIFE OF ROBERT LOUIS STEVENSON 10s. 6d. net.
Also, 3s. 6d. net.

BARKER (Ernest)
NATIONAL CHARACTER
　　　　10s. 6d. net.
GREEK POLITICAL THEORY 14s. net.
CHURCH, STATE AND STUDY
　　　　10s. 6d. net.

BELLOC (Hilaire)
PARIS 8s. 6d. net.
THE PYRENEES 8s. 6d. net.
MARIE ANTOINETTE 18s. net.
A HISTORY OF ENGLAND
In 7 Vols. Vols. I, II, III and IV
　　　　Each 15s. net.

BINNS (L. Elliott), D.D.
THE DECLINE AND FALL OF THE MEDIEVAL PAPACY. 16s. net.

BIRMINGHAM (George A.)
A WAYFARER IN HUNGARY
Illustrated. 8s. 6d. net.
SPILLIKINS : ESSAYS 3s. 6d. net.
SHIPS AND SEALING-WAX : ESSAYS
　　　　3s. 6d. net.
CAN I BE A CHRISTIAN ? 1s. net.

CHALMERS (Patrick R.)
KENNETH GRAHAME : LIFE, LETTERS AND UNPUBLISHED WORK
Illustrated. 10s. 6d. net.

CHESTERTON (G. K.)
COLLECTED POEMS 7s. 6d. net.
G.K.C. AS M.C.
THE BALLAD OF THE WHITE HORSE
　　　　3s. 6d. net.
Also illustrated by ROBERT AUSTIN. 12s. 6d. net.
AVOWALS AND DENIALS 6s. net.
ALL I SURVEY
ALL IS GRIST

CHESTERTON (G. K.)—*continued*
CHARLES DICKENS
COME TO THINK OF IT . . .
GENERALLY SPEAKING
ALL THINGS CONSIDERED
TREMENDOUS TRIFLES
FANCIES VERSUS FADS
ALARMS AND DISCURSIONS
A MISCELLANY OF MEN
THE USES OF DIVERSITY
THE OUTLINE OF SANITY
         Each 3s. 6d. *net.*
WINE, WATER AND SONG 1s. 6d. *net.*

CORTI (Count Egon)
THE DOWNFALL OF THREE
DYNASTIES
     Illustrated. 21s. *net.*

CURLE (J. H.)
THE SHADOW-SHOW   6s. *net.*
         Also, 3s. 6d. *net.*
THIS WORLD OF OURS   6s. *net.*
TO-DAY AND TO-MORROW   6s. *net.*
THIS WORLD FIRST   6s. *net.*
TRAVELS AND MEN   6s. *net.*

DRINKWATER (John)
THE KING'S REIGN : A Commentary
in Prose and Picture
     Illustrated. 5s. *net.*

EDWARDES (Tickner)
THE LORE OF THE HONEY-BEE
   Illustrated. 7s. 6d. and 3s. 6d. *net.*
BEE-KEEPING FOR ALL
     Illustrated. 3s. 6d. *net.*
THE BEE-MASTER OF WARRILOW
     Illustrated. 7s. 6d. *net.*
BEE-KEEPING DO'S AND DON'TS
         2s. 6d. *net.*
LIFT-LUCK ON SOUTHERN ROADS
         5s. *net.*

EINSTEIN (Albert)
RELATIVITY : THE SPECIAL AND
GENERAL THEORY   5s. *net.*
SIDELIGHTS ON RELATIVITY
         3s. 6d. *net.*
THE MEANING OF RELATIVITY
         5s. *net.*
THE BROWNIAN MOVEMENT
         5s. *net.*

EISLER (Robert)
THE MESSIAH JESUS AND JOHN THE
BAPTIST
     Illustrated. £2 2s. *net.*

FYLEMAN (Rose)
HAPPY FAMILIES
FAIRIES AND CHIMNEYS
THE FAIRY GREEN
THE FAIRY FLUTE   *Each* 2s. *net.*
THE RAINBOW CAT
EIGHT LITTLE PLAYS FOR CHILDREN
FORTY GOOD-NIGHT TALES
FORTY GOOD-MORNING TALES
SEVEN LITTLE PLAYS FOR CHILDREN
TWENTY TEA-TIME TALES
         Each 3s. 6d. *net.*
THE BLUE RHYME BOOK
     Illustrated. 3s. 6d. *net.*
THE EASTER HARE
     Illustrated. 3s. 6d. *net.*
FIFTY-ONE NEW NURSERY RHYMES
   Illustrated by DOROTHY BUR-
ROUGHES.   6s. *net.*
THE STRANGE ADVENTURES OF
CAPTAIN MARWHOPPLE
     Illustrated. 3s. 6d. *net.*

GIBBON (Edward)
THE DECLINE AND FALL OF THE
ROMAN EMPIRE
With Notes, Appendixes and Maps,
by J. B. BURY. Illustrated. 7 vols.
15s. *net* each volume. Also, unillustrated, 7s. 6d. *net* each volume.

GRAHAME (Kenneth)
THE WIND IN THE WILLOWS
     7s. 6d. *net* and 5s. *net.*
Also illustrated by ERNEST H.
SHEPARD. *Cloth,* 7s. 6d. *net.*
   Green Leather, 12s. 6d. *net.*
Pocket Edition, unillustrated.
       Cloth, 3s. 6d. *net.*
   Green Morocco, 7s. 6d. *net.*
THE KENNETH GRAHAME BOOK
(' The Wind in the Willows ',
' Dream Days ' and ' The Golden
Age ' in one volume).
         7s. 6d. *net.*
See also **Milne (A. A.)**

GREGORY (T. E.)
THE GOLD STANDARD AND ITS
FUTURE   3s. 6d. *net.*

HEATON (Rose Henniker)
THE PERFECT HOSTESS
   Decorated by A. E. TAYLOR.
7s. 6d. *net.* Gift Edition, £1 1s. *net.*
THE PERFECT SCHOOLGIRL
         3s. 6d. *net.*

4 Methuen's Publications

HEIDEN (Konrad)
A History of National Socialism
15s. net.

HERBERT (A. P.)
Helen   2s. 6d. net.
Tantivy Towers and Derby Day
in one volume. Illustrated by
Lady Violet Baring.   5s. net.
Each, separately, unillustrated
2s. 6d. net.
Honeybubble & Co. 3s. 6d. net.
Misleading Cases in the Common
Law   5s. net.
More Misleading Cases 5s. net.
Still More Misleading Cases
5s. net.
The Wherefore and the Why
'Tinker, Tailor . . .'
Each, illustrated by George
Morrow.   2s. 6d. net.
Mr. Pewter   5s. net.
'No Boats on the River'
Illustrated. 5s. net.

HOLDSWORTH (Sir W. S.)
A History of English Law
Nine Volumes. £1 5s. net each.
Index Volume by Edward Potton.
£1 1s. net.

HSIUNG (S. I.)
Lady Precious Stream :
An Old Chinese Play
Illustrated. 8s. 6d. net.
Limited and Signed Edition
£2 2s. net.

HUDSON (W. H.)
A Shepherd's Life
Illustrated. 10s. 6d. net.
Also unillustrated. 3s. 6d. net.

HUTTON (Edward)
Cities of Sicily
Illustrated. 10s. 6d. net.
Milan and Lombardy
The Cities of Romagna and the
Marches
Siena and Southern Tuscany
Naples and Southern Italy
Illustrated. Each 8s. 6d. net.
A Wayfarer in Unknown Tuscany
The Cities of Spain
The Cities of Umbria
Country Walks about Florence
Rome

HUTTON (Edward)—*continued*
Florence and Northern Tuscany
Venice and Venetia
Illustrated. Each 7s. 6d. net.

INGE (W. R.), D.D.
Christian Mysticism. With a New
Preface.   7s. 6d. net.

JOAD (C. E. M.)
Common-sense Ethics   6s. net.

JOHNS (Rowland)
Dogs You'd Like to Meet
Let Dogs Delight
All Sorts of Dogs
Let's Talk of Dogs
Puppies
Lucky Dogs
Every Dog its Day
The Rowland Johns Dog Book
Each, Illustrated, 3s. 6d. net.
So You Like Dogs !
Nurse Cavell : Dog Lover
Each, Illustrated, 2s. 6d. net.

'Our Friend the Dog' Series.
Edited by Rowland Johns.
The Airedale
The Alsatian
The Bulldog
The Bull-Terrier
The Cairn
The Chow-Chow
The Cocker Spaniel
The Collie
The Dachshund
The Dalmatian
The English Springer
The Fox-Terrier
The Great Dane
The House-Dog
The Irish Setter
The Labrador
The Pekingese
The Pomeranian
The Retriever
The Scottish Terrier
The Sealyham
The West Highland
Each 2s. 6d. net.

JOHNSON (Alan Campbell)
Growing Opinions : A Sympo-
sium of the Ideas of British
Youth   6s. net.

Methuen's Publications 5

KIPLING (Rudyard)
BARRACK-ROOM BALLADS
THE SEVEN SEAS
THE FIVE NATIONS
DEPARTMENTAL DITTIES
THE YEARS BETWEEN
Four Editions of these famous volumes of poems are now published, viz. :—*Buckram*, 7s. 6d. *net.*
Cloth, 6s. *net.* *Leather*, 7s. 6d. *net.*
Service Edition. Two volumes each book. 3s. *net* each vol.
A KIPLING ANTHOLOGY—VERSE
Leather, 7s. 6d. *net.*
Cloth, 6s. *net* and 3s. 6d. *net.*
TWENTY POEMS 1s. *net.*
A CHOICE OF SONGS 2s. *net.*
SELECTED POEMS 1s. *net.*

LAMB (Charles and Mary)
THE LETTERS OF CHARLES LAMB
Edited by E. V. LUCAS. Three volumes. *About* 45s. *net.*
THE COMPLETE WORKS
Edited by E. V. LUCAS. Six volumes. 6s. *net each.*
SELECTED LETTERS
Edited by G. T. CLAPTON.
3s. 6d. *net.*
THE CHARLES LAMB DAY-BOOK
Compiled by E. V. LUCAS. 6s. *net.*
THE BEST OF LAMB
Compiled by E. V. LUCAS.
2s. 6d. *net.*
LAMB'S ' BARBARA S——'
by L. E. HOLMAN. 6s. *net.*
LAMB ALWAYS ELIA
by EDITH C. JOHNSON. 7s. 6d. *net.*

LANKESTER (Sir Ray)
SCIENCE FROM AN EASY CHAIR
First Series
SCIENCE FROM AN EASY CHAIR
Second Series
GREAT AND SMALL THINGS
Each, Illustrated, 7s. 6d. *net.*
SECRETS OF EARTH AND SEA
Illustrated. 8s. 6d. *net.*

LODGE (Sir Oliver)
MAN AND THE UNIVERSE
7s. 6d. *net* and 3s. 6d. *net.*
THE SURVIVAL OF MAN 7s. 6d. *net.*
RAYMOND 10s. 6d. *net.*
RAYMOND REVISED 6s. *net.*
MODERN PROBLEMS 3s. 6d. *net.*
REASON AND BELIEF 3s. 6d. *net.*
THE SUBSTANCE OF FAITH 2s. *net.*
RELATIVITY 1s. *net.*

LODGE (Sir Oliver)—*continued*
CONVICTION OF SURVIVAL 2s. *net.*

LUCAS (E. V.), C.H.
READING, WRITING AND REMEMBERING 7s. 6d. *net.*
THE COLVINS AND THEIR FRIENDS
£1 1s. *net.*
THE LIFE OF CHARLES LAMB
2 Vols. £1 1s. *net.*
AT THE SHRINE OF ST. CHARLES
5s. *net.*
POST-BAG DIVERSIONS 7s. 6d. *net.*
VERMEER THE MAGICAL 5s. *net.*
A WANDERER IN ROME
A WANDERER IN HOLLAND
A WANDERER IN LONDON
LONDON REVISITED (Revised)
A WANDERER IN PARIS
A WANDERER IN FLORENCE
A WANDERER IN VENICE
Each, 10s. 6d. *net.*
A WANDERER AMONG PICTURES
8s. 6d. *net.*
E. V. LUCAS'S LONDON £1 *net.*
THE OPEN ROAD 6s. *net.*
Also, illustrated by CLAUDE A. SHEPPERSON,A.R.W.S. 10s. 6d. *net.*
Also, India Paper.
Leather, 7s. 6d. *net.*
THE JOY OF LIFE 6s. *net.*
Leather Edition, 7s. 6d. *net.*
Also, India Paper.
Leather, 7s. 6d. *net.*
THE GENTLEST ART
THE SECOND POST
FIRESIDE AND SUNSHINE
CHARACTER AND COMEDY
GOOD COMPANY
ONE DAY AND ANOTHER
OLD LAMPS FOR NEW
LOITERER'S HARVEST
LUCK OF THE YEAR
EVENTS AND EMBROIDERIES
A FRONDED ISLE
A ROVER I WOULD BE
GIVING AND RECEIVING
HER INFINITE VARIETY
ENCOUNTERS AND DIVERSIONS
TURNING THINGS OVER
TRAVELLER'S LUCK
AT THE SIGN OF THE DOVE
VISIBILITY GOOD
THE FRIENDLY TOWN
LEMON VERBENA *Each* 3s. 6d. *net.*
SAUNTERER'S REWARDS
'TWIXT EAGLE AND DOVE
ZIGZAGS IN FRANCE
PLEASURE TROVE *Each* 6s. *net.*

LUCAS (E. V.)—*continued*
  FRENCH LEAVES
  ENGLISH LEAVES
  ROVING EAST AND ROVING WEST
  THE BARBER'S CLOCK   *Each 5s. net.*
  'THE MORE I SEE OF MEN . . .'
  OUT OF A CLEAR SKY
  IF DOGS COULD WRITE
  '. . . AND SUCH SMALL DEER '
              Each, 3s. 6d. net.
  See also **Lamb (Charles)**.

LYND (Robert)
  BOTH SIDES OF THE ROAD
  THE COCKLESHELL   *Each 5s. net.*
  RAIN, RAIN, GO TO SPAIN
  IT'S A FINE WORLD
  THE GREEN MAN
  THE PLEASURES OF IGNORANCE
  THE GOLDFISH
  THE LITTLE ANGEL
  THE BLUE LION
  THE PEAL OF BELLS
  THE ORANGE TREE
  THE MONEY-BOX *Each 3s. 6d. net.*

McDOUGALL (William)
  AN INTRODUCTION TO SOCIAL
    PSYCHOLOGY   *10s. 6d. net.*
  NATIONAL WELFARE AND NATIONAL
    DECAY   *6s. net.*
  AN OUTLINE OF PSYCHOLOGY
                  10s. 6d. net.
  AN OUTLINE OF ABNORMAL PSYCHO-
    LOGY   *15s. net.*
  BODY AND MIND   *12s. 6d. net.*
  CHARACTER AND THE CONDUCT OF
    LIFE   *10s. 6d. net.*
  MODERN MATERIALISM AND EMER-
    GENT EVOLUTION   *3s. net.*
  ETHICS AND SOME MODERN WORLD
    PROBLEMS   *7s. 6d. net.*
  THE ENERGIES OF MEN *8s. 6d. net.*
  RELIGION AND THE SCIENCES OF
    LIFE   *8s. 6d. net.*

MAETERLINCK (Maurice)
  THE BLUE BIRD   *6s. net.*
  Also, illustrated by F. CAYLEY
    ROBINSON.   *10s. 6d. net.*
  OUR ETERNITY
  THE UNKNOWN GUEST
  THE WRACK OF THE STORM
  THE BETROTHAL   *Each 6s. net.*
  POEMS   *5s. net.*
  MARY MAGDALENE   *2s. net.*

MARLOWE (Christopher)
  THE WORKS. In 6 volumes.
    General Editor, R. H. CASE.
    THE LIFE OF MARLOWE and DIDO,

MARLOWE (Christopher)—*continued*
  THE WORKS—*continued*
    QUEEN OF CARTHAGE *8s. 6d. net.*
  TAMBURLAINE, I AND II
                  10s. 6d. net.
    THE JEW OF MALTA and THE
      MASSACRE AT PARIS *10s. 6d. net.*
    POEMS   *10s. 6d. net.*
    DOCTOR FAUSTUS *8s. 6d. net.*
    EDWARD II   *8s. 6d. net.*

MASEFIELD (John)
  ON THE SPANISH MAIN *8s. 6d. net.*
  A SAILOR'S GARLAND *3s. 6d. net.*
  SEA LIFE IN NELSON'S TIME
                  7s. 6d. net.

METHUEN (Sir A.)
  AN ANTHOLOGY OF MODERN VERSE
  SHAKESPEARE TO HARDY : An
  Anthology of English Lyrics.
          Each, Cloth, 6s. net.
          Leather, 7s. 6d. net.

MILNE (A. A.)
  PEACE WITH HONOUR   *5s. net.*
  TOAD OF TOAD HALL
    A Play founded on Kenneth
    Grahame's ' The Wind in the
    Willows '.   *5s. net.*
  THOSE WERE THE DAYS : Collected
    Stories   *7s. 6d. net.*
  BY WAY OF INTRODUCTION
  NOT THAT IT MATTERS
  IF I MAY   *Each 3s. 6d. net.*
  WHEN WE WERE VERY YOUNG
  WINNIE-THE-POOH
  NOW WE ARE SIX
  THE HOUSE AT POOH CORNER
  Each illustrated by E. H. SHEPARD.
        7s. 6d. net and 2s. 6d. net.
          Leather, 10s. 6d. net.
  THE CHRISTOPHER ROBIN VERSES
    (' When We were Very Young '
    and ' Now We are Six ' com-
    plete in one volume). Illustrated
    in colour and line by E. H.
    SHEPARD.   *8s. 6d. net.*
  THE CHRISTOPHER ROBIN STORY
    BOOK
    Illustrated by E. H. SHEPARD.
                    5s. net.
  THE CHRISTOPHER ROBIN BIRTH-
    DAY BOOK
    Illustrated by E. H. SHEPARD.
                  3s. 6d. net.

MILNE (A. A.) and FRASER-SIMSON (H.)
FOURTEEN SONGS FROM 'WHEN WE WERE VERY YOUNG'   7s. 6d. net.
TEDDY BEAR AND OTHER SONGS FROM 'WHEN WE WERE VERY YOUNG'   7s. 6d. net.
THE KING'S BREAKFAST   3s. 6d. net.
SONGS FROM 'NOW WE ARE SIX'   7s. 6d. net.
MORE 'VERY YOUNG' SONGS   7s. 6d. net.
THE HUMS OF POOH   7s. 6d. net.
In each case the words are by A. A. MILNE, the music by H. FRASER-SIMSON, and the decorations by E. H. SHEPARD.

MITCHELL (Abe)
DOWN TO SCRATCH   5s. net.

MORTON (H. V.)
A LONDON YEAR
   Illustrated, 6s. net.
THE HEART OF LONDON   3s. 6d. net.
Also, with Scissor Cuts by L. HUMMEL.   6s. net.
THE SPELL OF LONDON
THE NIGHTS OF LONDON
BLUE DAYS AT SEA   Each 3s. 6d. net.
IN SEARCH OF ENGLAND
THE CALL OF ENGLAND
IN SEARCH OF SCOTLAND
IN SCOTLAND AGAIN
IN SEARCH OF IRELAND
IN SEARCH OF WALES
   Each, illustrated, 7s. 6d. net.

MOSSOLOV (A. A.)
AT THE COURT OF THE LAST TSAR : Being the Memoirs of General A. A. Mossolov, Head of the Court Chancellery 1900–1916. Illustrated.   12s. 6d. net.

MUIR (Augustus)
SCOTLAND'S ROAD OF ROMANCE
   Illustrated. 7s. 6d. net.

OMAN (Sir Charles)
THINGS I HAVE SEEN 8s. 6d. net.
A HISTORY OF THE ART OF WAR IN THE MIDDLE AGES, A.D. 378–1485. 2 vols. Illustrated. £1 16s. net.
STUDIES IN THE NAPOLEONIC WARS 8s. 6d. net.

PETRIE (Sir Flinders)
A HISTORY OF EGYPT
In 6 Volumes.
Vol. I. FROM THE IST TO THE XVITH DYNASTY   12s. net.

PETRIE (Sir Flinders)—*continued*
Vol. II. THE XVIITH AND XVIIITH DYNASTIES   9s. net.
Vol. III. XIXTH TO XXXTH DYNASTIES   12s. net.
Vol. IV. EGYPT UNDER THE PTOLEMAIC DYNASTY By EDWYN BEVAN.   15s. net.
Vol. V. EGYPT UNDER ROMAN RULE By J. G. MILNE.   12s. net.
Vol.VI. EGYPT IN THE MIDDLE AGES By S. LANE POOLE.   10s. net.

RAGLAN (Lord)
JOCASTA'S CRIME   6s. net.
THE SCIENCE OF PEACE   3s. 6d. net.
IF I WERE DICTATOR   2s. 6d. net.

SELLAR (W. C.) and YEATMAN (R. J.)
1066 AND ALL THAT
AND NOW ALL THIS
HORSE NONSENSE
Each illustrated by JOHN REYNOLDS.   5s. net.

STAPLEDON (Olaf)
WAKING WORLD   7s. 6d. net.
A MODERN THEORY OF ETHICS   8s. 6d. net.

STEINBERG (Dr. I.)
SPIRIDONOVA : Revolutionary Terrorist. Illustrated.   12s. 6d. net.

STEVENSON (R. L.)
THE LETTERS Edited by Sir SIDNEY COLVIN. 4 Vols.   Each 6s. net.

STOCK (Vaughan)
THE LIFE OF CHRIST
   Illustrated.   6s. net.

SURTEES (R. S.)
HANDLEY CROSS
MR. SPONGE'S SPORTING TOUR
ASK MAMMA
MR. FACEY ROMFORD'S HOUNDS
PLAIN OR RINGLETS ?
HILLINGDON HALL
   Each, illustrated, 7s. 6d. net.
JORROCKS'S JAUNTS AND JOLLITIES
HAWBUCK GRANGE
   Each, Illustrated, 6s. net.

TAYLOR (A. E.)
PLATO : THE MAN AND HIS WORK   £1 1s. net.
PLATO : TIMÆUS AND CRITIAS   6s. net.
ELEMENTS OF METAPHYSICS   12s. 6d. net.

TILDEN (William T.)
THE ART OF LAWN TENNIS
Revised Edition.
SINGLES AND DOUBLES
Each, Illustrated.   6s. net.

TILESTON (Mary W.)
DAILY STRENGTH FOR DAILY NEEDS
3s. 6d. net.
India Paper.   *Leather*, 6s net.

UNDERHILL (Evelyn)
MYSTICISM   *Revised Edition.*
15s. net.
THE LIFE OF THE SPIRIT AND THE
LIFE OF TO-DAY   7s. 6d. net.
MAN AND THE SUPERNATURAL
3s. 6d. net.
THE GOLDEN SEQUENCE
Paper boards, 3s. 6d. net.
Cloth, 5s. net.
MIXED PASTURE :   Essays and
Addresses   5s. net.
CONCERNING THE INNER LIFE
2s. net.
THE HOUSE OF THE SOUL   2s. net.

VALETTE (John de la)
THE CONQUEST OF UGLINESS : A
Collection of Contemporary
Views on the Place of Art in
Industry. Illustrated. 8s. 6d. net.

WARD (A. C.)
TWENTIETH CENTURY LITERATURE
5s. net.
THE NINETEEN-TWENTIES   5s. net.
LANDMARKS IN WESTERN LITERA-
TURE   5s. net.
AMERICAN LITERATURE   7s. 6d. net.
WHAT IS THIS LIFE ?   5s. net.

WARD (A. C.)—*continued*
THE FROLIC AND THE GENTLE : A
CENTENARY STUDY OF CHARLES
LAMB   6s. net.

WHIPPLE (Sidney B.)
THE LINDBERGH CRIME   6s. net.
NOBLE EXPERIMENT : A Portrait
of America under Prohibition
5s. net.

WILDE (Oscar)
LORD ARTHUR SAVILE'S CRIME AND
THE PORTRAIT OF MR. W. H.
6s. 6d. net.
THE DUCHESS OF PADUA   3s. 6d. net.
POEMS   6s. 6d. net.
LADY WINDERMERE'S FAN
6s. 6d. net.
A WOMAN OF NO IMPORTANCE
6s. 6d. net.
AN IDEAL HUSBAND   6s. 6d. net.
THE IMPORTANCE OF BEING EARNEST
6s. 6d. net.
A HOUSE OF POMEGRANATES
6s. 6d. net.
INTENTIONS   6s. 6d. net.
DE PROFUNDIS and PRISON LETTERS
6s. 6d. net.
ESSAYS AND LECTURES 6s. 6d. net.
SALOMÉ, A FLORENTINE TRAGEDY,
and LA SAINTE COURTISANE
2s. 6d. net.
SELECTED PROSE OF OSCAR WILDE
6s. 6d. net.
ART AND DECORATION 6s. 6d. net.
FOR LOVE OF THE KING   5s. net.
VERA, OR THE NIHILISTS
6s. 6d. net.

METHUEN'S COMPANIONS TO MODERN STUDIES
SPAIN. E. ALLISON PEERS. 12s. 6d. net.
GERMANY. J. BITHELL. 15s. net.
ITALY. E. G. GARDNER. 12s. 6d. net.
FRANCE. R. L. G. RITCHIE. 12s. 6d. net.

METHUEN'S HISTORY OF MEDIEVAL AND MODERN EUROPE
In 8 Vols. *Each* 16s. net.

I.	476 to 911.	By J. H. BAXTER.
II.	911 to 1198.	By Z. N. BROOKE.
III.	1198 to 1378.	By C. W. PREVITÉ-ORTON.
IV.	1378 to 1494.	By W. T. WAUGH.
V.	1494 to 1610.	By A. J. GRANT.
VI.	1610 to 1715.	By E. R. ADAIR.
VII.	1715 to 1815.	By W. F. REDDAWAY.
VIII.	1815 to 1923.	By Sir J. A. R. MARRIOTT.

Methuen & Co. Ltd., 36 Essex Street, London, W.C.2